SURPLUS

A57-8627

5-17-61

HARVARD HISTORICAL STUDIES

Published under the Direction of the
Department of History

From the income of
THE HENRY WARREN TORREY FUND

VOLUME LXIX

Oscar Handlin, Editor

VASSOURAS

A Brazilian Coffee County, 1850–1900

STANLEY J. STEIN

PRINCETON UNIVERSITY

HARVARD UNIVERSITY PRESS

Cambridge, Massachusetts

1957

Library of Congress Catalog Card Number A57–8627

Printed in Great Britain

TO MY WIFE

PREFACE

THE economic development, population growth, and expanded trade of western Europe and North America affected Latin America radically in the nineteenth century. After 1850 the process of integrating Latin America into the world economy accelerated under the impact of commercial agriculture, railroad construction in limited areas, and new intellectual currents. The aim of this analysis of plantation economy and society in Vassouras, a community of the Parahyba Valley of south-central Brazil, is to examine at the local level the effect of the changing world economy upon Brazilian institutions.

Between 1850–1900 the Parahyba Valley was the scene of the greatest coffee production in the world. During the preceding thirty years a primeval forest had been transformed into a series of expanding settlements which spread up and down the valley, turning the region into large coffee plantations based upon slave labor. By the 1880's, however, coffee production was falling off rapidly in this area, and at the turn of the century the regions of virgin soil north and west of the city of São Paulo far outstripped the production of the wasted lands of the valley.

Coffee in Brazil has molded past and present social and economic patterns. The coffee plantation of the mid-nineteenth century was both root and branch of the national economy, its political, economic, and social core. Under the Empire it shifted the political and economic center from Bahia and Pernambuco southward, first to the province of Rio, and, later, under the Republic, to the state of São Paulo. Socially it sired a new aristocracy, the coffee barons of the Parahyba Valley, and brought an unprecedented influx of African slaves modifying the ethnic composition of central Brazil and stratifying society. Finally, the destructive course of coffee cultivation through the Valley in the past century and the crises of over-production in the early years of this century stimulated Brazilians to criticize economic dependence upon one staple subject to the vicissitudes of a world market controlled thousands of miles distant from centers of production. In large measure here are the roots of Brazilian nationalism of the 1890's and early decades of the twentieth century.

When research was begun, it was planned to study approximately ten *municípios** (municipalities or counties) throughout the valley. Unfortunately, it proved impossible with limited time and funds to perform a thorough job of interdisciplinary research in the history of scattered communities via uncatalogued municipal and notarial archives, not to mention establishing contact with local informants of all classes. On the basis of the Census of 1872, municipal histories and visits to several areas, the município of Vassouras was chosen as representative.

Emphasis on economic factors was dictated by the nature of the documentation encountered. Economic data were readily accessible in inventories, testaments, and other records. Regrettably such data cast only indirect light upon social relationships and political organization. Within this economic analysis the medium- and large-sized plantations take the limelight. Undertreatment of the smallholders (*sitiantes*) stemmed from the fact that the published and manuscript sources refer to them infrequently; their contacts with Rio commission houses were limited, their influence on events of the town or county, slight. Numerous as they were, the smallholders were dominated by the medium- and large-sized planters. After 1850, when the story of Vassouras begins for purposes of this analysis, they tended to restrict their production to subsistence crops. Nor could planter family relations receive extensive treatment, for it was difficult to obtain reliable information on planter families and their interrelationships, to weed fancy from fact, to appraise what was too often wishful reconstruction and to avoid emphasizing one family unduly.

* The *município*, Brazil's political and administrative unit at the local level corresponds in size and function to the county in the United States.

After an introductory chapter presenting the pre-1850 background, a section describes the economic organization and activity of the plantation from 1850 to 1864—the peak of Vassouras' prosperity. A third section shows the pattern of plantation life, while the last section attempts to analyze the period of decline in the last quarter of the nineteenth century. With emphasis upon change a cardinal objective, constant citing of events by year and even by month was unavoidable. Primary sources have been quoted extensively and as literally as possible to retain the thought pattern and phrasing of the period.

Source materials came from prefectural and notarial archives in the town of Vassouras, from interviews with aged residents of all classes, and from the National Library and National Archives in Rio de Janeiro. The *cartórios* or notarial offices in Brazilian county seats are the richest and perhaps most neglected repositories for historians, economists, anthropologists, and sociologists. Here are stored records of purchases and sales, mortgages and foreclosures of all property whether land, harvests, improvements, or slaves, as well as court proceedings of criminal and civil cases. Next in importance is the archive of the *Câmara Municipal* or Municipal Council whose deliberations, resolutions, and correspondence were packaged by year. Wherever possible, successive inventories of the same plantation were utilized to obtain a pattern of growth and decline of property over the years. Documentary photographs of the Vassouras area supplemented archival and oral sources; recordings were made of work songs and slave *jongos*, rhymed commentaries closely related to work songs, for their comments on slave society.

This study, based upon eighteen months of research in Brazil, was made possible by grants from the Woodbury-Lowery Fund of Harvard University and the Social Science Research Council, both generously providing sufficient funds to permit my wife and daughter to accompany me. Clarence H. Haring, who has guided so many graduate students in Latin American history, supported the research loyally and suggested changes in the manuscript. I am also indebted to

Melville and Frances Herskovits and to Charles Wagley for guidance and encouragement. The Committee on the Institute for Brazilian Studies, Vanderbilt University, and the editors of the *Hispanic American Historical Review* have graciously consented to the use herein of material they have published.

To those hospitable residents of Vassouras, Luciano Alves Ferreira da Silva, jurist and accomplished storyteller, to the prefect of Vassouras, José Bento Martins Barboza, to Pedro Costa of the Cartório do Primeiro Officio, my thanks for their cooperation. Raúl Fernandes, Edgard Teixeira Leite, Maurício and Carlos Lacerda furnished valuable letters of introduction. Josué Montello placed at my disposal many facilities of the National Library, particularly the use of the microfilm laboratory, and Antonio Caetano Días provided a place to work when the National Library was not open to the public. In the National Archives, Eugenio Vilhena de Moraes aided my work as he has done for so many researchers. And my thanks to those informants, mainly former slaves and their descendants, who patiently answered my innumerable questions.

It is a pleasure to acknowledge the insight, patience, and hard work of my wife, Barbara Hadley Stein. Her training in Brazilian history and her never failing encouragement made her my invaluable assistant.

S. J. Stein

Princeton, New Jersey
July 24, 1957

CONTENTS

xi

TABLES

GRAPHS

ILLUSTRATIONS

PART ONE

FROM WILDERNESS TO PLANTATION

SOUTHEASTERN BRAZIL

MUNICIPIO de VASSOURAS

CHAPTER I

Introduction

An abandoned Vassouras *fazenda* which still dazzles the eye
with its coat of deteriorating whitewash, its Imperial Palms
standing sentinel-like over the entrance way, reflects a per-
manence, stolidity, and strength that recent decades have not
erased. Dating from about 1850, as a rule, these impressive
sprawling structures were not the first buildings on the site.
They developed from humble beginnings when but a handful
of settlers inhabited the hills covered with primeval forest and
when the pioneer planter could easily see the end of his clearings
of corn, beans, and cane from the earthen terrace of his modest
establishment.

The change from wilderness traversed by one or two mule
paths and sparsely settled by a few planters and way-station
proprietors to a municipality of extensive coffee plantations
with some 35,000 free and slave residents in 1850 was wrought
in two generations; its rapidity impressed even contemporaries.[1]
As early as 1835 one observer remarked that a few decades
before the inhabitants lived miserably, without slaves, eating
manioc, beans, and bananas and earning a little cash by selling
bacon to the city of Rio de Janeiro. Noting that the settlers had
passed from a state close to indigence to one of opulence he
concluded: "Who would have thought less than forty years
ago that one product, not even mentioned in the commercial

---

[1] Joaquim José Teixeira Leite to Câmara Municipal of Vassouras (hereafter
referred to as CMV). In Arquivo da Prefeitura de Vassouras (APV), 1850. A
report of 1808 described one portion of what later became a busy road as useful to
"two residents who dwell in this wilderness." Sargento-Mor Ignácio de Souza
Wernek to Vice-Roy, March 9, 1808. In Manuscript Section, National Library,
Rio de Janeiro.

circles of Rio de Janeiro, would gradually become the largest export of this province?" [2]

At the start of the nineteenth century, coffee had been an exotic bush grown in gardens on mountain slopes around the capital and prepared mainly for local consumption. Shortly thereafter coffee cultivation on a commercial scale spread from the environs of Rio de Janeiro to the highlands immediately north.[3] Here the bush adapted itself so well to the local topography, soil, and climate that its cultivation spread rapidly —first along the roads already worn by mule trains traveling between the mining centers of Minas Geraes and the capital, and later up and down the Parahyba Valley. It was to Vassouras and the neighboring upland areas along the Parahyba that the observer of 1835 referred.

The Parahyba River, which forms the northern boundary of the *município* of Vassouras, flows in a general southwest-to-northeast direction parallel to the coast. At Vassouras, the river's south, or right, bank drains the area from the escarpment of the Serra do Mar northward; a few miles to the north of the river the Serra da Mantiqueira rises abruptly. In comparison with the hot, moist climate of the coastal lowlands, the climate of the Parahyba Valley, including the upland area between the river and the escarpment of the Serra do Mar, is moderate the year round. Winter months are dry with relatively cold nights; summer months bring heavy rainfall and higher temperatures. Rainfall varies between forty and sixty inches annually and comes in torrential downpours. "Rare is the day from September to April," wrote a Vassouras resident

[2] *Recopilação do Custo, Despezas e Rendimento de Hum Estabelecimento da Cultura do Caffeeiro* (Rio de Janeiro, 1835), pp. 5–6. To emphasize the rapid transformation, this unknown author added that the tithes for the Serra Acima (uplands) in 1788 had been about Rs. 500$000 for a three year period, growing to Rs. 59:720$000 by 1820. *Ibid.*, p. 5.

[3] A contemporary of the migration of coffee to the highlands claimed that many coffee seedlings were taken from the fazenda of Padre Antonio do Couto da Fonseca in the Campo Grande area. Francisco Freire Allemão, "Quaes São as Principaes Plantas que Hoje se Acham Acclimatadas no Brazil?" *Revista do Instituto Histórico e Geográphico Brasileiro*, XIX (1856), 571. In the *Recopilação* it was reported that muleteers on their return trip to the highlands "passed by the [plantation of] Padre Antonio do Couto to load their animals with coffee seedlings." P. 5.

in 1852, "when there do not come thundershowers accompanied by copious rains." [4] Little rain falls during the remainder of the year. Characteristic of the winter months are the morning mists which rise from the water courses and burn off as the sun warms the earth.

In common with other areas of the plateau of southeastern Brazil the topography of Vassouras displays the knob-like hills which have caused some to describe it as a "sea of hills." These domes or "half-oranges," as they are termed locally, are strung in loose chains which parallel the general southwest–northeast axis of the Serra do Mar and the Parahyba River. The whole município of some 1,400 square kilometers is slightly inclined downward toward the northeast corner where the Ubá River meets the Parahyba, while between the escarpment of the Serra do Mar and the Parahyba there is a series of drops to a chain of hills (Serra de Matacães) found south of the town of Vassouras, and from there two more drops to the Parahyba. At the escarpment the altitude is roughly 600 meters, while at the river it varies from 357 meters at the western-most point to 259 meters at Ubá.

Aside from the inclination of the município and the drop from 600 to 300 meters, the higher southern portions around Sacra Família have steeper hills which disappear in the rugged terrain of the Serra do Mar; there the streams have practically no bottom land. Looking north or northeast along the strings of half-oranges the hills tend to become more rounded, the streams grow wider and bottom lands appear until at Ubá the ridges nearest the Parahyba end in low widely spaced mounds. The whole area is well watered and drained by streams which flow between the ridges in a general southwest–northeast direction, meeting the Parahyba in the eastern part of the município near Ubá. A few streams, varying from this pattern, cut across the ridges to join the Parahyba further upstream.

Nineteenth-century coffee planters of the Parahyba Valley appraised the suitability of their lands for coffee cultivation on a pragmatic basis. Indeed no chemical analysis was available

[4] Alexandre Joaquim de Siqueira, *Memória Histórica do Município de Vassouras* (Rio de Janeiro, 1852), p. 2,

then, nor even today, of the coffee soils of the area.[5] Left to their own devices, planters fell back upon the common agricultural lore that developed with the spread of coffee cultivation: the color of the soil, elevation of the terrain, and its exposure in relation to the sun. Through decomposition caused by tropical heat, humidity, and acids of vegetal origin, the soil cover of the rounded hills of the region had a generally reddish aspect to one nineteenth-century traveler.[6] Certain localities of the valley substituted the indefinite terms "good" or "cold" for color. Since coffee grown on high, hence cold, mountain slopes did not match the yield of coffee planted on lower slopes, "the majority of planters avoid the soils called 'cold.'"[7] Slopes receiving sunlight were favored over the shadier ones. A mid-century writer reported on local judgments of soil conditions: between the escarpment of the Serra do Mar and the Serra de Matacães running south of the town of Vassouras "all the lands . . . are generally exceedingly poor in quality, and the saying goes that such lands will 'only raise snakes.'" On the other hand, the lower and less inclined lands between these hills and the Parahyba River were of "better quality."[8]

The clay loam and sandy loam soils of the Parahyba Valley produced flourishing coffee groves, but their fertility was only temporary. It was noted that virgin forest often had little vegetable mold, a condition ascribed to loose, gritty soil which permitted decomposed organic matter to seep through in

[5] According to an observer of 1858, "there exists no soil analysis to determine where coffee, sugar cane or manioc produce best." G. S. Capanema, *Agricultura. Fragmentos do Relatório dos Commissários Brazileiros á Exposição Universal de Paris em 1855* (Rio de Janeiro, 1858), p. 8. This was the situation when Delden Laerne toured the area in 1884. C. F. Van Delden Laerne, *Brazil and Java. Report on Coffee Culture in America, Asia and Africa* (London, 1885), p. 258. A more recent comment sums up present conditions: "It is practically impossible to describe accurately the coffee soils of Minas Gerais, Rio de Janeiro and Espírito Santo from observation. There is no published information on these soils." Henry W. Spielman, "The Coffee Future of Brazil" (MS U.S. Embassy, Rio de Janeiro. Report No. 249, 1946), p. 21.

[6] Delden Laerne described the three gradations of red he found: very dark purple-hued (*terra vermelha*), yellowish and brownish red (*massapé*) and very red (*terra roxa*). *Brazil and Java*, pp. 255, 260.

[7] Agostinho Rodrigues Cunha, *Arte da Cultura e Preparação do Café* (Rio de Janeiro, 1844), pp. 42–43. "Cold" lands included all elevations above 2000 feet.

[8] Siqueira, *Memória Histórica*, p. 1.

combination with water instead of remaining on the surface.[9]
More recently it has been observed that these lateritic Brazilian
soils, despite the fact that they are often extremely fertile, are
"liable to become rapidly impoverished by loss of some of their
essential constituent elements, such as organic matter which is
present in great quantities while they are virgin." [10]

(2)

From the discovery of the first mines in Minas Gerais late in
the seventeenth century, it was gold and gold alone that
fascinated native-born Brazilians and immigrant Portuguese,
attracting them magnetically to the desolate, forbidding hills
of Ouro Prêto, Marianna, and Sabará. In their passage from
the coast to the interior they had eyes only for the far-off gold
fields; the intervening forest which they traversed from Rio de
Janeiro, up the Serra do Mar, down to the Parahyba and
across the Serra da Mantiqueira until they reached their
destination, drew little attention until the end of the mining
boom forced them to turn elsewhere for a livelihood. Then, in
effect, the first wave of settlement rolled back upon itself, back
upon the neglected areas which had been gradually furrowed
by the tropeiro-worn trails to bring in supplies and take out gold.

Early in the eighteenth century at the beginning of the
mining boom the first line of communication between Minas
and Rio de Janeiro via the port of Paraty southwest of Rio[11]
proved unsatisfactory and new passages over the escarpment
were sought. One of these roads, the New Road or *Caminho
Novo*, left the river town of Parahyba do Sul and entered what

[9] Delden Laerne, *Brazil and Java*. p. 259.

[10] Escritorio Técnico Paulo de Assis Ribeiro, *Settlement Possibilities in the State of
Paraná* (São Paulo, 1949), p. 25. After only a brief period of cultivation, it was seen
in the Rio area that the layer of humus or vegetal earth "was already unfit for
vegetation" and contained "clay mixed with water." Rodrigues Cunha, *Arte da
Cultura*, p. 36.

[11] Leading north to Minas from Paraty, the road was called the Estrada da
Serra do Facão and was the first road over which passed the "golden riches and
precious stones torn from the wilderness." One of the reasons given for its later
abandonment by the royal government was the ease with which gold and diamonds
could be smuggled out. José de Souza Azevedo Pizarro e Araujo, *Memórias
Históricas do Rio de Janeiro e das Provincias Annexas* (9 vols., Rio de Janeiro, 1820–
1822), III, 54, note 19.

is now the município of Vassouras at Caburú; then following
the Ubá River upstream to the Serra do Mar and descending
to the lowlands, it arrived at the port of Estrella on the Bay of
Guanabara. On this path immediately north of the Sapé Pass
in the Serra do Mar was founded the parish of Paty do Alferes
(1726),[12] Vassouras's first. Variants of the Caminho Novo were
subsequently established in order to avoid the trip across the
bay and perhaps the over-zealous check points of the royal
government. By cutting in a westerly direction after leaving
the clearing (*roça*) of the Alferes, a route was opened to a pass
in the Serra do Mar and down the escarpment to the way-
stations of Iguassú, Jacotinga, and Inhaúma overland to Rio
de Janeiro. The new road drew many travelers, and in 1750
another parish was established, Sacra Família do Caminho
Novo do Tingúa.[13]

Road-builders and way-station proprietors who mushroomed
along the narrow path of the Caminho Novo were enclosed by
primeval forest, cutting off any landmarks that might serve as
points of reference. Two frequently mentioned points on contemporary maps were the Serra do Mar—often called the
"serras do mar" because of the variety of local names used—
and the Parahyba River. Between these lay the wilderness
(*certão*) of rolling, forested hills which might hold precious
minerals for all that was known.[14] Proprietors identified them-

[12] André João Antonil (João Antonio Andreoni, S. J.) left a description of the
Caminho Novo in the first decade of the eighteenth century. He cited the "roça"
or clearing of the Alferes and a hill, "Cabarú." *Cultura e Opulencia do Brasil por
suas Drogas e Minas* (A. d'E. Taunay, ed., São Paulo, 1923), p. 243.

[13] For discussion of the roads that opened Vassouras and neighboring areas
during the eighteenth century, see José Mattoso Maia Forte, "Introdução à
Corografía de Vassouras," *Revista da Sociedade de Geografía do Rio de Janeiro*, XLVIII
(1941), 24–33; José Mattoso Maia Forte, *Memória da Fundação de Vassouras* (Rio
de Janeiro, 1933), pp. 5–7; Basílio de Magalhães, "García Rodrigues Paes,"
Revista do Instituto Histórico e Geográphico Brazileiro, LXXXIV (1918), 9–40.

[14] During the eighteenth century the Portuguese crown was constantly on the
lookout for new discoveries of valuable metals. In 1743, for example, the brothers
João de Godoes and José de Moraes received a *sesmaría* of land paralleling the
Caminho Novo. It was stipulated in the grant that such concession "will not
comprehend ownership of Mines or any kind of metal whatsoever that may be
discovered there. . . ." Carta de Sesmaría in Medição Judicial da Fazenda das
Palmas, 1837. Cartório do Primeiro Offício de Vassouras (hereafter cited as
CPOV).

selves as owners of "half a league of frontage on each side of the Caminho Novo," but the road itself was the center of activity where each day's journey ended with a tiny nucleus of life, the trading-station (*venda*) and its neighboring shelter (*rancho*) at which passing muleteers (*tropeiros*) could stop for the night and purchase corn for the animals and for themselves beans and *cachaça*, "fine and transparent like water and in taste resembling Scotch whisky." [15]

Three new developments operated to complete the settlement of Vassouras during the last quarter of the eighteenth century and the first quarter of the nineteenth: the exhaustion of the mines to the north, the extension of coffee cultivation to the uplands of the Parahyba Valley, and the elimination of a small group of Coroado Indians in what is now Valença on the north bank of the Parahyba. Back from the mines and from the towns situated on the roads which had thriven on mining trade[16] came those who had enriched themselves, the contingents from Barbacena and São João d'El-Rey with one eye on the virgin hills dotted with occasional squatters and the other on the nearby market in the city of Rio de Janeiro for sugar, rum, corn, pork, beans, and bananas. Dominated by the speculative background and get-rich-quick psychology of a mining economy, they saw great opportunities in the Vassouras area. Meanwhile the Indians of Valença had been placed in a mission (*aldeia*) and quickly deprived of their lands.[17] Opening the

[15] Reverend R. Walsh, *Notices of Brasil in 1828 and 1829* (2 vols., London, 1830), II, 8. Walsh's equally noted contemporary, French traveler Auguste de Saint-Hilaire, remarked that cachaça kept the "taste of copper and smoke," developed in the course of distillation. *Voyage dans les Provinces de Rio de Janeiro et de Minas Geraes* (Paris, 1830), I, 65.

[16] On a visit to the mining areas of Minas in 1816 Saint-Hilaire described Barbacena, one of the towns which sent many of its sons to Vassouras, as owing its existence solely to the passing "caravanes." He saw no intensive agricultural activity in the environs of the town. *Voyage*, I, 118.

[17] Writing in 1850 an observer noted bitterly that the aldeia of Valença had been an example of "laxity in educating the Indians, of abandonment of their interests, and of their dispersion." He flayed both Jesuits and those who succeeded them in the administration of Indian interests in general of the province of Rio. "The reduction of the Indian to the Faith," he wrote, "was the mask that gave a moral tone to their captivity. . . ." Joaquim Norberto de Souza Silva, "Memória Histórica e Documentada das Aldeas de Indios da Província do Rio de Janeiro,"

combined areas of Valença and Vassouras required new roads that could tap more closely the mounting exports of corn, cane, bacon, and coffee. In quick succession there appeared two new roads, both originating north of the Parahyba: the Estrada do Commércio opened in 1813, which entered the município of Vassouras at Commércio on the river and traversed the central part of Vassouras; and the Estrada da Polícia, inaugurated in 1820. The latter crossed the Parahyba at Desengano, passed through the town of Vassouras and descended the escarpment near Sacra Família.[18]

(3)

Two types of pioneer appeared early along the roads and each established his claim in a different way. There were those who asked and received *sesmarías* or grants of land from the Portuguese crown because they had helped in opening a road or because the grant would permit the grantee to be of public service, probably referring to the growing of crops which could be sold to the tropeiros.[19] Existence of large amounts of unclaimed land on both sides of the road was frequently emphasized. By law the grants along the Minas road and its variants could not be longer than a half-league on each side of the road,

Revista do Instituto Histórico e Geographico Brazileiro, XVII (1854), 112. By midcentury so many settlers and their families had become established on lands formerly in Indian hands, it was almost impossible to repair the damage. *Relatório do Presidente da Província do Rio de Janeiro*, May 4, 1862, pp. 35–36. According to a rumor still current in Vassouras, one of the "benefactors" of the Valença mission, an important landholder, removed his Indian charges by free distribution of poisoned cachaça.

[18] Walsh traveled this road in 1828 and recorded the town as "Bassura." *Notices of Brazil*, II, 41. Two Mineiros, Luciano Leite Ribeiro and Joaquim José Teixeira Leite, held contracts for repairing the sections of the Estrada da Polícia in the limits of the município of Vassouras. Letter of provincial president Paulino José Soares de Souza to CMV, November 5, 1839. APV, 1839.

[19] A typical *Carta de Sesmaría* granted for settlement along the Caminho Novo do Tinguá in 1743 read: ". . . that they had maintained diligently the road of Minas Geraes that went overland to wit to the place called the clearing of the Alferes where they intended to establish themselves with their slaves, that they were the possessors of cultivated land not only for public utility but also in the interest of His Majesty's Fifths in transporting them by land without running the risk of the sea." Carta de Sesmaría granted to João de Godoes and José de Moraes in Medição Judicial da Fazenda das Palmas, 1837. CPOV.

with an equal distance back into the wilderness. Grants were to follow each other, each square league fitting on to the preceding one. Royal admonitions to measure and cultivate these grants do not seem to have been carried out for many sesmarías were sold almost immediately without signs of land boundaries or cultivation of crops and it seems likely that the sesmarías were often sought purely for their negotiable value.[20] Only in the geographically more favored eastern section of the município in the wide bottom lands of the Ubá and Sacco rivers and their tributaries sugar cultivation and processing early brought a number of plantation nuclei. Here the Ribeiro de Avellar and Werneck extended families (kinship groups) established themselves effectively on huge grants along the Caminho Novo in the third quarter of the eighteenth century.

Another type of land occupation developed along the mule paths later opened in the higher areas of the município. Attracted by the lively market provided by the pack trains, squatters (*posseiros*) built ranchos for tropeiros and their pack-animals and made small clearings for the corn, beans, cane, and pasture required by the trade. Some of these squatters subsequently obtained sesmarías, others sold out to newcomers, and still others continued undisturbed in the occupation of considerable tracts of land. The legal rights of such holders were embodied in a series of Portuguese dispositions protecting effective cultivators of the soil from eviction.[21]

[20] Speculation in royal land grants was conspicuous at this time. For example, in return for sixteen land grants the Portuguese crown around 1700 assigned to García Rodrigues Paes the construction of the Caminho Novo from the Parahyba river to the escarpment and down to the coastal lowlands. The crown, exasperated by Rodrigues Paes's slow pace, wrote to the governor-general of Rio de Janeiro in 1725: ". . . García Roiz Paes had failed to open the caminho novo to Minas where he desired to get possession of land grants which he says were promised him, on the pretext that his age no longer permitted him to bear the inclemencies of the wilderness, and he sold them after perpetrating this deception, and did not open the said road." Basilio de Magalhães, "García Rodrigues Paes," pp. 28, 32–33, 39–40. For further examples of similar speculation, see José Mattoso Maia Forte, A Fazenda do "Secretario" em Vassouras. Sua Origem e Fim. Ms. in Archives, Serviço do Patrimonio Histórico e Artístico Nacional, Rio de Janeiro.

[21] A recent study by Virginia Rau illustrates the importance of effective cultivation of the soil as the primary condition of royal land grants in Portugal in the form of *presúria* during the reconquest and the sesmaría in the post-reconquest period.

As long as there remained ample tracts of unclaimed land in the Vassouras area and no highly profitable crop to inflate land values, few difficulties arose between those who bought or received large grants and those titleless proprietors interested in subsistence agriculture. The development that interrupted large landholders and squatters in their efforts to establish themselves as producers of subsistence crops and growers of the colonial staple, sugar, and that moved them from an era of contemplation of virgin forest to one of bitter defense of each yard of land, each vague boundary marker, each tortuously worded scrap of signed paper, was the irresistible advance of the coffee bush. From the turn of the century onward coffee appeared in the inventories of deceased planters under various names: first as a garden (*horta*), then as an orchard (*pomar*), and later as a coffee grove (*cafesal*), it began to be counted in the hundreds and later in the thousands of bushes. Its spread throughout the município intensified the fight over the possession of land, a struggle whose roots were imbedded in the previous hundred years of vaguely marked grants embracing scores of square kilometers, and of equally vague legislation.

In 1809 the Portuguese government, then exiled in Rio de Janeiro, ordered that no unclaimed public lands be left between concessions in the course of their measurement, presumably a blow at squatters. This measure further complicated the confused situation of land tenure, a situation described by one historian as an "impenetrable maze of textual incongruence, of contradictory dispositions . . . an impossible conglomeration of doubts and pitfalls." [22] An attempt was made to clarify the muddled situation in 1817 when the measurement and registration of all holdings were requested whether title to them was sesmaría, inheritance, purchase, or squatting.[23] It seems

Sesmarías Medievais Portuguesas (Lisboa, 1946), pp. 23–24, 127–128. A law of 1767, particularly applicable to Brazil, assumed that the squatter had some right to his otherwise titleless property and in 1795 a royal order, more specific than that of 1767, was promulgated to protect those who "possessed lands without any title other than the daily use of their holdings." Ruy Cirne Lima, *Terras Devolutas* (Porto Alegre, 1935), p. 44.

[22] Lima, *Terras Devolutas*, p. 43.

[23] Affonso d'Escragnolle Taunay, *História do Café no Brasil*. (15 vols. Rio de Janeiro, 1939–1943), III, 65. This was the Tombamento or land registry of 1817.

probable that the results of this legislation showed numerous posseiros and sesmeiros living side by side, for in 1822 the government abolished the granting of sesmarías and instituted the recognition of titleless holdings if squatters could establish proof of effective cultivation.

The opportunity to establish effective land rights through unmolested occupation and cultivation of unfrequented portions of huge plantations lured squatters at this time. If any public lands remained unclaimed after 1822, they did not continue so for long. Replying to a questionnaire, in 1843 the Câmara Municipal of Vassouras informed the president of the province of Rio that the município had no unoccupied public lands.[24] But with the disappearance of the last unclaimed land in Vassouras and the rapid expansion of cultivation during the second quarter of the nineteenth century, litigation increased.

Lawsuits between those who considered themselves rightful titleholders and those they termed "intruders" were particularly frequent in the western portions of Vassouras where roads which were developed in the first quarter of the century attracted squatters.[25] Titleholders of lands never adequately measured nor marked remained fearful of anyone entering, clearing, and planting unmolestedly on their lands, then erecting almost irrefutable signs of "undisturbed and pacific possession"—houses for slaves and master as well as machinery sheds. Often such interlopers, if left undisturbed, sold the cleared land and buildings to a third party and made eviction a more complicated process.[26]

By the 1830's the presence of squatters menaced the development of coffee cultivation on the large fazendas to the point

[24] CMV to João Caldas Vianna. APV, 1843.

[25] As one planter complained in 1828: "On my plantation where there have been erected large sugar and coffee processing works, with immense cultivation of other crops which I have developed for many years and where I cultivate and enjoy pacific and never interrupted nor altered ownership, it happens that about one month ago Luis de Lace intruded within the confines of the said fazenda to clear underbrush and cut down trees in the area called Matta-Caens . . . in my forest reserves . . . which was always known by all as part of my plantation and where I have many farmers who are my renters. . . ." Colonel Ambrozio de Souza Coutinho vs. Luis de Lace. APV, 1828.

[26] Manoel Francisco Bernardes vs. Simão da Rocha Loureiro. APV, 1829; Conselheiro José Clemente Pereira vs. Manoel de Avellar. APV, 1834.

where those who had consolidated large holdings through numerous purchases or through possession of eighteenth-century grants resolved to establish unquestionable legal title to their domain. This they could accomplish through supervised measurement, description, and demarcation of the sesmarías.[27] The judicial measurement of the Fazenda das Palmas in the western sector was typical of the process which was to culminate in the undisputed dominance of the large plantation in Vassouras coffee economy.

According to the petition directed in 1834 to the local judge, the proprietors of the Fazenda das Palmas, all heirs of Bento de Oliveira Braga,[28] asked the court to take appropriate steps to "measure, describe and mark the sesmarías" that provided title to the plantation's lands. All residents of the area were by law to be notified officially of the legal measurement. Fully aware, however, of the subterfuges used by the titleless squatters, the heirs added to their petition that "Since it may well occur that several of the parties to be cited may conceal themselves, let your Honor be pleased to order that such parties be advised of the time of the action through the persons of their families, neighbors, employees, or overseers." As the legal case unfolded, the sesmeiros submitted proof of ownership: bills of sale and copies of royal grants obtained from notarial offices in Rio de Janeiro. The stumbling block appeared later when the residents through whose lands the new markers ran rebutted the documents presented by the sesmaría-holders and stressed the fact that no one had ever disputed their residence. Said one posseiro of his father: ". . . he came and established himself

[27] The legal process was known as judicial measurement (*medição judicial*). In charge of the work was a surveyor (*agrimensor* or *pilôto*) who employed compass and chains. The chains were graduated in lengths of five or ten *braças* (approximately eleven or twenty-two meters). Every planter preserved certain documents to prove ownership or distinguish the boundaries of his plantation: papers included a copy of the original sesmaría, or any bills of land purchases (*escrita*), a map of the plantation (*planta*) and the surveyor's account (*derrota*) of the terrain and the markers encountered in following the plantation's boundaries. These items were preserved in tin tubes and kept on the plantations. See J. M. P. de Vasconcellos, *Livro das Terras* (4th ed., Rio de Janeiro, 1885), pp. v, 114–117.

[28] Oliveira Braga and his wife had purchased two sections of lands (*datas*) in 1813 from a land surveyor, Simão Antonio da Roza Pinheiro, and his wife. In Medição Judicial da Fazenda das Palmas, 1834, CPOV.

in this parish in 1822, bought a small holding where he constructed quarters and learning in that year that the forest there belonged to the Fazenda da Santa Cruz,[29] known publicly as the King's Wilderness, and taking the liberty to establish himself wherever he wished and without the slightest opposition by anyone, he came to this place at the headwaters of the Ribeirão do Pocinho . . . created a holding which he improved with buildings, and planted and cultivated fields." Then came the crux of his case against the sesmaría-holders: "Since I was left in undisturbed and peaceful possession of these lands through just titles of inheritance and succession from my father for many years and without the slightest opposition of anyone, unquestionably the measurement which took a different course and unduly entered the lands of the complainant on the sole pretext of measuring, describing and marking the Fazenda das Palmas can never, must never be upheld." [30] A second complainant accused the Palmas' proprietors of "Machiavellism" when they claimed that their titles were older than those of the residents there, whether possessors of royal grants or as proprietors over long and uninterrupted periods. Through the fog of verbiage, of point and counterpoint, it is clear that the struggle involved grants and squatting rights never described, measured, nor marked, each grant made to follow the "square" of earlier grants and without lines or points of reference ever having been established. When the legal battle ended, the Palmas plantation emerged relatively unaffected by the charges leveled by the small holders.

Partly to terminate litigation and partly to ascertain the status of public lands for purposes of colonization, in 1854 the Imperial Government issued a decree confirming the rights of titleholders and creating machinery whereby squatters might legitimize their holdings.[31] However well intentioned this

[29] This fazenda was originally one of the holdings belonging to the Jesuits and was transferred to the Portuguese crown at the time of the expulsion of the Jesuits by the Marquês de Pombal. The lands of the Fazenda da Santa Cruz ran from the coastal area around Itaguahy north to the Parahyba river.

[30] Joaquim José Furtado in Medição, 1834.

[31] Charles Reybaud, *Le Brésil* (Paris, 1856), p. 203–206. On the confused situation of land tenure in the 1850's, see Charles Ribeyrolles, *Brasil Pitoresco* (2 vols.,

legislation, it came too late. Despite the determined and sometimes scornful stand of the small posseiros, they could not long
continue the fight against powerful opponents with friends in
Rio, ample funds for lawyers, and time to travel to and from
the town center of the município. Although a large number of
small holders continued to exist in the period from 1830 to 1850
and afterwards, their position grew increasingly subordinate as
the wealth of the município became synonymous with the coffee
production of the large fazenda. Sandwiched between the large
planters, the small planters turned their efforts to the growing
of foodstuffs.

A registry of landed property in each of the three parishes
of the early fifties revealed that approximately eighty-two
plantations controlled the most productive of the 1,400 square
kilometers of the município of Vassouras.[32] A few clans owned
a majority of these plantations. In the western area, there were
the extended families of the Paes Leme, the Correa e Castro,
and the Araujo Padilha; the middle sections were under the
influence of the Santos Werneck, Avellar e Almeida, and
Caetano Alves clans; and in the eastern section there were the
Lacerda Werneck, the Souza Werneck, and the Ribeiro de
Avellar family groups.[33] Although division of estates among
heirs created a legal force working toward division of the land,
in fact the dominant families preserved and extended their
holdings by intermarriage within and between clans, by
partnership arrangements (*sociedades*), and later by consortiums
(*consórcios*) set up among planters and their children.[34] Concentration was further encouraged by the "immunity of land from
taxation and the heavy tax on transfers (6 per cent)." [35] Both

Gastão Penalva, tr., São Paulo, 1941), II, 12; Richard Burton, *Explorations of the
Highlands of the Brazil* (2 vols., London, 1869), I, 42, note; Lima, *Terras Devolutas*,
p. 54 and *Relatorio do Presidente da Provincia do Rio, 1855*, pp. 39–40.

[32] Maia Forte, "A Fazenda do 'Secretario'," *passim*.

[33] Maia Forte, "A Fazenda do 'Secretario'," pp. 35–36. Maia Forte obtained
his data from parochial land registers.

[34] Pedro Días Gordilho Paes Leme and others, "Organização Agrícola; Parecer
sobre a Organização Agrícola do Estado do Rio de Janeiro," *Revista Agrícola do
Instituto Fluminense de Agricultura*, XXII (June 1891), 15.

[35] Consul-General Adamson, November 30, 1878. *Report on the Commercial
Relations of the United States and Foreign Countries for the Year 1878* (Washington, 1879),
p. 192.

the extension of coffee cultivation and progressive exhaustion of virgin soil fostered what one planter described as the "almost superstitious spirit . . . of the individual agricultural proprietor whose general tendency is to augment his territorial property" and made of the município an area where a few large family-proprietors controlled thousands of acres.[36] It was with these families and the use to which they put their lands that plantation economy in Vassouras was associated.

(4)

Not only did coffee cultivation establish the pattern of large landholdings, it also required new sources of capital and credit. In an epoch of self-sufficiency, most early coffee planters purchasing lands, stocking plantations with slaves who had to be fed, clothed, and furnished with iron tools, or obtaining a few necessities such as salt from outside their immediate area found operating funds available within the limits of the município. They utilized long-established institutions. Inheritance and the marriage dowry frequently provided both lands and slaves. Nearest of kin or even the more distantly related by birth or marriage were often in a position to meet the demands. Moreover, where a limited number of planter families owned vast stretches of land in a município of restricted outside social contact, inter- and intra-family marriage tended to blur the distinction between moneylending and a family helping hand.[37]

There were neighboring planters ready to help out for a price and a few fazendeiros acquired considerable fortunes in cash as well as in land by judicious loans, as revealed in inventories of their estates. Failing to tap these sources or desiring to supplement them, there was final recourse to be found in the local capitalists, such as the members of the Teixeira Leite family. For the better part of forty years this family played an important role in supplying the credit needs of the município of Vassouras. The fact that one of the most

---

[36] Paes Leme, "Organização Agrícola," p. 15.

[37] A common practice among early planters, many of whom were illiterate, was the presentation by the borrower of a hair of the beard in recognition of a financial obligation.

prominent members of the clan, Francisco José Teixeira Leite, settled in the area in 1820 and lived there until his death in 1884 accounted to a considerable degree for the role played by the family. Even more important, however, was the fact that this member, as well as others, arrived with the financial backing of an established family of Minas Gerais.[38] Family solidarity and mutual help were vital in widening the family's financial influence, and Francisco José—"Cousin Chico" to members of the extended family who occasionally visited Vassouras from the province of Minas—urged upon his descendants the continuation of this tradition in his last will and testament: "Let each of you be a friend to the other, always united and aiding mutually, imitating the fine example of your grandparents and uncles; be . . . diligent, orderly, and economical so that you will not fall into misfortune." [39]

Loans made by such capitalists were secured by mortgages. Default ultimately involved many members of the creditor family in real estate transactions, although neither Francisco José nor his brothers ever accumulated or long administered any sizable agricultural property.[40] A surer way of collecting debts was through the planter's factor in Rio, and the Teixeira Leites maintained close contacts with the expanding business community of the capital where members of the family acted as factors (commissários). In 1839, for instance, Thomas Rufino da Silva Franco borrowed from Joaquim José Teixeira Leite to buy twelve newly arrived African slaves whom he supplemented with nineteen more through another loan. The slaves were sick when bought, as he discovered shortly thereafter when fifteen of them died, leaving him with slight means of repaying the large debt. Some installments were paid through

[38] Francisco José came to Vassouras at the age of sixteen in the company of his uncle, Custodio Ferreira Leite, who contracted for the construction of segments of the Estrada da Polícia on which the town of Vassouras was founded. Francisco José and his brother, Joaquim José, were both sons of the Barão de Itambé, who left a large fortune earned in banking.

[39] Inventory, 1884, deceased: Francisco José Teixeira Leite, executor: Alfredo Carlos Teixeira Leite, CPOV.

[40] Francisco José acquired the Fazenda da Cachoeira as part of his first wife's dowry, but the plantation was maintained largely as a residence rather than as an agricultural enterprise.

the consignment of coffee to a Rio factor, Joaquim José's brother-in-law, Luciano Leite Ribeiro, who then paid the lender from the proceeds of the coffee's sale. In 1844, however, "judging the debt if not wisely contracted, at least insufficiently guaranteed," Joaquim José proposed that Silva Franco mortgage his property and the latter complied.[41] In a later case (1859), the estate of Evaristo da Silva Franco, perhaps the son of Thomas Rufino, showed a debt of twenty-three contos to Francisco José Teixeira Leite's brother-in-law, Francisco José Teixeira e Souza, and a ten-conto debt to the Rio commissário, Caetano Furquim de Almeida, who was Francisco José Teixeira Leite's son-in-law.[42]

A fourth source of credit frequently tapped by planters during the years of prosperity was found in the Rio factors or commissários, many of whom were related or became related to Vassouras families. During the heyday of Vassouras coffee production, in the fifties and early sixties, Rio factors willingly advanced credits to their clients on the security of future harvests at interest rates varying between 12 per cent and 18 per cent per annum. Financial conditions in Rio were not favorable to the continued independence and prosperity of commission houses, however, and, with the declining importance of the município, the financial fortunes of Vassouras planters became increasingly linked to a new and far less personal institution: the banks.

Until the feverish activity of the 1850's first developed a capital market for mortgage loans on a large scale, the few banking institutions dealt only in discount and deposits.[43]

---

[41] João da Costa Coelho vs. Joaquim José Teixeira Leite, APV, 1863. Costa Coelho bitterly attacked the mortgage because the property evaluation was unnecessarily low in view of the small allowance granted for property appreciation ("increase in slave prices, progress, and improvement in cultivation of the land") between 1834 and 1844.

[42] Inventory, 1859, deceased: Anna Thereza Goulart, executor: Evaristo da Silva Franco, Fazenda Unknown, APV, 1859.

[43] The first Banco do Brazil functioned from 1808 to 1829. Nine years later François Ignace Ratton opened the Banco Commercial do Rio de Janeiro, which eventually became a bank of discount and deposit. Later two other banks appeared to meet the growing demands of the Rio market: Irineu Evangelista de Souza's (later Barão do Maúa) Banco do Brazil (1851) and the Banco Rural e Hypothecário. In 1853 the government merged the Banco Commercial and the Banco do

After 1850, when the slave trade was terminated, the release of capital hitherto employed in the African slave trade flooded the investment market, and planters found their resources expanded almost overnight as their slave property's value doubled. On the basis of this new security, commissários extended new credits to their clients and turned to the banking institutions mushrooming on all sides for funds to carry them until the coffee harvests of their clients would be marketed.

In view of the highly speculative character of these banking houses, the Imperial Government hesitated between rigid control of the financial structure maturing too quickly for its former slow growth, and a policy of *laissez faire*. After a few years of attempting to control paper money issue, the policy was reversed and five new banks of issue were authorized by finance minister Bernardo de Souza Franco. One of these was the Banco Commercial e Agrícola which in 1859 opened a branch in the town center of Vassouras and in other coffee-growing areas of the Parahyba Valley. President of the Banco Commercial and intimate friend of Souza Franco,[44] João Evangelista Teixeira Leite was also the brother of Vassouras's leading capitalist, financier Francisco José Teixeira Leite. To local planters it was probably appropriate as well as a sign of stability that the first president of the Vassouras branch of the Banco Commercial happened to be Francisco José, and two of the directors, his son-in-law and a Rio factor in his own right, Caetano Furquim de Almeida, and brother-in-law, Francisco José Teixeira e Souza.[45]

Brazil into the second government sponsored Banco do Brazil. For the nature of banking activity in the first half of the century and subsequent economic expansion of the fifties and early sixties, see Sebastião Ferreira Soares, *Elementos de Estatística comprehendendo a Theoría da Sciencia e a sua Applicação a Estatística Commercial do Brasil* (2 vols., Rio de Janeiro, 1865), I, 159 ff., and his *Esboço ou Primeiros Traços na Crise Commercial da Cidade do Rio de Janeiro em 10 de Setembro de 1864* (Rio de Janeiro, 1865), pp. 37 ff.; also, the report of the parliamentary commission of inquiry into the Souto crisis of 1864, *Relatório da Commissão encarregada pelo Governo Imperial de Proceder a um Inquérito sobre as Causas Principaes e Accidentaes da Crise do Mez de Setembro de 1864* (Rio de Janeiro, 1865). A more concise sketch of early Brazilian banking can be found in Luiz Rodrigues d'Oliveira, "Banques et Institutions de Crédit," in F. J. de Santa-Anna Nery, ed., *Le Brésil en 1889* (Paris, 1889), pp. 351–352.

[44] Jorge Pinto, *Fastos Vassourenses* (Vassouras, 1935), p. 271.
[45] Ignácio Raposo, *História de Vassouras* (Vassouras, 1935), p. 151.

INTRODUCTION

(5)

Engrossed in clearing patches of forest to plant foodstuffs and in trying a new crop, coffee, the pioneer planter had little leisure to look beyond immediate necessities. Once his crops were sown, his next preoccupation was getting a roof over the head of his family, his slaves, his water-driven machinery, and his harvests. The nearby stream served for drinking water; he planted his crop of cane along its banks; from it he diverted the water to drive his primitive processing equipment, a grist mill (*moinho de fubá*) and a pounding mill (*monjollo*).[46] If he prospered at the spot, he added a small water wheel to run a mill for grinding cane. Once these tasks were finished, he planted along the roads and on the borders of his fields rows of fruit trees, oranges, bananas, and others including, too, an orchard for the "enjoyment and recreation of himself and his family." [47]

In the midst of forest that encroached on all sides, in touch with the outside world only when travelers stopped for the night, the early fazendas were more than the way-stations surrounded by tiny clearings typical of the years before 1800. They were nuclei of settlement. From these pinpoints of population there went out each day the free and the slave to clear the forest, to plant and harvest. In exchange for coffee and other products sent to Rio they received iron for implements worn in the siege with the forest, and slaves to wield them, also

[46] Francisco Peixoto de Lacerda Werneck (Barão do Paty do Alferes), *Memória sobre a Fundação e Costeio de uma Fazenda na Província do Rio Janeiro* (4th ed., Rio de Janeiro, 1878), pp. 1, 3–4. The first edition was written before 1847 according to documents relating to the Werneck Family in the National Archives, Rio de Janeiro, and was entitled *Rudimentos de Agricultura Brazileira contendo Utilíssimas Noções Indispensaveis para a Applicação e Cultura de Café, Chá, Milho, Feijão, Canna de Assucar, etc.*, Rio de Janeiro, no date. When the Barão do Paty died in 1861 he left one of the largest landed fortunes amassed to that time in the município of Vassouras, a fortune obtained through the inheritance and purchase of six plantations as well as way-stations on the Estrada do Commercio. His grandfather, Sargento-Mor Ignácio de Souza Werneck, had drifted back from the Minas center of Barbacena prior to 1750 and was at mid-century residing in the parish of Parahyba do Sul, founded as a way-station on the Caminho Novo das Minas. Francisco Klörs Werneck, *História e Genealogía Fluminense* (Rio de Janeiro, 1947), p. 60.
[47] Lacerda Werneck, *Memória*, p. 5.

cotton goods and salt. In common with all pioneer plantations, everything was temporary: the essential job was to feed, clothe, and house the people of the settlement.

Early fazendas, like the later ones, were planned as functional squares. Living quarters for the free (*casa de vivenda*) were set up against the base of a hill with dwelling units located over an incomplete ground floor or cellar partially dug out of the hillside. Around the square were aligned the slave quarters (*senzallas*), the storehouses (*armazens, tulhas*), the cribs (*paióes*), mule sheds (*casas de tropa*), stables (*estribarías*), and the pigpens (*chiqueiros*). In the center of the square there was nothing but a wide expanse of beaten earth called the *terreiro*, dusty in the winter sun, a quagmire in the torrential summer rains. This nucleus of buildings was known as the fazenda's *sede*. Since most of the fazendas were situated near falls on the streams where a marked drop could supply water power for the primitive fazenda machinery, the sound of the falls was constant. For this reason so many of the fazendas were called "Cachoeira" (waterfall) or "Ribeirão" (stream); others were named after the patron saint of the founder, after a topographical feature or after one of the awe-inspiring forest giants growing in the neighborhood.[48]

These early structures were utilitarian, primitive to an extreme. Walls were made of wooden corner posts, rough-hewn, the spaces filled with uprights of *palmeira* wood across which were tied strips of the same wood. As metal was hard to come by and had to be laboriously and expensively hauled in by mule, a wirelike liana (*cipó de São João*) was used to tie the palmeira crossbars to the poles. Over this framework was thrown mud, producing the mud-and-wattle construction (*pau-à-pique* or *sopapo*) common to this day in the Brazilian interior. All construction was roofed with *sapé*, a common grass. Bare earth was the floor of rooms constructed over the rear of the incomplete cellar, for time and labor could be diverted

[48] Typical of those named after the patron saint of the founder: São Francisco (owned by Francisco Luis dos Santos Werneck), São Fernando (owned by Fernando Luis dos Santos); for those referring to a topographical feature: Boa Vista, Lagoa, Vargem, Ribeirão; and for those named after trees: Sucupira, Pau Ferro, Palmeiras, Pau Grande, Guaribú.

only to flooring storage bins to keep crops from moisture and rats.

Primitive surroundings and the need for self-sufficiency produced the mentality characteristic of frontier psychology. During this period of expansion, 1800–1830, each small improvement in the standard of living, each modest luxury, received careful attention. Inventories of the time are filled with minutiae: the number of squared logs, the precise weight of copper pans, the three-legged stools, the wooden bowls of all sizes, the available billhooks, axes, digging sticks, and hoes, the implements of the fazenda's smithy, the contents of the fazenda's chapel, the number of doors and windows in the dwelling house of the fazendeiro. Perhaps strangest of all, each roof tile burnt in the fazenda's kiln (*olaría*) was counted; a typical inventory stated that the roof of the dwelling house had 5,200 tiles.[49] Seldom were wheeled vehicles of any type mentioned, for the narrow trails could offer passage over long distances only to mules.[50] This was the period of small-scale cultivation carried on by a few slaves when coffee was slowly, hesitatingly adapted to the highlands, when fazendeiros learned the agricultural know-how that they were to follow for the rest of the century.

In the development of techniques, fazendeiros had few manuals and such as they had were based on inadequate practice and poor theory.[51] Even those few were restricted in

[49] Inventory, 1825, deceased: Antonio Vieira Machado, executrix: Isabel Ignacia do Nascimento, Fazenda unknown, CPOV.

[50] On the larger plantations ox-carts with fixed axles were used to haul in the harvests.

[51] Borges de Barros in one of the first Brazilian coffee manuals offered a short bibliography of French authors who wrote on coffee planting in the Antilles. In closing his articles he gave advice which was practiced by the more empirically minded planters of Vassouras. "It's not wise to read these materials without first understanding the necessary principles for reasoning with them, and to avoid following blindly what they say, for otherwise it is very easy to lose time and money because there are authors who publish readily what they imagine without the stamp of experience . . . we must therefore read carefully but never practice what we get from our reading without studying the local situation." "Memória sobre o Café," *O Patriota*, VI (June 1813), 43. Padre João Joaquim Ferreira de Aguiar, who lived in the municípios of Vassouras and Valença, attacked the most important Brazilian agricultural periodical of the time, the *Auxiliador da Indústria*

influence, for the number of literate fazendeiros was small.[52] Consequently the methods used by early coffee growers were those of trial and error. Fazendeiros probably saw their neighbors receive a few seedlings (*mudas*) from muleteers on their return from the lowlands.[53] Within three or four years new mudas sprouted beneath the first bushes and these were given to the fazendeiros of the neighborhood whose interest was aroused by the high prices paid for coffee and its lighter weight in shipping compared to that of other crops.[54] Coffee planting was tried in various types of soil and terrain, at first probably being put into former corn and sugar cane fields until experience taught that virgin soil and well drained land were essential to its profitable cultivation. Such experiments took a toll in worn out land and prematurely aged or unproductive bushes. Inventories of many fazendas of this early period report coffee

Nacional, because it had published "fine theories, and the practices of foreigners; but said nothing on the theory and practice of Brazilians." *Pequena Memória sobre a Plantação, Cultura e Colheita do Café na qual se expõe os Processos seguidos pelos Fazendeiros d'esta Província desde que se planta até ser exportado para o Commercio* (Rio de Janeiro, 1836), pp. 5–6. Other manuals available to fazendeiros at this time included: C. A. Taunay, *Manual do Agricultor Brazileiro, Obra Indispensavel á Todo o Senhor de Engenho, Fazendeiro e Lavrador* (2nd ed., Rio de Janeiro, 1839), and Augustinho Rodrigues Cunha, *Arte da Cultura e Preparação do Café* (Rio de Janeiro, 1844).

[52] A large number of fazendeiros signed petitions during this period with an "X".

[53] Ferreira de Aguiar described this process in considerable detail. "On the establishments of Desengano Feliz, where I live, it was at first necessary to order mudas from spots one or two days distant, as soon as the neighbors' supply gave out; many of them died on the trip, and constancy was required lest we lose courage; we can say that as many were lost as are alive today." *Pequena Memória*, p. 7. Compare Francisco Freire Allemão, "Quaes São as Principaes Plantas que Hoje se acham acclimatadas no Brazil," p. 571.

Borges de Barros claimed that the first coffee bush that appeared in the city of Rio de Janeiro belonged to "Jopeman, a Dutchman, who established himself in this City." "Memoria sobre o Cafe," V (May 1813), 12. The National Archives contain the request of a Norberta Joaquina Hopman in 1789 who claimed she had "several slaves and no lands granted by sesmaría." She wanted a grant in what is today part of the município of Vassouras. In Sesmarías do Estado do Rio, Caixa 130, Arquivo Nacional.

[54] Wrote Rodrigues Cunha on the motivating forces behind expanding coffee production in the Province of Rio: ". . . if its price will more than repay the labor which its cultivation and processing demand, and if in addition the capital invested will give a return superior to any other branch of industry, it is natural that its production spreads as rapidly as possible." *Arte da Cultura*, p. 106.

bushes with no value usually near the dwelling house.[55] Sometimes these bushes were pruned to within inches of the ground in the hope of saving them.

But planting went on, the profits of the successfully grown bushes returning to the fazenda in the form of more slaves to undertake ever greater plantings. Fazenda self-sufficiency[56] coupled with cheap, plentiful land and a growing labor force

TABLE I. Slave imports into Brazil, 1840–1851.

Year	Number	Year	Number
1840	30,000	1846	50,324
1841	16,000	1847	56,172
1842	17,435	1848	60,000
1843	19,095	1849	54,000
1844	22,849	1850	23,000
1845	19,453	1851	3,287
		Total	371,615

Source: Based upon Liverpool statistics cited in Sebastião Ferreira Soares, *Notas Estatísticas sobre a Producção Agrícola e Carestia dos Géneros Alimentícios no Imperio do Brazil* (Rio de Janeiro, 1860), pp. 134–135.

placed a floor under the experiment and soon coffee took its place beside sugar and subsistence crops as a pillar in the growing economy of the município.

By the middle thirties coffee cultivation was no longer a haphazard venture. In Vassouras as in the neighboring municípios the number of coffee trees had become the measure of a planter's wealth[57] and was a clear indication of the number

[55] Inventory, 1824, deceased: Luisa María de Jesus, executor: Francisco Quirino da Rocha, Fazenda Morro Azul, CPOV. "One coffee orchard of 1500 trees behind the house on a very steep and stony hillside, and the coffee very yellow and moribund; one orchard of 6000 trees on the other side of the river . . . very poorly tended."

[56] "A careful fazendeiro always has a splendid dinner, which costs him in cash only wine and salt . . . his establishment provides the rest and in great profusion." Lacerda Werneck, *Memória*, p. 10.

[57] In 1836, according to a resident of both Valença and Vassouras, there were "establishments of 500, 600, 800 thousand coffee bushes . . . so that the municípios sometimes export annually more than 300 thousand arrobas of coffee . . ." Ferreira de Aguiar, *Pequena Memória*, p. 6.

of slaves in his labor force. By the fifth decade of the century, as the taste for coffee spread among Europe's and America's expanding urban populations, the demand for slaves and the hunger for virgin forest grew among the coffee planters of the Parahyba Valley.

In response to the demand, at least 371,615 African slaves were openly smuggled into Brazil between 1840 and 1851 (Table 1). Vassouras fazendeiros with ample land and credit made enormous additions to their labor force in these years.

At the same time, as coffee production augmented, the large plantation emerged as the dominant producer of the crop, tending to absorb in its land hunger small and medium sized holdings. This tendency was to be intensified in the succeeding decade of the fifties, years of unprecedented prosperity.

PART TWO

THE ECONOMY OF PROSPERITY

CHAPTER II

Plantations in the Fifties and Sixties

THE decade of the 1850's was the golden age of coffee and the society based upon it in Vassouras. The fears and failures of these years were forgotten in the nostalgia evoked but three decades later when only their optimism and exuberance were remembered.

Strangely, although the spurt in the slave trade had made possible the rapid extension of coffee culture in the previous decade, it was the end of that trade that sparked the prosperity and opulence. To those whose holdings were small and poorly stocked with slaves the rapid rise in slave prices after 1852 proved a calamity. But for the landholders who had gone into debt in the purchase of large lots of slaves in the period of lower prices the end of the trade was a boon. It doubled the security which could be offered for further loans and permitted them to break down the primitive self-sufficient economy that characterized the early plantations. Furthermore, it is doubtful if the shortage of slave labor was felt immediately, for one contemporary economist explained that until 1860 the migration of slave property from the northern provinces of Brazil to the coffee-growing areas compensated for the absence of new levies from Africa.[1]

Meanwhile the slave traders who had previously invested their *contos* in ships and human cargoes now turned their large capital to banking, to importing and exporting ventures, and

---

[1] Sebastião Ferreira Soares estimated that the planters of Rio de Janeiro, São Paulo and Rio Grande do Sul provinces received approximately 14,774 slaves from the African coast annually between 1840–1851 after deducting possible losses through disease, flight and those who remained in urban centers. From 1852 to 1859 Rio de Janeiro received 5,500 slaves annually from northern Brazil, which he thought compensated for the extinction of the traffic because "they began to work immediately in the fields." *Notas Estatísticas*, pp. 135–136.

to the financing of enterprises to bring material improvements to the country, particularly transportation companies.[2] New fortunes were also being made by coffee merchants and the economic life of the Province of Rio de Janeiro as a whole experienced an upsurge of activity.

Vassouras, its prosperity already committed irrevocably to one-crop agriculture, was ready to expand further its coffee acreage. With ample credit in Rio, the Vassouras planter undertook to improve and embellish his establishment and to bring to it some refinements, a desire fostered by his closer contact with the seaboard capital. Conscious of his new economic status and importance as a coffee planter, he never doubted his ability to pay off debts incurred with new crops of coffee; thus the vicious circle of destroying virgin forest to plant coffee, to pay debts to get credit for the purchase of slaves to destroy more forest and plant more coffee, closed upon the economy of Vassouras.

(2)

The Brazilian forest, with its mystery, solemnity, and brilliant color, fascinated many visitors of the nineteenth century. Entranced by his first views of the forest near Rio de Janeiro, the French botanist Saint-Hilaire wrote that to perceive the beauty of "equinoctial forests one must go deep into fastnesses as old as the world" where there was little of the monotony of European woods of oak and pine. Particularly impressive were the trees "rising perfectly straight to prodigious heights," some with smooth bark, others protected by spines. There were the enormous trunks of wild fig trees whose composite vein-like structure reminded him of flying buttresses, and the lianas such as the "cipó d'imbê" encircling the tree from

---

[2] Annual provincial reports are excellent sources for the changes that occurred during the fifties. Especially informative is the *Relatório do Presidente da Província do Rio de Janeiro, May 3, 1852*. Also Caetano Furquim de Almeida, "Carestía de Géneros Alimentícios," Annexo K, *Relatório do Presidente da Província do Rio de Janeiro, August 1, 1858*, p. 2. Affonso d'Escragnolle Taunay, *História do Café no Brasil*, IV, 71 has a brief analysis. One of the best analyses is Sebastião Ferreira Soares, *Esboço ou Primeiros Traços na Crise Commercial da Cidade do Rio de Janeiro em 10 de Setembro de 1864*, pp. 22–54.

which it drew its sustenance and the "cipó matador" which supported itself by trailers to nearby trees.[3] The "sublimity and grandeur" of the virgin forest which impressed Saint-Hilaire also affected the British chaplain Walsh who passed through the Vassouras area in 1829. Traveling the Estrada da Polícia near the crest of the escarpment of the Serra do Mar, he noted in his diary: "The road, or rather path, winded along the edge of deep vallies and ravines, from the bottom of which trees shot up to a most extraordinary height; and some of them could not be less than 400 feet . . . when they have attained that eminence, many of them begin then, and not till then, to send out lateral branches . . . forming a canopy" over the heads of their neighbors.[4] Describing the virgin stands of timber in the neighboring município of Parahyba do Sul a Brazilian botanist noted the graceful names of the trees: brown *sucopira*, white *jacarandá*, *cabiuna* and the "elegant" *jequitibá*. He marveled at the huge convoluting roots which spread down the slope, that of the sucopira twelve meters long and one of a Brazilian *cedrela* measuring forty-one meters.[5] From the size of the roots and towering crowns of these trees it is clear that the hills of Vassouras were covered with trees well spaced by nature and with sparse undergrowth to hinder the cutting down of the forest.

Little science was used by planters in selecting those portions of the forest to be cleared for planting.[6] In a tract written by one affluent fazendeiro for his European-educated son, ignorant of Brazilian agricultural practices, an empirical correlation was made between various trees and the soil in which they grew. "From afar the quality of the land can be judged by the

[3] Saint-Hilaire, *Voyage*, I, 11.
[4] Walsh, *Notices of Brasil*, II, 30–31.
[5] José de Saldanha da Gama, *Configuração e Estudo Botânico dos Vegetaes Seculares da Província do Rio de Janeiro e de Outros Pontos do Brazil* (2nd ed., Rio de Janeiro, 1872), pp. 12–13, 31–32, 34, 38, 45–46.
[6] Sources for the reconstruction of the techniques of clearing virgin forest, planting, cultivating, harvesting and processing of coffee are based upon consultation of agricultural manuals deposited in the National Library, Rio de Janeiro and upon local customs as described by aged ex-slaves, former plantation overseers and foremen and elderly residents of Vassouras. Where any doubt arose, local custom took precedence.

foliage, especially in spring, when blossoming aids the classifi-
cation of vegetation," he wrote. "Give attention to the foliage,
the shape and height of the branches, the color of the flowers,
if there are any." [7] An old ex-slave who took part in the felling
(*derrubada*) of virgin forest recalled the advice: "If the ankle
and half the calf sink into the humus beneath the tree, the soil
is good."

As a preliminary step the fazenda's carpenter looked over
the standing timber for hardwoods to fill construction needs.
Then "on the waning moon of the months without 'R,' "
when the hollows were covered with mist and the chill air
brought shivers to slaves assembling before dawn, the felling
began. Underbrush and entangling vines were cut with billhooks to clear the way for the axmen who followed. Only
slaves who handled the ax and billhook well and *caboclos* or
aggregados were detailed to this work.[8] After cleaning the ground
immediately around a large tree, the axmen began chopping
at waist-high level or sometimes from a scaffolding. A watch-
man warned the axmen when to leave an almost-cut tree to
move up the slope to another. When it trembled they left it,
and when all the trees on the slope were weakened, the more
experienced cutters chose one which they calculated would
bring down all those below it, tied as they were by the upper-
most lianas. With a roar heard for miles one tree after another
toppled, a huge wave of trees crashing to the ground. "The big
timber on the hilltop would clean out everything." This work
produced a sense of exhilaration for it was one activity where
the usual monotonous work chants of the field slaves were
replaced by songs.

To hasten drying the crowns and any branches were cut
leaving the trunks previously marked by the master carpenter

[7] F. P. de Lacerda Werneck, *Memória*, p. 11.

[8] In this dangerous task planters often substituted the labor of valuable slaves
with that of free, landless squatters who lived in tiny clearings in the forest and who
were skilled woodsmen. During the early period of settlement they were usually
halfbreeds (*caboclos*). As unclaimed land diminished the propertyless forest dweller
was joined by the dispossessed settler who had squatted along the roads, and later
by escaped slaves. This group furnished occasional day laborers (*camaradas*) and
from it planters chose a few non-rent-paying tenants (*agregados*).

to be pit-sawed on the spot. Only hardwoods were chosen for sawing boards and beams for the main plantation buildings, posts for the corral, jacarandá for bridge beams, red-grease (*oleo vermelho*) for the fixed axle of the ox-cart—"it won't catch fire because the wood has grease in it." Next a firebreak was cut around the lumbered section of forest and after the trunks or boards were dragged out by oxen, cart, and chain, the rest was left to dry until shortly before the September rains. With a rumble the wood which the "tenth generation to follow would not encounter on the devastated earth," [9] the creepers and the colorful parasitic plants went up in flames and smoke. The stumps smouldered for days and the earth was often warm when slaves came to prepare for the planting.

Planting and cultivation of coffee in the fire-blackened clearing littered with burnt and half-burnt logs, roots, and high stumps was a laborious process in which the hoe was the only feasible tool. Experience had shown that coffee rows which climbed the slopes vertically gave easy access to the coffee trees and simplified weeding and harvesting for the slave gangs.[10] Into the holes went the seedlings ripped from the ground where they had sprouted near parent bushes, for seedlings matured quicker than coffee beans planted directly. "Thrust a seedling into the hole," said one former field hand, "tamp it lightly with the hoe; thrust in the other seedling and tamp it too; throw red earth on the root. Fill the hole and tamp it hard." This same ex-slave estimated that one field hand hoed and planted daily three rows, each one hundred to one

[9] Lacerda Werneck, *Memória*, p. 13. According to this author, many planters ordered their forests burnt "with sang-froid, as if they were committing a heroic act." Not many years before, Walsh in fact praised the patriotism of the "enterprising agriculturists" near Vassouras who "displayed . . . that improving spirit, which seems everywhere we passed, alive in Brazil. The sides of the mountain were cleared by fire, and the vegetation of useful esculents substituted for forest trees." Walsh, *Notices of Brasil*, II, 41.

[10] The practice of planting coffee in rows that climbed and descended the hillsides evolved from local experience. There are signs that early groves had little symmetry. C. A. Taunay suggested in 1839 that an orderly system be followed and not discarded. *Manual*, p. 36. Agostinho Rodrigues Cunha believed that "the way of planting coffee groves without order . . . was rejected because it made hoeing and harvesting difficult; then there came the system of planting in lines." *Arte da Cultura*, p. 29. Compare Lacerda Werneck, *Memória*, p. 46.

hundred fifty meters long and containing from thirty to forty
seedlings.

At the end of the third year the young trees produced fruit,
reaching full production at six years of age. During the period
when the plants were small it was frequently the practice to
interplant the rows of coffee with crops such as corn, beans,
and manioc thus shielding the young coffee plants from the hot
sun and providing the mainstay of the slaves' diet.[11]

At least two weedings were required annually. Men and
women slaves, old and young, were sorted into gangs and
directed to move from the bottom to the top of the hill. Each
male was equipped with a four-and-a-half to five pound hoe;
women wielded a slightly lighter one. Shortly after the first
heavy rains of late September and October came the first
weeding. Weeds and grass were hoed away from the coffee
bushes, the land beneath the trees scraped clean and all the
trash then spread around the trees to provide fertilizer during
the period of growth. Toward the end of March and early
April the gangs returned for the second weeding. The main
purpose of this cultivation was to prepare the soil for the
harvesting which followed almost immediately when the last
of the rains had passed. Instead of respreading the trash it was
piled in the center of the alley between the coffee rows where
it could not interfere with the gathering of the berries which
fell during the picking.

Planting coffee in vertical rows up and down the hills
proved a mixed blessing. The heavy tropical rains coursing
down the steep slopes tended to follow the line of coffee holes
where the earth had been depressed in planting and left the
roots of the trees "exposed to the air and the sun." One critical

---

[11] Interplanting subsistence crops helped reduce the cost of cultivating coffee
groves during the three to four years before they began to produce adequate
harvests. Hoeing of corn and manioc, for instance, also coincided with weedings
needed for coffee groves, thus eliminating a duplication of labor. Interplanting
continued until the lower branches of the bushes or "skirt" shadowed the intervening rows. When the skirts had grown smaller as coffee aged the practice of
interplanting was renewed. Planters were sure that interplanting had little effect
on coffee yields. Lacerda Werneck, *Memória*, p. 36; Ferreira de Aguiar, *Pequena
Memória*, p. 9; C. A. Taunay, *Manual*, p. 36.

writer remarked. "Look at any planted hillside after copious and continuous rains," he said, "and you will see the sad aspect it offers." [12]

The seasonal cycle that began with the clearing of forest and planting of coffee and subsistence crops, that continued with successive weedings to the tune of monotonous slave work songs, closed with the harvesting, drying, storing, and milling of the mature coffee beans. Starting in May, each dawn saw every available slave out on the hills where coffee trees showed branches heavy with reddish-brown cherries. By this time the three-year-old coffee groves had their roads which spiraled the steep sides of the hills, some wide enough for laden mules to pass, a few even wide enough for oxcarts. Slaves deposited their coffee baskets at the lower end of the row assigned to them and began picking into a screen of woven bamboo which was tied around the waist. Each branch was encircled by thumb and index finger, the hand then being pulled down and outward thus "stripping the branch in one swift motion" and filling the screen with leaves, dead twigs and coffee berries. When the strainer was heaped, the contents were thrown into the air. Coffee berries fell to the bottom of the strainer while the leaves and twigs which remained on the top were swept to the ground with a wipe of the hand. What berries fell to the ground were swept up, dropped into the screen and sifted.[13] Into the bag went the berries and what leaves and twigs remained and when the bag was filled the slave carried it to an open-air shed (*rancho*) nearby where it awaited transport to the drying

[12] Rodrigues Cunha, *Arte da Cultura*, p. 31. Earlier, C. A. Taunay wrote that in his opinion "the heavy torrential rains which sweep down the steep slopes where most Brazilian coffee is cultivated . . . carry off a portion of the humus which gave to the clay its fertility leaving it as though 'caput mortuum.' " *Manual*, pp. 35–36.

[13] There is a wide divergence of opinion between what the manuals say and what local informants recounted on the subject of harvesting methods. According to the former, the coffee berries were pulled or beaten to the ground, then picked up and winnowed. Local custom has it that every picker tried to get as many berries into the screen as possible. Ferreira de Aguiar's comment is typical of what the manuals say: the slave "will throw on the ground all the ripe cherries . . . and afterward he will pick up the clean ones from the ground . . ." *Pequena Memória*, p. 12. This technique may have been the decisive factor in producing coffee of poor quality.

terrace or *terreiro*. On an average each slave gathered between five and seven *alqueires* daily.[14]

Hurried picking—there was an established amount each slave was expected to pick daily—made for quantity but not quality in the berries gathered. Dry, green, and mature cherries were piled together on the terreiros for drying. During daylight hours a thin layer of coffee was turned several times with wide wooden hoes and at nightfall was piled in small heaps. When the beans were dry and could be "easily cracked when squeezed"[15] they were carried to the storage bins where they remained until they were shipped to Rio in leather bags on muleback. Where labor was available, however, the beans were processed on the fazenda.

In the fifties the most advanced milling machinery in which the outer shell and inner parchment of the dried coffee bean were removed was the massive *engenho de pilões*.[16] Its size and cost of manufacture in terms of skilled labor still prohibited its use by any except the large-scale planters. Hence there still existed the methods from which it had evolved. Most primitive of these was the beating of coffee by hand with wooden rods; then came the water-driven pounding mill or monjollo. Those who found the latter too slow employed two slaves each equipped with a pestle who pounded the coffee bean in a mortar (*pilão*), a technique long used to hull rice and grind corn. In this process the dried beans were pounded in the mortar and later tossed into the air on a screen to separate the bean from its outer shell. To remove the inner husk which still enclosed the two halves of the bean the coffee was returned to the pilão where it was pounded again and polished. This coffee brought a higher market price. The engenho de pilões developed the mortar and pestle principle further: a number

---

[14] Lacerda Werneck, *Memória*, p. 37. At measuring time "the overseer should be present to order any slave who did not fill the daily quota to be punished . . ." An alqueire held roughly 13.5 liters.

[15] Ferreira de Aguiar, *Pequena Memória*, p. 15.

[16] The term "engenho" was used on coffee plantations in two ways: (1) as a particular machine such as the engenho de pilões, and (2) as the building in which all machinery was housed, the casa de engenho. The engenho de pilões was built on the fazenda.

of pestles were staggered in action and powered by a large waterwheel. Meanwhile hand-driven ventilators or winnowers (*ventiladores*) and a few water-driven ones blew away the chaff, replacing the screens.

The coffee was now ready for sorting on tables or, more often, on the smooth floor of the engenho. This was a task at which slave women with infants, and old folks were most employed. A thin layer of coffee was spread out; rejects consisting of broken, spotted, and undeveloped beans were separated by hand to be sold at a low price or to be consumed on the fazenda. Each slave sorted up to four *arrobas* (or one sack) daily.[17]

Sometimes cynical, sometimes humorous, the "Memoirs of a Coffee Bean" written for the *O Vassourense*, a local newspaper, reduced to simplest terms the harvesting and processing on an average plantation. "Uncle Tom picked me. The overseer looked disgusted when I fell out of the harvesting basket and considering us a poor job, he whacked the old man and kicked him twice in the seat of the pants. It rained. Then the sun dried me. For two days a stupid wooden hoe fell heavily upon me as though it wanted to break open my shell each time it rolled me. They finally thought I was dried and winnowed me in a *taquara* screen. Then to the monjollo. (By now you can see that my owner is not a member of the rural aristocracy) . . . I was thrown into the ventilator whence I came out ready to be bagged . . . from the plantation to the middleman at the station and on to Rio." [18]

With increased production and profits in the fifties some fazendeiros could afford to improve the quality of coffee by replacing the earthen terreiros, often covered with "piles of rubbish and pools of stagnant water . . . where animals, principally pigs, wallowed," [19] with those of brick, cut stone,

[17] Ferreira de Aguiar, *Pequena Memória*, p. 17. An arroba weighed 14.4 kilos.

[18] Nuno Alvares (pseud.), December 10, 1882.

[19] Padre Antonio Caetano da Fonseca, *Manual do Agricultor dos Géneros Alimentícios* (Rio de Janeiro, 1863), pp. 9–10. This manual was written to improve agricultural practices and living conditions on worn out soils and closes the cycle that was ushered in by the works of Borges de Barros and F. P. de Lacerda Werneck who spoke in terms of virgin soils.

and cement.[20] On the larger terreiros with their improved drainage system, coffee could be dried more quickly and with less spoilage.

As early as 1852 one Vassouras planter boasted a steam engine on his plantation and the inventory of the São Fernando plantation of 1855 detailed another. These were isolated indices of attempted modernization; until the late sixties most milling machinery consisted of the water-driven engenho de pilões. Adoption of power-driven winnowers probably increased the dust of the engenhos, creating an occupational hazard where coughing and spitting revealed the effect on the respiratory passages of slave laborers.[21]

Yet there existed no reason for radical changes in the techniques of producing coffee. A blind faith in ever-continuing prosperity seemed to be the general feeling. Ferreira Soares, an otherwise alert observer of the economic scene, could envision no end to the plateau of prosperity. Writing in 1860, he expressed the sentiments of planters who had seen in the previous decade great changes in their localities as the larger plantations remodeled their buildings or built new ones, and stocked them all with some of the luxury goods of Europe. "None of the provinces of the Empire equals in wealth and industry the province of Rio de Janeiro which by its great coffee and sugar production as well as by its foreign commerce will always prosper." [22] And how could it fail to, for in the words of a later observer, "Coffee pays for everything." [23]

[20] Prior to the 1850's no mention was made of "terreiros" and it may be presumed that since those required were merely beaten earth, no value was given to them in the inventories. In 1855 there was the first mention of a "paiol (crib) no terreiro" but no value was given the terreiro, probably earthen. In 1856 there was mentioned a "terreiro cercado de pedras" and in the same year a "terreiro cercado de achas" with practically no value attached. A "terreiro de pedra" appears in 1862 and in 1865, a "terreiro de cimento."

[21] "The very fine dust is extremely irritating, it attacks the lungs . . . the slaves during the whole period sicken quite often, and I have been able to note that it was always a chest ailment. . ." Rodrigues Cunha, *Arte da Cultura*, pp. 91–92.

[22] *Notas Estatísticas*, p. 203.

[23] Quintino Bocayuva, *Mensagem do Governador do Estado do Rio de Janeiro*, *September, 1902*, p. 43.

(3)

During the boom certain external features of plantation life were transformed. A few plantations had been established on poor locations near bottom lands or on badly drained terrain which left stagnant water near the living quarters. To the planters who would not recognize the evils of such conditions one observer wrote that because of negligence many planters "suffer immense damage not only to their slaves but also to their cattle." [24] On other fazendas, owners had allowed tile roofs to deteriorate and under heavy rainfall unprotected mud-and-wattle walls rapidly disintegrated.

There were motives other than the purely economic for changing a plantation site or for adding to and remodeling older buildings. The more sophisticated children of well-to-do planters were more conscious than their parents of isolation and primitive surroundings. Said Luis Peixoto de Lacerda Werneck of his position as administrator of a Vassouras fazenda which he had accepted in behalf of his debt-ridden mother-in-law:

> In accepting the proposal I had to move from Rio de Janeiro to the Plantation, abandon and perhaps lose a commercial, financial, and political career which had been well begun and exile myself and my family to a clearing far from the nearest hamlet, beset with all the burdensome tasks of agriculture, without distractions or rest and far from schools where I could educate my children; all of which, without becoming immodest, is not an insignificant sacrifice on my part.[25]

Notwithstanding the opinion of Luis Peixoto, the larger coffee plantations of the time of his writing were an improvement over those of the previous quarter-century. It had been difficult to change fazendas in the forties when eyes were riveted on the expansion of cultivation and the purchase of slaves. But in the fifties the opulence of Vassouras and neighboring coffee centers drew Portuguese craftsmen—carpenters, stonemasons, cabinetmakers as well as an occasional French artisan—who found employment on the plantations and in the

[24] Caetano da Fonseca, *Manual*, pp. 9–10.
[25] Inventory, 1862: deceased: Anna Joaquina de São José Werneck, executor: Ignacio José de Souza Werneck, Fazendas Recreio, Pindobas, Palhas, CPOV.

towns which were rapidly developing a civic consciousness and the arts.[26] Small furniture shops sprang up in Vassouras at this time and slaves became skilled in woodworking.[27]

The materials used in construction, the basic requirements of food and shelter, the methods of agriculture from planting to processing—all imprinted upon coffee plantations a similarity of pattern that the boom years ornamented and added to, but could not change. This is evident in the general uniformity in plantation layouts and house plans, a uniformity that was even more marked among the fazendas of one family.[28]

Before undertaking major improvements there was often some reappraisal of the plantation's situation with respect to water and roads. Some planters moved their buildings lower down on the same stream and to this day the sites of the "Old Pau Grande" and that of the "Old Guaribú" are locally known. Other planters moved away from the roads which had first brought them to the area. Still others, perhaps seeking a better water supply and drainage, moved to higher ground.[29]

Wood, stone, and red earth that earlier planters had found in plentiful supply, now in the hands of more skilled craftsmen,[30] both free and slave, became the sprawling and sometimes pretentious residences of the newly titled rural aristocracy of the coffee zone. Starting with a rectangular building, one side of which often rested on a slope, the other separated from the ground by a half-cellar,[31] improvements usually began with the

---

[26] The archive of the prefecture contains a document referring to the tools of a Victor Pagnon and to a cabinetmaker, Victor Helm, both Frenchmen. APV, 1853.

[27] Raposo, *História de Vassouras*, p. 104. In 1863 there were five furniture shops. P. 158.

[28] Three plantations built by the Ribeiro de Avellar family—Pau Grande, Bôa Sorte, Glória—contained a long, glassed-in veranda running the length of the front of the main residence. The fazendas were all built in the northeastern corner of the município.

[29] Caetano da Fonseca, *Manual*, pp. 9–12.

[30] Before 1847 a Vassouras planter suggested: "If, from the earliest moment, you will have a few young slaves trained as carpenters, smiths and stonemasons, you will soon have skilled workmen on your own establishment. . ." Lacerda Werneck, *Memória*, pp. 34–35.

[31] A typical entry in inventories was: "A dwelling-house, two-storeyed in front and in the rear one-storeyed. . ." Inventory, 1873, deceased: Estevão Pimenta de Moraes, executor: José Voyano, Fazenda Fortaleza, CPOV.

construction of two ells extending backward. Sometimes the main residence (*casa de vivenda*) with its two ells was turned into a square around a small *páteo* by the addition of a shed between the ells. Occasionally the half-cellar was enlarged by excavating the hillside, windows added, and the former basement storehouses divided into rooms. The net effect of the latter improvement created the impression of a two-storey house when viewed from one side.

Almost as often, however, a new and larger main residence was built next to the old one, which was thenceforth referred to in inventories as the "old house" and might serve as a slave infirmary or a storehouse.[32] Suggestive of the work of transformation are such inventory entries as "a residence in state of alteration, including páteo, garden, stone sustaining wall, and staircase," [33] "forty-five boards for floors and ceilings" [34] and the recurrence of the phrase "finished wood" in contrast to the earlier "unfinished logs."

From the quarries scattered throughout the Vassouras area, many within a stone's throw of some plantation center (*sede*), came the granite for house foundations, gutters to carry off to the nearby stream the torrential rains of summer. From the new clearings, on two-wheeled carts drawn by several yoke of oxen, came the hand-squared beams for corner posts (*esteios*) to be erected on stone foundations or sunk into the ground with part of the trunk still bark-covered for protection against rot. Other beams (*vigas*) often as much as two and one-half feet square were laid atop the stone foundations to form the base of the outside walls; crosswise went the beams supporting the floor

---

[32] For example: "One dwelling house, one very old dwelling house adjacent." Inventory, 1848, deceased: Manoel d'Avellar e Almeida, executor: Unknown, Fazenda Boa Vista do Matto Dentro, APV. "One dwelling house, one old house with a veranda to store coffee." Inventory, 1858, deceased: Bernardino da Silveira Dutra, Fazenda do Rio Bonito (or da Cachoeira), CPOV. "One old house adjoining the main residence." Inventory, 1862, deceased: Barão do Paty, executrix: Baroneza do Paty, Fazenda de Sant-Anna, CPOV. "One ruined dwelling house, one main residence under construction." Inventory, 1865, deceased: Barão do Paty, executrix: Baroneza do Paty, Fazenda da Piedade, CPOV.

[33] Inventory, 1855, deceased: Jesuina Polucena d'Oliveira Serra, executor: João Arsenio Moreira Serra, Fazenda São Fernando. APV.

[34] Inventory, 1854, deceased: Antonio Soares da Costa, executrix: Fausta Bernarda de São José, Fazenda dos Taboões, CPOV.

(*barrotes*) in turn supported by the center beam (*viga madre*) on piled stone. Care lavished upon the foundations paid dividends in summer when the rains could turn the ground floor into mud, and when the dank cellar (*porão*) cooled the bottom apartments. Most walls continued to be made of mud-and-wattle as in earlier days, refinements consisting in the care with which the palmeira wood uprights (*paus de prumo*) were placed in specially drilled holes in the bottom and top beams and with which the finishing layer of mud and sand (*revestimento*) and the final whitewash (*caiação*) were applied. More rare were outer walls of oblong blocks of adobe and those of rammed earth (*taipa*) although such were common in the town.

Frames for the hip roofs were assembled on the terreiro, then taken apart and remounted on top of the walls. Unlike modern construction, a scissors-support was not employed; main walls (*paredes mestres*), built on the cross beams or barrotes, stretched from floor to roof.[35] From the fazenda's kiln came the fifteen-inch long canal tiles which were laid in alternate convex and concave positions upon the roof poles. When nothing held the tiles to each other the roofing was said to be of "telha vão" and had the advantage of allowing air to penetrate. Tile gradually replaced the shorter-lived grass on the other buildings of the plantation center—first the engenho and storehouses, then the cribs and finally the pigpens and slave quarters.[36]

The wood and earth construction of the walls was sturdy, cool and extremely practical but required an over-hanging eave to protect upper walls from beating rains and the base from splash of drip water. A series of wooden corbels anchored the eaves to the outer wall and were sometimes decoratively worked, sometimes covered by a board extending from the eave to the wall. Embellishment in the neo-classic style popular

---

[35] The space between the paredes mestres in the center of the house was divided into windowless bedrooms (*alcovas*).

[36] "A dwelling house roofed with tile, a house which serves as kitchen, roofed with tile, a storehouse roofed with tile, a paved pigpen fenced with boards and roofed with tile, a house which serves as slave quarters divided into twelve compartments and roofed with grass." Inventory, 1850, deceased: Luis de Franca, executor: Severino José de Franca, Fazenda São Luis da Bôa Vista, CPOV.

in this period often took the form of an elaborate wooden molding on the board which usually ended abruptly at the back of the house, where the eyes of the visitor would not notice the economy. Such minor changes in façades gave rise to the expression attributed to nouveau-riche planters: "Give me two hundred milreis worth of decoration."

Steep roofs cooled the inner apartments of the central block in the intense summer heat and, as the wide eaves curved slightly upward, they produced the characteristic sunken roof faintly reminiscent of oriental pagodas; while imitation columns at the corners of the building, hip roofs, and the many false transom windows produced a Brazilian or "dechimneyed" tropical Georgian architectural style.

Plantation interiors also underwent expansion and elaboration in this period. Aside from the added ells, however, basic changes in floor plan were limited by the location of walls which sustained the heavy tile roof. The principal rectangle of the house was generally divided by thinner walls.

From a small veranda approached by wooden stairs or granite steps with wrought-iron railings, the visitor might enter a large room or ante-chamber (*sala de espera*), from which doors opened to right and left on other rooms which usually included a formal reception room (*salão nobre*), a chapel, and perhaps another small room. In the rear, doors led to rooms of the central section, usually windowless alcovas, and to a corridor leading to the third section, a large dining hall with rooms at each end and doorways leading to the ells. The dining room looked out on the páteo which the ells also faced. One ell might include a number of sleeping rooms off a corridor, the other housing the kitchen and various storerooms. In the shed which closed the four sides of the páteo various ovens and open-air cooking facilities were located. Kitchen floors were earthen or paved with red brick; other rooms of the house had plastered ceilings and wooden floors.

The slave quarters changed little in the face lifting of the plantation: a tile roof, perhaps a cooling outside corridor enclosed by strong wooden bars, never any flooring. The narrow windowless cubicles of the mated slaves—single men and women slaves lived in separate undivided senzallas—contained the few possessions a slave could have: a bed or *tarimba* of boards supported on two sawhorses, covered with a mat of woven grass, perhaps a small wooden chest; and on the wall a few pegs and several gourds or *cuías* for storing beans, rice, or pork fat.

In the mid-fifties a few inventories of well-to-do plantations still revealed the humble furnishings which the early settlers had brought along or made on the spot: hair-trunks of wood and rawhide, wooden chests for storing food and clothing, stools, simple cot-like beds, an occasional armoire and the appurtenances of the chapel.[37] To these elements was now added furniture of Regency and Directoire inspiration. Though more elaborate and finished than those of the earlier period, these pieces embodies a simple elegance in the gracefully curved arms and backs of the chairs, sofas, and ottomans and in the austere caning which suited the furniture of a warm climate. Unfinished hardwoods predominated: heavy jacarandá, mahogany, the light brown textured vinhático bordered with strips of dark brown cabiúna—timber from the nearby clearings transformed by slave or itinerant carpenters. Dining tables were often called "elastic" to indicate that there were as many extra leaves as there were chairs available to accommodate guests and family—anywhere from ten to thirty. Bathrooms were not a feature of most plantations; tub-like "basins for baths" and countless urinals "with" and "without covers" [38] suggested the affluence of a particular household.

Fine porcelain, a mark of distinction, also made its appearance in purchases of English china, porcelain tea and coffee services[39] which replaced the older chocolate servers. Lettered

[37] "One kitchen table, two large hair-trunks, one pair of wicker baskets, a small oratory, one old chest to store clothes for the Blacks." Inventory, 1850, deceased: Escolástica Cándida Ferreira, executor: Unknown, Fazenda Conceição, CPOV. "Cots, ottomans, benches, three pairs of wicker baskets, oratory with its images." Inventory, 1854, deceased: Antonio Soares da Costa, executrix: Fausta Bernarda de São José, Fazenda dos Tabões, CPOV.

[38] "One tin bathtub, six blue urinals with covers, seven white urinals without covers." Inventory, 1855, deceased: Polucena d'Oliveira Serra, executor: João Arsenio Moreira Serra, Fazenda São Fernando, CPOV.

[39] "One porcelain tea service, one modern porcelain coffee service minus four cups and saucers." Inventory, 1850, Escolástica Cándida Ferreira, executor: Luis

with initials of the newly created rural aristocrat—*commendador* or *barão*—these services, which were kept for gala occasions when everyday white stone china was put away, sometimes showed the planter's recognition of the close tie between his title and the soil, for the initials of the plantation often replaced his own. Glassware and silverware were other indications of affluence in this period of difficult transport, and wine glasses in large numbers often appeared in inventories. The total number of luxury items even in the more elaborate households was not large, however; the mechanics of plantation life still moved on a very simple plane.

(4)

"Neither man nor his land rested." This is the way the restless cycle of transient coffee agriculture was described, the cycle of tearing from virgin soil as much as possible in the shortest possible time to move on to new clearings. But just as the older plants furnished seedlings for new plantings, so reaching the plateau of prosperity brought the first signs of the decline which was to shadow the years that followed. Foremost among these were the reduction in the available supply of land, the aging of slave labor and its increased cost to fazendeiros, and the end of plantation self-sufficiency.

It was at the close of the prosperous decade that there appeared a recognition of the approaching end of virgin forest. For the first time land evaluations began to discriminate between virgin forest (*mata virgem*), secondary growth (*capoeira*, *capoeirão*), and pasture (*pasto*).[40] The disappearance of virgin forest was by no means restricted to the small or the medium-sized fazendeiros. Wrote the Baroneza do Paty in 1862 of the immense holdings left her and her children by the Barão do Paty do Alferes: "The absolute shortage of land for planting coffee did not allow me to increase any plantings. . . . Regretfully I must report that on all our fazendas which cover an

Caetano Alves, Fazenda Conceição, CPOV. Or, "One tea service of French silver." Inventory, 1855, deceased: Manoel Rodrigues dos Santos, executrix: Maria Eufrasia dos Santos Goulart, Fazenda da Mantiqueira, CPOV.

[40] Inventory, 1861, deceased: Joaquim Francisco Moreira, executrix: Maria Magdalena de Castro Moreira, Fazenda da Floresta, CPOV.

area equal to 21,104,000 square braças or almost two and
one-half square legoas . . . we do not have 200 square *braças*
of virgin forest of first quality." [41]

Under such conditions many planters saw their agricultural
techniques, characterized by the use of poorly chosen seedlings,
insufficient maintenance of coffee groves, and careless harvesting by slaves, turn to plague them. The short life of the
coffee trees now threatened the economic basis of their society.
Estimates of the life span of a coffee bush were various in this
period. While Domingos Borges de Barros, writing before the
cultivation of coffee had spread throughout the highlands of
the Parahyba Valley (1813), estimated that a bush lasted from
twenty-five to forty years in good soil,[42] Ferreira de Aguiar
somewhat later (1836) and basing his assertion on observation
in Vassouras claimed that it gave little fruit after twenty
years.[43] "When they reach the age of twenty to twenty-five
years, they are considered old," wrote Rodrigues Cunha in
1844.[44] Burlamaque in 1860 dropped the figure lower: "It's
not worth picking after fifteen years." [45] New plantings and
the exclusion of subsistence crops as competitors for virgin soil
could alone compensate for the inevitable drop in coffee
production.

Tied closely to the problem of reduced forest lands was that
of the aging of slave labor, a key factor in a society based
entirely on the slave. It was especially serious to those planters
who had stocked their plantations with slaves in the thirties and
early forties. The period of maximum productivity in the life
of a slave was relatively short—from eighteen to thirty years of
age—and fazendeiros had never enjoyed what they considered

[41] On the basis of a legua of 3,000 braças or 6,600 meters the total plantation
area was approximately 81 square kilometers. "Relatorio do Estado da Nossa
Caza desde 6 de Dezembro de 1861 até 6 de Dezembro de 1862," page 105 in
Inventory, 1862, deceased: Barão do Paty, executor: Francisco de Assis e Almeida,
Fazendas Monte Alegre, Manga Larga, Piedade, Sant'Anna, Palmeiras, Monte
Lybano, Conceição, CPOV.
[42] "Memoria sobre o Café," VI, 42.
[43] *Pequena Memória*, p. 11.
[44] *Arte da Cultura*, pp. 49–50.
[45] F. L. C. Burlamaque, *Monographia do Cafeseiro e do Café* (Rio de Janeiro, 1860),
p. 33.

an adequate labor force even during the busiest days of the slave trade. After 1850 the constant complaint of the planters concentrating more and more upon coffee became the "lack of hands for field work."

Stemming from the increasingly evident disappearance of virgin forest and the diminishing supply of labor was the end of plantation self-sufficiency. Before the early 1850's both large coffee planters and small agriculturists had grown foodstuffs for personal consumption, with the surplus going to the local markets.[46] Attracted by high coffee prices in the early fifties and alarmed by the diminishing labor pool now partially drained by the road-building and maintenance companies which sprang up after 1850, large fazendeiros (*grande lavoura*) had reduced foodstuff acreage and concentrated their labor force upon coffee production.[47] This concentration was natural because planters' credit depended solely upon the arrobas of coffee shipped to factors (*commissários*) in Rio and because coffee alone left a handsome profit after paying costly transport by mule.[48] Erroneously, fazendeiros believed that the previous abundance and low price of foodstuffs would endure.[49] When they reduced their acreage in subsistence crops, however, even the slightest variation in their harvests forced them to turn to the formerly bountiful local market which had been supplied in recent years principally by the small agriculturists (*pequena lavoura*).[50] These—sitiantes, renters, and aggregados—had been unable to compete with the big planters in producing coffee which demanded abundant labor, land, and credit.

Small planters, in their turn, had not maintained any interest in subsistence crops because the rise in slave prices prevented them from purchasing new slaves and forced them to sell those they had to the big planters and to the road companies. The increasing absorption of the available slave labor by the large plantations resulted in the gradual disappearance of the small

[46] Furquim de Almeida, "Carestía," p. 1.

[47] Furquim de Almeida, "Carestía," p. 2.

[48] Manoel Joaquim da Silva, "Carestía de Géneros Alimentícios," Annexo K., *Relatório do Presidente da Província do Rio de Janeiro, August 1, 1858*, p. 15.

[49] Ferreira Soares, *Notas Estatísticas*, p. 133.

[50] Furquim de Almeida, "Carestía," p. 2.

plantations and farms.[51] The plight of the aggregados attracted the notice of Luis Peixoto de Lacerda Werneck. "They have been reduced to dependents of the big planters," he said. "Today the best lands are denied them and they may no longer cut any forest lands." The planters intended to devote their land exclusively to coffee and the aggregados now watched the coffee rows of the large planters arrive at their doorsteps. Hence, precisely where coffee progressed most, there the cost of foodstuffs was highest.[52]

Fazendeiros who had formerly produced their own basic foods—cornmeal, manioc flour, beans, jerked beef, and bacon—were now shocked by the drop in production and the rise in price of these commodities that followed in the late fifties. A certain amount of monopolistic practice by Rio dealers seems also to have contributed to the scarcity. Between 1852 and 1859 the price of basic foods more than doubled at the wholesale level (Table 2) and quadrupled at the retail level (Table 3), while from the United States were imported "bacon and lard cheaper than that produced locally." Warned one observer: "We will shortly import the food of our lowest class, beans, cornmeal and jerked beef from the United States" just as "we already import foreign cheese and butter." [53]

Caught thus between the rapidly diminishing forest reserves and the rising price of foodstuffs and slaves, the planters were now criticized for their traditional, unquestioned agricultural methods which were termed in the aggregate "routinism" (rotina). Writing in 1848 that the "routinism to which the majority of our planters have condemned themselves" was a factor in lowering the quality of Rio coffee, the president of the province sounded a theme repeated throughout the rest of the century.[54] Eleven years later another provincial report censured the "spirit of routinism which dominates many of our

---

[51] Furquim de Almeida, "Carestía," pp., 2–3; Augusto-Emilio Zaluar, *Peregrinação pela Província de São Paulo, 1860–1861* (Rio de Janerio, 1862), p. 57.

[52] *Ideas sobre Colonisação precedidas de uma Succincta Exposição dos Princípios Geraes que Regem a População* (Rio de Janeiro, 1855), pp. 36, 39.

[53] G. S. Capanema, *Agricultura. Fragmentos do Relatório dos Commissários Brazileiros à Exposição Universal de Paris em 1855*, p. 3.

[54] *Relatório do Presidente da Província do Rio de Janeiro, April 1, 1848*, p. 2.

TABLE 2. Rio wholesale prices, 1850–1859

Commodity	1850–1851		1854–1855		1858–1859	
	Price	Index No.	Price	Index No.	Price	Index No.
Rice (arroba)	1$520	100	1$410	93	3$300	217
Sugar (arroba)	1$770	100	2$050	116	3$750	212
Jerked beef (arroba)	2$720	100	2$830	104	5$500	102
Beans (alqueire)	2$300	100	3$980	173	4$980	216
Corn (alqueire)	1$150	100	1$530	132	3$750	326
Bacon (arroba)	3$540	100	7$980	225	8$500	240

According to the old weights followed in the area, an *arroba* was the equivalent of 14.4 kilograms while the *alqueire* approximated 13.5 liters. For metric equivalents of capacity used in Brazil at this time, see Appendix.

Source: Adapted from "Demonstração dos Preços Medios . . . dos Géneros Comestíveis conforme as Pautas Semanaes da Mesa do Consulado desta Corte nos Exercícios de 1858–59," in Ferreira Soares, *Notas Estatísticas*, p. 288.

TABLE 3. Vassouras retail prices, 1850–1861.

Commodity	1850–1851		1855–1856		1860–1861	
	Price	Index No.	Price	Index No.	Price	Index No.
Rice (kg)	0$150	100	0$300	200	0$600	400
Sugar (arroba)	2$200	100	5$400	245	8$800	400
Fresh meat (kg)	0$110	100	0$320	291	0$400	364
Corn (alqueire)	1$600	100	2$500	156	8$000	500
Bacon (kg)	0$180	100	0$500	277	0$800	444
Cod (kg)	0$150	100	0$300	200	0$600	400
Minas cheeses	0$800	100	1$280	160	1$600	200
Garlic (bunch)	0$200	100	0$500	250	1$000	500
Salt (alqueire)	0$100	100	2$560	256	—	—

Source: Bills presented for collection and included in inventories. CPOV, APV.

planters." [55] Asked another commentator: "With the same labor force, how can we produce as much in soil now worn out and supposedly useless as we did in land when it was virgin, without changing the system to which our planters are so attached?" [56] Rare but trenchant was a local protest against the "spirit of routinism . . . rooted prejudices . . . complete repugnance for the examination and study of agriculture as a science." [57] A few years before, a merchant with interests both in Vassouras and in Rio despaired of the system of converting fertile slopes into barren mounds: "Since no attempt is made to improve the soil, no fertilizer, no irrigation nor any other system, the land is quickly exhausted." He summed it up by commenting that "The soil is cultivated with the methods and instruments of 300 years ago." [58]

From the average planter's point of view, there were grounds for complacency, adequate justification for the way lands were cultivated. During the previous half-century a new crop had been successfully adapted where formerly there had been only wilderness. Ever-rising prices and the rapid growth in coffee production justified continued expansion and even if "enlightenment" had been more general it is doubtful whether techniques could have progressed beyond the perfected routinism advocated by Vassouras' Francisco Peixoto de Lacerda Werneck, Barão do Paty, in his *Memória*. In this situation foreign ideas could make little impression upon fazendeiros who could sometimes barely sign their names, much less take time to read a manual which was often pure theory when not a mere compilation of techniques evolved in foreign lands. Others asked why they should concern themselves with agricultural developments which might be inapplicable in the virgin soils of Brazil.[59] Had not some of the writers of manuals warned against the agricultural theorists anyway?

[55] *Relatório do Presidente da Província do Rio de Janeiro, August 1, 1859*, p. 23.
[56] Francisco de Paula Cándido, *Clamores da Agricultura no Brazil* (Rio de Janeiro, 1859), p. 6.
[57] Baroneza do Paty, "Relatório do Estado da Nossa Caza," p. 114 in Inventory, 1862, CPOV.
[58] Furquim de Almeida, "Carestía," pp. 12–13.
[59] Quintino Bocayuva, *Mensagem*, p. 77.

Isolation and its attendant individualism further strengthened routinism. Poor communications between plantations created an "impassable barrier founded partly upon the total absence of any knowledge of what happens beyond local limits." It was inevitable that the outlook of the father should be transmitted to the son, along with the property. Noting that immobility and not progress had become the motto of agriculture, the Baroneza do Paty sarcastically remarked: "The son's ideas are still those of the father, which the grandfather instilled . . . we can still see establishments set up more than sixty years ago directed by the same methods which leave to nature and the slow action of time the work of production." [60]

There were factors beyond the manipulation of even the best planters and their overseers. "The efforts employed in improving the coffee groves will be, thanks to Divine Providence, crowned with a most satisfactory result," commented the Baroneza do Paty in 1863, but she added: "May it please God to preserve us from the evil that caused so many apprehensions last year." [61] The evil referred to was a pest which attacked the coffee trees. Sudden blights complicated the life of the planter wedded to routine or not. To Vassouras in May and November of 1861 came inquiries sent by the provincial government to ascertain the extent of the "evil which menaced coffee plantations which provided the principal income of the Empire and the Province." [62] A year later it was reported that the groves more than twenty years old were "irremediably lost" to the "butterfly blight." [63] Other pests were always present to shorten the productive life of the coffee covered slopes of the município. Once bird pest (*erva de passarinho*), a semi-parasitic plant borne by birds feasting on coffee cherries, got a foothold on coffee trees left untended, it spread from branch to branch and drew away sustenance that might have gone into producing

[60] Baroneza do Paty, "Relatório," p. 114 in Inventory, 1862, CPOV.
[61] Baroneza do Paty, "Relatório," p. 113.
[62] Letter from José Ricardo de Sá Rego, President of the Province of Rio de Janeiro, Nictheroy, May 27, 1861 to CMV. APV; Letter from Luiz Leite d'Oliveira Bello, President of the Province of Rio de Janeiro, Nictheroy, November 4, 1861 to CMV. APV.
[63] *Relatório do Vice-Presidente da Província do Rio de Janeiro, September 8, 1862,* p. 14.

coffee cherries. There was also the saúva ant (Atta Sexdens) which plagued planters soon after the forest was opened and first crops put in by eating the leaves of the coffee bush. From the 1830's onward, municipal and provincial reports referred to the necessity of combatting this plague more effectively.[64] Planters who could afford the expensive bellows used to eradicate the ant nests, trained a slave (*matador* or *formigueiro*) whose job it was to seek out spots where red earth had been laid bare. Smouldering fires were built at the mouths of the canals and the smoke blown through them. The method was expensive and not very successful while it took its toll of nearby coffee trees whose roots often overheated and withered.

In addition to such contingencies the fictitious stability of the coffee planter was undermined by his accumulation of debts. Even in the forties before the financial boom, a planter paid 60 per cent interest on the money advanced him until newly planted coffee could pay off after four years.[65] During the fifties, coffee production rose to new heights (Table 4) as the end of the slave trade turned loose a torrent of funds producing the inflation of 1854 to 1857.[66] The credits which coffee factors in Rio put at the disposal of up-country planters were extended in the form of purchases which the planter and his family ordered the factor to make. Little cash passed between the commissário and the fazendeiro. But poor harvests in 1857 and 1858 reportedly caused a run on the banks of the capital as factors sought to cover the excessive imports ordered through them by their clients. At the same time the Imperial Government tried to tighten credit facilities by obliging banks of emission to have a gold reserve for conversion on sight.[67]

[64] Relatório do Fiscal, 1834; Relatório do Fiscal Supplente, Lúcio José de Paiva, May 6, 1842; Relatório do Fiscal Supplente Lúcio José de Paiva, July 2, 1844; Joaquim José Teixeira Leite, Antonio Torquato Leite Brandão, Christiano Joaquim da Roca to CMV, May 5, 1859; Relatório do Fiscal, September 6, 1858. All in APV: provincial Decree No. 980 of October 13, 1857 and *Relatório do Presidente da Província do Rio de Janeiro, June 1, 1860*, p. 22.

[65] *Relatório do Presidente da Província do Rio de Janeiro, March 1, 1841*, p. 15.

[66] Ferreira Soares, *Crise Commercial*, pp. 56, 60–61; Luiz Torquato Marques d'Oliveira, *Novo Méthodo da Plantacão, Fecundidade, Durabilidade, Estrumação e Conservação do Café* (Rio de Janeiro, 1863), p. 6.

[67] Ferreira Soares, *Crise Commercial*, pp. 68, 51–52, 60.

This measure proved unsuccessful; the total of mortgaged property in the Province of Rio and the other principal coffee producing provinces doubled between 1859 and 1864.[68]

TABLE 4. Production, export, and price of coffee of the Rio area, 1792–1860.

Year	Export Port of Rio (arrobas)	Production Province of Rio (arrobas)	Price per arroba
1792	160		
1817	318,032		
1820	539,000		
1826	1,304,450		
1830	1,958,925		
1835	3,237,190		
1840–41	4,982,221		3$519
1845–46	6,720,221		3$028
1849–50	5,706,833		3$866
1851–52	9,673,842	7,535,844	3$396
1852–53	8,312,561	6,535,113	3$764
1853–54	10,128,908	7,988,551	3$896
1854–55	12,024,063	9,369,107	3$890
1855–56	10,918,148	8,602,658	4$301
1856–57	10,426,449	8,097,879	4$627
1857–58	9,415,843	7,593,200	4$167
1858–59	10,286,504	8,082,953	5$199
1859–60	10,606,394	8,746,361	5$829

Sources: Francisco Freire Allemão, "Quaes são as Principaes Plantas que Hoje se acham Acclimatadas no Brazil," p. 570; Ferreira Soares, *Notas Estatísticas*, pp. 208–209; A. d'E. Taunay, *História*, III, 62–63.

Fazendeiros had always taken a dim view of such advice as Burlamaque's admonition to "keep a reserve for calamitous times." [69]

Despite the storm warnings, however, from the vantage point of the 1860's, the Vassouras planter surveyed a half-century of remarkable progress. The establishment he had founded and

[68] A. d'E. Taunay, *Historia*, IV, 155.
[69] F. L. C. Burlamaque, *Catechismo de Agricultura* (Rio de Janeiro, 1870), p. 92.

supplied with an expensive labor force had grown phenomenally. Some luxury goods had arrived from abroad to soften the essentially primitive life of the plantation centers. It seemed clear that a new generation, the sons of the founders, would take over the establishments that had sunk roots into the soil of the steep slopes. There was little doubt of the successful future of large-scale agriculture which "is and will be for many years the principal source of public and private wealth, the most efficient auxiliary of our progress, participating in the evolution which has brought us to the present state of civilization." [70] On the momentum of this success the economy of Vassouras rolled on toward troubled times.

[70] Miguel Antonio da Silva, "Agricultura Nacional," *Revista Agrícola do Imperial Instituto Fluminense de Agricultura*, X (March 1879), 3–4.

CHAPTER III

Plantation Labor

"My property consists of land and slaves." [1] With these words innumerable testaments throughout the nineteenth century down to 1888 began the statement and distribution of what Vassouras planters had inherited, purchased, and mortgaged, and ordered built or cultivated in their lifetimes. The linking of land and slaves, the pillars of plantation society, was more than fortuitous; not only was slave labor indispensable in working the land, its ownership in adequate amounts had been a perquisite in obtaining the sesmaría from the Portuguese crown.

Back into the earliest days of the settlement of Vassouras went the roots of the problems which vexed the province of Rio de Janeiro and other coffee-growing areas once large-scale coffee production established itself: first, how to insure a steady supply of slave labor to work the plantations; second, how to employ slave labor and keep it in line. Free labor as an alternative hardly existed in the minds of the settlers. And when the prospective gains of commercial agriculture were presented to settlers in the form of high coffee prices and an expanding market, forces set in motion years before precluded even the possibility of free labor in agriculture.

Among these forces one of the most important was the sesmaría or royal land grant. When the Portuguese crown confirmed, on March 8, 1749, the request of Gaspar de Godoes for a grant on the road to Minas, it stated clearly that it understood Godoes had "sufficient slaves to cultivate any lands." [2] Forty years later the request of Norberta Joaquina Hopman for a grant in the same area repeated three times in the space

---

[1] "Os bens que possuo são terras e escravos."

[2] Letter of Confirmation. In Medição Judicial da Fazenda das Palmas, 1834, CPOV.

of three pages in order to satisfy the crown of her ability to use the land sought, that "she has more than ten slaves belonging to her, and enough wealth to buy those slaves which may be necessary to cultivate the grant of land." [3] And in 1802 Vicente Ferreira produced a witness to testify that "he possesses a few slaves and has possibilities of buying more to cultivate the lands which are his by sesmaría." [4]

The Portuguese background of the early Vassouras settlers and the nature of Brazilian economic development during the colonial period inured planters to slave labor.[5] "Why, Master," requested the Disciple in Burlamaque's nineteenth-century catechism, "why hasn't the plow replaced the hoe in our agriculture?" Replied the Master: "Because of habit and ignorance. Habit, because your fathers inherited both the slave and his hoe." [6]

At the end of the eighteenth century and in the early decades of the nineteenth, many of the large grants were growing sugar cane with the use of slave labor. Thus the sugar engenho of the area contributed to the establishment of the slave-operated plantations. Manoel Joaquim de Azevedo declared, in his request for more lands in 1822, that he "had established a sugar engenho containing considerable equipment and maintained more than 130 slaves" on the north bank of the Parahyba River near Vassouras.[7] Within the município of Vassouras the sugar plantation worked by slaves had been started even sooner. When Manoel de Azevedo Ramos died on the Fazenda do Sacco in 1795 he left his wife and children almost two sesmarías, cane fields and a water-driven sugar mill, a distillery, several

[3] Auto da Justificação a Requerimento da mma. Justificante D. Norberta Joaquina Hopman. In Sesmarías do Estado do Rio, Caixa 130, Arquivo Nacional. Variations of the statement appear on pages 6, 8, and 8 reverse. Compare the statement of Manoel de Azevedo Ramos: ". . . has enough slaves to cultivate and plant the aforementioned lands which are unclaimed. . ." In Sesmarías do Estado do Rio, Caixa 130, Arquivo Nacional.

[4] In Sesmarías do Estado do Rio, Caixa 130, Arquivo Nacional.

[5] The importation of African slave labor into Portugal from the fifteenth century onward, and the role of slave labor in the sugar and mining episodes of the Brazilian colonial economy are well presented and documented by Maurício Goulart, *Escravidão Africana no Brasil (Das origens a extinção do tráfico)*, São Paulo, 1949.

[6] Burlamaque, *Catechismo de Agricultura*, pp. 81–82.

[7] In Sesmarías do Estado do Rio, Caixa 130, Arquivo Nacional.

hogsheads for storing aguardente, and twenty-five slaves, twenty of whom came from the African coast.[8] A similar state of affairs was described by Saint-Hilaire and Walsh when they traveled through the município during the 1820's. Saint-Hilaire spent several days at the Fazenda Ubá and noted the few free folk directing the lives and labor of the large slave labor force.[9] The Coroado Indians living in the area he considered useless in working the plantation.[10]

Once the advantages of coffee cultivation became apparent, the only possible remaining source of free labor, squatters and other small holders, was eliminated. Without adequate funds to hire lawyers, unable to proceed to the town of Vassouras to defend their lands before the local judge, without connections —official or social—in the capital, the squatters and small holders became hangers-on of the planters. They lingered as aggregados[11] who lived isolated from the plantation centers, less often as renters of small plots where they could raise subsistence crops and a little coffee, as overseers (feitores) of the ever-growing slave gangs of men and women, as hired hands (camaradas), and as artisans in the town.

A Vassouras planter whose travel in Europe acquainted him with the exodus of Europeans to the New World examined in 1854 the system of land ownership to determine how to channel immigrants to Brazil. "Our rural property," he commented, "is the privilege of one class" and those who could not purchase land lived "as aggregados of the large landholders under precarious conditions since they can be evicted at the pleasure of the proprietor. Their land is delimited and they are told what to plant." [12] One aged Vassouras planter depicted aggregados as free white men or manumitted blacks to whom

---

[8] Inventory, 1795, deceased: Manoel de Azevedo Ramos, executrix: Anna Maria Verneck, Fazenda do Sacco, CPOV.

[9] Saint-Hilaire, Voyage, I.

[10] Walsh, Notices of Brazil, II, 13–15.

[11] The degree to which planters tolerated aggregados was based upon the support both physical and moral, of the latter at election time. Vassouras' local newspaper often carried vignettes caricaturing the aggregado's role at election time. Macedonio [pseudonym of Domiciano Leite Ribeiro], "Um Votante," O Município, August 18, 1878.

[12] L. P. de Lacerda Werneck, Ideas sobre Colonisação, p. 36.

planters gave "house and land" where they raised corn and beans for their own consumption, sometimes selling the surplus to the planter or a local country storekeeper. When called upon to help in clearing virgin forest, a task which planters sought to spare their expensive slave labor, they received wages and worked with the hired hands.[13] In the 1880's their conditions of dependence were relatively unchanged compared with those of a quarter-century before. One observer traced the "misery and ignorance" of the landless rural population of the coffee zones to the fact that "in a country so large, they cannot acquire territorial property which belongs exclusively to the planters who will admit them only as aggregados, reserving the right to order their wretched hovels burnt when they consider it convenient to their interests to expel them from their property." [14]

There are signs that aggregados in the coffee zones often reacted strongly to their landless condition. On the plantation of the Barão do Piabanha in Vassouras' neighboring município of Parahyba do Sul, word spread among the Barão's aggregados during the early months of 1858 that the Imperial Government would allow them to "legitimize the lands which they had cultivated for ten years with the permission of the proprietor." Meanwhile the rumor spread to other planters' aggregados who "in identical circumstances made common cause." Presumably at the Barão's request the local judge ordered the imprisonment of several of the aggregados who" had invaded and cleared the lands of the said Barão." The aggregados then took law into their own hands. Twenty-nine or thirty, carrying arms, forced the police authorities to release the seized aggregados, then massed before the Barão's residence where they

[13] See above, p. 32, note 8.

[14] Henrique de Beaurepaire Rohan in the *Jornal do Commercio* of Rio de Janeiro, reprinted in *O Vassourense*, July 2, 1882. Louis Couty who held a chair at the Polytechnical School in Rio termed all free rural labor in Brazil—which he estimated at approximately 7,000,000 in 1881—as "plantation aggregados, caboclos, caipiras" who, he thought, "are lackadaisical, with few needs and share only one characteristic of the European peasant, residence far from the cities." *L'Esclavage au Brésil* (Paris, 1881), p. 87; and *Étude de Biologie Industrielle sur le Café. Rapport Adressé à M. le Directeur de L'École Polytechnique* (Rio de Janeiro, 1883) p. 92.

"threatened the life of one of the proprietor's sons." When the local chief of police rounded up a force and marched to the plantation, the affair had already quieted down; he arrested eleven of the "mutineers" while the rest dispersed.[15]

Following the end of the transatlantic slave trade (1850), large-scale attempts to introduce foreign laborers, both European and Asiatic, occurred in the coffee-growing areas of the provinces of Rio and São Paulo.[16] Doubtless the supremacy of large property throughout the Parahyba Valley as in the município of Vassouras deeply influenced the course of colonizing ventures; for planters accepted the new labor force arriving in the fifties and later decades solely on a basis compatible with large landed property—that of share tenancy or *parcería*. One planter of Vassouras even ascribed the large influx of immigrant labor in 1852 to the fact that share tenancy was then put into practice on a wide scale for the first time.[17] In the province of Rio the immigrant laborer or *colono* remained synonymous with sharecropper or salaried laborer, never with small proprietor.[18]

[15] *Relatório do Presidente da Província do Rio, 1858*, pp. 3–4. When the need for agricultural schools to improve rural living was felt in the 1870's, attempts were made to give such technical instruction first to the children of aggregados. For example, vacancies in the Agricultural Asylum or Practical School of Agriculture were to be filled by the "sons of the aggregados of this province. . ." *Revista Agrícola do Imperial Instituto Fluminense de Agricultura*, V (March 1874), 50.

[16] The failure of early colonization schemes involving Swiss and later Azorean immigrants who refused to fulfill their contracts and fled elsewhere throughout the area became apparent during the twenties and thirties. In 1825, the Imperial Secretary of State asked for any information on the whereabouts of Swiss *colonos* who broke their contracts and scattered through the Province of Rio. An attempt to force immigrants to fulfill their obligations was reported in 1830; and in 1837 the president of the province informed the CMV that Azoreans had "fled from road construction gangs on the Estrella road and could be captured and compelled to live up to their contracts." Also, there was before 1850 the tendency of the only steady supply of Europeans—the Portuguese—to consist of "merchants, artists, overseers . . . but no or very few day laborers in agriculture, mining, or other heavy manual trades." Few coffee planters felt they could afford to pay free rural laborers and their families, were they available, because the planters "by habitually discounting the purchase price of slaves, in view of the way they subsequently handle them, see no advantage nor even the possibility of paying day wages to free men. . ." Documents in APV; C. A. Taunay, *Manual*, pp. 126–127.

[17] L. P. de Lacerda Werneck, *Ideas sobre Colonisação*, p. 169.

[18] Wrote the British secretary of legation in Rio in his report for 1862: ". . . the valley of the Parahyba is a district which affords no opening for foreign colonists.

While sharecropping was never wholly rejected in the Parahyba Valley, it did not prove attractive to either free immigrants or patriarchal fazendeiros as long as slave labor gangs were available for working coffee fazendas. When, in 1854, Vassouras planters first discussed the advantages of introducing free immigrants on their slave-worked plantations, colonos were proposed only as "elements of resistance" in a "system of caution and vigilance" against possible slave insurrections, rather than as potential small coffee producers.[19] And twenty-four years later, at the Agricultural Congress of 1878, a planter from another município near Vassouras similarly urged planters to found nuclei of colonos to "preserve public order, counter-balancing the brutal force of slave elements which will then continue to produce as they have heretofore." [20]

Equally discouraging to the popularity of share tenancy was the fact that provincial legislation failed to provide the newcomers with adequate "guarantees of liberty, security and property, without which they will encounter here only bitter deception instead of the improvement of their fortunes." [21] According to an analysis of sharecropping in São Paulo during the early seventies, the colono was "always suspicious and therefore always convinced that the proprietor wished to cheat in any of the operations such as weighing, shipping, selling, etc., any of his production." The colonos considered themselves "merely partners in the profits, and the proprietor's share an intolerable tax upon the laborer which takes from him any hope in the future whatsoever." [22] Couty, writing five or six years later, agreed with this statement. Share tenancy on coffee

The lands are parcelled out among a few planters where the labor employed is exclusively slave-labour. . ." *Report by Mr. Baillie.* Rio de Janeiro. February, 1862. Gr. Britain. C 3222. LXX (1863), 5.

[19] *Instrucções para a Commissão Permanente nomeada pelos Fazendeiros do Município de Vassouras* (Rio de Janeiro, 1854), pp. 5–6. A proportion of free to slave on each fazenda was suggested as follows: "one free person per 12 slaves; two per 25; five per 50; seven per 100; ten per 200; and beyond this number two more free persons per 100 slaves added." *Ibid.,* p. 6.

[20] *Congresso Agrícola. Collecção de Documentos.* (Rio de Janeiro, 1878), p. 238.

[21] *Relatório do Presidente da Província do Rio, August 1, 1859,* p. 21.

[22] José Vergueiro, *Memorial acerca da Colonisação e Cultivo do Café* (Campinas, 1874), cited by Henrique de Beaurepaire Rohan, "O Futuro da Grande Lavoura e da Grande Propriedade no Brazil," *Congresso Agrícola,* p. 244.

fazendas was comparable to "métayage or perhaps a bastard and insufficient system of fourths. . . The colono will never substitute the slave as long as the fazendeiro . . . wishes to intervene in the simplest acts of his life." [23] Indeed on one of the fazendas in the município of Valença, the sharecropping colonos "became insubordinate and threatened the public peace" in 1853 because of excessive patriarchalism.[24]

Salaried colonos fared little better. Accustomed to working their slaves long hours daily and to expending meager sums for their food, clothing, and shelter, Rio planters would not condition themselves, as long as slavery existed, to the "labor of the free man who desires . . . an increase in salary and constantly aspires to rise out of his position of lowly day laborer to obtain a higher one more independent and convenient." [25] More than the problem of paying ever-rising wages which depended upon the general price level, planters resented the fact that the salaried laborer worked "as little as possible, with no other incentive than his daily wage . . . without a care for his employer's losses. In this sense he produces less than the slave who, equally disinterested in his master's profits, is nonetheless forced to work by those violent means which are now employed and which imprint upon our morality so black a stigma." [26]

[23] Couty, *Pequena Propriedade e Immigração Europea* (Rio de Janeiro, 1887), p. 36. Similarly pessimistic over the problem of parcería on coffee fazendas was Ribeyrolles. *Brasil Pitoresco*, II, 114–117, 131. Reflecting on the need of fazendeiros to obtain European labor in preparation for eventual slave emancipation, one of Vassouras' schoolmasters wrote of his experience in promoting private colonization. "I was unfortunate when I tried to substitute free men for my slave labor in 1856. I contracted two Portuguese. One fled at the end of the second week, the other worked for the school three months. I lost all the money I spent to bring them from Portugal to Vassouras." Antonio José Fernandes, "Lavoura e Colonisação," *O Município*, November 16, 1873.

In 1890 a French journalist's comments on immigrant agricultural labor in São Paulo corroborated Couty's views. The São Paulo planters, he wrote, saw in the immigrant "only a substitute for the slave, an instrument of their wealth and nothing more. It is therefore by a strange abuse of words that they call these immigrants colonos; they are perpetuating the old colonial system, slightly modified, but that is not colonization." Max Leclerc, *Lettres du Brésil* (Paris, 1890), p. 107.

[24] *Relatório do Vice Presidente da Provincia do Rio, August 1, 1853*, p. 25.

[25] Furquim de Almeida, "Carestía de Géneros Alimentícios," p. 6.

[26] Beaurepaire Rohan, "O Futuro da Grande Lavoura," p. 243.

Accepted in Brazilian rural society only on these grounds and confronting the "resistance of the owners of the land" in their attempts to set themselves up independently, immigrant colonos left the Parahyba Valley for frontier regions in São Paulo. Conditions in Vassouras were never propitious for European colonos, who continued to depart for more promising areas. When Vassouras fazendeiros awoke to the dangers of imminent abolition in the latter months of 1887 and finally sought to establish on their plantations nuclei of north Italian colonos with their families, the Imperial Government warned that it would reimburse planters for the immigrants' passage "only after they have been definitely established on the above-mentioned plantations as workers with or without contract." [27]

By tradition, example, and the fact that African slaves—cheap and in abundant supply—adjusted to conditions of coffee cultivation, Negro labor was responsible for the clearing of virgin forest and planting of coffee, construction of large plantation houses, and so many other contributions to Brazilian civilization that one coffee baron had to remark bitterly that it was a civilization that "came from the coast of Africa." [28] Once the type of labor force had been settled, the problem revolved about the assurance of a steady and inexhaustible supply of slaves. Consequently, as long as they could, planters remained inalterably opposed to any effective curtailment of the slave trade.

(2)

Until the end of the eighteenth century the African slave trade was an unquestioned integral part of Brazilian life. With

[27] Letter from the provincial government to Manoel Peixoto de Lacerda Werneck, October 19, 1887 and to Carlos Sebastião Pegado, Fazenda das Antas, October 25, 1887. APV, 1888. A few years later a Vassouras planter vehemently denounced the provincial government for the failure to stimulate immigration. "The State of Rio, badly oriented by those in charge, nearsightedly refused to treat immigration questions." Characteristically, he placed little blame on the planters. Pedro Días Gordilho Paes Leme, and others, "Organização Agricola," p. 5.

[28] *Congresso Agrícola*, p. 234. In a less embittered vein José Cesário de Farfa Alvim wrote that "the opening of the forest and the founding of important centers and . . . large fortunes" was due exclusively to African immigration. *Relatório do Presidente da Província do Rio*, March, *1885*, p. 12.

the opening of the nineteenth century, however, Portugal became involved in the European issue regarding abolition of the trade, a movement in which, for reasons of her own, England took the initiative. At the Congress of Vienna in 1815, Portugal, whose economic relations with England had long been close, agreed to "cooperate with His Britannic Majesty in the Cause of Humanity and Justice, by adopting the most efficacious means for bringing about a gradual abolition of the Slave Trade." [29] On its separation from Portugal, Brazil recognized this commitment, and its implementation was a major factor in the negotiations for recognition of the Brazilian Empire by England. Finally, in 1827 a convention was ratified stating that after three years the trade would be considered equivalent to piracy. Belatedly the Brazilian Regency passed, in 1831 and 1832,[30] laws carrying severe penalties for indulgence in the trade; three years later these provisions, never enforced, were replaced by milder ones providing that captured contraband slaves instead of returning to Africa at the cost of the importer be auctioned in the Rio market to persons of probity paying the highest yearly rent for them. Through use and abuse of this and subsequent legislation a large number of these "Free Africans" were permanently added to the slave population. Lip service to the principle of enforcement was largely for English eyes.

In these years of uncertainty and negotiation the Brazilian slave market responded to any threatened cessation of the trade. "To date speculation in the African trade has been a sort of furor, and with the idea of the end of that commerce there are few who do not care to invest a few *doblas* in the slave traffic," an article in the *Aurora Fluminense* of 1828 reported. An

---

[29] Article IV stated: "The High contracting Parties reserve to themselves, and engage to determine by a separate Treaty, the period at which the Trade in Slaves shall universally cease, and be prohibited throughout the entire Dominions of Portugal." *Tratado da Abolição do Tráfico de Escravos em todos os lugares da Costa de Africa.* . . (Rio de Janeiro, 1818), p. 6. This agreement in principle was implemented by the Additional Article of 1817 which called the continuance of the trade after this treaty "piracy." *Artigo Separado da Convenção Assignada em Londres aos 28 de Julho de 1817.*

[30] Goulart, *Escravidão Africana*, pp. 246–247; Agenor Roure, "A Escravidão (De 1808 a 1888)," *Jornal do Commercio*, September 28, 1906.

unexpected and bizarre rumor that the English had requested an extension of the trade for another ten years caused the bottom to drop from the market; the crowding of newly disembarked Africans "sick and infected with contagious diseases" in warehouses in the center of Rio brought widespread fear for the health of the city.[31] Determined action by the Regency in 1831, seconded by demands forwarded to municipal governments for vigilance against the entry of Africans, created a new situation and "the slave trade sunk into perfect stagnation for some months until one dealer landed a cargo with impunity, which led to an immense revival of the traffic." [32]

Modification and relaxation of enforcement measures by the Imperial Government reflected the growing strength of coffee interests, both of exporters and planters. By the mid-thirties the finances of the Empire were based upon the prosperity of the coffee planter, a dependence stronger than pressure of English diplomacy applied for twenty years. Increased slave imports in the forties profited planters and government coffers alike; in 1848 roughly 60 per cent of Vassouras' tax contribution to the province of Rio came from a tax on the sale of slaves.[33]

At strategic points along the coast, often on the outskirts of Rio, landings of contraband slaves were made. Even when apprehended on the scene, local juries were quick to exonerate the parties involved. Certain planters and merchants had their depots of Africans at isolated coastal spots; in the barracoons, slaves were provided with clothing and food before trekking to the interior. Since the ability to speak Portuguese was the only test of the recency of arrival—and a doubtful one, the internal slave trade could be constantly and surreptitiously supplied with new levies.

---

[31] May 5, 1828.

[32] E. Wilberforce, *Brazil Viewed Through a Naval Glass: With Notes on Slavery and the Slave Trade* (London, 1856), p. 233.

[33] Of all the municípios in the province of Rio only the large sugar-raising município of Campos forwarded a larger amount from its tax on slave sales. Vassouras sent a total of 9:989$800 of which 6:000$000 was the "meia siza da venda de escravos." "Tabella explicativa do orçamento da receita para . . . 1848–1849," *Relatório do Presidente da Província do Rio, April, 1848.*

Slave importations reached an all-time peak when in 1848 60,000 Africans arrived. Thereafter a conjunction of factors seems to have operated to discourage and eventually to halt slave landings. Increased activity of English cruisers[34] which seized ninety slave-laden ships between 1849 and 1851 and the resultant loss of capital invested by traders crippled the trade. The Imperial Government now adopted effective

TABLE 5. Estimated slave imports into the Province of Rio from other provinces, 1852–1859.

Year	Number	Year	Number
1852	4,409	1856	5,006
1853	2,090	1857	4,211
1854	4,418	1858	1,993
1855	3,532	1859	963
		Total	26,622

Source: Ferreira Soares, Notas Estatísticas, pp. 135–136.

measures to halt it: those apprehended for landing contraband slaves were tried by Admiralty Courts which replaced the ineffectual local juries; and the principal slavers, mostly Portuguese, were deported. Although a few landings occurred after 1850, for all practical purposes the trade ceased. But many planters believed that it would be resumed. "It is indispensable that planters convince themselves of one thing, whether they like it or not . . . the slave trade has ended and will not return," a commission of Vassouras planters stated in 1854.[35]

Following cessation of the slave trade, prices for slaves almost doubled in the short space of two years, 1852–1854.[36]

[34] Goulart, Escravidão Africana, p. 259.

[35] Joaquim Nabuco, Um Estadista do Imperio (2nd. ed., 2 vols., Rio de Janeiro, 1936), I, 166–167; Instrucções para a Commissão Permanente, pp. 7–8. For a detailed account of the role of the slave trade in Anglo-Brazilian relations, see A. K. Manchester, British Preeminence in Brazil. Its Rise and Decline (Chapel Hill, N.C., 1933).

[36] See below, p. 229 (Figure 3).

This sudden increase in slave evaluations did not inhibit the expansion of coffee production,[37] for a new source of slaves was found in northern Brazil. Effective replenishment of aging and dying slaves came from the interprovincial trade which brought an estimated 5,500 slaves annually into the province of Rio from 1852 to 1859 (Table 5).[38] In the seventies Nature, too, took a hand in stimulating the torrent of northern slaves moving southward to Rio de Janeiro and São Paulo, as a series of long droughts parched northeastern lands and forced planters to dispose of slave property.[39]

Desirable as they were to the slave-hungry planters of the south, the new arrivals created the specter of a nation potentially divided into a slaveholding south and a slaveless north. Conselheiro J. J. Teixeira Junior warned his fellow parliamentarians in 1877 that São Paulo, Rio de Janeiro, and Minas Gerais contained 776,344 slaves, or more than half the total in all other provinces of the Empire.[40] Three years later it was revealed that the ten provinces from Espírito Santo south, held twice the number of the eleven provinces from Bahia, north, roughly 920,921 to 498,268.[41] Reminding his readers that lack of homogeneity in interests had set slaveless groups in the northern United States against Southern planters and had led to the imposition of emancipation, Rafael P. de Barros warned that, by opposing limitations on the inter-provincial slave trade, Brazil's northern deputies in the General Assembly of 1880 justified fears of the south that, once northern slaves were profitably sold, they would be indifferent to emancipation. However compelling such reasoning may have been, when the

---

[37] According to Ferreira Soares, production rose 75 per cent in the decade following the end of the trade. *Notas Estatísticas*, p. 131.

[38] Ferreira Soares reached this figure by computing the average annual importation from the northern provinces (3,430), those northern slaves sold unofficially (1,765), and those brought from the provinces of Minas Gerais and Rio Grande do Sul (305). Figures are approximate. *Notas Estatísticas*, pp. 135–136.

[39] São Paulo's slave population swelled from 80,000 in 1866 to 200,000 in 1875. Joaquim Floriano de Godoy, *A Província de São Paulo* (Rio de Janeiro, 1875), p. 136, cited in Nícia Vilela Luz, "A Administração Provincial de São Paulo em face do Movimento Abolicionista," *Revista de Administração*, VIII (December 1948), 85, note 26; A. d'E. Taunay, *História*, V, 166.

[40] *O Município*, June 7, 1877.

[41] Rafael P. de Barros, *A Província de São Paulo*, September 11, 1880.

Rio provincial assembly voted restrictions on the trade in 1881, fear of insurrection—not unexpected emancipation—was the official explanation.[42]

Last, and far less important as a factor affecting the supply of slaves in the southern provinces, was legislation provoked by the growing emancipationist sentiment, reflecting the theory that complete abolition could be met by successive and progressive measures. This legislation proposed to diminish slave property gradually without disturbing the foundations of plantation society and economy. The first significant measure, the Rio Branco law of 1871, provided, among other things, for emancipation of slave children (*ingénuos*) born after passage of the law, and for emancipation of adult slaves through a specially created fund. Planters were given the option of freeing ingénuos at the age of eight with indemnification, or freeing them at twenty-one without compensation. Fourteen years later there followed passage of the Sexagenarian law, freeing sixty-year-old slaves, although their services could be claimed for three more years if their masters so desired.

The fate of both pieces of legislation was identical: few slaves were affected. In the case of the Rio Branco law few planters took the option of freeing their ingénuos at the age of eight, accepting indemnification from the Imperial Government. Instead they incorporated the children of their slave women into their slave labor force; of the 9,310 ingénuos registered in Vassouras between 1873–1888, 64 were freed—and only because they accompanied their mothers liberated by the Emancipation Fund. As for the Emancipation Fund, in fourteen years (1873–1887) it freed 370 adult slaves of the município of Vassouras whose slave population in 1882 numbered 18,790 (Tables 6, 7, 8).[43] In the face of passage of the Sexagenarian

---

[42] "This wisely inspired law ought to maintain order and tranquility on rural establishments by impeding entry of more slaves into this province to whose fazendas they bring neither that resignation nor contentment with their fate which is essential to good discipline." *Relatório do Presidente da Província do Rio de Janeiro, August 1881*, p. 7; Luz, "A Administração Provincial de São Paulo," p. 90.

[43] From the table on page 68 it will be seen that the effect of the Emancipation Fund was similarly negligible at the provincial and national levels.

TABLE 6. Adult slaves and ingénuos of Vassouras freed by the Emancipation Fund of the Rio Branco law of 1871.

Slaves		Freed		Mortality	
Year	Number	Year	Number	Year	Number
		Adults			
1873	20,168	1873–1882	94	1873–1882	3,521
1882	18,790	1873–1887	370		
		Ingénuos			
1873–1888	9,310	1873–1882	49	1873–1888	3,074
		1873–1887	64[a]		

[a] Freed with manumitted mother.

Sources: Recenseamento, *1872; O Vassourense,* February 19 and May 7, 1882; "Appenso," *Relatório do Presidente da Província do Rio, September 1887,* pp. 35–37; Delden Laerne, *Brazil and Java,* pp. 120–121; "Mappa Estatística dos Filhos Livres de Mulher Escrava Matriculados na Collectoría de Vassouras de Accordo com o Artigo 40. do Regulamento Approvado pelo Decreto no. 4835 de Dezembro de 1871." APV.

TABLE 7. Adult slaves and ingénuos of the Province of Rio freed by the Emancipation Fund of the Rio Branco law of 1871.

Slaves		Freed		Mortality	
Year	Number	Year	Number	Year	Number
		Adults[a]			
1873	301,352	1873–1883	2,439	1873–1883	54,705
1883	263,755				
		Ingénuos			
1872–1881	97,739		?	1872–1881	30,576

[a] Excluding slaves imported into the province from northern Brazil as well as those freed by individual initiative.

Sources: Relatório do Presidente da Província do Rio, 1884; O Vassourense, April 9, 1882.

law, planters simply refused to register their sixty-year-old slaves.[44]

While legislation failed to halt slave imports to the areas of economic expansion in nineteenth-century Brazil, it heightened the speculative nature of the commerce which continued in

TABLE 8. Adult slaves and ingénuos of the Empire of Brazil freed by the Emancipation Fund of the Rio Branco law of 1871.

Slaves		Freed		Mortality	
Year	Number	Year	Number	Year	Number
		Adults			
1873	1,541,000	1872–1884	18,900	1872–1885	214,860
		1882–1885	23,147		
		Ingénuos[a]			
1872–1884	363,307	1872–1884	113		

[a] Freed at age of eight years.

Source: Luz, "A Administração Provincial de São Paulo," p. 81, notes 5 and 7.

Rio and in Vassouras until shortly before abolition in 1888 ended all discussion. The center of the trade in slaves for the municípios of the Parahyba Valley remained in and around the port of Rio de Janeiro.[45] Here, until 1850, were sent slaves bought on the African coast; here arrived slaves shipped south

[44] According to the slave registration (*matrícula*) of June 30, 1886, the slave population of the Province of Rio totaled 238,631. Following the new registration ordered by the Sexagenarian law, only 162,421 were re-registered, a drop of approximately 32 per cent. It had been estimated on the basis of the 1886 matrícula that the new registration would reveal approximately 25,800 slaves over sixty years old or more; only 9,496 were reported. *Relatório do Presidente da Província do Rio, September 12, 1887,* p. 40.

[45] Coastal ports of the province of Rio were also the scene of numerous slave debarkations. Most prominent of such ports were Angra dos Reis and Paraty; the Souza Breves family with extensive coffee plantations between the coast and the valley is reported to have used the Restinga de Marambaia as a slave depôt where African arrivals were rested and fattened for the trip to the fazendas. A. d'E. Taunay, *História*, VIII, 270. The largest slave markets were found in the capital, Rio.

from Maranhão, Fortaleza, Pernambuco, and Bahia when the inter-provincial trade replaced African importations. To serve up-country planters who lacked good roads to the coast and cash once they arrived in Rio, a host of middlemen developed. Despite the heavy risks involved, "few were the slave dealers who did not amass a colossal fortune." [46] Especially prominent were the Portuguese whose ample credit facilities and knowledge of business techniques, generally absent among rural Brazilians, prepared them for the commerce in slaves. Slave-bearing ships from Africa put into Rio under the Portuguese flag; in 1831 more than twenty Portuguese ships were so engaged. [47] The trade in slaves—a "very considerable branch of commerce"— resembled other business enterprise, the purchaser carefully reserving the right to examine the good or bad qualities of the "merchandise" before closing a sale. [48] Dealers maintained a dispassionate attitude toward their trade: one retailer bought slaves landed on the coast and sold them to planters of the province of Rio in the same way he "used to retail mules" in the southern provinces. [49] With the dealer interested solely in disposing of his lot of slaves as quickly and profitably as possible (often "selling them loaded with incurable diseases"), [50] planters had to know and recognize the signs of a good slave capable of withstanding hard labor, poor feeding, and poor clothing in a climate of variable temperature. For plantation conditions were such that it was common for a planter to have twenty-five acclimated and trained slaves left three years after buying a lot of one hundred. [51]

Among the first questions a prospective purchaser asked

[46] Ferreira Soares, *Crise Commercial*, p. 30. ". . . a business carried on with frock coat, leather gloves and large bank credits." Luiz Correa de Azevedo, "Da Cultura do Café," in F. P. de Lacerda Werneck, *Memória*, p. 222. See also J. J. von Tschudi, *Viagem às Províncias do Rio de Janeiro e São Paulo*. Biblioteca Histórica Paulista. V (Eduardo de Lima Castro, transl., São Paulo, 1953), pp. 15–16, 79.

[47] *Aurora Fluminense*, May 27, 1831.

[48] Jean Baptiste Auguste Imbert, *Manual do Fazendeiro ou Tratado Doméstico sobre as Enfermidades dos Negros, Generalisando as Necessidades Médicas de Todas as Classes* (2nd ed., Rio de Janeiro, 1839), p. 1.

[49] Charles Hubert Lavollée, *Voyage en Chine* (Paris, 1853), p. 35.

[50] F. P. de Lacerda Werneck, *Memória*, p. 23.

[51] Ferreira Soares, *Notas Estatísticas*, p. 135.

concerned the tribe and region in Africa whence the slave came. Certain tribal groups, such as those from the Gold Coast (*Alto Guiné*), were considered the best because of height, strength, and ability to bear hard labor. Those from Angola (*Baixo Guiné*) were thought "by nature enemies of work." [52] Since women were put to work beside the men, Congo women were desirable because it was rumored that in their native land they were accustomed to agricultural labor.[53] A thumbnail correlation was established between unwillingness to work and evil character, denoted by "too curly hair, small head, or low forehead, deep-set eyes and large ears." [54] Important also was the condition of mouth and nose, chest and abdomen, legs and feet. "A healthy Negro who will endure heavy work," prescribed Imbert, must show "smooth black, odorless skin, genitals neither too large nor too small, a flat abdomen and small navel or hernias may develop, spacious lungs, no glandular tumors under the skin—signs of scrofulous infection leading to tuberculosis, well-developed muscles, firm flesh, and in countenance and general attitude eagerness and vivacity; if these conditions are met, the Master will have a slave with guaranteed health, strength, and intelligence." [55] Visiting by night a slave market on the outskirts of Rio, Lavollée entered a fetid, stable-like building where he found recent African arrivals lying on dirty and worn mats; at an order they rose, washed and dressed in shirts and trousers prepared for the

[52] Imbert, *Manual do Fazendeiro*, p. 2.

[53] Imbert, *Manual do Fazendeiro*, p. 2. Imbert's observation on the advantages of Congo women is supported by comments published in Rio in 1860. Manioc, beans, peanuts ("mendobim ouginguba"), were reported grown in the Congo, as well as corn and sugar, on small plots. "All this labor and the rest is performed by the women; they are the ones who work in the fields, who prepare various flours and the food for themselves and their families; and finally they also buy and sell foodstuffs at their stands (*quitandas*)." Antonio María de Castilho Barreto, "Impressões sobre Africa Occidental," *Revista Luso-Brazileira*, I (July 1860), 58.

[54] Imbert, *Manual do Fazendeiro*, pp. 2–3. Older residents of Vassouras still repeat the expressions current in their fathers' days for interpreting physical characteristics among slave field hands. A "tall, thin, small-calved Negro" was sure to be a good worker. Large buttocks or calves, on the contrary, were signs of laziness. Strong, healthy Negro slaves were supposed to have a bright, brilliant black skin and the wise fazendeiro who desired to sell his older slaves used "pangrease" rubbed into the skin to give a healthy appearance.

[55] Imbert, *Manual do Fazendeiro*, p. 3.

inspection. In a yard they lined up, about twenty Negroes from eight to twelve years old, girls to one side. "Even trading in slaves," commented Lavollée dryly, "has its modesty." Then came the inspection where "face, eyes, ears, arms, legs . . . all the parts of the body underwent a minute examination which made more horrible the low jokes of the seller and his cynical language in hiding a defect or in pointing to a good quality." Their senses numbed by the long sea voyage in cramped quarters, the Negroes resembled "animals sold as though they were horses." Finally the lot was rejected by the astute French dealer who had taken Lavollée there—because the youngsters were too young for work on coffee plantations and had developed an eye infection. Noted Lavollée, "It's not easy to be a good merchant of humanity." [56]

The inter-provincial trade differed only in minor details. An ex-slave related that he was raised on a cotton and castor bean plantation in Maranhão in the north. Fearful of sudden emancipation without compensation, the master sold him to a passing slave dealer who, in turn, sold him to a commissário in the city of São Luis do Maranhão. He and other slaves remained there until a sufficient number were collected, then embarked on a steamer and landed on the Niteroi beach opposite Rio de Janeiro. He was then fourteen, according to his calculation. Along with other slaves, he was lodged in a large house where he received two meals daily, every detail of which he carefully recalled. Doctors looked over the arrivals, asked them how they felt; if anything was reported, doctors advised that it was not serious and supplied medicine. Planters who had come down to Rio to buy for their own plantations or to fill the requests of neighboring planters, examined them. They would approach the lined-up slaves and ask: "Boy, do you want to work for me?" A planter of Ubá, in the município of Vassouras, finally purchased him along with others, placed them on a train of the Dom Pedro Segundo railroad and sent them to the station at Ubá where they were quartered until called for.

Peddlers of slaves (*comboieiros*) often led their gangs up from

<hr />

[56] Lavollée, *Voyage en Chine*, pp. 36, 40.

the Rio market to sell directly to Vassouras planters. Another ex-slave repeated the story told by his parents: how they came from the African coast, how they marched along the dusty roads ahead of the comboieiro. Nearing a fazenda, they were lined up "like cattle" for the inspection of the planter and his overseer. The planter chose the slaves he desired, paid cash, gave the Africans new names, and sent them to the slave senzallas.[57]

In the latter years of the century, when Vassouras' coffee boom was over and the heirs of planters preferred hard cash to an inheritance of depreciating lands, coffee trees, buildings, and slaves, slave sales were frequent and planters could obtain field hands at public auctions. On the day appointed, usually announced in the local newspapers, buyers appeared and examined slaves drawn up in groups on the terreiro according to age and type of services they could perform. A contemporary journalist described one such gathering. The slaves stood with bowed heads, dispirited, now and again conversing with the prospective buyers who asked questions "more or less repugnant." No buyer offered to purchase all the slaves in one lot, and they were therefore sold in groups. Families were broken up and with "consternation they said goodbye to each other." Last to go were the disabled slaves and one old Negro who had been separated from the others because his former master had kept him as the sole surviving witness to the founding of the fazenda decades before.[58]

Unlike a few wealthy planters who had time and money to go down to Rio to purchase slaves, many planters had to rely upon the men who made a profession of buying and selling slaves locally, as well as upon those who had contact with the Rio marts, the commissários and mule-drivers.

Among the earliest Vassouras settlers were Mineiros who came south to the "forest of Rio" from São João d'El-Rey and

[57] Among more diligent fazendeiros it was the practice to list ". . . in a registry book the names of male and female slaves as well as of the offspring . . . and the names of those who died and those . . . freed when baptized. . ." Inventory, 1874, deceased: Barão do Tinguá, executor: Antonio Agrícola de Pontes, Fazenda do Tingúa, CPOV.

[58] Augusto-Emilio Zaluar, "Um leilão na Roça," *O Vassourense*, April 9, 1882,

Barbacena with enough capital to furnish credits to the first coffee planters for the purchase of slaves.[59] The development of the plantation economy of Vassouras was partially ascribed to the arrival of slave dealers "who brought and sold slaves to planters extending payments over five years, a fifth of the payment made annually without any security but that of the coffee trees planted. I knew a Mineiro, my close friend, João Francisco Junqueira, who sold in this fashion more than 2,000 slaves in those parishes once coffee was introduced there." [60] With the appearance of a local press in the seventies, local dealers employed newspaper advertising. Typical of such notices were "Antonio Carvalho de Goes, dwelling at Praça do Aquidaban no. 5, buys slaves of both sexes provided they are skilled and healthy; sellers please appear at the street and number above"; [61] or, "Propício Bernardes Cardoso, who has resumed residence in this city and wishes to announce that he prices slaves, ingénuos and any other services of the same type at Rua Augusta, 17." [62] Ranking in importance with the local traders, were the planters' commissários or factors who from an early date marketed the coffee consigned via mule team to the coastal ports, first Iguassú and later Rio, forwarded provisions and credits, and logically assumed the function of supplying slaves from the coastal marts to their up-country accounts. Between March 1832 and December 1834, Manoel Ferreira da Silva, a Vassouras planter, consigned to his commissário in Iguassú, 17:916$000 in coffee. Antonio Ferreira Neves, the commissário, debited to this account more than 41:577$000 in salaries paid to Ferreira da Silva's mule-driver and overseer, luxury foodstuffs such as Port wine, codfish, butter, and other necessities—meat, salt, and cotton cloth, as well as in coffee commissions and the cost of transshipping

[59] Vassouras local archives contain records of such transactions. There is a record of the sale of two slaves, to be paid in installments, made by Francisco José Teixeira Leite, February 28, 1822; by Custodio Ferreira Leite in 1826; another sale by Joaquim José Teixeira Leite of four "new slaves" to Antonio da Silva in 1833; and still another by Captain Florianno Leite Ribeiro in 1828—all members of the same clan originating in Minas Gerais. APV.

[60] Recopilação do Custo, p. 6.

[61] O Município, December 23, 1877.

[62] O Vassourense, August 13, 1882.

coffee in his launch to Rio across the bay. But of the total balance left, 23:661$000, 14:400$000 was a "credit granted for the purchase of twenty-four untrained Africans." [63]

A final source of slave labor—one which was common in the large urban centers of the coast—was found in the renting of slaves, both in the town of Vassouras and on surrounding plantations. Construction and maintenance of public works required slave labor, and the município rented slaves for this purpose. So-called "Free Africans"—slaves confiscated in the suppression of the slave trade—were rented to public authorities and private contractors.[64] Moreover, as a scarcity of labor developed on the plantations after 1850, planters proceeded to hire neighbors' slaves or even to rent out their own. Inter-family renting became common as evidenced by the following executor's report: "The growing disproportion between needs of the fields and the number of field hands available for cultivation obliged the executor to hire the slaves of several of the estate's heirs and even the labor of the estate's slaves on Sundays and saints' days." [65] And equally frequent were advertisements such as: "For rent. One young girl suitable as wetnurse. Healthy." [66]

The large slave labor force which developed Vassouras plantations was no working force chosen at random. From data

---

[63] Inventory, deceased: Manoel Ferreira da Silva, executrix: Escolástica Cándida Ferreira da Silva, Fazenda da Conceição, 1837, CPOV.

[64] By a law of 1853 contraband slaves were to work fourteen years after which they were to be freed. Roure, "A Escravidão." In 1851 and 1855 the Câmara Municipal of Vassouras requested the provincial government to send a few of these "Free Africans." To the latter request the provincial authorities replied that the Imperial Government had ceded them to the provincial government and that they could not be turned over to municipalities because they were needed on other projects and because "among the Africans were a number of children." Letter from the President of the Province of Rio de Janeiro, November 24, 1855. APV. For an account of what happened to "Free Africans" hired out to road-building contractors only to disappear in the mass of agricultural slaves of the province see *Relatório Apresentado ao Exm. Snr. Primeiro Vice Presidente da Província do Rio de Janeiro, February 15, 1864.*

[65] Inventory, 1876, deceased: Francisco Ribeiro de Avellar and wife, executor: João Ribeiro dos Santos Zamith, Fazenda unknown. CPOV. Several of the executor's expenses are revealing: "Payments to slaves for harvest labor" and "Payments to slaves for ending the cleaning (hoeing) of the coffee groves."

[66] *O Município*, May 9, 1879.

gathered on slave property listed in 93 plantation inventories totaling 6,701 slaves for the period 1820–1888, certain tentative conclusions may be drawn as to the nature of the labor force

Figure 1. Ratio of African male to female slaves, 1820–1888

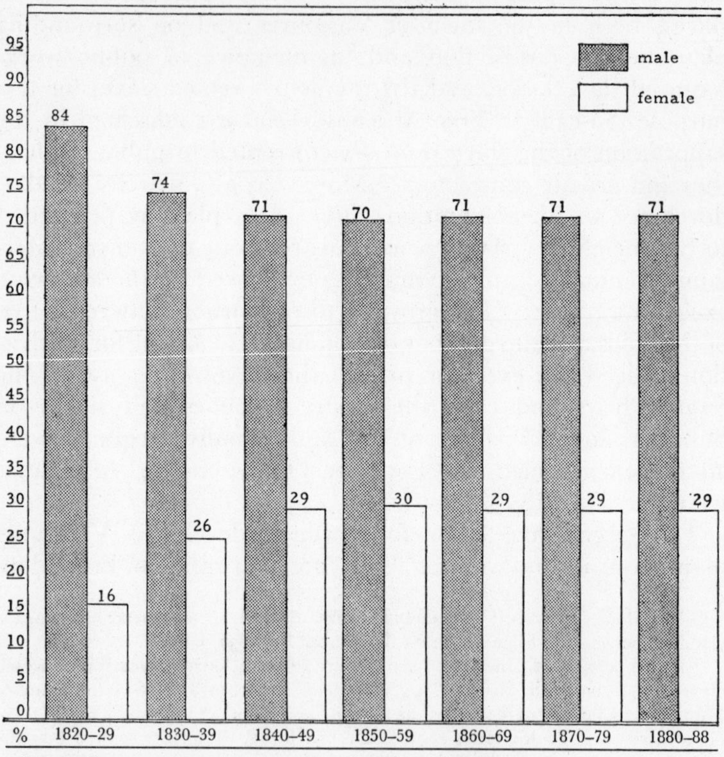

Sources: Inventories and testaments, CPOV and APV.

employed, with particular attention to provenience, proportion of sexes, and size of the working age groups.

Planters recorded the provenience of African slaves according to the port of embarkation, not tribal origin, and only after 1860 was the detailed listing of provenience dropped in favor of the general heading of "Africano" or "Nação." More than 50 per cent of African slaves had their proveniences given as "Angolla," "Benguela," "Congo," and "Cabinda," with the next largest group termed "Mossambique." Approximately 30 per cent came from "Cabundá," "Cassange," "Ganguella," "Inhambane," "Mocena," "Mossambe," and "Rebollo."

Figure 2. Ratio of male to female slaves, 1820–1888

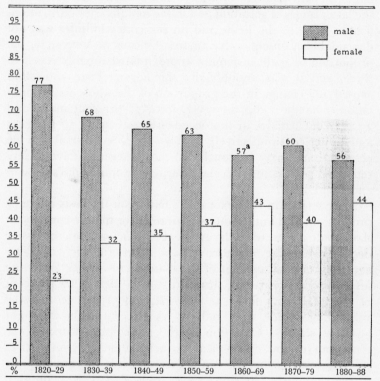

Sources: Inventories and testaments, CPOV and APV.

[a] Based on *Recenseamento, 1872.*

Very few were classified "Mina" or "Calabar." Location of these ports reveals that the African provenience of Vassouras slaves was limited to the area now embraced by the twin Portuguese possessions of Angola and Moçambique.[67]

[67] For similar provenience of African slaves entering the Rio de Janeiro custom-house in 1821 and 1822, see Maria Graham, *Journal of a Voyage to Brazil and a Residence There during Part of the Years 1821, 1822 and 1823* (London, 1824), p. 228, note.

Until the end of the slave trade forced planters to look more carefully to the physical needs of their slaves to prolong their working existence, planters sought field hands whom they could work out efficiently and replace with new levies. Under such circumstances planters preferred males to females for, during the latter stages of gestation and in the months after parturition, female labor in the fields and on the coffee hillsides was not dependable. Consequently, among Africans in Vassouras, the proportion of male to female approximated roughly seven to three, and it was undoubtedly the normal birth ratio that caused any change in the proportion of the whole slave population. Change it did, however, from 77 per cent males and 23 per cent females in the decade 1820–1829, to 56 per cent and 44 per cent respectively in 1880–1888. So gradual was the change that it may be concluded that Vassouras slave society remained predominantly male during the município's growth and decline.

More serious in its inexorable effect upon the costs of coffee production, and important as a stimulus for the interprovincial slave trade almost until the eve of abolition, was the progressive decline in the size of the slave population of efficient working age. This crucial segment of the plantation working force, the fifteen-to-forty-year-olds, dropped from a high of 62 per cent of the total labor force in 1830–1849 to 51 per cent in the succeeding decade, and finally to 35 per cent in the last eight years of slavery. Evolution of the slave labor force of the Fazenda Guaribú, an atypical but not unique case, emphasizes the reduction of the size of the most efficient age group: fully 64 per cent of the Guaribú's slaves from 1839 to 1847 consisted of fifteen-to-forty-year-olds. From then on the decline was precipitous for by 1863 it had plummeted to 25 per cent and by 1885, three years before abolition, to 19 per cent. Meanwhile, the rising proportion of aged and aging slaves on the same plantation—those above the age of forty—was no less spectacular. From 12 per cent in 1839–1847 it rose to 48 per cent in 1863 and to 61 per cent in 1885. Although the rise in the number of aged slaves on the Guaribú was not represen-tative of conditions obtaining throughout the area, nevertheless it is highly indicative of slave population trends. In this connection it is necessary to point out that of 183 slaves on the Guaribú in 1885, fully 79 were above the age of 70.[68]

Figure 3. Ratio of slave working force aged fifteen to forty years to total slave force, 1820–1888

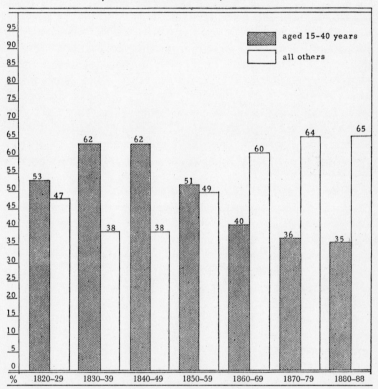

Sources: Inventories and testaments, CPOV and APV.

It was the unavoidable requirement of renewing the aging and dying slave labor with younger, more active slaves that led planters in the latter years of the century to supplement the

[68] Most plantations did not keep as large a proportion of incapacitated and senile slaves, preferring to turn them upon public charity by voluntary manumission on the part of the planter-owners. It was typical of the Ribeiro de Avellar family, a group most patriarchal in its outlook, that it preferred to support its slaves.

labor force inherited from their planter-fathers. When Lucio Soares da Costa entered his 54 slaves in the obligatory registration of 1872, only 40 per cent had been raised on the plantation while 14 per cent had come through inheritance and in a dowry, and 46 per cent by purchase.[69]

[69] Relação No. 1235 dos Escravos Pertencentes a Lucio Soares da Costa. September 22, 1872. CPOV.

Town of Vassouras, 1859

Fazenda do Secrétario, Vassouras, 1859

Fazenda São Fernando, Vassouras, 1949

Old slave and apprentice weaving baskets, 1859

Slaves preparing food, 1859

CHAPTER IV

Marketing, Provisioning and Transport

BEFORE the construction of the Dom Pedro Segundo railroad, Vassouras' large planters sent several times each year their train of pack mules (tropa) in charge of an *arreiador* (pack-leader) and slave muleteers on the difficult, often dangerous haul to Iguassú near the bay of Rio or to the capital itself. Here the coffee sacks enclosed in rawhide bags were deposited in the warehouse of the fazendeiros' urban factotum, the commissários or *correspondentes*, for sale to foreign coffee exporters established in Rio de Janeiro.

As middlemen sandwiched between the up-country planters and the coffee exporters, commissários or factors performed a multitude of services for their isolated clients. In the first place it was to the planters' advantage that the returning pack-trains arrive laden with articles not produced on the plantation: foodstuffs—codfish, jerked beef, salt, and bacon—as well as iron goods and some luxuries. The commissário was the logical purveyor of these articles, for the funds credited to planters from the sale of their coffee were employed in purchasing articles requested by the planters. Secondly, the commissário was favorably located in the port capital where a wide variety of imports were available at prices cheaper than those quoted by commercial houses of the towns of Vassouras and Paty, or by vendas along municipal roads. Describing the lack of contact between planters and commercial houses in the town of Vassouras, one member of the Câmara Municipal of Vassouras explained: ". . . because Iguassú and Rio are near, and because they each have packmule trains, large fazendeiros consider it more practical to maintain direct commercial relations with those towns." [1]

[1] Joaquim José Teixeira Leite in his Relatório de Administração Municipal presented to the newly elected CMV, January 7, 1849. APV, 1849.

By word of mouth, as one fazendeiro advised another, and via elaborate descriptive billheads, commissários built an up-country clientele. From Iguassú in 1845, Pimenta & Ribeiro announced that they had "facilities for receiving shipments for further consignment, and supply other goods." [2] On their billhead, Amaral & Bastos advertised that they were ". . . large-scale merchants in Rio de Janeiro where they have a dry-goods store for wholesale and retail customers on cash or credit basis, furnishing and supplying their clients not only with their own goods but those bought in other shops, and with monies as well." [3] A planter might decide to forward his harvest to a certain factor, who, without knowing the planter, accepted the coffee and sold it. He then opened a current account (*conta corrente*), entered the balance and, in a note handed to the arreiador, informed the fazendeiro of his balance. Through years of contact, fazendeiro and factor developed mutual trust; on his part the planter accepted prices entered for sale of his coffee as well as provisions ordered, and he "drew more or less at will upon his factor, and not a few used up all their credit before the new harvest was ready." [4] The trust was mutual, and almost always with good reason. A commissário had to be careful to sell consigned coffee at the highest possible price despite daily fluctuations and not to overcharge on provisions; if found cheating, the word soon spread to other planters who would refuse to deal with him. Before extending too large a credit on provisions requested, commissários ascertained through their planter clients the financial situation of a new account. Despite the trust, both employed certain devices in handling coffee. Very dry coffee absorbed moisture in the descent from the highlands to the more humid Rio lowlands, with the gain in weight accruing to the planters' account. To counter this, commissários bought bagged coffee on the basis of an arroba of fifteen kilos and

---

[2] From a bill sent to Alexandre Michaude. APV, 1845.

[3] Libello Civil de Dívida . . . contra RR. D. Carolina Julia Ferreira Dias e Seos Filhos Menores, Viuva e Herdeiros do Fallecido Antonio Thomaz Ferreira Dias. APV, 1849.

[4] *Correio da Manhã*, August 9, 1949.

weighed it to exporters on that of the slightly smaller "English" arroba.[5]

Very few were the fazendeiros or fazenda administrators who maintained accounts of coffee shipments and purchases requested of their factors. Conspicuously lacking was the careful bookkeeping of Luis Peixoto de Lacerda Werneck who reported that "from the beginning he resolved to conduct all fazenda business with his factors, Furquim & Brother, to make all business negotiations as legal as possible. He sent orders stating specifically the why and wherefore of every request. The letters were copied by letter-press . . . while the factors replied when they fulfilled the requests." [6] On the contrary, most planters were unwilling to use "complicated processes of commercial accounting" [7] and preferred to await reports occasionally forwarded by the more zealous commissários prompt to "attend to the orders of Your Excellency" and hopeful that "Your Excellency will honor me with your trade which I esteem highly and which I will always diligently serve." [8] In reports on their current account, fazendeiros ascertained what they had ordered, whether bills had been settled or mortgages paid as they had directed, all carefully classified by debit or credit. Over a two-year period, 1835–1837, a Vassouras fazenda received from Iguassú, among other things, two pairs of linen stockings, two arrobas of meat, two dozen spoons and two dozen plates, a trunk-lock, nails, two arrobas of bacon, a ream of paper, and a leather bag of salt.[9] Wrote a Rio factor to his Vassouras client: "With your most esteemed favor of February 22nd we received via the launch of Manoel José Lopes Tavares a shipment of coffee whose bill of sale and full payment of

[5] Moreover, when coffee arrived noticeably soaked, the price quoted by commissários was slightly lower than the normal for the day. Inventory, 1847, deceased: Luiz Gomes Ribeiro, executrix: Joaquina Mathilde d'Assumpção, Fazenda Gurubú, Sitio dos Encantos, CPOV.

[6] From his Prestação de Contas in Inventory, 1862, deceased: Anna Joaquina de São José Werneck, executor: Ignacio José de Souza Werneck, Fazendas Recreio, Pindobas, Palhas, CPOV.

[7] "Contabilidade Rural," *O Município*, September 27, 1874.

[8] Letter from Rio merchants Motta & Cia. to Anna Maria da Luz Jordão, November 22, 1858. APV.

[9] Bernardo Teixeira Pinto Machado to Manoel Gomes Coelho, 1837. APV.

Rs. 882$255 we have credited to your account. At your order, included in your letter of February 12th, we paid Agostinho José Vieira Rs. 1:498$400 which we have debited to your account. We append a receipt, also the debt to Snr. Jordão which the above-mentioned Snr. Vieira handed us." [10]

Generally speaking, commission houses—considered the "only branch of business left to Brazilians" [11]—knew far better than planter clients the financial status of their agricultural establishments. As clients over many years of financial prosperity and vicissitude, planters were considered friends for whom commissários supplied "sumptuous" lodgings whenever they arrived at Rio de Janeiro.[12] On both sides of the Rua dos Benedictinos, do Rosário, da Praínha, do Visconde de Inhaúma, narrow streets lined with commercial establishments from whose wide doors came odors of coffee and sacking, were located commission houses which accepted the coffee production of Vassouras' large fazendeiros: Teixeira Leite & Sobrinhos, Teixeira Leite & Bastos, João Baptista Leite & Cia., Furquim, Joppert & Cia., Teixeira de Castro & Malafia, Faro & Irmão, Bernardo Ribeiro de Carvalho, Ortigão & Cia., Roxo, Monteiro & Lemos, Alves & Avellar, and Gracie, Ferreira & Cia. Here and on nearby streets centered the trade in coffee of the municípios of the Parahyba Valley; and from here and other large commercial houses went out provisions for coffee fazendas, and to stock the shelves of local business

---

[10] Motta & Cia to Anna María da Luz Jordão, March 5, 1859. APV.

[11] Quintino Bocayuva, *Mensagem do Governador do Estado do Rio, September 1902*, p. 49.

[12] Bocayuva, *Mensagem do Governador*, p. 49. Although written shortly after 1900 Pierre Denis' portrait of the fazendeiro on his visits to the city was undoubtedly true of previous decades. "In the country rich and poor lead much the same life," he observed. "So long as the planters remain on their estates they have no occasion for personal expenditure. If business or pleasure take them to the city, it is at most only for a few days. More often than not they are personally unknown in the cities; and the simplest means of inspiring respect and esteem is to spend royally, in good, ringing, coin. Considerations of economy are needless; the purse once empty, they have but to return to their houses and their fields. They do not like calculation; they prefer not to count the expense. During the days of comparative idleness which they pass in the city they display a tendency to prodigality which gains by contagion on the people of the city." *Brazil.* Bernard Miall, trans. (New York, 1911), p. 136.

houses—ranchos, vendas, tabernas, botequins, as well as the packs of itinerant peddlers.

Vassouras' local commerce which supplied the small planter thrived on the trade with pack trains traveling the Estrada da Polícia—in the 1840's the "most extensive and important in Brazil . . . stretching four hundred leagues from Cuiabá to Rio de Janeiro."[13] From muleteams going south to Rio and Iguassú, business houses purchased Minas' production of heavy cotton cloth, bacon, and hides which they supplemented with imported goods picked up on the coast by returning mule-teams.[14] Stock-in-trade consisted of coarse textiles, dry goods (cornmeal, jerked beef, bacon, rice, beans, codfish, cheese, biscuits), liquors (aguardente, inexpensive Portuguese wines), knick-knacks (ribbons, combs, wallets, nail- and tooth-brushes, perfumed soap), and iron goods (axes, hoes, billhooks, iron pots, tin dishes).[15] To this list were sometimes added ready-made clothes and hides.[16] Typical of a prosperous establishment of the forties, a rancho and taberna on the Estrada da Polícia near Vassouras was a family enterprise where the "taberneiro sold alcoholic beverages, raw sugar (*rapadura*), corn, iron goods . . . and in his leisure hours played cards. His wife prepared meals, coffee for travelers, cornbread, and biscuits."[17] Other establishments bordered on the bare subsistence level as seen by a request in the fifties for a low license fee on the ground that the proprietor was "sick and miserable, and has no other recourse to maintain his family if not by his small casa de negocio."[18] Such small tradesmen dealt with the muleteers and to a considerable extent with those free members of society "not favored by fortune"[19]—small proprietors, renters,

---

[13] Joaquim José Teixeira Leite to the Presidente da Provincia do Rio, March 1846. APV, 1846.

[14] *Ibid.*; Siqueira, *Memória Histórica*, p. 26.

[15] Bill presented by José Thomas da Silva to Domiciano Antonio de Souza Monteiro, 1849. APV, 1849; advertisement of Ferreira da Costa & Franca, *O Vassourense*, August 13, 1882.

[16] Bill of Padilha & Athaíde, 1852. APV, 1852.

[17] Macedónio, "Hercules e Omphalia," *O Municipio*, August 22, 1878.

[18] Dated February 23, 1858, to CMV. APV, 1858.

[19] Letter of merchant protesting his high licensing fee to CMV, January 29, 1883. APV, 1890.

aggregados, poor free folk (*pobreza*) eking out an existence at trades subsidiary to the large planters—and with the large slave population on roads outside the municipal centers. With such retailers large planters had little business contact, with the exception of one or two large retail houses in the town of Vassouras. To prevent slaves from congregating at the doors of liquor-selling tabernas which dotted the short roads (*travessías*) feeding into main highways and which tended to outnumber drygoods stores,[20] a very few planters permitted their aggregados to sell drygoods and liquors. In 1849, Silverio Gomes Leal who styled himself a "dweller on the Fazenda Old Pao Grande situated on the Estrada Geral de Minas, an aggregado of the owner, Barão do Capivary," requested the lowest possible license to sell dry goods, vinegar, olive oil, and liquors." [21] Similarly an aggregado of the Fazenda do Secretário bought beans and corn for sale to slaves of the fazendeiro, Christóvão Correa e Castro.[22] Most planters throughout the century complained that isolated vendas and tabernas traded in goods stolen by slaves,[23] sold goods of inferior quality at excessively high prices, offered poorly prepared or "falsified" liquors to trusting slave customers, and beguiled the sick with sales of "small or large doses of poisonous, corrupt, and strange medicines." [24] During the peak years of Vassouras agricultural

[20] In 1836 there were 71 tabernas against 20 drygoods stores on the roads of the município. Relatório of Fiscal João Luis de Lima, September 11, 1836 to CMV. APV, 1836.

[21] Silverio Gomes Leal to CMV. Granted on August 11, 1849. APV, 1849.

[22] Dated April 29, 1867. APV, 1867.

[23] In one of his regionally flavored tales, Macedonio turned a light upon the psychology of the local businessmen who dealt in stolen articles. "One slave brought a silver spoon, knife, and fork," Macedonio wrote with his tongue-in-cheek, "and to help the little Darkie the shopkeeper bought them at a reasonable price, in view of the risks of the operation." Reasoned the shopkeeper on the ethics of the deal: "If the Negro sells this, it must be his; if it is not his, we may consider him reimbursed for his labor which the planter does not remunerate." Macedonio expressed the view of a Portuguese shopkeeper on accepting stolen coffee from slaves: "The poor Negroes . . . also have their own coffee plots and when they cannot have them, the plantation's groves are the product of their sweat. The slaves plant, weed, harvest and prepare coffee while the boss-planter sits idly by with one foot crossed over the other." "Negocio é Negocio," *O Município*, October 4, 1877.

[24] *O Município*, October 4, 1877; Posturas da CMV do Paty do Alferes, Artigos

prosperity tabernas and vendas clustered within easy radius of coffee plantations, and in exasperation one municipal authority compared them with the equally damaging coffee pest: "They are sucking the sap of the fazendeiro and are a pest perhaps worse than the coffee blight." [25] Nor were planters immune to the practice of short-weighting prevalent among local shops. "Twelve arrobas of meat," wrote a local planter, "arrived packed in three packages of four arrobas each. As soon as they arrived I ordered them weighed; two packages gave three arrobas, a third gave three arrobas and 16 pounds." Most damning of all, the packages arrived in "perfect condition." "Now you see," the planter concluded, "why I have to order certain things from Iguassú, for when they come from local stores . . . there is no charge for shipping but the tradesmen more than make up for it." [26]

To still another enterprising businessman, the itinerant peddler (*mascate* or *pombeiro*), the large potential market provided by fazenda slave population proved irresistible. Unlike taberna or venda proprietors who traded over the counter, mascates tramped the roads of the município of Vassouras with small wooden or tin trunks strapped to their backs to sell directly to planters and their slaves; others employed burros or even a porter to carry merchandise. Pack peddlers sold notions on wooden trays or glass-topped cases (*caixas vidraças*) and usually included in their assortment of goods striped and checked cloth.[27] Some included lottery tickets;[28] others, who were required to post a bond of two contos to "indemnify those who might be defrauded by the

15, 21; Pharmacist Manoel José Monteiro de Barros to CMV, January 23, 1847. APV, 1847; Antonio Correa e Castro, Eloy José d'Avila and others to CMV as reported in *O Vassourense*, June 25, 1882.

[25] Joaquim José Teixeira Leite, attacking a complaining taberna-keeper, José Fernandes Gorito. To Presidente da Província do Rio, September 6, 1862. APV, 1863.

[26] Barão do Paty (F. P. de Lacerda Werneck) to his commissário, Bernardo Ribeiro de Carvalho. Fazenda Monte Alegre, December 9, 1853. Documentos Referentes a Familia Werneck. Arquivo Nacional.

[27] Disposições da Organização da Tabella, Artigo 7, January 10, 1861. APV, 1861.

[28] Pedido de licença para mascatear bilhetes, February 14, 1853. APV, 1853.

seller," [29] offered articles of gold and silver, even diamonds and the decorations newly created barons could sport in button-holes.[30] There were a few who specialized in peddling shoes, tin, and tinware or aguardente.[31]

Wisely the peddler concentrated first on the fancies of female members of the planter's family by displaying eye-catching textiles, ribbons, shiny jewelry, and notions. Such techniques and the fact that he was a bearer of welcome news of the outside world usually won the master's approval to sell to his slaves, the real object of a large number of pack peddlers.[32] On them he unloaded his assortment of shiny notions and inexpensive, coarse textiles. When he had exhausted this market, he pushed his measuring rod into his walking stick, hoisted the trunk to his back, picked up a hand valise, and moved on to the next fazenda. His stock-in-trade exhausted, he returned to a rented room in the town center of Vassouras and restocked by purchases from the town's larger business houses.

Later in the century other types of salesmen appeared. Vassouras stores occasionally employed their own peddlers. Joaquim José da Silva paid for two licenses in 1853 when he had a "small trade in the town" and desired to "send someone out for a little peddling." [33] Cardoso Pereira de Lima & Cia explained to the Câmara Municipal that "they do not carry merchandise for sale to any customer. Only at the end of each semester a clerk customarily visits clients to liquidate accounts and take the opportunity to exhibit samples of new merchandise our House offers its Clientele." [34] At about the same time the

---

[29] *Posturas da Câmara Municipal de Vassouras, 1857*, Artigo 36.

[30] From a list of articles found in the tin trunk of a mascate fined in 1875 for non-payment of his license. APV, 1875.

[31] Auto de Multa contra Daniel Esposito, January 17, 1877. APV, 1877; Pedido de Licença de Affonso Bandeira para Mascatear Folha de Flandres, February 13, 1878. APV, 1878; Letter from Secretaría do Governo da Província do Rio, July 5, 1873. APV, 1873.

[32] Americo Werneck, *Graciema, Romance Brasileiro* (2 vols. 2nd ed., Rio de Janeiro, 1920), I, 26; ". . . the real motivation of most of the peddlers is to trade with slaves." Relatório do Fiscal Antonio José Eneas da Frequesía do Paty do Alferes, December 31, 1862. APV, 1863.

[33] Pedido de Licença, 1853. APV, 1853.

[34] Pedido de Licença, January 26, 1891.

cometa appeared with articles he bought in Rio, shipped to the town of Vassouras, and then forwarded to dispersed clients throughout the município. Clients paid cash or in coffee and furnished him with new requests for the return trip.

Since peddlers entered the trade with a shoestring capital, the onus of a municipal license irked considerably and they took pains to avoid the Câmara's inspectors. A few tried the expedient of halting their peddling to deceive the *fiscal*, before surreptitiously returning to it.[35] Venancia Portore and Francisco Caputo tried a more ingenious scheme: they formed a mascate company, acted "as if they were partners, then separated as soon as they paid for one license, and engaged new partners." The loss of revenue annoyed the fiscal plagued with the problem of catching up with shifting peddlers, and he complained: "I know a few such peddlers who last year changed partners three or more times." [36]

Great as was their usefulness in supplementing channels for distribution of goods, particularly to poor free folk and slaves dispersed far from commercial centers, peddlers were the target of surveillance and constant control by municipal authorities from the early years of the nineteenth century. Many manumitted African slaves or libertos apparently turned to peddling to earn a living in the 1830's and, as the jittery Imperial Government stated in its printed circular of 1830, there was every "presumption and suspicion that such Blacks, male or female, are the inciters and provocateurs of tumults and commotions which have influenced those who live in slavery." No liberto could leave "City, Town, Hamlet, Fazenda, or Building in which he dwells to trade . . . without a passport obtained from the Juiz Criminal or Justice of the Peace" for which he needed three witnesses who vouched for his good conduct, and without stating his destination.[37] The following year Vassouras' municipal regulations extended similar control over those who could act as mascates to include

[35] APV, 1867.

[36] Relatório do Fiscal Antonio José Eneas, December 31, 1864. APV, 1864.

[37] This Law of December 14, 1830 repeated the Resolution of the General Council of the Province of Bahia. APV.

any Brazilian or foreigner.[38] Five years later the provincial president ordered every câmara municipal to change or add such controls over mascates whether "slave or liberto, foreign or national."[39] Rigorous controls were relaxed in the forties, presumably since the number of incoming Portuguese peddlers reduced any possible threat of liberto "troublemakers" masquerading as peddlers.

It was now the turn of the foreign peddlers. When rising foodstuff prices in the fifties disturbed Brazilian planters, some of the blame fell upon the many immigrants, including peddlers. "The new mouths . . . are foreigners who now run about the country as peddlers, without any intention of settling here but only to profit by selling cheap jewelry and worthless trash and then to retire when their pockets are full. Behind them come others, for there is always a large number of these fortune-seekers."[40] In 1859 there were fifteen licensed peddlers in Vassouras, almost all Portuguese.[41] By 1864, the number of Italian peddlers had grown large enough to bring exaggerated complaints from the local retail stores:

> They block the streets, the roads, the plantation yards, the kitchens, and even the slave quarters, a swarm of Italians with their trunks and hand valises, without home or hearth; and as small mascates or pombeiros they pay a mere twenty milreis for a license. They have no expenses and can sell their drygoods cheaper; because they have neither reputation nor credit to lose, they deceive here and move there and when they have a certain amount which they feel will make them happy they go home.[42]

Within a quarter of a century the Italians were replaced by Syrian and Lebanese, called indiscriminately *Turcos*, whose business tactics were similarly criticized.

[38] Posturas da Câmara Municipal de Vassouras, 1831, Parte 3, Título 2, Artigo 12.
[39] Paulino José Soares de Souza in distributing Decree no. 18, 1836. APV, 1836.
[40] Pedro Ramos da Silva, "Carestía de Géneros Alimentícios," Annexo K, *Relatório do Presidente da Província do Rio, August 1, 1858*, p. 21.
[41] *Tabella*, 1859. APV, 1859.
[42] Merchants of Vassouras to CMV, 1864. APV, 1864.

(2)

For the dispatch of coffee and maintenance of a supply of provisions, Vassouras planters paid a high price. Although many fazendeiros believed that slave labor, including that of slave muleteers, was gratis once the original purchase price was paid, there remained the upkeep of a pack-mule train demanding a steady outlay of cash and frequently involving losses in maimed or drowned mules and water-soaked or mud-spattered coffee. Until the Pedro Segundo railroad changed the problem radically, the fazendeiro resigned himself to the inescapable: "without your pack-train you cannot be a fazendeiro of Serra-Acima (highlands)." [43]

That "very important person of coffee fazendas" [44]—the pack leader or arreiador—was entrusted with the management of the slave muleteers (tropeiros or tocadores) and with responsibility for safe arrival of the valuable coffee cargo at the warehouse of the commissário leagues away on the coast. For such positions Vassouras planters employed immigrant Portuguese from the Azores, almost invariably bachelors. Very typical was the arreiador who described himself in court as "José de Menezes Vasconcellos, a White man, born on Ilha Terceira, 24 years old, and unmarried." [45] For his services to the proprietor of the Fazenda São Fernando during 1850–1851 an arreiador received approximately Rs. 30$000 monthly, one-third more than the salary paid another "free employee," the overseer supervising the drying of coffee on the terreiro. Undoubtedly the proprietor did not assess it this way, but the fact remains that fully 20 per cent of the plantation's effective male working force ("always chosen from among the best" [46]) or seven of thirty-five Negro slaves was taken from field labor and channeled to the job of muleteer. Nor did expenditures on the pack team end here. Typical accounts included such entries as Rs. 45$000 paid for "a cargo mule substituting the

[43] F. P. de Lacerda Werneck, *Mémoria*, p. 94.
[44] A. d'E. Taunay, *História*, IV, 371, quoting Jules d'Assier.
[45] From testimony in case of Francisco Aleixo vs. José Lourenço. APV, 1847.
[46] Alfredo de Barros e Vasconcellos, Capitão de Engenheiros, in *Relatório do Presidente da Província do Rio, June 1, 1860*, p. 70.

one which died," the cost of two specially carved wooden harness pieces totaling Rs. 6$000, plus the price paid to "João Benguella for rent of one cargo mule, Rs. 12$500," not to mention the "cost of men and animals in the Rancho do Alto" over a period of five months or Rs. 300$220.[47] Moreover, where planters shipped coffee to Iguassú, they were billed by their factors for the overwater transhipment of their coffee via launch to the Rio de Janeiro market[48] and for food and pasture while awaiting a return load to be assembled.[49]

According to the account of an ex-slave muleteer, on the morning of a trip to the coast, mules were brought around to the plantation storehouse. A large leather bag (*broaca*) was weighed on the plantation scales and into it went four arrobas of coffee. A pack harness was placed on the mule to carry eight arrobas equally distributed on both sides; if the mule bucked when loaded, an extra arroba of coffee was thrown on top "to calm it down." For protection against heavy rains and unforeseen falls on the trail, a heavy rawhide coverlet was thrown over the leather bags and bound with a rawhide strap tightened with a tourniquet on top of the load. Two slave muleteers supervised each troop (*lote*) of seven burros. Horses were never used for bearing cargo in pack trains because "experience shows they cannot bear forced marches of thirty-seven to fifty miles daily" over poor roads and were not as "surefooted in the endless mudholes formed during the rainy season."[50]

---

[47] Conta Corrente da Receita e Despeza do Cazal do Finado Fernando Luis dos Santos Vernek até o Dia 19 de Septembro de 1851. Inventory, 1855, deceased: Jesuina Polucena d'Oliveira Serra, executor: Dr. João Arsenio Moreira Serra, Fazenda São Fernando. APV, 1855. See A. d'E. Taunay, *História*, IV, 356–358.

[48] Usually listed in the current account forwarded by the factor as "frete de lancha," in 1850 charged at the rate of Rs. 0$080 per arroba. Conta de Venda e Líquido Rendimento . . . de Café que de sua Fazenda São Fernando me consignou o Illmo. Snr. Dr. João Arsenio Moreira Serra. Inventory, 1855, deceased: Jesuina Polucena d'Oliveira Serra. APV, 1855. Launches had sails and carried between eight and thirty-five tons with a crew of three to five. *Relatório do Presidente da Província do Rio, 1855*, p. 56.

[49] Motta & Cia to Anna Maria da Luz Jordão in bill of November 22, 1858. APV, 1859.

[50] Siqueira, *Memória Histórica*, p. 4. Most mules came from São Paulo's Sorocaba Fair held in the south each year during April and May just before the coffee harvest. A. d'E. Taunay, *História do Café*, IV, 342, 361, 371, 375. As late as 1877 reports of the progress of the Sorocaba Fair were reprinted in Vassouras newspapers.

After receiving last-minute instructions from the fazendeiro and a slip of paper giving the weight of the coffee cargo, the trip began. Out in front walked the lead mule, slave muleteers trudging beside their pack mules sometimes carrying in their hands a "calabash full of black beans bedded in white farinha" eaten on the march.[51] Muleteers and arreiador who brought up the rear were armed, the latter with pistols and the former with long-bladed knives thrust behind and secured by the belt.[52] By late afternoon the pack team was on the lookout for a rancho or way-station to halt for the night. Failing to locate one, the weary travelers often made camp in the middle of the road or trail, unloading coffee bags and harness and building a fire to heat their beans, rice, and coffee.[53] Days later the dust and sweat covered men arrived at the doors of the commissário in Rio or Iguassú where unloaded coffee was weighed immediately and the total compared with the list made by the planter. A few days' rest and the return trip with provisions began.

More than the expensive maintenance of fazenda pack trains, the damage to coffee during shipment and to animals brought unending complaint from up-country fazendeiros. "The inhabitants of this município must struggle with terrible roads, mud holes and precipices which consume most of the profit accruing from their products . . . and cause the death of their animals," wrote one planter in 1835.[54] Another complained in 1850: "We have had heavy rainfall . . . the animals are frightened as they wade through mud as high as their chests, or fall by the wayside. Wretched muleteers cover themselves with mud as they try to save coffee bags which most of the time become damp and spoil the coffee. Of a troop of mules very often four or five drown in this sea of mud." On a particularly difficult stretch the "hardworking muleteer excommunicates the hour when he was born!!" [55] Mud and deep holes were

[51] Walsh, *Notices of Brazil*, II, 27.

[52] According to municipal posturas arreiadores and muleteers were permitted to bear arms when working. Posturas da Câmara Municipal de Vassouras, 1831, Parte 2, Titulo 3, Artigo 1.

[53] *Posturas da Câmara Municipal de Vassouras, 1857*, Artigo 65.

[54] APV, 1835.

[55] Barão do Paty to Bernardo Ribeiro de Carvalho, Fazenda Monte Alegre, 1854. Documentos Referentes a Familia Werneck. Arquivo Nacional.

recurrent themes in other complaints: "When the rains come the roads dry out with difficulty; daily rains, lack of sunlight, and the constant march of mule teams and cattle turn roadbeds into gruel-like mud, so deep that frequently many animals are found drowned in it." All too obvious were the consequences of this situation in "tremendous damages to the fazendeiro who not only loses the animals for which he had expended considerable capital, but who still must suffer a loss in the price of his coffee spoiled by contact with mud." [56] So bad did the situation become that, in 1854 and the first months of 1855, it was reported to the provincial assembly that transport costs absorbed more than one-third the value of coffee shipped from up-country plantations.[57]

As producers and shippers of coffee to the coastal ports, planters insisted that the "most desirable improvements" be "ease of communication above all else" and that roads be prepared for the heavy torrents of November, not "just for the dry period." [58] By mid-century it was all too evident that participation of fazendeiros in road maintenance, municipal *posturas* to the contrary, was entirely inadequate. Indeed, penury of the early municipal treasury and vagueness of municipal regulations rendered difficult assessing where responsibility for local road construction and maintenance fell —whether upon planter or municipality.[59] In 1830 a non-public hence non-municipal road was defined as "privately used by a few residents" to be maintained by users as far as its junction with any highway (*estrada geral*) maintained by provincial or Imperial funds.[60] Failure to define precisely "a few residents" brought a proposed regulation in 1831 stating that all property owners were to "maintain . . . drain . . .

[56] Siqueira, *Memória Histórica*, p. 5.

[57] *Relatório do Presidente da Província do Rio, 1855*, 59; *Relatorio da Commissão encarregada da Revisão da Tarifa . . . apresentado . . . as Governo Imperial* (Rio de Janeiro, 1853), p. 279.

[58] Siqueira, *Memória Histórica*, p. 5.

[59] Ambrozio de Souza Coutinho to Câmara Municipal of Paty do Alferes, December 13, 1829, Artigo 9. "Since the Câmara has no funds for repairing public roads. . ." APV, 1829.

[60] Posturas da Câmara Municipal do Paty do Alferes, 1830, Artigo 11. APV, 1830.

and clear" roads on which they had any frontage.[61] Four years later municipal authorities increased planters' responsibility by specifically demanding that they also clear their frontage on provincial or Imperial highways.[62]

Brought up again for settlement in 1853, the thorny problem posed by the vague language of ordinances relating to road maintenance was handled by a municipal commission which declared that "since we found in no law a definition of what constitutes a public or private road we must give these words their popular meaning according to which a road serving a few planters cannot be considered public." [63] Final word as far as municipal regulations were concerned appeared in 1857. Fazendeiros were ordered to maintain in good condition any municipal road fronting on their property, such a road being defined as any "frequented road leading to hamlets of the município, to any neighboring municipalities or to any provincial or Imperial roads intersecting them." This time, however, an attempt was made to pin down those elusive terms, "a few" and "frequented"; classified as municipal roads were those private roads leading to the same places giving "transit to ten or more persons who live in as many houses for a period of five years with knowledge and tolerance of respective owners of fronting property." [64]

The indifference of the Câmara Municipal to road maintenance had its roots in divergent economic patterns of town and countryside. Vassouras, the town, depended upon the commercial activity of the highway passing through its narrow streets. At a suggestion in the 1840's that the highway be rerouted to shorten its length, the president of the Câmara hastened to explain that its first effect would be "annihilation of the town of Vassouras." "Everybody knows," his petition continued, "the road is the sole fount of life and prosperity." Then in a prophetic tone he warned that "If you remove this

[61] Projecto de Posturas da Câmara Municipal de Vassouras, 1831, Parte 3, Título 3, Artigo 2. APV, 1831.
[62] APV, 1837.
[63] Joaquim José Teixeira Leite and Camillo de Carmo to CMV, April 20, 1853.
[64] Posturas de Câmara Municipal de Vassouras, 1857, Título 5, Artigos 68, 69.

road from the town, the town will have to move too." [65] Planters maintained stronger social than economic ties with the town where they sent their families to spend part of the year in town houses, to take part in church festivities and in the social life of the landed and commercial gentry. Their coffee production, on the other hand, went directly out of the município to Iguassú and Rio. Thus town prosperity was linked closely to the traffic of the Estrada da Polícia and to sales to small proprietors and poor folk in the vicinity, to a lesser degree to the economic life of the coffee plantations. The seeming paradox of municipal inspectors pestering planters for failure to maintain their sections of municipal roads[66] while the Câmara Municipal used mounting revenues solely for town public works is to a great extent understandable from the fact that such revenues derived from taxes on commercial, not agricultural activity: town business houses, tabernas, vendas, peddlers, hotels, barber and tailor shops, cabinet-makers and cobblers, butchers and vendors of lottery tickets. Approximately 66 per cent of total municipal revenue for the prosperous year of 1859 came from licenses and fines paid by commercial establishments; meanwhile the Câmara Municipal extended fully 54 per cent of its revenue on town public works (Table 9).

Fazendeiros had to use their own resources to construct and maintain feeder roads through their own and neighbors' property until they met the highways of the provincial government.[67] And often zealous fazendeiros ran into obstructions

[65] Joaquim Jose Teixeira Leite to the Presidente da Provincia do Rio, March 1846. APV, 1846. Almost the same statement appeared eighteen years later when a municipal finance commission stated that commerce was the "principal fount of this chamber's revenues." João Ribeiro dos Santos Zamith to CMV, November 22, 1865. APV, 1864.

[66] Relatórios of Fiscals to CMV; Joaquim Antonio de Macedo Tupinambá, January 15, 1856; Antonio José Eneas, January 27, 1857; Fabianno Carlos de Araujo, September 3, 1857; Antonio José Eneas, 1860 and Antonio Florencio Pereira do Lago, Chief of the 4th district of Public Works of the Province of Rio de Janeiro to CMV, December 11, 1862. All in APV.

[67] With the expansion of coffee and increased commercial activity between Minas and the coastal ports the município of Vassouras boasted of at least six parallel provincial roads crossing the município to the Serra do Mar and descending to the Rio lowlands: Estrada de Marcos da Costa, do Pilar, do Vernek, do Commercio, da Polícia, and the Estrada do Rodeio. Siqueira, *Memória Histórica*, p. 11.

raised by their neighbors. Bernardo Caetano de Freitas ordered a "rough" path opened from Rio Bonito to the banks of the Parahyba River by linking the trails that his neighbors used for

TABLE 9. Income and public works expenditures of Câmara Municipal de Vassouras, 1838–1879.

Year	Total local income	License fees	Per Cent of income	Total public works expended	Per Cent of income
1838	5:042$327	2:836$400	56		
1843	6:348$730	3:739$200	59	4:468$000	70
1844	6:283$300	3:966$600	63	13:505$000	210
1848	6:070$000	4:400$800	72	6:700$000[a]	110
1849	12:007$380	5:480$000	46	7:100$000	58
1852	12:982$246	7:749$440	60	9:150$470[b]	70
1855	16:960$031	14:280$000	84	10:567$403	60
1859	27:879$260	18:683$220	66	15:189$513	54
1862	30:928$533	29:491$573	97	20:871$833	67
1863	24:639$996	22:810$137	90	6:539$000	25
1865	28:466$152	21:727$003	76	18:637$000[c]	65
1866	23:099$435	20:122$500	87	5:375$000[d]	23
1867	23:239$832	21:238$669	91	8:500$000	36
1869	20:778$723	18:023$436	87	9:082$335[e]	43
1872	35:509$357	19:832$403	53		
1875	23:469$650	26:741$008	94		
1879	4:940$010	3:809$000	77		

[a] Represents construction cost of town fountain.

[b] Construction of local bridge.

[c] Contribution of município to construction of railroad station at Estação de Vassouras on Pedro Segundo railway.

[d] Construction of road from town center to Pedro Segundo railway and construction of station there.

[e] Construction of road from town center to Pedro Segundo railway.

Source: Balanços Resumidos das Receitas e Despezas da CMV. APV.

communicating between their plantations. Once the path was concluded, he found that "all my neighbors neglect their sacred duty to maintain the roads fronting on their property." Even more galling, they failed to clear sections of the path where trees cut in virgin forest were left athwart the path. Custodio

Coelho, to whom Freitas paid a small sum to open a short cut, proceeded to use the money for clearing his land, leaving trees cluttering the path.[68] It took four months to get the municipal authorities to check Freitas's complaints.

There was the case of Salvador Lopes de Figueiredo who announced that for two years he had not cleared his section of a road because he "persuaded himself that by law and common sense Proprietors ought to conserve only those roads useful to the public transit of travelers and not for the personal comfort of two or three fazendeiros." Since he did not have extra slave labor to clear the road he had to "beg his Friends to order it done at his expense . . . unless they kindly wish to pay for it themselves." With a flourish he ended his peroration: "However it is done I will accept it as a Great Favor and Charity." [69] A spirit of cooperation was conspicuously lacking when Honório Francisco Caldas sent slaves to repair a portion of road which his overflowing dam had ruined. Here they met an enraged planter who insisted that the level of the dam be permanently lowered and that Caldas pay him for damages. Caldas recalled his slaves and left an "immense mudhole" which impeded all traffic. Queried the diligent inspector of the Câmara: "Will this Respectable Corporation decide to fill the hole or reopen the old road?" [70] When inspectors worried planters with complaints about their lack of road maintenance, they retorted that "in the old days the road was conserved by provincial coffers" [71] or "the Câmara should take care of such necessities," [72] or they took refuge in legal loopholes left in the posturas by intimating that a road remained private, not municipal, because it had been used without their "knowledge and tolerance." [73] Where most fazendeiros neglected roads, others hungry for land incorporated them into their holdings

[68] Bernardo Caetano de Freitas to Câmara Municipal of Paty, January 14, 1830. APV.

[69] Salvador Lopes de Figueiredo to CM of Paty do Alferes, Fazenda do Cordeiro, December 31, 1830. APV, 1830.

[70] APV, 1867.

[71] Fiscal Joaquim Antonio de Macedo Tupinambá to CMV, 1856. APV, 1856.

[72] Tupinambá to CMV, March 12, 1855. APV, 1855.

[73] Supplicante: Francisco Gomes d'Assumpção, Supplicado: Salustriano de Souza Freitas, March 1879. APV, 1879.

by "ruining bridges, digging ditches or piling wood in the middle of the roadbed," [74] offering an unedifying example to their neighbors if unpunished. And after the slaves were freed, the good intentions of the fazendeiros with regard to road maintenance were inadequate because they lacked labor and money.[75]

As an elected body, the provincial assembly responded to powerful pressures exerted by electors of a province of expanding agricultural production and widespread prosperity. Logically planter electors solicited from provincial representatives adequate funds to maintain those highways within convenient distance of developing coffee fazendas. Also, fazendeiros were not averse to the possibility of turning an easy penny by supplying timber cut from their forests and sold at "excessively high prices" for use in local bridge construction on provincial roads.[76] Restive under the constant pressure for roads throughout the province, mid-century provincial presidents hammered at the roads which had mushroomed everywhere, and at the burden their maintenance laid upon provincial budgets. Within the município of Vassouras there were numerous examples of parallel highways, one substituting the other in importance and—when its usefulness disappeared—in abandonment. Joaquim José Teixeira Leite was undoubtedly motivated by the successive abandonment in a period of fifteen years of the Caminho Novo, Estrada do Vernek, and Estrada do Commercio, when he reproached provincial authorities. "There are so many roads not merely useful but of imperious necessity for whose conservation there are no funds" while "staggering outlays are begun without any certainty they will do good, rather, with clear signs of their inadvisability." "Certainly," he pleaded, "experience should have taught that it is a great error to construct innumerable roads and immediately abandon them." In a philosophical vein he concluded: "This Câmara . . . knows by experience that there are two

[74] Antonio Florencio Pereira do Lago to CMV, December 11, 1862. APV, 1862.
[75] Fiscal report, January 7, 1889. APV, 1889.
[76] Relatório do Presidente da Província do Rio, March 1, 1841, p. 24.

classes of individuals always prompt to promise miracles rarely fulfilled: discoverers of mines and of shortcuts." [77]

Throughout the Province of Rio, Vassouras' road problems were duplicated year after year and outlined with similar phraseology. The provincial president's report for 1841 attacked the diversion of road maintenance funds, leaving little for the completion of major arteries and complicating any official supervision.[78] "The old roads followed defective plans," wrote a president in 1854, "and the proof lies in the fact that it would be hard to find in all our country a territory traversed by as many roads as is our province." [79] Four years later another president bemoaned the "costly roads satisfying purely local pressures and very limited interests when our nation's life demands construction of those great arteries to lay out the cardinal lines of our transport system." [80] Highlighted the following year were the defects and strains within the provincial administrative hierarchy where the president probed at the "lack of administrative continuity, rapid succession of presidents, annoyances, and feuds met by one who decides to oppose thousands of individual interests and thereby loses his zeal and dedication." [81] Months later another report criticized the situation where "many parallel roads compete with each other, connecting terminal points without meeting at an important point. . ." in the intervening sections.[82] Surveying more than a half-century of road construction, the provincial report for 1861 noted that "almost all roads have been built on unstable ground and have deteriorated because of the constant passage of mule teams and other vehicles. . ." and the damage of "copious summer rains which can be repaired only at the end of the season. . . To make repairs in summer would be spending funds for pure loss." [83] To the theme of "no over-all

[77] Joaquim José Teixeira Leite to the President of the Province of Rio, March 1846. APV, 1846.

[78] *Relatório do Presidente da Província do Rio, March 1, 1841,* pp. 22–24.

[79] *Relatório do Vice-Presidente da Província do Rio, August 1, 1854,* p. 8.

[80] *Relatório, 1858,* p. 83.

[81] *Relatório, April 25, 1859,* p. 43.

[82] *Relatório, August 1, 1859,* p. 48.

[83] *Relatório, April 16, 1861,* pp. 14–15.

plan," "chance local interests," and the "provisional character of road construction"—a twenty-year cycle of complaint—returned the presidential report of the following year, although it mitigated its criticism with the observation that such practices were common among "young countries which, lacking experience, try to hurry down the path of material progress." [84]

In their desire to get roads built quickly, without an adequate public works labor force, provincial authorities turned over to contractors the construction and maintenance of roads. This system set in motion two conflicting interests, the contractor's desire to obtain greater profits versus better road maintenance. The struggle was an unequal one, as provincial reports reminded the Assembly. Poorly phrased contracts overestimated costs, permitted speculation, and left loopholes for the wily who were also tempted by the few supervising engineers assigned to cover large areas.[85] Little policing of roads existed to prevent and correct the malpractices of muleteers and wagon drivers. In fact, the reliance of the province upon contractual faith without safeguards of supervision during construction and maintenance forged a circle of irresponsibility. Called to account for his road's terrible state, the construction contractor would defend himself by citing contract clauses or by accusing travelers for damage he had repaired "just the day before"; the travelers claimed the damage was unavoidable because they had to keep clear of deep mudholes and the tardy contractor observed that the weather was the *force majeure* of "so many evils." Such irresponsibility profited only the maintenance contractor who followed the "orthodox precept of saving his own skin" and waited patiently for the "sun to repair all the damage the rains had brought." [86] From this administrative and financial morass a railroad seemed to promise a ready exit.

(3)

A gilt-edged prospectus of the "Great National Railroad" accompanied by an enclosure—"Map of a Railroad from the

---

[84] *Relatório, May 4, 1862*, p. 68.
[85] *Relatório, May 3, 1864*, p. 7.
[86] *Relatório, 1858*, pp. 84–85.

Court to the Villa of Rezende"—appeared in the 1840's, offering some hope for amelioration of transport difficulties. With paeans designed to stimulate the nationalism of the young Empire of Brazil, the prospectus opened: ". . . we propose a company which, consecrating all its goodwishes to the prosperity of the heroic Brazilian Empire, has chosen for its enterprise the stimulation of the largest possible sum of commercial advantages for the Empire, and commences with the opening of a railroad from Pavuna in the município of Rio de Janeiro to Campo Bello, a district of Rezende." It followed this effusive prologue with two paragraphs protesting "vibrant love" for the future "prosperity and glory of the Brazilian People" which it compared with the "happy well-being" of Great Britain where the "wonder-working key of industry" depended upon the steam engine first employed in coal mines and then by the Stockton and Darlington Railroad of 1825. Dazzling readers with promises of speedy shipment and consequently cheaper distribution of Rio's imports of salt, textiles, and wines (one railroad car was pictured with consignments of pianos and glass), the prospectus promised to solve planters' transport difficulties. "There will no longer be any need for costly mule teams, risks, and damages due to incompetent pack leaders and moribund, pasture-starved animals." [87]

Despite the promises of cheaper transport which the railroad prospectus brought to Vassouras planters and to those of the Parahyba Valley, fifteen years elapsed before construction began. Thomas Cochrane, who prepared the prospectus of 1839, failed to implement his concession.[88] Above all, the backers of a railroad through the coffee-growing districts lacked political influence and a financial climate favorable for investment.

They did not have to wait long. By 1852, foreign and national developments radically changed the situation. Growing facility

[87] *Plano de Huma Estrada de Ferro desde o Município da Corte até a Villa de Rezende.* Rio de Janeiro, 1839, na Typographia da Associação do Despertador dirigida por F. de S. Torres Homem. APV, 1840; *Artigo de Officio. Caminho de Ferro Entre o Município da Corte e a Provincia de São Paulo.* Rio de Janeiro, 1840. APV, 1840.

[88] C. B. Ottoni, *Esboço Histórico das Estradas de Ferro do Brazil* (Rio de Janeiro, 1866), p. 5.

of communication with Europe, and newspaper reports of French parliamentary debates over a railroad network revived Brazilian interest. The end of the African slave trade created a reservoir of capital; and a swing of the political pendulum put into power the Conservative Party in which Vassouras' leading citizens were influential. Yet many planters of the Parahyba Valley remained dubious, dreading the financial drain of railroad construction. Others insisted there would be adequate traffic for only one day per month.[89] Many Vassouras planters doubted that the difficult project would ever be realized. "In ten years the railroad should be over the Serra do Mar in search of points where it may receive our products," penned the Barão do Paty to his factor. "I am still doubtful about it. Our hopes have failed us many, many times and men do not change."[90] Nevertheless the Teixeira Leite brothers of Vassouras—Joaquim José, João Evangelista, Francisco José, and a member by marriage, Caetano Furquim de Almeida—with large financial investments in local planters and Rio commission houses pushed the project. Undoubtedly they hoped their initiative would bring the concession for the construction of the railroad.[91] Certainly Joaquim José Teixeira Leite perceived the commercial advantages if the railroad passed through the center of the município, for a centrally located station would serve as a transfer point for cargo and passengers traveling from the city of Rio and from the neighboring provinces of São Paulo and Minas. After all, as a leader of Vassouras commercial interests and an official of the Câmara, he had stated a decade earlier that the vital Estrada da Polícia was the "sole fount of life and prosperity" and "if you remove this road from the town, the town will have to move, too."

The Dom Pedro Segundo railway through the Parahyba Valley was constructed after 1855, but the Teixeira Leites

<hr />

[89] Ottoni, *Esboço Histórico*, p. 6.

[90] Barão do Paty to Bernardo Ribeiro de Carvalho, 1854 [?]. In *Documentos Referentes a Familia Werneck*, Arquivo Nacional.

[91] Members of the family hired English engineers to make preliminary surveys of a possible route. Ottoni, *Esboço Histórico*, p. 6, and José Matoso Maia Forte, "A Fazenda do 'Secretario,'" pp. 11–12.

failed to receive their concession, and American engineers
resolved to surmount the coastal range to reach the level lands
along the Parahyba River at Barra do Pirahy, bypassing the
center of the município of Vassouras.[92] From Barra do Pirahy
eastward through the município of Vassouras, the tracks hugged
the banks of the Parahyba with stops at Ypiranga, Vassouras,
Commercio, and Ubá—a series of stations which skirted the
northern perimeter of Vassouras leaving untouched the commercial and agricultural core. The only concession the commercial interests of the town of Vassouras could wring from the
railroad administration was the construction of a station to
serve the town of Vassouras on the south or Vassouras bank of
the Parahyba River, rather than one across the river to serve
the interest of a politically influential planter.[93]

Immediate and far-reaching was the effect of the Pedro
Segundo railroad upon the Vassouras road pattern. Here the
railroad gave impetus to changes dimly discerned as early as
1853, when the inconveniences of the Estrada da Polícia's steep
descent of the Serra do Mar via the hamlet of Botaes contrasted
with the advantages of a new provincial highway further
westward, the Estrada do Presidente Pedreira.[94] The advantages of the Presidente Pedreira evoked even the grudging
approbation of Vassouras' Câmara, wedded to the Estrada da

[92] On the bitter struggle over where to locate the tracks over the coastal range,
the sources vary from the frankly partisan to the ambiguous. See Ignacio Raposo,
História de Vassouras, p. 156; Ottoni, *Esboço Histórico*, pp. 6–7; *Relatório apresentado
pela Directoria aos Acciónistas da Estrada de Ferro de D. Pedro II em 31 de Janeiro de 1857*
(Rio de Janeiro, 1857), pp. 10–12.

[93] Joaquim José Teixeira Leite to Directory of the D. Pedro II Railroad, July 3,
1862. APV, 1863; *Relatório do Vice-Presidente da Província do Rio, September 8, 1862*,
pp. 42–43; C. B. Ottoni to CMV, July 3, 1863. APV, 1863.

[94] Possibilities of the Presidente Pedreira road, previously called the "Estrada da
Bocaina dos Mendes," were first studied by provincial engineers under orders from
a provincial president, José Clemente Pereira. By marriage to a wealthy widow,
the Portuguese-born Clemente Pereira became proprietor of the extensive Fazenda
das Cruzes located in the western corner of the município of Vassouras near
Ypiranga. The Presidente Pedreira crossed the Parahyba River at Ypiranga,
traversed the município of Vassouras to descend the Serra do Mar via the headwaters of the Ribeirão dos Macacos; on it passed the agricultural production of
Valença and, later, of Vassouras in the fifties. Luiz Antonio Barbosa de Almeida
to CMV, March 14, 1854. APV, 1854; *Relatório do Presidente da Província do Rio,
August 1, 1859*, pp. 51–52.

Polícia, as testified by one municipal councilor who admitted that the former was "in many respects superior to other roads cutting through the Município because it descends the Serra do Mar where it is least steep and because its inclination accommodates carts, even four-wheeled ones." [95] To planters of Vassouras at this period, the Presidente Pedreira offered the paramount advantage of cart-borne over mule-borne cargo, and in response to this growing awareness came a second comment from the Câmara in 1853 that the Presidente Pedreira was "not only especially advantageous but even absolutely necessary for the Town of Vassouras and the greater portion of the Município which to date lack a single cart-road on which to travel to the Court [Rio de Janeiro] and to transport certain voluminous cargo." [96] Even the provincial report for that year echoed planters' desire to ship coffee in carts on the Presidente Pedreira.[97] Loath to see the commercial center stagnate as muleteers, cart drivers, and cattle herders favored the new road, the Câmara urged construction of a branch road from the town to Mendes on the Presidente Pedreira.[98]

When railroad tracks neared the town of Belém at the foot of the coastal range, the wisdom of the province's financial support for the Pedro Segundo railroad became apparent. In laying tracks through the lowlands to Belém, original plans had called for stations "at junction points with roads carrying heavy traffic." [99] Now, on the second section of the railroad, between Belém and Barra do Pirahy, the Presidente Pedreira could channel its cargo at successive points onto freight cars as the tracks climbed the coastal range via the headwaters of the Ribeirão dos Macacos, the path both of the railroad and the highway. Originally a through highway from Minas to the port of Rio de Janeiro, the Presidente Pedreira now became a feeder

[95] CMV to the Presidente da Província, July 4, 1853. APV, 1853; Luis Peixoto de Lacerda Werneck, "Breves Considerações sobre a Posição Actual da Lavoura de Café. Difficuldade do Transporte. Estado Ruim das Estradas," *Jornal do Commercio*, October 12, 1854.

[96] CMV to Presidente da Província do Rio, September 16, 1853. APV, 1853.

[97] *Relatório do Presidente da Província do Rio, August 1, 1853*, p. 7.

[98] CMV to Presidente da Província do Rio, October 16, 1853. APV, 1853.

[99] CMV to Directory of the Pedro Segundo Railroad, July 3, 1862. APV, 1863.

line for the railroad.[100] Moreover, the further the tracks
climbed the coastal range, the more quickly the provincial
treasury cut back maintenance programs on abandoned
portions of the Presidente Pedreira. To avoid a swampy portion
of the road, the Pedro Segundo ran a trunk line to Macacos in
1861; promptly the province saved 2:526$400 annually in
maintenance funds.[101] In 1862 the provincial president proposed complete abandonment of all portions of the Presidente
Pedreira traversing the município of Vassouras "as soon as
construction of the Pedro Segundo Railroad is completed
there." [102] Seven years later, portions of the untended Presidente Pedreira road were pictured: "The roadbed is in terrible
condition and almost all its bridges are down. . ." [103]

Equally disastrous to road conditions within the município
of Vassouras as provincial road maintenance funds were cut off,
was the junction of the Pedro Segundo with other once heavily
trafficked roads. When the railroad intersected the Estrada da
Polícia on the banks of the Parahyba at the station of Vassouras,
several miles from the town center, it was prophesied the third
section, still in use, would soon follow the fate of the other two
sections.[104] Of the Estrada do Commércio wrote one small
merchant as the railroad came to the station of Commércio,
where the road entered the município: "Only its ruins remain
because of its lamentable state of abandonment. There is no
trade and no road maintenance. Only those proprietors who
cannot abandon it, remain." [105] To be sure, the provincial
authorities were fully cognizant of what was happening.
Commented a report: "Many of the roads laid out before the
construction of railroads . . . have lost their former importance
to a great degree." [106] Sixteen years after the first rail of the
Pedro Segundo was laid, the road pattern of the province had

---

[100] *Relatório do Presidente da Provincia do Rio, October 7, 1856*, pp. 12–13.
[101] *Relatório, April 16, 1861*, pp. 23–23.
[102] *Relatório, May 4, 1862*, p. 84.
[103] Relatório do Fiscal do 2o. Districto de Sacra Família to CMV, May 1869.
APV, 1869.
[104] *Relatório, May 21, 1867*, p. 17.
[105] APV, 1864.
[106] *Relatório, October 4, 1866*, p. 32.

changed radically from a number of parallel highways essentially for pack mules to a system wherein two railroads, the Pedro Segundo and the Cantagallo, were "principal arteries" into which fed short cart roads.[107]

Yet the Pedro Segundo was no panacea for Vassouras planters' transport difficulties. If it minimized obstacles nature created in pre-railroad days when mud-filled and precipitous highways seemed main obstructions to coffee shipments, the railroad also introduced Vassouras coffee planters to a new whipping boy: administrative red-tape and incompetence. Signed "An Important Fazendeiro," a letter appealed to the editors of *O Município* for "support in finding out if railroad officials take pity on the poor planter!" "Every day new difficulties are invented to plague the transport of merchandise which is forwarded us from Rio or which we consign there." One bureaucratically minded stationmaster had refused to accept coffee for shipment because identifying tags were old-style ones. The complainant hurried a slave to a station down the line where a few new tags could be bought. "I was surprised," ran the letter, "that the sole modification consisted of a new entry to be filled out—'Declared Value.' " The "Important Fazendeiro" finished his letter in despair: "Now, Mr. Editor, how can a fazendeiro who forwards coffee to factors in Rio declare on his tags the value of his coffee, when this depends entirely upon the price prevailing when sold in Rio? How can we declare a value which we find out only after we hear from our factors!" [108] And to older fazendeiros the railroad age probably offered other drawbacks when they read of derailments covered in detail by local newspapers to beguile the monotony of fazenda life. "We are informed that two days ago between the stations of Ubá and Parahyba do Sul, five railroad cars were derailed when the locomotive ran over an ox running in front of the train." The human interest theme came in the last paragraph. "Our informant told us there were a number of deaths and several people hurt." [109] Four days

[107] *Relatório, March 15, 1871,* p. 10.
[108] June 17, 1877.
[109] *O Município,* July 15, 1877.

later another encounter between engine and ox near Barra do Pirahy left an engineer with "shattered legs and crushed abdomen, and he died immediately. . . He was married and leaves a wife and children." Now the newspaper editorialized by commenting that "Such facts, which recur frequently, demand every attention and solicitude of the railroad administrative hierarchy." [110]

Planters quickly reoriented to changing conditions of local transport, the rate of adaptation varying with the distance separating their plantations from the nearest railroad station. Four years after the Pedro Segundo reached the Parahyba Valley, the change from pack animals to ox-drawn carts was well under way. To a provincial request of 1868 on types of transport animals used in the município, a Vassouras councilor replied that "Oxen and pack animals are employed in this município for transport work. Planters who are near stations of the Pedro Segundo and have cart roads at hand use oxen." [111] More indicative of the altered transport pattern was the increasing number of oxen on fazendas and the corresponding decrease in pack animals over a thirty-year period commencing in 1850. After the mid-sixties, oxen rapidly displaced pack mules; shortly after 1873 the price per head of oxen surpassed that of pack animals, within a few years attaining twice, sometimes three times their value.[112]

To fazendeiros the advantages of the new transport system were clear. Ox-drawn carts required a fraction of the funds formerly expended on pack mules and on free and slave personnel. While slave muleteers were transferred into the dwindling field gangs, at a pace of two or three miles per hour oxen hauled close to one hundred arrobas (roughly 1,500 kilos) of bagged coffee; under the direction of a lone slave master driver (*mestre-carreiro*), a fixed-axle cart pulled by two or three ox-teams would start its whining journey before sunrise and return after sunset, eliminating rancho bills including food for personnel and pasture for animals. On the return, carts brought

[110] *O Município*, July 19, 1877.
[111] CMV to Presidente da Província do Rio, 1868. APV, 1868.
[112] Inventories, CPOV and APV.

goods ordered from the factor in Rio and forwarded on the railroad. And a final advantage: plantation isolation, hitherto enforced by narrow and tortuous mule paths, began to break down as funds were spent on feeder roads accommodating wheeled vehicles, not only ox-carts but lighter, horse-drawn two- and four-wheeled wagons, shays, and carry-alls.

Many fazendeiros entertained hopes for railroad trunk lines which might reduce the distance their ox-carts covered to reach stations of the Pedro Segundo on the município's perimeter. Such ideas were especially popular in the two key coffee-producing areas of the município—the Massambará Valley and the Paty do Alferes region—where large planters could foresee "great backwardness and hopelessness among fazendeiros situated far from the Pedro Segundo . . ." because they lacked ". . . easy means to transport their agricultural produce." As they reasoned, where the "motive force of civilization"—the Pedro Segundo—ran, there agriculture prospered, while removed areas sank into "shameful apathy." [113] Before tracks reached Rodeio on the headwaters of the Ribeirão dos Macacos, fazendeiros petitioned for a road from Paty to Rodeio or Mendes;[114] and they maintained the campaign for nine years until the provincial government consented in 1870 to construct a cart road from Paty over the Serra do Mar to Belém.[115] Fazendeiros of Massambará were cheered the following year when wealthy commercial interests in the town of Vassouras circulated plans for a narrow-gauge railroad to tie Massambará to Mendes on the Pedro Segundo.[116] In 1874 the railroad fever captured Paty too, and a wealthy planter and Rio factor of that area, Joaquim Teixeira de Castro, formed a company to run tracks from Paty to Belém, although no construction materialized. In the see-saw struggle between the two agricultural areas of the município to obtain provincial backing for railroad trunk lines, Paty bested Massambará. The

---

[113] *O Vassourense*, July 16, 1882.

[114] *Relatório, April 16, 1861*, p. 24.

[115] *Relatório, October 9, 1864*, p. 51. Proposal of Councilor A. B. Moura to CMV, July 19, 1865. APV, 1865; Provincial Government to CMV, July 29, 1870. APV, 1870.

[116] Raposo, *História*, pp. 192–193; *O Município*, July 6, 1873 and July 27, 1873.

provincial government decided in 1882 that the Mendes-Mas-
sambará narrow gauge project was not feasible, then awarded
to two engineers, Luis Raphael Vieira Souto and Henrique
Eduardo Hargreaves, a contract for railroad construction from
Paty to Belém.[117] Planters of Paty had won their right to a
railroad; they waited sixteen years for the right to become an
actuality.[118] As for fazendeiros of the Massambará area, several
—including the barons of Cananea, of Massambará, of Avellar
e Almeida, Zeferina Adelaide das Chagas Werneck, Luis
Caetano Alves, and João Ribeiro dos Santos Zamith—had seen
the handwriting on the wall in the late seventies, and at their
cost built a railroad station at Concordia on the Pedro Segundo
which their coffee reached by cart. Until Paty residents obtained their railroad in 1898 they had to ship their production
via cart and pack mule to the Pedro Segundo station at Ubá,
below Concordia on the Parahyba River.[119]

(4)

The chain reaction touched off by railroad construction,
redistribution of road maintenance funds, and abandonment of
parallel north–south pack train roads for short cart roads
leading from plantations to rail stations on the município's
perimeter, struck at the município's most sensitive spot—its
commerce with highway travelers and local residents. Solace,
in 1865, from the retiring provincial president—"You deserve
our full support against the pitfalls the new railroad has visited
upon you" [120]—could not compensate for signs of commercial
decay on all sides. Town houses in Paty on the old Caminho
Novo were sold because the hamlet was "completely decadent" [121] in 1865. Paty continued moribund for the next
twenty-two years, and its road was last reported "with hardly

[117] *O Vassourense*, May 7, 1882 and December 7, 1882.
[118] Max Vasconcellos, *Vías Brasileiras de Communicação* (Rio de Janeiro, 1928),
pp. 14–15.
[119] Raposo, *História*, pp. 207–208; Pedido dos Moradores do Paty do Alferes para
Conservação da Estrada . . . onde transitam tropas e gentes a Estação de Ubbá,
August 1881. APV, 1881.
[120] Bernardo de Souza Franco to CMV, October 11, 1865. APV, 1865.
[121] Inventory, 1862, deceased: Barão do Paty, executor: Francisco de Assis e
Almeida, Fazenda das Palmeiras, CPOV.

any travelers, due to the enormous number of Pedro Segundo stations which dot the edges of this município and eliminate a road where once there passed all kinds of Minas produce which went to the capital of the Empire." [122] Spectacular were the effects on the valuation of buildings erected for trade along now abandoned highways: between 1862 and 1865 a store, residence, two ranchos, and billiard-hall at Quilombo on the Werneck road lost 75 per cent of their value, another store and dwelling dropped 87 per cent, and a third such group of buildings, 47 per cent.[123] Vendas on the Estrada da Polícia near Sacra Família informed the Câmara in 1863 that the area was "decadent" as consumers went to buy at the Rodeio railroad station. The company of Braga & Pires demanded a lower license fee since "the decadence of Sacra Família at Graminha is all too evident due to the new commercial center established . . . at the Rodeio station where all customers hasten." [124] And in the disastrous year of 1863, another merchant, this time in Vassouras, submitted a similar request "in view of the . . . woeful condition to which commerce in this town has been reduced." [125] A few small tradesmen left the town of Vassouras on the heels of the "large number of workmen who have to seek employment in other municípios because there is none here." [126] When railroad tracks reached the station of Vassouras on the Parahyba River, wagon drivers went there directly without entering the town.[127] Even the herds of cattle which had once crossed the município on the way to Rio slaughter-houses left the Estrada da Polícia to meet freight trains at Rodeio; the province therefore refused to cover any repairs on that now useless road.[128] Nor did the prosperity of perimeter railroad stations endure. Rodeio was reported to be suffering from "commercial apathy" in 1867 as consumers preferred to

[122] Torquato de Macedo Silva to CMV, February 16, 1887. APV, 1887.

[123] Inventory, 1862, deceased: Barão do Paty, executor: Francisco de Assis e Almeida, Fazenda das Palmeiras, CPOV.

[124] Braga & Pires to CMV, 1863. APV, 1863.

[125] APV, 1863.

[126] Exposição, December 1864. APV, 1864.

[127] Joaquim José de Souza Lopes to CMV, 1865. APV, 1865.

[128] Alfredo de Barros e Vasconcellos, Director de Obras Públicas da Província do Rio, to CMV, November 26, 1870. APV, 1870.

buy directly in Rio. The most important factor behind commercial decline came up in the annual report of the Câmara Municipal in 1869 when João Ribeiro dos Santos Zamith emphasized "the advance of the Pedro Segundo Railroad which allowed consumers to obtain provisions in the Rio markets." [129]

Many merchants tried to keep their businesses going in spite of the reduced volume of trade, receiving help from tolerant municipal authorities who lowered license fees. By 1870, however, hope for an eventual return of prosperous years dwindled and the exodus began. Felipe Laport, peddler, advised the Câmara in 1870 that he was leaving "after peddling drygoods and notions in this Municipio from 1863 until last year." [130] The exodus moved into high gear by 1877 when departure notices of all kinds of businessmen filled columns of the local newspaper. "Domingos Carvalho Guimarães is selling his food and liquor business because he wishes to leave." "Torquato Villarinho begs his customers kindly to settle accounts as soon as possible." [131] A week later Augusto Christiano de Freitas, "former owner of the Four Columns Hotel begs his debtors via this newspaper to go to the hotel to settle accounts so that he may pay his debts." [132] The following month a local artist, Antonio Joaquim Pereira Falcão, announced his intention to leave Vassouras for Campos where he was establishing a shop. [133] Those who tried to weather the creeping depression gave municipal authorities a dismal picture of commercial decay throughout Vassouras in 1878 and 1879. Manoel Martins da Silva sought a cheaper license fee on February 28, 1878 because business along the railroad between Commércio and Cazal was "decadent"; Antonio Lopes Cancella advised in March that his license fee was not warranted, for business conditions at Commércio were "decadent"; from the foot of the Serra do Mar José Teixeira da Fonseca Bastos described the "decadence of Macacos" in December 1878 and, from Sacra Família, José

[129] APV, 1869.
[130] Felipe Laport to CMV, February 9, 1870.
[131] *O Município*, August 9, 1877.
[132] *O Município*, August 19, 1877.
[133] *O Município*, September 2, 1877.

Furtado Domingues d'Oliveira echoed with "the decadence of this place" in March 1879.[134] Commercial decline affected lovers too, since local wage scales paid clerks by business houses could not support bodies and souls of two. Stoutly declared one young hero of a short story: "I'll go to Rio and there I'll get a job which will provide enough for us to live together modestly." [135] The decline entered the conversation of two godmothers who gossiped one morning about the news of a railroad and telephone line rumored on the way to link the town of Vassouras to the railroad station on the Parahyba River. "And what are you wondering about?" inquired one. "Our Progress and Activity," replied godmother Paula. "On second thought, it's our Activity—now a rare fruit hereabouts." [136]

Dwindling social ties between planter families and townsfolk followed declining commerce. The cost of a railroad ticket was negligible, the trip was brief enough to quiet the most faint-hearted, and in a matter of hours planter families could vacation in Rio. Sooner or later, as Raposo wrote, everyone had to vacation in the capital to hear the opera or, where the ladies were concerned, to buy a new "toilette." [137] Those townsfolk, who remembered the struggles of municipal authorities to maintain municipal independence in the fifties from the expanding bureaucratic controls of the Imperial capital, saw in the commercial and especially in the social decline of the town center another sign of what they castigated as "centralization." Less than a quarter-century after its greatest prosperity, others spoke of the town as entering upon its "period of decadence." Gone was the "life, the animation, the bustle of twenty years ago," nostalgically recalled a town resident in 1882. "Then there were the rumble of carts, the trot of animals, children's shouts, the streetsongs of hawkers of every kind of fruit and sweets . . . the howling of dogs on the roads which led to this former emporium of merchandise." More sadly he

---

[134] APV, 1878, 1879.
[135] "O Juramento," *O Município*, July 22, 1877.
[136] "Uma Visita," *O Vassourense*, April 30, 1882.
[137] Raposo, *História*, p. 208.

ended with "Today Vassouras is not what it used to be." [138]

Yet the melancholy, the tears, and the romantic journalistic reconstructions of the bygone halcyon years in the late seventies and early eighties reflected only one aspect of the município's economy—the commercial. Curtailment of local commerce brought economic decline to the town center and small hamlets before signs of wide-scale decadence appeared in the agricultural countryside whose slower pattern of decline was based on aging and depleted slave labor forces and the wearing out of the soil. When townsfolk wrote that the município had been "knifed in the breast" [139] by the railroad, they confused the town with the countryside. For the town of Vassouras lamented its fate before agricultural decadence became glaring. Indeed, in its outward aspects, plantation life showed an apparent increased affluence as a result of closer contact with the coast and easier transport abroad. A somewhat more elaborate pattern of living, a greater emphasis upon social amenities, and upon the consumption of imported goods—furniture, clothing, food, household utensils, and books—for a time and to a degree shrouded the slow paralysis which affected agricultural production. Plantation premises were made more prepossessing by the construction of gardens or *parques* directly in front or behind the dwelling house, where drying terraces had once been. Wallpaper, curtaining, marble-topped tables, pianos, rocking chairs, sewing machines, heavy French beds, bathhouses, and iron-topped tile and brick stoves gradually altered the austere simplicity of the affluent households. Less well-to-do planters, whose contacts and credit in Rio were more limited, continued to live as they always had.

[138] *O Vassourense*, February 19, 1882.
[139] *O Município*, May 24, 1877.

PART THREE

PLANTATION SOCIETY

CHAPTER V

The Free

A SOCIAL as well as a productive unit, the slave-operated plantation shaped relationships among all classes of Vassouras society: the planters and their slaves and—sandwiched between them—the merchants and tradesmen, lawyers, doctors, and the free poor (pobreza). The institution of slavery, moreover, colored not only relations between masters and slaves and among classes, but even those established between mothers and fathers, parents and children. And along with slavery the plantation cast its shadow over the life of the município, not only in the routine of daily life but in patterns of change.

Roughly 35,000 to 40,000 slave and free folk inhabited the município in the second half of the nineteenth century. The first and most reliable census of those fifty years, that of 1872, showed a total of 39,253 residents, including 20,168 slaves and 19,085 free persons of all colors and origins. While the município's population was almost equally divided between slave and free in 1872, distribution of free and slave within the large county was not uniform. More than half of Vassouras' population was located in two of the five parishes which, in turn, held the largest percentage of the município's slaves. These parishes, Nossa Senhora da Conceição and Paty do Alferes, were the most important plantation and commercial districts. Together they included 64 per cent of the município's total population and 71 per cent of all slaves. On the other hand, the parish of Sacra Família do Tinguá, which contained the rugged terrain of the coastal range (Serra do Mar), had a far less dense population with a higher proportion of free folk (almost 75 per cent). Many of the free were ex-slaves, and more than 50 per cent of all free Africans in the município lived in this economically marginal parish (Table 10). Finally, since more than half

TABLE 10. Population of Vassouras, 1872.

Parish	Free			Slave			Total
	Male	Female	Total	Male	Female	Total	
Conceição	2,474	1,987	4,461	3,632	2,571	6,203	10,664
Mendes	965	682	1,647	961	732	1,693	3,340
Paty	3,361	2,992	6,353	4,567	3,520	8,087	14,440
Ferreiros	1,223	900	2,123	1,428	1,115	2,543	4,666
S. Familia	2,341	2,160	4,501	891	751	1,642	6,143
Total	10,364	8,721	19,085	11,479	8,689	20,168	39,253

Source: *Recenseamento, 1872.*

the society was slave, it is not surprising to find that three-quarters of the population was colored (black or mulatto). Again, only the parish of Sacra Família, where free men outnumbered slaves, showed a lower proportion (66 per cent) of colored to white (Table 11).

TABLE 11. Racial composition of Vassouras, 1872.

Parish	White	Mulatto	Black	Indian or half-breed
Conceição	2,764	1,789	6,103	8
Mendes	756	929	1,623	32
Paty	3,288	3,812	7,328	12
Ferreiros	1,239	1,338	2,079	10
S. Familia	1,947	2,292	1,489	55
Total	9,994	10,160	18,622	117

Source: *Recenseamento, 1872.*

Planters were only part of the general group of agriculturists or *lavradores*, the largest and most important group by occupation in Vassouras (Table 12). The term lavrador included large and small agriculturists, property owners, and landless farmers.

First, there were the fazendeiros (possessors of plantations over thirty alqueires in size), then the sitiantes (proprietors of holdings—*sitios* or *situações*—up to thirty alqueires). Lavradores also included the aggregados, free men whom planters permitted to reside and farm on their lands, without any property rights. Colonos, or hired laborers, rounded out the group known as lavradores. Depending upon the size of holdings and the number of slaves, the lavradores numbered both the very

TABLE 12. Occupational distribution in Vassouras, 1872.

Parish	Agriculturists	Merchants	Capitalists, Proprietors	Civil servants	Medical[a]	Lawyers and judges
Conceição	685	239	55	36	22	18
Mendes	717	44	7			
Paty	1,945	81	1	7	10	2
Ferreiros	720	17	1	1	4	
S. Familia	1,202	93	3	3	4	2
Total	5,269	474	67	47	40	22

[a] Includes doctors, surgeons, midwives, and pharmacists.

Source: adapted from *Recenseamento, 1872.*

wealthy and those bordering on the pobreza. The leadership of this heterogeneous group was vested in a small but influential segment of the planters. Numerically insignificant, the planters and their kinfolk dominated each parish effectively by means of elections, administration of justice (they were elected justices of the peace),[1] and as officers in the National Guard. Among the planters a few families or clans exercised a dominant role in county affairs.

(2)

The origins of the plantation families exercising social, economic, and political hegemony in nineteenth-century Vassouras go back to the eighteenth century, either to the

[1] For detailed treatment of the jucidial and electoral importance of the *juizes de paz* in the Brazilian interior, see Victor Nunes Leal, *Coronelismo, Enxada e Voto* (Rio de Janeiro, 1949), pp. 140–145, 160–163.

Portuguese mainland or island possessions, to the cities of the Minas gold fields, or to areas in and around Vassouras itself. The forebears of Vassouras planters engaged in trade, were small proprietors working small holdings or, in a few cases, were military men.

To generalize on the origins of these planters is difficult. It is only possible to ascertain some details of those families which played significant roles in the heyday of Vassouras. One of the most influential families, the Correa e Castro, which held vast estates in the parishes of Conceição and Ferreiros, reportedly sprang from a group of obscure lavradores located on the Fazenda Pau Grande at the end of the eighteenth century. The means by which three Correa e Castro brothers came into possession of large plantations by the 1830's is obscure.[2] The holdings of other influential families were in evidence by 1800. Both the Werneck and Ribeiro de Avellar clans were the nineteenth-century "owners" (*donos*) of the rich coffee-producing parish of Paty do Alferes founded astride the Minas road. Ignácio de Souza Werneck, Vassouras' chief local administrative and military officer (*sargento-mor*) from 1790 to 1820, was largely responsible for surveying and initiating the construction of the Estrada do Commércio and for herding the local Indians into a reserve. His extensive royal land grants and his twelve children entrenched the Werneck clan in the município. The Wernecks shared control of Paty with the Ribeiro de Avellar family, whose first residents were merchants who purchased the lands of the Fazenda Pau Grande and of the nearby Fazenda Ubá in the last quarter of the eighteenth century. The marriage of two cousins—the bridegroom was a Portuguese returning enriched from the Minas gold fields—produced the most important branch of the clan, the Gomes Ribeiro de Avellar group.[3] Important in the parish of Sacra Família was the Paes Leme family whose members were pro-

---

[2] Francisco Klörs Werneck, *Historia e Genealogía Fluminense* (Rio de Janeiro, 1947), p. 55; Pinto, *Fastos Vassourenses*, p. 256.

[3] Antonio Gomes Ribeiro de Avallar, "A Prole da Familia Avellar a contar de Antonio Ribeiro de Avellar e sua mulher D. Antonia da Conceição," pp. 1–2. Manuscript in possession of D. Marianna de Albuquerque, Avellar, Estado do Rio; F. K. Werneck, *História*, pp. 34–38.

prietors of vast holdings mainly in the Rio lowlands at the foot
of the coastal range; their properties were also obtained in
return for opening a road through the município. In the town
of Vassouras, the Teixeira Leite family occupied a position of
equality with the rural aristocracy, although its wealth was the
product of the financial activities of several brothers who
settled in Vassouras in the 1820's.[4] The Correa e Castro, the
Werneck, the Ribeiro de Avellar, Paes Leme, and Teixeira
Leite families were the most prominent of Vassouras; only
slightly less so were the Avellar e Almeida family, the Araujo
Padilha, and others. Certain families of importance in the early
nineteenth century, the Monçores and the Gomes Leal for
example, gradually receded into obscurity as the century wore
on. Most of the large number of lavradores clustered about one
or the other of these rural clans.

Thus Vassouras planter society had few aristocratic roots.
In the nineteenth century it was based upon the rapidly
accumulated wealth provided by coffee, and the planters were
aware how swiftly many had earned large fortunes. They
recognized that many planters "get along well as simple
lavradores and go to ruin once they receive a title" [5]—an
obvious recognition of modest origins.

If planters had no aristocratic background to fall back upon,
their pride found other channels of expression. As the município's prosperity increased, wealth in any form—particularly
slaves, land, and coffee—conveyed prestige and was assiduously
cultivated. A planter who informed his colleagues that the
yield per 1000 coffee bushes on his property reached 200
arrobas could rest assured his neighbors would call him a
"very, very important planter." [6] As one planter wrote to his
son: "All is egoism, and 'keep-your-eye-on-money.' Hereabouts
the motto is: 'If you can make money, go ahead at any cost.' " [7]

[4] The Teixeira Leite group and their cousins, the Leite Ribeiro and Furquim
de Almeida clans, were financiers and coffee factors in Rio de Janeiro. Pinto,
Fastos Vassourenses, pp. 267–268, 272–273.

[5] Macedonio, "O Filho do Capitão-Mor" *O Município*, September 30, 1877.

[6] Delden Laerne, *Brazil and Java*, cited in Taunay, *História*, VII, 184.

[7] Undated letter, probably 1854. Documentos References a Familia Werneck.
Arquivo Nacional. Compare Delden Laerne, *Brazil and Java*, p. 192.

Associated with the social criterion of wealth were conspicuous consumption, which one planter called the squandering of sums upon "futile and ostentatious objects," and excessive hospitality. Well-stocked wine cellars, liberal expense accounts for wives, children, and parents, jewelry, and a well supplied table at mealtimes—all attested to the high scale of living adopted by affluent Vassouras planters.

Recognition of the economic role of coffee planters came in the form of baronies, much sought by Vassouras landed gentry.

TABLE 13. Estimated distribution of baronies and other titles in Brazil, 1840–1889.

Year	Coffee barons	All barons	Total titleholders[a]
1840–49	15	61	70
1850–59	20	75	92
1860–69	35	127	133
1870–79	51	192	204
1880–89	—	347	372
Total	121	802	871

[a] Includes barons, viscounts, counts, marquesses, dukes.

Source: A. d'E. Taunay, *História*, VIII, 228, 230, 232, 235–240.

The Imperial Government conferred these non-hereditary titles upon coffee fazendeiros from the first year of Pedro II's reign (1840) to his last (1889). Coffee planters' financial contributions in the Paraguayan War, or their local or national prominence in supporting the Imperial regime, or their philanthropic acts, earned a share of titles. Approximately 14 per cent of all titles were bestowed upon coffee planters including all the influential planters of Vassouras (Table 13), while about 30 per cent of all titles went to planters, their bankers and their factors.[8]

Despite the general absence of interest in literary or scientific matters, the planters joined in a number of local associations. The first of such organizations, organized in 1832, was the

[8] A. d'E. Taunay, *História*, VIII, 229.

Society for the Promotion of Civilization and Industry of Vassouras. On the first meeting's agenda were the proposed construction of a school, awarding contracts for the town prison, and a resolution urging the town fathers to make necessary repairs on one of the main roads. Later that year a subscription was begun to establish a local newspaper, but, although part of the equipment was purchased, funds ran out and the enterprise was abandoned until the 1870's.[9] The Society dissolved by unanimous consent in 1850. Two years later, planters and town merchants joined to form a Masonic lodge (the "Eastern Star") adopting the Scottish rite; the organization lasted until 1881 when it was disbanded and its property donated to the município.[10] Perhaps the local organization that united all Vassouras planters most effectively was the *irmandade* or brotherhood attached to the local church. Through the years this religious association of Catholic laymen followed closely church affairs and supervised both the administration of the cemetery (its main source of revenue) and the maintenance of the local charity hospital or *Santa Casa de Misericordia*.

Of more immediate interest to local planters were the agricultural clubs or associations prominent in Vassouras and neighboring municípios in the critical years prior to the abolition of slavery. The spread of abolitionist influence and the threat which emancipation posed to the survival of the coffee plantation reinforced planter apprehensions already sharpened by the agricultural depression of the seventies. The agricultural congress held in 1878 under the auspices of the Imperial Government aimed to elicit planters' opinions on what could be done in their behalf. To canvass them for practical recommendations and to choose local representatives for the congress, a group of the most influential planters and local merchants proposed a meeting be held in the town hall. After electing a ten-man committee, the assembled planters also resolved to establish a "Vassouras Agricultural Club." [11]

[9] *O Município*, June 3, 1877.
[10] Raposo, *História*, pp. 108–109.
[11] *O Município*, June 20, June 30, 1878.

In 1886, two years before the abolition of slavery, another planter association was proposed by planters and merchants, several of whom had taken the lead in 1878.

Such planter organizations, educational, agricultural, medical, and mortuary, do not exhaust the list of group activities. They were, however, more long-lived than the ephemeral local social groups—Jockey Clubs, dancing societies, literary and musical clubs—that appeared in the seventies and eighties to "lighten the spirits" and to "banish the gloom of a period when the deepest despair hovered over the heads" of planters and their families as the land gave out and emancipation of slaves grew imminent.[12]

(3)

The esteem planters accorded to Rio factors was not extended to the medium and small businessmen operating in or around the town of Vassouras. For planters did not consider as their social equals the local artisans and shopkeepers who dwelt and worked in the município. Those who earned a living at these occupations came from Portugal, Italy, Spain, France, and Germany, although a majority were Portuguese. Very few rose to local importance, although some, as freemen and Whites, managed to marry into the ranks of the less affluent landholders, modest planters and small proprietors.

Vassouras' few professional men—judges, lawyers, public notaries, doctors, schoolmasters, and municipal civil servants—provided the small intellectual core of the middle class. A handful in comparison with the rest of Vassouras society and almost invariably limited in financial resources, the professionals nevertheless were respected by planters, who paid deference to the European tradition of the university-trained man, the "doutor." From colonial times, possession of a degree represented a step upward in the Brazilian social hierarchy, a tradition reinforced in the nineteenth century. Further, once the limited circle of eligible men was exhausted, parvenu planter families grasped at the opportunity to marry their

---

[12] Raposo, *História*, pp. 229–230; *O Município*, July 27, November 30, 1873, June 10, July 1, November 15, 1877.

daughters to Brazilian or European professional men who went to rural Brazil in search of fortune. In the early part of the century there were men like the lawyer and politician José Clemente Pereira whom one traveler described as a man of "eminence and married to a rich widow" of a Vassouras planter family.[13] More humble in origin was a local youth for whom a local planter acted as patron. The proprietor-director of a widely recognized Vassouras private school accorded him free tuition and board whence the youth proceeded to the São Paulo law school. In rank-conscious Brazil the career of this youth was not smooth. "Under the conditions molding our society," wrote the director of the Vassouras school he attended, "a man who does not proudly possess a gallery of illustrious ancestors, a man who has only ability and respects his backbone so highly that he refuses to curve it, that man is almost always mad." [14] While there was a tendency for professional men to become planters by marriage or purchase of land, there was little tendency for planters to send their sons to professional schools in the heyday of Vassouras' prosperity. Consequently the professional class was recruited mainly from graduates of European schools in the case of doctors and, in the case of lawyers, from aspiring young Brazilians of other classes aided by the patronage of the well-to-do.

These men not only attended the legal and medical needs of the community and made up the ranks of the administrative bureaucracy, they were also the teachers and the publishers and editors of the short-lived local newspapers filled with stories and comment on the local scene and reports on national politics.[15] Carried along by the leisurely pace of rural Brazil

[13] Walsh, *Notices of Brazil*, II, 133.

[14] Antonio José Fernandes and Alberto Brandão, *O Município*, November 23, 1873.

[15] Perhaps the most outstanding of the professionals was Domiciano Leite Ribeiro (1812–1881), jurist, politician and man of letters. Born in São João d'El-Rey, Minas Geraes, he attended the São Paulo Law School, then participated actively in the abortive Liberal revolt of 1842 which attempted to prevent excessive executive centralization by the emperor. Subsequently, he settled in Vassouras where he practiced law. Under the pseudonym of "Poeta Vassourense" he was a frequent contributor to the *Correio Mercantil* of Rio; under the name of "Macedonio" he published in Vassouras newspapers innumerable sketches of life in the

tied to the outside world by pack teams and irregular train arrivals, the professionals had both the time and interest for poetry, for reading John Stuart Mill and for publishing (as did one editor) a "small, elegant volume of four charming brief poems by Henry Wadsworth Longfellow, the inspired author of Evangeline. . ." [16] Several Vassouras private schools for upper-class Brazilians achieved more than regional recognition, and the men who directed them were responsible for the training of several Brazilians who achieved prominence under the Republic inaugurated in 1889. Thus, although closely associated with the plantation and commercial economy of Vassouras, these professional men were also cognizant of a larger world and were themselves to some degree the vehicles of change.

The Portuguese, the largest free immigrant group in Vassouras, furnished merchants, doctors, lawyers, teachers, and, in a lower status, clerks, plantation overseers, and skilled and unskilled workers. Aside from the factor of language, the path of the nineteenth-century Portuguese immigrant was smoothed by the fact that many of the ancestors of local planters had come from the same areas of Portugal. They were hard-working, penny-conscious and trustworthy.[17]

Many were the indigent Portuguese who, like José Rodrigues da Rosa, emigrated from the Azores around the middle of the nineteenth century and, as soon as he disembarked in Rio, "left directly for Vassouras to seek work and make a home." [18] Until the recent arrivals could afford better quarters, they lived

município, in which he satirized gently the foibles of plantation and small-town society. Several of his *costumbrista*-like vignettes have been used in this study to illuminate aspects of life in nineteenth century Vassouras. *O Vassourense*, July 23, 1882; A. d'E. Taunay, *História*, III, 109, 111–112.

[16] *O Vassourense*, September 17, 1882. Except for the insertion of occasional innocuous articles usually reprinted from the columns of Rio newspapers, the editors of local papers avoided the institution of slavery.

[17] A. Lazzarini, *O Município*, March 15, 1874.

[18] José Rodrigues da Rosa, July 14, 1873. APV, 1873. The names and description of Rosa's witnesses at the time of his naturalization provide a tableau of Vassouras' Portuguese immigrants. "Manoel de Souza Teixeira, 30, married, housepainter, born on the Island of St. George." "João de Azevedo Jordão, 28, married, tradesman, born on the Island of St. George." "Francisco Tessa Vargas, 30, single, cigarmaker, born on the Island of Fayal."

on the outskirts of the town in what was picturesquely and appropriately called "Portuguese Gully." Others came from the mainland, generally from the area of Traz-os-Montes. One such immigrant arrived at sixteen years of age and became a pack-peddler in Vassouras, hauling his wares from plantation to plantation. Later he purchased a horse to aid in his journeys, and then, a small piece of land. On his many trips back to the homeland he returned with one or more relatives or friends. A nephew also started as pack-peddler; to this enterprise he soon added a tailor shop for planters, taking measurements on his trips and returning with finished suits; in time he branched out into the sale of watches and jewelry. Probably because of his numerous business contacts, this Portuguese immigrant became a representative of the Rio house of Marinho, Pinto & Cia., coffee factors and wholesalers of foodstuffs and liquors, and eventually became a partner in the concern. In 1900, when Vassouras plantations were up for auction at a fraction of their former value, he already owned four or five in the area where he had first peddled. A distant relative became the administrator of a large plantation in the 1890's and later married the daughter of his employer. Of one Portuguese merchant, born in the Madeiras in 1832, who commenced as a clerk in a Vassouras store at the age of fifteen, became the wealthiest local merchant, and educated a son at the São Paulo law school, it was fittingly inscribed: "He is a Portuguese of the old school, resolute and fair, incapable of guile or falsehood; strong in his religious beliefs and a perennial treasurer of the Brotherhood." [19]

In the seventies, approximately a quarter-century after the great influx of Portuguese immigrants, many Portuguese terminated their commercial activities in Vassouras to retire to their homeland, applying "patiently accumulated savings to the purchase of homes and vineyards." On the eve of their departure they inserted such notices in the local newspapers as: "João Francisco da Costa Torres is soon returning to Europe and cannot bid adieu to his many Vassouras friends. . . Through the columns of this newspaper he thanks all who

[19] Pinto, *Fastos Vassourenses*, p. 285.

during his long residence in this city aided and honored him with their friendship; they may rest assured he will remain grateful eternally to them and he will always be at their disposition in Lisbon, where he will make his residence." [20]

The entry of penniless Portuguese and their subsequent retirement to the homeland on Brazilian earnings inspired considerable nativist resentment. Part of the resentment can be traced to the colonial period when the Portuguese "like ants, came to carry off Brazil's rare and costly products, to digest them abroad and to raise children who would continue the Conquest, the Colony." [21] Later the export of capital earned in Brazil by Portuguese brought the bitter comment by a nineteenth-century Brazilian economist. "Unbelievable as it may seem . . . a large percentage of the Portuguese capital acquired in Brazil is invested in the industries and general improvements of Portugal . . . Rare is the Portuguese who fails to invest his earnings in his native land." [22]

(4)

The large and heterogenous class of penniless freemen or pobreza existed in an economic twilight zone limited on the one hand by the lower fringes of the middle class and on the other by the multitude of slaves. Some of this group were descendants of free landless squatters of various racial origins; others were dispossessed settlers, joined by escaped and manumitted slaves and by indigent Portuguese. Congregating in small hamlets or in the town center, they did not form an integral part of plantation life. For the pobreza were reserved the many menial and often the most dangerous jobs; among them were the artisans, the aggregados, the rural and town laborers, the homeless and indigent. The group also included slaves freed by self-purchase, or by an owner's act of charity which became more common in the third quarter of the nineteenth century when antislavery ideas filtered into the countryside or when

[20] *O Município*, March 1, 1874.
[21] Juiz de Paz, Mattosinhos, Parahyba do Sul, October 26, 1831. APV, 1831.
[22] Ferreira Soares, *Crise Commercial*, pp. 22–23.

planters frequently discarded their infirm or aged slaves. Because their situation was almost always precarious, many were hangers-on of both the planters and the middle class of merchants and professionals.

A sure sign that a person belonged to the pobreza was his begging, usually on Saturdays when country folk came to town to sell their produce and to make their purchases. Among the upper class, especially among women, it was also considered evidence of religious fervor and self-dedication to "care for the poor," generally considered "loyal and honest because they are ingenuous . . . unaware of hypocrisy"—in brief, as child-like charges of the benevolent wealthy.[23] The town of Vassouras was the center of alms seekers because planters and prosperous merchants maintained town residences there, the church provided a spiritual focus, while adjoining it was the charity hospital for the indigent sick. During two outbreaks of yellow fever, in 1880 and in the following year, when the economic life of the town came to a standstill and brought hardship to the pobreza, a Vassouras planter ordered the largest mercantile establishment to furnish foodstuffs for the poor at his expense.[24]

Other Vassouras citizens did not look favorably upon the Saturday "hordes of beggars who make the procurement of alms their sole occupation." One irate citizen wrote to the local editor that he knew of one man who accepted a job on condition he work only five days per week in order to reserve Saturday for begging. The letterwriter opined that those who labored

[23] *O Vassourense,* June 11, 1882.
[24] *O Vassourense,* May 28, 1882. To demonstrate their gratitude to the charitable planter, the presentation of an oil portrait of their benefactor was arranged. One evening "all the social classes converged at the residence of the vicar, including doctors, lawyers, notaries, merchants, artisans, farmers, and an immense crowd of the poor" and marched through the streets to the planter's town house preceded by a brass band. Amid fireworks and shouts of "Long Live the Barão de Cananea, Long Live the Father of the Poor," the marchers arrived at the residence where the "pobreza elbowed, pushed, and gesticulated its way through the doors which on this occasion were open to all." After the stairways and richly furnished salons of the residence were filled with the poor, they quieted to hear the prepared speeches. When these were over and the poor departed, the "higher classes were invited to the salons upstairs where a ball began, made resplendent by the elegance of the ladies' and gentlemen's clothes. . ." "Uma Festa da Pobreza," *O Vassourense,* June 11, 1882.

should not open their purses to those who could be useful citizens but preferred to idle.[25]

The increasing number of beggars in the 1870's, perhaps a result of the economic dislocation caused by completion of the Pedro Segundo railway, inspired a few residents to reconsider the problem of local charity. Here the initiative came from the wife of a deceased merchant and coffee factor. During residence in Vassouras, the merchant Furquim de Almeida (related by birth and marriage to the Teixeira Leite family) served as president of the Câmara Municipal; on his death, his wife resolved to donate their town house to the município, providing the local authorities maintained the residence as a free school for poor girls.[26] She and her children reasoned that among the first obligations of modern society was the guarantee of individual rights, and that it was a "sacred duty" of all citizens to contribute when society failed to provide for the aged and to protect the young. It was the duty of the "collective Entity—the State or Commune—to remedy as quickly as possible the faults of nature," they argued, and these could be undertaken by charitable organizations. This was not a duty to be left solely to well-wishing individuals: "Society would indeed fail to fulfill one of its most necessary obligations were it to abandon exclusively to private initiative the establishment and improvement of such charitable organizations." "The power and assistance of the State or Commune," the Furquim de Almeida family declared in 1882, must join the efforts of private citizens, and they warned that the school for poor girls was made all the more pressing in view of the inevitable transition from a slave to a free labor force in Brazil.[27]

The município, however, refused to assign any revenue, and proposed to loan the building to a schoolmistress in return for her maintenance of six poor girls. Then the schoolmistress reduced the offer to four girls and, in disgust, the Furquim de Almeida family tried to raise funds privately. At the end of

[25] *O Município*, April 20, 1879.
[26] Letter, María Furquim Teixeira de Almeida and others to CMV, July 9, 1881. APV, 1881.
[27] "Asylo Furquim," *O Vassourense*, April 23, 1882.

1882 it seemed evident that the original aim of a publicly supported primary and secondary school for poor girls was unfeasible and that sooner or later the Câmara, alleging inadequate local revenues, would hand the building to private individuals to operate as a paying institution. Some contested this viewpoint and blamed not the lack of funds but the "self-interest which seems to dominate the present epoch." [28] In 1882, Vassouras' leading citizens were as unwilling and unprepared to assume responsibility for the "less favored of fortune" as they were to make citizens of their newly-free slaves six years later.

[28] *O Vassourense*, December 17, 1882 .

CHAPTER VI

Planter and Slave

"GREATER or lesser perfection . . . of discipline determines the greater or lesser degree of prosperity of agricultural establishments." [1] Constant supervision and thorough control through discipline joined to swift, often brutal punishment were considered an absolute necessity on coffee plantations. Proper functioning of a fazenda varied directly with the steady application of the working force; in an epoch of little machinery, slave labor or what Brazilians termed "organized labor," had to be guided carefully and supervised closely.

It seemed that apparently slow-witted slaves had to be driven to produce. In a day's work conscientious planters had to "look for a fugitive slave, consider punishing a second, decide to send a third to help a neighbor—check the weeding . . . complain about the escolha . . . explain each morning in detail to a flock of slaves the nature of extremely simple tasks they were to accomplish, check each evening to see if they have been barely achieved." [2] In their reasoning, the needs of production dovetailed with concepts of slave character. "Only with constantly exercised vigilance under military-like discipline" would slaves work hard and earnestly, was a widespread opinion. The Negro slave was "by nature the enemy of all regular work," the "passive partner" in the transaction that entrusted him to his owner at the time of purchase. His salary? The purchase price and food and clothing provided by his master.[3]

Those Brazilian planters who failed to find in the nature of their plantation economy sufficient justification for slavery could find support in the writings of foreigners, both resident

---

[1] C. A. Taunay, *Manual*, p. 7.
[2] Couty, *Biologie Industrielle*, p. 113.
[3] C. A. Taunay, *Manual*, pp. 11–12.

and transient. In 1839 planters were informed, for example, that the Negro was a "man-child" with the mental development of a white man fifteen or sixteen years of age. To the French émigré, Charles Auguste Taunay, the "physical and intellectual inferiority of the Negro race, classified by every physiologist as the lowest of human races, reduces it naturally as soon as it has contact and relations with other races (especially the White race) to the lowest rung and to society's simplest tasks. One searches in vain for examples of Negroes whose intelligence and works merit admiration." He felt that Negroes' inferiority obliged them to live in a state of perpetual tutelage and that therefore it was "indispensable that they be kept in a state of servitude, or near servitude." [4] Another Frenchman assured Brazilian slaveholders that the Negro was intellectually inferior to the white because the Negro's cranium was smaller and therefore he could not develop his "moral intelligence to a comparable degree." [5] In defense of these writers it must be noted that their line of reasoning was akin to that of many Brazilian slaveholders who taught their sons that Negroes were not humans but different beings "forming a link in the chain of animated beings between ourselves and the various species of brute animals." [6] This conception of Negro inferiority was generally universal, although some planters and town residents did not share it.[7] A description of a Parahyba Valley planter published shortly before the abolition of slavery, underscores the prevalence of prejudices, the effect of routinism, and the absence of scientific knowledge. Though a planter might be capable of displaying compassion and pity for whites, toward his slaves he was "harsh and very cruel" for he refused to see in them the "nature and dignity" of men. The slave was little

[4] C. A. Taunay, *Manual*, p. 6.

[5] Imbert, *Manual*, p. xix.

[6] Caetano Alberto Soares, *Memória para Melhorar a Sorte dos Nossos Escravos lida na Sessão Geral do Instituto dos Advogados Brazileiros no dia 7 de Septembro de 1845* (Rio de Janeiro, 1847), p. 4.

[7] In 1873 a local newspaper printed that it was foolish to disparage Negroes, and local subscribers were informed that Negroes were like other humans, neither inferior physically nor mentally to the whites, nor created separately by God. Carlos Pradez, "Negro," *O Município*, November 30, 1870.

more than an "animated object, a tool, an instrument, a machine." [8]

(2)

On isolated fazendas, amid numerous slaves, planters perceived the precariousness of their situation. Many declared openly "The slave is our uncompromising enemy." [9] And the enemy had to be restrained and kept working on schedule through fear of punishment, by vigilance and discipline, by forcing him to sleep in locked quarters, by prohibiting communication with slaves of nearby fazendas, and by removing all arms from his possession. Where fazendeiros judged that one of their number did not maintain adequate firmness toward his slaves, they applied pressure, direct or indirect. Manoel de Azevedo Ramos discovered this when he brought charges against the overseer of a nearby plantation for beating unmercifully one of his slaves. Neighbors testified that Azevedo Ramos enforced little discipline on his establishment, and the case was dropped since witnesses refused to testify in his behalf.[10] To judge by tasks assigned him, the model planter was an omnipotent, omnipresent, beneficent despot,[11] a father to his "flock" of slaves when they were obedient and resigned, a fierce and vengeful lord when transgressed.[12] And, unlike the

[8] A. E. Zaluar, *O Vassourense*, November 19, 1882.

[9] *Instrucções para a Commissão Permanente*, p. 7.

[10] Supplicante: Manoel de Azevedo Ramos, supplicado: Sabino José dos Santos. APV, 1850.

[11] Slaves played skillfully upon planter paternalism to escape or mitigate punishment for minor transgressions. A slave might ward off a lashing by fleeing immediately upon committing an offence to the proprietor of a neighboring plantation. On arrival, the slave would request the planter to "adopt" him (*tomar padrinho*). If the planter accepted, the slave returned to his master with a note or else the planter personally escorted him back. Then the slave would be admonished not to repeat his offence lest he suffer the consequences.

[12] "The master of a number of rural slaves fills only half his task when he is a competent agriculturist; for he must also possess and exercise those qualities which make him the kindly head of a small kingdom where although governing despotically and accumulating attributions of legislator, magistrate, commander, judge and sometimes executioner, he is still responsible for the good management on which his family's prosperity depends." C. A. Taunay, *Manual*, p. 4. Wrote Caetano da Fonseca in a similar vein: "Slaves, unfortunate creatures, must always look upon their masters as fathers and benefactors, not as tyrants." *Manual*, pp. 98–99.

urban slaveholder whose punishments were somewhat regulated by law, "on the fazendas of the interior the master's will decided and the drivers carried it out."[13] Lightest of punishments might be the threat "Mend your ways or I'll send you to the Cantagallo slave market," more serious might be the age-old instruments of corporal punishment.

Most visible symbol of the master's authority over the slave, the whip enjoyed several names: there was the literate term *chicote* for what was usually a five-tailed and metal-tipped lash, colloquially known as the "codfish" or "armadillo tail."[14] Probably because Portuguese drivers went armed with such cat-o'-nine-tails, slaves tagged it with the name of the favorite article of Portuguese diet—codfish. It was felt that sometimes it was used too much, sometimes too little, for often masters had the "very poor habit of failing to whip on the spot, and prefer to threaten the vexatious slave with 'Wait, you'll pay for this all at once' or 'The cup is brimming, wait 'til it pours over and *then* we'll see'—and at that time they grab and beat him unmercifully; why? because he paid for his misdeeds *all at once*!!!!"[15] It was difficult to apply legal restraints to the planters' use of the lash. When one of the founding fathers of Vassouras, Ambrozio de Souza Coutinho, proposed, as one of the municipal regulations of 1829, that "Every master who mistreats his slaves with blows and lashes, with repeated and inhuman punishment proven by verbal testimony. . ." be fined, fellow-planters refused to accept it.[16] Not sheer perversity but the desire to drive slaves to work longer and harder motivated liberal use of the lash. "Many inhuman fazendeiros," wrote Caetano da Fonseca, more than thirty years after Souza Coutinho, "force their slaves with the lash to work beyond physical endurance. These wretched slaves, using up their last drops of energy, end their days in a brief time." And, he added, "with great financial damage to their barbarous

[13] Ribeyrolles, *Brasil Pitoresco*, II, 35.

[14] Bill of Mello & Irmão to Lieutenant Felix do Nascimento Costa. "1 chicote (rabo de tatú) . . . 3$000." CPOV.

[15] F. P. de Lacerda Werneck, *Memória*, p. 26.

[16] Ambrozio de Souza Coutinho to Câmara Municipal of Paty do Alferes, December 13, 1829. In APV.

masters." [17] Indeed there were masters who believed "their greatest happiness was to be considered skillful administrators, men who force from their slaves the greatest amount of work with the smallest possible expense." [18]

Whipping was not done by the senhor himself who "ordered his overseer to beat the slaves." [19] The whipping over, overseers rubbed on the open wounds a "mixture of pepper, salt and vinegar," probably as a cauterizer but interpreted by slaves as "to make it hurt more." An ingenious labor-saving variation of the whip was reported by ex-slaves. This was a water-driven "codfish" by which a whip secured to a revolving water-wheel lashed slaves tied to a bench.[20] So widespread was use of the lash, that terms such as "fulminating apoplexy" and "cerebral congestion" [21] were employed as medical explanation for death induced by whipping. Typical is an eye-witness account of a beating told by an ex-slave. On orders from the master, two drivers bound and beat a slave while the slave folk stood in line, free folk watching from further back. The slave died that night and his corpse, dumped into a wicker basket, was borne by night to the slave cemetery of the plantation and dropped into a hastily dug grave. "Slaves could not complain to the police, only another fazendeiro could do that," explained the eye-witness.[22]

---

[17] Caetano da Fonseca, *Manual*, p. 103.

[18] Pradez, *Nouvelles Études*, p. 81.

[19] The expression frequently used by ex-slaves: *O senhor mandava bater.*

[20] "Bacalhao de arame tocado a agua."

[21] The slave of Geraldo de Souza Correia was found beaten to death in the coffee groves of the neighboring plantation of Felix do Nascimento Costa. Costa's driver, "Manoel the Islander," was reported to have received orders to whip all slaves using a nearby path to return to their fazendas from a country store. The municipal coroner reported that the slave died of a "cerebral congestion"—exactly the terms used when another medical examiner looked at the corpse of Constança, a slave woman, ordered beated to death by her mistress, wife of an Oliveira Barcellos. In APV, 1858 and 1860. Observed another doctor of the cause of death of a slave beaten severely: "dead . . . by 'fulminating apoplexy,'" frequently observed by doctors "who practice on fazendas of the interior." APV, 1883.

[22] Recommended C. A. Taunay: "Vigilance without punishment is an illusion. Punishment must be determined with moderation, applied reasonably according to the quality of the crime and the conduct of the delinquent, then executed in full view of all the slaves accompanied with great solemnity so that one slave's punishment will teach and intimidate the others." *Manual*, p. 12.

Only slightly less brutal than the whippings were the hours spent by male and female slaves alike in the *tronco*, a form of heavy iron stock common on plantations. Arms and legs were imprisoned together forcing the victim to sit hunched forward with arms next to ankles, or to lie on one side. This was the *tronco duplo*; the *tronco simples* merely imprisoned legs. One ex-slave claimed that she had been told that the fazendeiro placed her to her mother's breast to nurse while her mother served her punishment in a tronco duplo. Another variation was the long wooden stock (*tronco de pau comprido*) into which were locked the feet of four or five slaves. For inveterate offenders an iron hook or collar (*gancho*) was used to encircle the neck. For less important offenses the slave's open palm was slapped with a hardwood palm-slapper (*palmatorio*). Inveterate runaways were chained to each other and put into field gangs, or forced to wear a heavy iron weight on one foot. Such chain gangs were part of the *pena de galés* prescribed by the Imperial Criminal Code of 1830.[23] This form of punishment may have inspired the jongo:

> Pretty little canary, kept in a cage
> Why the little chain on your leg, please tell why?[24]

The worst offender of all was the unregenerate, rebellious slave. If the planter did not kill him outright, he wisely preferred to sell him far away. With evident regret at losing a field hand as well as a skilled artisan, F. P. de Lacerda Werneck wrote his Rio factor: "I authorize you to sell my slave Ambrosio for the highest price you can get. He is a first-class carpenter, axman and field hand, with health like iron; you may say I sell him because he refuses to work for me."[25] If a planter owned more than one establishment, often it proved feasible to

[23] The *pena de galés* obliged criminals to walk singly or in groups with a shackle on the foot and an iron chain, and to be employed on public works in the province where the crime was committed. *Codigo Criminal do Imperio do Brasil*, 1830, Parte I, Titulo 2, Artigo 44.

[24] "O canarinho tão bonitinho, que está preso na gaiola
P'ra quê correntinha está no pé, p'ra quê?"

[25] Letter to Bernardo Ribeiro de Carvalho, Fazenda Monte Alegre, October 6, 1858. In Documentos Referentes a Familia Werneck, Arquivo Nacional.

shift the offender to another fazenda to conserve among slaves "ideas of order and obedience." Wrote the Baroneza do Paty: "I decided to transfer our mulatto slave, Ciro, because he is a pernicious influence on the maintenance of good discipline." [26] Zeferina Adelaide das Chagas Werneck sold an African slave south to Rio Grande do Sul because "it is necessary to remove him from the fazenda and to sell him because he is insubordinate and will not work and he may serve as a bad example to the other slaves." [27]

As a complement to supervision, to discipline, and to fear of corporal punishment, fazendeiros hoped that the local priest, on visits to plantations of his parish, would use the sermon to "rehabilitate the Negro's condition, to consecrate his relations with his master, who would thereby no longer appear as proprietor or tyrant but rather as father, as a portrait of God, whom he should love and serve with the sacrifice of his toil and sweat." [28] The Barão do Paty suggested that the conscientious confessor instil in the slave "love for work and blind obedience to his masters and to those who control him." [29] Such an attitude other Vassouras planters expressed laconically as "religion is a restraining force and teaches resignation" and therefore planters should "push by every means the development of religious ideas." [30] Planters were not to quibble over the costs of the visiting priest, for "in addition to being necessary for the good, the spiritual grazing of souls, such expenses contribute heavily to maintain the morality, order, submission and proper discipline of . . . slaves who cannot be kept in hand and controlled merely by temporal punishment." [31] Padre Caetano da Fonseca advised that "confession is the

[26] "Relatório do Estado da Nossa Casa desde 6 de Dezembro de 1861 ate 6 de Dezembro de 1862," 104 reverse, in Inventory, 1862, deceased: Barão do Paty, executor: Francisco de Assis e Almeida, CPOV.

[27] Inventory, 1875, deceased: João Barbosa dos Santos Werneck, executrix: Zeferina Adelaide das Chagas Werneck, Fazenda São Luis de Massambará, CPOV.

[28] C. A. Taunay, *Manual*, p. 15.

[29] F. P. de Lacerda Werneck, *Memória*, p. 24.

[30] *Instrucções para a Commissão Permanente*, p. 11.

[31] Inventory, 1855, deceased: Fernando Luis dos Santos Werneck, executrix: Polucena d'Oliveira Serra, Fazenda Sao Fernando, CPOV.

antidote of slave insurrections," that the confessor was to teach
the slave to see in the master a father and therefore owed him
"love, respect and obedience." Through the confessor, explained this priest, the slave learned that "this life is as nothing
compared to eternity" and that "the slave who bears his
captivity patiently finds recompense in the heavenly kingdom
where all are equal before God." [32] Reflecting his nineteenth-
century liberal outlook, Ribeyrolles demanded sarcastically:
"And what do these pastors of the Negroes preach? Absolute
obedience, humility, work, resignation. Some go as far as to
say that Negroes are the sons of Cain—sons of the accursed—
and that there is no possible rehabilitation for their condemned
race." [33]

In a society, half free and half slave, many Vassouras
planters maintained harmonious relations with the individual
members of their labor force. Strong attachments based upon
affection and mutual respect often obscured the harsh reality
of slavery. A notable difference developed between the affluent
planters and the proprietors of small holdings with regard to
this relationship. While the large planter had to employ intermediaries to direct the activities of his labor force, the sitiante
directed his few field hands personally, resided in unpretentious
quarters hardly better than those of his slaves, even "maintained his slaves as part of his family and fed them on the
same fare." [34]

It appears, however, that slaves bore perennial animosity
toward planters as a group. While slaves in general accommodated themselves to the conditions of their existence, few
were ever reconciled to them.[35] Range of reaction was wide—
from merely verbal acquiescence to masters' orders to violent,
organized insurrection.

[32] Caetano da Fonseca, *Manual*, pp. 107–108.
[33] Ribeyrolles, *Brasil Pitoresco*, II, 35.
[34] Couty, *Pequena Propriedade*, pp. 40–41.
[35] Suggestive of a common attitude is a story recounted by an ex-slave. Two old
Negroes were sitting in the sun exchanging stories when one questioned the other.
"Oh, Uncle John, what's the best thing that God put into this world of ours?"
"Women," retorted his companion. "No," came the reply, "it was the burro.
Because if we didn't have *him*, we'd have to lug the master's son around on *our*
shoulders."

To defend themselves against masters trained to "absolute dominion" [36] who were always ready to interpret independent thought as insubordination, slaves responded automatically "Sim-Senhor" to any positive command or opinion and "Não-Senhor" to the negative. "Slaves never resist outwardly" and although "apparently obsequious and attentive, refusing to argue over an unreasonable order . . . they use any means at their command to defend themselves," Couty observed. Where a command demanded no immediate execution, "the slave considers it a law permitting him to do nothing." Mistresses knew they could not order a cook to perform other household tasks. Slave washerwomen or nurses "refuse to wash floors, or they will do so sloppily, soiling walls and curtains; their retort is ready: 'that's not my work.' " Or, in more subtle form of reaction similar to a slowdown in effect, they forced the master "to repeat several times each new detail." [37]

Not always as subtle or restrained was the reaction to a regime where "fear and coercion" [38] were believed the only techniques for obtaining work. Portuguese overseers, as symbols of authority constantly in the view of slaves, suffered much violence. "A slave of the widow, Dona Joaquina, shot Manoel, overseer of the house and land of the widow, and it is necessary that he be severely punished to avoid repetition of similar acts which are extremely poor examples especially in places where the slave population considerably exceeds the free," was reported in Vassouras in 1837.[39] On the São Roque plantation a slave who "lost control over his feelings when his overseers refused to stop beating his wife, seized a shotgun and shot him." [40] In the last two decades of slavery, attacks on overseers mounted as rumor spread that imprisoned slaves received food and clothing without work.[41] Such ideas could

[36] C. A. Taunay, *Manual*, p. 117.

[37] Couty, *L'Esclavage*, pp. 44–45. In his *Pequena Propriedade e Immigração Europea*, written later, Couty used the phrase "passive refusal to obey" (p. 40).

[38] C. A. Taunay, *Manual*, pp. 11–12.

[39] Instructions forwarded by the President of the Province of Rio to the Juiz de Direito of Apparecida, January 10, 1837. APV, 1837.

[40] *Relatório do Presidente da Província do Rio, September, 1873*, p. 6.

[41] *Annexo ao Relatório do Presidente da Província do Rio, September, 1872*.

not be extirpated and the local newspaper advised its readers that "there is an erroneous belief that under the penalty of perpetual 'pena de galés', which is almost always imposed for slave crimes, slaves' existence is less harsh than that which they bear under private ownership." When a crime was committed, slaves surrendered voluntarily to the police, confessed the crime "with cynical disdain and tranquilly awaited inevitable condemnation." [42] Thus, Faustino, "slave of Dr Antonio José Fernandes, killed his overseer with a billhook at 8:30 P.M. and them gave himself up," recorded the same local newspaper which concluded: "Rare is the week when such facts are not registered." [43]

Where slaves could not bring themselves to react by passive resistance or violence, many committed suicide. "Eva, slave of Francisco Soares Torres, a planter of the parish of Mendes, committed suicide on April 7th with a knife blow in the abdomen." [44] Similarly, "on the morning of November 3rd, Maximiano, slave of José Manoel Teixeira Coelho, committed suicide by cutting open his stomach." [45] According to an ex-slave, some slaves hung themselves "to avoid a beating" and others "to make themselves useless to the master." "On May 23rd, on the left side of the Commércio road in land belonging to Senhora D. Maria Francisca das Chagas Werneck, there was found hanging the corpse of Henrique, who belongs to Senhora D. Zeferina Adelaide das Chagas Werneck, also a fazendeira of the same locality." [46]

Many slaves escaped to the woods until accidentally discovered or rounded up by local police and planters helped by agregados and slaves. Since coffee groves were usually prepared near virgin forest, slaves working in gangs asked permission to leave to attend to physical necessities then fled. Others chose to flee in the dusk as gangs returned from the fields. Others managed to crawl from their locked quarters during the night. As early as 1824 so troublesome were slave flights that planters

[42] "A Condemnação de Escravos," *O Município*, July 15, 1877.
[43] *O Município*, October 7, 1877.
[44] *O Município*, April 12, 1874.
[45] *O Município*, November 9, 1873.
[46] *O Vassourense*, May 28, 1882; August 6, 1882.

requested the Câmara Municipal to hire a slave-catcher (*capitão do mato*) to hunt down and recapture fugitives.[47] Once in the woods, the fugitive built a shelter and might prepare a small patch for growing corn and beans. It was probably more common to obtain supplies by stealing from nearby plantations. Hunting parties might run across a slave refuge, as occurred when several free men encountered "a rancho which seemed to have a fugitive slave, and there they waited to ensnare anyone who came. Shortly there appeared a Black man and, when José Barboza tried to hit him, the said Negro resisted. The Negro fell on the ground. Barboza shouted to his companion to help, bashed in the Negro's head while his companion knifed him twice." [48]

Frequently slave runaways lived in organized communities or *quilombos*, a name applied to more than one locality in the município of Vassouras.[49] When thefts of cornmeal, sugar, or other foodstuffs became too frequent, planters called in the local authorities. One summer morning a police chief and five municipal policemen joined a planter, thirty of his slaves, and several neighbors—all well-armed. Moving through abandoned land gone to brush, they came upon a grass-roofed rancho where there were a mulatto and two Negro women. A fourth *quilombola* fled when warning shots were fired. In the rancho they found "iron pots, candles, a bag of cornmeal, vegetables, a suckling pig quartered and salted, and several articles of clothing." More than six months previously the mulatto had fled his master; the Negro women had left their master three months before. This quilombo, vouchsafed the fugitives, originally formed part of another quilombo established on the land of the São Fernando plantation. But two weeks earlier it had been attacked, the eleven quilombolas had split up with four setting themselves up in the brush on the nearby Limoeiros

---

[47] Request from Parahyba do Sul to the Câmara Municipal of Paty, December, 1824. APV, Vassouras.

[48] Autor: Justiça, Reo: Ignacio de Nação, Autos de Crimes de Corpo de Delicto. APV, 1832.

[49] A request for a bakery license informed the Câmara Municipal that the shop was located near the railroad station of Belém "in the place called 'little Quilombo.'" APV, 1858. Many coffee slopes were also called quilombo.

plantation of José Caetano Alves. Pressed further, they admitted that some of the articles in their rancho were bought "after midnight in the venda of João de Mello near Indayá" in exchange for foodstuffs stolen from grist mills and sugar mills on nearby plantations. "They were kept alive with stolen goods," the local reporter explained.[50]

In a society where manumitted slaves were common, apprehension of fugitives was not easy. Recapturing fugitives gathered in quilombos was one thing, finding them after they had fled to other coffee growing towns, another. An unknown Negro was likely to be sent to the local jail "on suspicion of being a runaway," [51] inasmuch as manumitted slaves (*libertos* or *forros*) were hard to distinguish from runaways who passed themselves as freedmen and sought employment as rural salaried labor. Masters carried the names of fugitives on their plantation accounts for years in the hope they could someday be recaptured. One inventory listed "Little John, African, forty-nine years old, a fugitive about 10 years" and "Clemente, Brazilian-born, thirty-six years old, a runaway about 6 years." [52] Slave holders placed advertisements in local newspapers describing their runaways with extraordinary care to distinguish them from thousands of others. There were African fugitives: "The slave Mariano, African, has fled from this town. His color is a bit lighter than black, average height, thick beard with bald spots, no front teeth, small eyes, speaks well, dressed in blue cloth blouse and trousers of the same material, madapollam shirt with a worn linen center, cloth cap of military cut. He also wears a black alpaca coat much used, cotton duck trousers, a cotton shirt. Stumbles when he walks because he was locked up in Vassouras' jail for a long time. Wears his cap or hat pulled forward." [53] There were creoles or Brazilian-born fugitives: "The slave Laurentino, creole, has fled from the Fazenda da Diligencia. He is tall, fleshy, his right hand is

---

[50] "Diligencia Importante," *O Município*, December 30, 1877.

[51] "Por suspeito de captivo." Inspector da 1a. quarteirão, Joaquim de Sant' Anna Passos to the jailer of Vassouras. May 30, 1845. APV, 1845.

[52] Inventory, 1880, deceased: Ezequiel de Araujo Padilha, executrix: Alexandrina de Araujo Padilha, Fazenda Sta. Eufrazia, CPOV.

[53] *O Município*, September 30, 1877.

crippled and twisted, he has a hernia, talks well and quickly, plays the guitar. Whoever befriends him will be prosecuted to the full extent of the law." [54] There were women fugitives: "On December 1st the slave Mariá José fled from her master, Bernardino Alves da Cruz. Bears the following marks: light color, twenty-six years old, average height, short hair, round face, speaks well, is a seamstress, wore light calico dress and a colored cotton shawl. Was formerly the slave of Captain Laureanno Correa e Castro. Whoever apprehends and hands her over to her master in Massambará, or in Vassouras to Antonio José de Abreu Cesar, will receive . . . Rs 100$000." [55] There were married fugitives: "50$000. The slave named Antonio fled on June 29th from the farm Tatuhy of Paty do Alferes. He is a carpenter, African from Benguella, pock-marked, tall, large feet, thick lips, fleshy, white beard. With him fled the slave Damiana, African from Benguella, wife of the aforementioned slave, very dark, short, very stout, lacks three fingers on the right hand, speaks well. These slaves are known in Parahyba do Sul, Bemposta and Piabanha where they have worked, and in the município of Vassouras. Whoever befriends them will be prosecuted to the full extent of the law. Above reward for whoever returns them to their mistress, D. Luiza Rosa Sampaio at Tatuhy, or can give definite information of their whereabouts." [56] Thus, whether they were born in Africa, or in Pernambuco, or in Minas, or in Rio Grande, or in the Province of Rio de Janeiro, whether they were male or female, they fled with their clothes, their knowledge of trades, or their physical deformities. If they fled repeatedly, their apprehension could be expensive, too. A master wrote of two slaves who refused to work and kept fleeing for a whole year: ". . . the estate has suffered important damages not only by the loss of their services, but particularly by the expenses that repeated searches and apprehension demand." [57]

Individual slave reactions to discipline could readily be kept

[54] *O Município*, September 29, 1877.

[55] *O Município*, December 14, 1873.

[56] *O Município*, July 5, 1877.

[57] Inventory, 1884, deceased: Josué Torres de Albuquerque, executor; Augusto Coelho d'Oliveira, Fazenda Ubá, 1885. CPOV.

within manageable proportions. It was the haunting fear of mass reaction, insurrection, that terrorized masters and their families throughout the period of slavery. Many could recall the revolting slaves of Manoel Francisco Xavier who formed an organized group more than 300 strong in 1838 and supplied with "all the tools sufficient to form a new fazenda . . . withstood the musket fire" of local police and planters until troops from Rio under the command of the then Marquez de Caxías defeated them on the Fazenda Maravilha.[58] The dramatic impact of this episode brought the adoption of a stringent slave code in the same year, regulating the movement and assembly of slaves and their possession of any arms.[59] These measures failed to inhibit repeated abortive uprisings during the forties, the decade when the largest number of Africans arrived at Vassouras plantations. What one aged resident of Vassouras termed a "zum-zum" or threatened insurrection was noised abroad by slaves in 1848, then quickly squelched by masters who circulated warning letters to neighbors.[60] Mindful of the violent slave revolts in Bahia during the 1830's,[61] Vassouras planters dreaded that among the northern slaves sold southward when African importations ceased, unscrupulous planters would include those who "least suit their owners because of their evil disposition and incorrigible comportment." [62] The commission of Vassouras planters formed in 1854 instructed its members to use every means to convince planters of the "danger of insurrections and of the need to take measures which hinder and prevent so terrible a misfortune as soon as possible." "If the fear of a general insurrection is perhaps still remote, nevertheless the fear of partial uprisings is always imminent, particularly today when our plantations are being

[58] A tantalizingly brief summary of the insurrection with some details of its organization is furnished by Pinto, *Fastos Vassourenses*, pp. 133–134. A letter from Ignácio Pinheiro de Sousa Vernek, dated November 13, 1838, affords details on the local action before Caxías arrived. APV, 1838.

[59] Reorganização das Posturas. Posturas da Câmara Municipal da Vila de Vassouras. Parte III, Título 2, Artigo 8, 9; Título 3, Artigo 5, 6, 7, 8. APV, 1840.

[60] Joaquim José Teixeira Leite to Paulo Gomes Ribeiro de Avellar, sub-delegate of police in the parish of Paty, April 19, 1848. APV, 1848.

[61] *Instrucções para a Commissão Permanente*, p. 5.

[62] *Relatório do Presidente da Província do Rio*, August 1, *1859*, p. 7.

supplied with slaves from the North who have always enjoyed an unfortunate reputation. We have had partial insurrections in various spots, and unfortunately they will not be the last." [63] In following years isolated references in municipal archives to group resistance may be largely attributed to the exaggerated fears of planters, to malicious statements by quarreling slaves eager to settle accounts with their fellows, or to incitement by a few slave leaders. Despite planters' fears, Vassouras slaves are reported to have harbored animosity toward the northerners or *Bahianos*, who felt themselves culturally superior. To this element of division among slaves may be added the activity of slaves who curried favor with their masters by offering to help catch fugitives or by informing on their companions. Slaves are reported to have ostracized the slave tale-bearers (*chaleiras*), refusing to speak to them or to aid them in their work. Furthermore, when the chaleira could be enticed from under the overseer's eye, a group of slaves might maul him unmercifully.

Passage of the Rio Branco law (1871), the rising tide of abolitionist sentiment, and discussion of abolition at masters' dinner tables and over the counters of country saloons and stores frequented by slaves, spread among slaves "hopes never before felt, spurring them with the prospect of a smiling future around the corner" and apparently made slavery less tolerable.[64] The worsening situation forced a newspaper of the province of Rio to announce in 1877 that in one town "all planters and their families dread attacks at any moment. In view of the attitude of the slaves their existence and personal security run great risk." [65] By the early 1880's, Couty, undoubtedly bearing in mind the social ferment in Europe at that period, expressed fear of a "frightening . . . social revolution" foreshadowed by the isolated slave attacks everywhere, particularly frequent assassinations of overseers. There was a permanent undercurrent of insubordination ("refusals to obey, passive disobedience") that slaveholders tolerated to avoid

---

[63] *Instrucções para a Commissão Permanente*, p. 5.

[64] "A Condemnação de Escravos," *O Município*, July 15, 1877.

[65] "A Situação dos Fazendeiros em Relação aos Escravos," *A Patria*, December 5, 1877, cited in *O Município*, December 13, 1877.

"aggravating the crisis." "The slave no longer obeys or obeys reluctantly, and even runaways are protected by the tacit or avowed complicity of a large segment of the population." [66]

At this point, the problem of mounting slave reaction to forced labor and to the master became more than a matter for local repression. It became the problem of Brazilian labor in general, linked closely to the spread of transportation lines, decline of older coffee plantations, and the rise of an urban middle class. The protest of slaves against their status in a changing society now became part of the nationwide movement for abolition.

(3)

Although the plantation gave Vassouras society a well-defined class structure, the bonds of patriarchalism, the *compadre* system, and the various types of union between the sexes both legal and extralegal formed a web of social contacts drawing together members of the society often irrespective of class lines.

All plantation residents—the planter's wife, sons and daughters, nephews and nieces, dependent relatives, aggregados, overseers, and slaves—owed obedience to the planter. Even the municipal authorities avoided any infringement of the large landholder's suzerainty. Wives deferred as submissively as did their children; for fourteen years one planter "prohibited" his wife from "visiting her mother to receive her blessing, and without cause . . . always treating her as he would a slave, using curses and filthy language." [67] A wife who fled from her husband did not leave his "bed and board," rather in the words of the husband, "for thirty years she has lived outside my control." [68] The submission of children was symbolized by their request for the father's blessing mornings and evenings. On the arrival of a child's godparent, the father would order his offspring to request that visitor's blessing too.

[66] Couty, *Pequena Propriedade*, pp. 40–41.

[67] Luiza Maria de Carvalho vs. João de Souza Vieira. APV, 1853.

[68] Inventory, 1846, deceased: Manoel Francisco Barboza; executrix: Ignacia Maria de Jesus, Fazenda Unknown. CPOV.

Since children were married young and parents supplied land and slaves for the newlyweds, the arm of the patriarch was respected even after a youth attained maturity. Whether deeply felt or superficially accorded, respect to the patriarch had to be observed.

Among slaves there existed a comparable respect for the elders, the "wise ones." But since Negro slave elders or god-parents had no property whose disposition brought deference, the threat of sudden death by supernatural intervention enforced respect. A young slave failed to ask the blessing of an aged Negro, and his mother beat the child unmercifully until the old slave ordered her to stop. When the old man had left, the son wished to know why he had been beaten for his forget-fulness. The mother replied that if she had not done so, the child would have died by morning.

Supplementing the usual family relationships were the ties of godparenthood (*compadrío*). These formed a triangle of child-ren, parents, and godparents. Relatives or close friends could become godparents. Their responsibility for and authority over godchildren were comparable to those of the parent; con-sequently, at the time of baptism, parents chose their children's godparents (*padrinhos*) only after careful deliberation. The obligations of godparents protected children in the event parents were unable to provide adequately. Furthermore, where marriage was common within the clan, the godparent relation-ship strengthened family ties. A godparent, whether relative or friend, not only assumed a close tie with his godchild (*afilhado*), he formed simultaneously a new tie to the child's parents, who became his compadres.

Religious overtones entered, too, since the relations were established at baptism. " 'Compadre' and 'comadre' so called in relation to the afilhado or afilhada, the godchild," Burton observed during his residence in Brazil, "still form in Brazil a religious relationship as in the days when our gossip was a God-sibb, or 'akin in God.' I have heard brothers address each other as compadre. These brothers and sister sponsors may legally marry, but public opinion is as strongly pronounced against the union as the wise of England regard 'confarreation' with the deceased wife's sister. . . In small country places, for instance, all the inhabitants are connected by baptism if not by blood. . ."[69]

Social security benefits of the compadre system were widely distributed by some of the wealthy women of the plantations. Because of pious and charitable inclinations, planters' wives were not only the madrinhas of children in their own families, they became the godmothers of friends' children or of the offspring of poor free parents, and "protected" others. "I leave one conto to my following godchildren," ran the will of a Vassouras woman, and she added the provision that "To all the godchildren I may have henceforth, if they are my relatives, I bestow another conto."[70] When the time came to settle the estate of a generous godparent, the executor often inserted a notice in the local newspaper asking all the deceased's godchildren to appear at the executor's plantation or at the lawyer's office along with a certificate of baptism to collect the inheritance.[71]

The godparent–godchild relationship apparently existed among slaves too, although infrequent marriages and the annual mass baptism of infants probably made the relationship less important. Slave godparents gave the newly baptised infant a towel, soap, nightshirt, and bonnet, purchased from passing pack peddlers with the small change earned by the sale of their own produce or poultry. When a boy reached puberty and was about to shave for the first time his godfather presented him a razor, the godmother bought or made a towel. If the slave mother died, the grandmother or the godparents were expected to look after the orphaned child or children; disrespect for godparents brought the inevitable beating. After abolition, members of upper-class families often became the godparents of infants born to their former slaves. These were frequently raised in the godparents' homes in the expectation that they would become dedicated household servants.

[69] *Explorations*, I, 80, note. Compare Charles Wagley, *Amazon Town. A Study of Man in the Tropics* (New York, 1953), pp. 150–159.

[70] Inventory, 1885, deceased: Antónia Ludovina Mascarenhas, Fazenda Unknown, CPOV.

[71] "Edital," *O Vassourense*, July 16, 1882.

(4)

The years of infancy, childhood, and early adolescence on the plantation were the same for the children of the planter and of his slaves. Negro midwives attended their mistress in childbirth, and she reciprocated; Negro "aunts" nursed their own children and those of the mistress, and took charge of the infants as first they crawled, then toddled, and finally walked and talked. The constant loving attention of the slave women nurtured in the planters' children the image of the "Black Mother," which many carried through life.

Awareness of the functioning of a slave society was gradually acquired by both free and slave children. In the early years, the master's children played with slave children. Most of the people they observed were slaves: in the kitchen or serving the table, their Negro companions, the men working on or around the drying terraces. Then, at the age of property-consciousness, when the planter's child began to speak, he probably learned to say "my slave" or "Papa's slaves." Later, he observed that his parents undertook certain tasks but ordered slaves to perform others; and, simultaneously, "little master," commenced ordering his slave companions. It was then that differentiation occurred: the master's children, especially the girls, wore better clothes, and the master's son went to school or was tutored. Growing up in a slave society, the planter's children learned their role gradually, perhaps as unconsciously as they grew accustomed to the splashing of the water-wheel and the thumping of the coffee milling machinery.

The Negro slave child, on the contrary, learned that he had few rights, that he could be ordered by the master's children, that he—not they—was expected to be saddled, ridden, and switched in play. His reaction to inferior status was expressed mainly in the form of impassivity; if he failed to do so, he "caught it." At the close of early adolescence, between ten and twelve years of age, a break sharper than any previous occurred. The slave boys were sent off to handle a hoe and to take part in the multifarious jobs of the coffee plantation; the planters' sons were prepared for school, possibly as resident students in Vassouras' private primary or secondary schools, while families began to consider eligible bachelors for their rapidly maturing daughters. This was the period when planters' wives began to wonder about "moral miscegenation" and the consequences of their children's formative years "spent among the Blacks." [72] Planters' wives worried about the contacts of the young mulatto girls with their daughters and their main "preoccupation" was to "watch . . . and not permit . . . intimate talks" between them.[73]

The role of free and slave women on the nineteenth-century plantation differed markedly. At the level of the planter, merchant, and professional groups, free married women were usually molded into passive creatures. They took charge of the household, they bore sons and daughters, they watched their girls through the brief period of adolescence (the boys' education falling largely to the province of the fathers). In planter families, the dowry and behind that the inevitable inheritance that fell to the wife through her parents' death were the main considerations in marital arrangements. Yet, with such factors, the wife herself had little to do, for her inheritance came legally and as a matter of course.

On the slave level, women were far more independent economically. They performed the work of men—weeding, hoeing and harvesting—on the coffee slopes. They raised foodstuffs on their patches of land for sale; in this fashion, a few, sometimes aided by outsiders, purchased their freedom. Of the latter, many were seamstresses. In many respects, Negro women, both before and after emancipation, enjoyed an independence denied their upper-class sisters. There were exceptions, of course. Although women of the planter class depended upon their fathers and, after marriage, upon their spouses, there frequently came a time when they became economically and intellectually emancipated. Such an opportunity might come when a husband died, leaving the wife free to make the dispositions she thought necessary. In some cases, when the wife was middle-aged, she administered her property with a wisdom and acumen absent in her deceased spouse. Aid

[72] Couty, *Biologie Industrielle*, p. 114.
[73] Macedonio, "Em Uma Reunião," *O Município*, January 13, 1878.

and advice came from parents, sons, sons-in-law. Other women remarried men of their own choice, although it seems that the sheltered lives they led until the death of their husbands left them naïve, unprepared for the blandishments of the calculating fortune-seeker.

If this situation developed, planters had themselves to blame. For many fathers, bachelors, and husbands, a woman's life was only a tale of "affection . . . the love of a delicate woman is always timid and silent even when she is happy." Accepting a woman's life as "monotonous, lonely, meditative," Vassouras upper-class male society considered a man a "creature swayed by self-interest and ambition . . . Love is merely an ornament of the dawn of his life." [74] A local schoolmaster expressed the status of free plantation women in 1873 in less florid terms. "A woman in Brazil is still the image of what she used to be; she still bears on her wrists the marks of chains; she has not yet taken the place which is rightfully hers as a powerful agent of social progress." Dependent solely upon their "powers of physical beauty or of wealth," women were judged inferior to men.[75] Young girls learned to cut, sew, embroider and make lace, to prepare cakes and sweets, and to supervise the cooks, chambermaids, waiters, and seamstresses of the plantation. Less frequently they were taught to sign their names and to keep household accounts. In the second half of the nineteenth century it became more common for the wealthier planters to permit their daughters to read, write, play the piano, and speak French, although practical planters derided these innovations on the grounds their daughters would have little occasion to use such abilities. This upbringing produced wives, mothers, and grandmothers whose horizons extended to the limits of the fathers' property or at farthest to those of the extended family. Breaks in the monotony of plantation existence came when birthdays, baptisms, and weddings provided an opportunity for planters' daughters to visit grandparents, uncles, aunts, first, second, and third cousins, and to display the results of sewing, embroidery, and perhaps a few jewels.

[74] *O Vassourense*, June 18, 1882.
[75] Alberto Brandão, *O Município*, July 13, 1873.

Easter brought planters and their families to their town houses in Vassouras to participate in the ceremonies centering around the church. During the daylight hours there would be excursions on horseback for sisters, brothers and cousins always chaperoned; the spacious main salons of plantation and town houses accommodated numerous families at the formal soirées— social gatherings designed to bring together the marriageable of local society.

Since the administration of a coffee plantation demanded no apprenticeship period for the proprietors' sons, adolescence was brief, generally culminating in early marriage. Favoring early marriage too, was early economic maturity—the lands and slaves placed by planter parents behind their children. Equally significant was the factor of plantation continuity through unbroken property transmission. Mortality was high and it behooved the practical planter to insure conservation of wealth within the family. Love was a secondary consideration; in affairs of the heart it was more practical to overlook the bride's beauty and to ascertain instead, as did a young local merchant, if the "father is financially sound and can provide a good dowry." Equality of the fiancés' financial standing or social status received careful consideration lest the parties concerned degrade themselves. A widow whose fifteen-year-old daughter was to marry a doctor practicing in a prosperous locale of the município, wrote that the "marriage has my full approval, and that of the affianced and of all the relatives; moreover, they are equal in every respect." [76] A prominent banker decided to marry off his ward, aged seventeen, to her cousin, a "marriage very gratifying to the two contracting persons and to all their relatives, and which is perfectly equal both in family, position, and fortune, for it is commonly recognized that the fiancé has commenced with dignity and respect his career in the Law." [77] Where local prosperity and improved communications brought Portuguese and other European intellectuals, largely doctors and lawyers, some

[76] Letter, María Euphrasia dos Santos, November 22, 1856 in Inventory, 1856, deceased: Manoel Rodrigues dos Santos; executrix: María Eufrasia dos Santos, Fazenda Unknown, CPOV.
[77] Letter, Francisco José Teixeira Leite. APV, 1863.

planter fathers accepted them as sons-in-law. Affluent families often displayed similar preoccupation with status and income in marrying off the daughters of poor freemen whom they had "protected." The Baroneza do Amparo raised "in her company" a girl for whom a suitor appeared and she consented in a letter to the local authorities, "in view of the fact the boy is honest and hard-working and very equal to the girl in birth and goods, and therefore in a position to wed her." [78]

Wedding festivities were among the most important social events, and wealthy planters spent liberally to refurbish the plantation house completely. At one wedding a small orchestra played during the ceremony and at its conclusion the parents and grandparents of the bride and groom solemnized the occasion by granting three slaves their "letters of liberty." "There followed," recounted the local newspaper, "an ample supper in the French style" and a "sumptuous ball that lasted until six a.m. the following morning. The ballroom was richly decorated, and expensive toilettes were in evidence, all characterized by the good taste, elegance and 'chic' of the wearers." [79]

The elaborate nuptial festivities of Vassouras planters' children did not alter the fact the unions were essentially marriages of convenience. Analysis of the sixty-two marriages of seven generations (1780–1900) of one family reveals thirty-six unions between participants not recognizably related, twenty among first cousins, three involving uncles and nieces, and one between an aunt and her nephew. Two marriages occurred where brothers married the wives of their deceased brothers.[80] It was therefore not rare for a wife to address her husband as "uncle" or in other cases as "cousin."

Such planned marriages did not always bring domestic felicity and the abundant love poetry of the period may have emphasized its absence in actual relationships. It was the observation of one Vassouras resident that "you can establish the following rule: a marriage planned at birth is soon

[78] Letter. APV, 1872.

[79] O Vassourense, February 19, 1882.

[80] A. G. Ribeiro de Avellar, "A Prole da Familia Avellar." Note the case of one of Vassouras' earliest and largest landholders who married his mother's granddaughter by her first marriage. F. K. Werneck, História, p. 58.

undone." [81] Reared to accept the traditional submission of the female to father, husband, uncle or godfather, the planter's wife was expected to tolerate the mate picked for her as well as his extra-marital relations with female slaves.

The interest and planning that planters lavished upon the marriage of their children were absent where slaves were concerned. Married slaves, according to one early manual, were to live apart, meeting briefly at night in the slave quarters. "As for the passing unions, these must remain completely secret and unknown . . . the proprietor of a plantation does not want priests or nuns, but a race of robust, obedient and docile workers; and he should therefore shut his eyes to anything that does not disturb decorum or discipline. The duties and quarters of both sexes should be separated; there must be difficulty but not the impossibility of their meeting; and as the Spartans punished not theft but its discovery, so must planters punish not the action but the scandal thereof." [82] Thirty years later, ten years after the end of the slave trade, another writer stressed the absence of marriage among slaves as a factor in their low reproductive rate. He appealed to planters' self-interest by pointing out that the offspring of married Negroes enriched the planter.[83] And Couty observed that planters permitted their slaves to be together two or three hours each evening with the result that "most of the slave children have only one parent, the mother." [84]

These conditions helped foster among Brazilian Negroes the passing union or *amazia* that replaced the African tradition of polygyny. The pattern of temporary union was reinforced by economic equality between male and female slaves, by the importance of the mother in African polygymous society and by the disproportion between male and female slaves in Vassouras until the closing decades of slavery.[85] Fights over women were

---

[81] *O Município*, April 27, 1879.

[82] C. A. Taunay, *Manual*, p. 171.

[83] Caetano da Fonseca, *Manual*, pp. 101–102.

[84] *L'Esclavage*, p. 25.

[85] "The enormous difference of one-third less women than men among the slaves. . ." *Resumo Chorográphico da Província de Rio de Janeiro* (Rio de Janeiro, 1841), pp. 18–19.

a constant source of friction among male slaves, and undoubtedly were more frequent until the normal reproductive ratio equated the number of female to male slaves.[86] Nor were planters perturbed by the problem of paternity. Drawing an analogy between the slave mothers and cows, one ex-planter explained that if another man's bull inseminated his cow, the cow and calf were his.

Amazia, most common among slaves, existed in all classes of Vassouras society and cut across class lines. According to

TABLE 14. Marital status in Vassouras, 1872.

Parish	Unmarried	Married	Widowed
Conceição	8,945	1,419	270
Mendes	2,299	723	318
Paty	11,639	2,597	204
Ferreiros	3,673	874	119
S. Familia	4,932	1,049	162
Total	31,488	6,662	1,073

Source: Recenseamento, 1872.

the census of 1872, for 6,662 married persons (presumably 3,331 couples) there were 31,488 unmarried persons not including 1,073 widowed (Table 14). Although most of the unmarried were undoubtedly children and slaves, it would appear that many were among the adult free poor. The Portuguese, so often hired as overseers and in other supervisory capacities, were generally single and were said to have a "taste for Negro women."[87] Most arrived poor, clerked for meager wages

[86] For a typical account of such slave conflict, see *Relatorio do Presidente da Provincia do Rio, October, 1876*, p. 15.

[87] Comparing them with other European immigrants, Couty noted in 1881 that the Portuguese "lacked completely racial prejudice." "Today," Couty added, "Brazil receives annually many Portuguese immigrants who have the defects and good qualities of the early colonists; today just as a century ago, the Portuguese immigrant has a taste for Negro women." *L'Esclavage*, pp. 20–21. Examination of National Guard membership rolls revealed that at least 75 per cent of Vassouras plantation overseers were unmarried in 1872.

in the city of Rio de Janeiro, or moved into the rural areas where they worked on railroads, public roads, or in the towns and on plantations. For these lower-class Portuguese the possibility of marriage to daughters of wealthy planters was small. They arrived in Brazil unaccompanied and were in constant contact with Negro and mulatto women, slave and free. They could ill-afford racial prejudice.

Planters' wives were naturally aware of their husbands' and sons' proclivities toward slave girls. A planter and his wife, so a satiric tale went, lived blissfully together. The husband, however, had an "innate flair for beauty, and he purchased male and female slaves, horses, cattle, sheep and pigs provided they were beautiful." His wife was unconcerned with male slaves, horses, cattle, sheep, and pigs—beautiful or ugly. But toward the female slaves she followed the precept that the "uglier they are, the better." Whenever any slave trader appeared at her home, she cast an eye over the lot and invariably felt well-disposed toward all the "big-lipped, toothless, flat-nosed, or crippled female slaves." She noted too that on the plantations where there were many "beautiful, well-kept black and mulatto slave women, guests kept arriving like grasshoppers during a plague. She dreaded plagues, she wanted her husband and sons undisturbed and her plantation not a guest house. So, she always bought slave women whose faces would frighten nursing infants." [88] In other cases planters' wives might desert their mates, as happened to one planter who complained to the local authorities that it was a matter of common knowledge that his wife "lived as the concubine of the defendant . . . and that she lived in her mother's home, cohabiting [with her new mate] scandalously and fleeing from her husband without cause. . ." [89] Or a wife "separated" from her husband

[88] "O Maná," *O Município*, December 23, 1877. What planters assumed as an unquestioned right in their own lives, they denounced vigorously as adultery when practiced by their wives. Returning to his plantation one evening, a planter chanced to pass by his slaves' quarters and overheard reports that his wife was *amaziada* with a slave, and that she had induced an abortion because the child was the slave's. It is probable that such relations between slave men and free white women were rare. APV, 1870.

[89] APV, 1835. For comparable cases, see APV, 1852 and *O Município*, October 4, 1877.

and "went to live in the company" of another whom she married upon the death of her abandoned spouse.[90]

In occasional cases of extreme abuse of marital vows, wives resorted to legal separation. After twenty-three years of marriage, during which she bore eight children, one wife could not "tolerate her husband or cohabit with him." "Indulging in a dissolute life, her husband had amazias all the time, and spent large sums on them. About ten years ago (1843) he purchased the freedom of the dark mulatto, Rosa, and her brother, and taking her as his amazia, he fed and clothed her and built her a house where he spent four months on end. . . Many times she felt grief and shame on finding him in their bed with his own slave women. . . Unable to tolerate his demands and insults, she tried to flee first to her mother's residence, then to her relatives." Once he attacked her with a knife, forcing her to flee to the home of her mother-in-law. Then, in 1851, two years before her request for a divorce, he took a new amazia "for whom he built a tile-roofed house, floored and whitewashed, and installed her as his concubine, along with her relatives." He even hired a servant for her. The wife lost her "patience, hope, and Christian resignation" when the husband took his amazia to mass in the "full view of the public, which denounced so immoral an action." [91] Her divorce was granted by the Church.

With good reason planters feared the vengeance their repressed and outwardly submissive wives often turned upon slave women suspected of relations with their husbands. The wives of planters were raised in a society based upon obedience obtained by force. When the opportunity was presented, when a husband was absent, the frustrated wives could turn upon the suspects, ordering their overseers to brand faces, or whip them to death. Planters hid their slave amazias in remote corners of their plantations "to avoid domestic misunderstanding," [92] sent them to their friends for safekeeping, or freed them; or

---

[90] Letter, Agostinho Pinheiro de Souza. APV, 1864.

[91] Luiza Maria de Carvalho vs. João de Souza Vieira. APV, 1853.

[92] Testament, José Correa e Castro. APV, 1876.

they established them on small plots of land and supplied them with one or two slaves.[93]

Actually, the brunt of illegitimate yet countenanced miscegenation fell upon the offspring. If these escaped the enmity of the planter's wife as the "children fathered by the Portuguese overseer," or by an itinerant pack peddler, or were shipped off to other plantations, their status did not differ in general from that of other slave youngsters. Many received no special attention from their fathers, were whipped for misdemeanors or even sold to passing slave traders. Some planters, and Portuguese and other immigrants, more conscience-stricken, included in wills and testaments provisions for the upbringing of illegitimate children with varying success. Pedro Correa e Castro went through life a bachelor, freeing his "Black slave, Laura, from the Congo" and the "five females and one male" she bore him and whom he raised with "solicitude and in the Christian doctrine." His three executors were all free men married to several of his daughters by slave women; to his children he left slaves and cash.[94] "I beg my dear wife," penned another planter in his testament, "to educate your young slave girl, Sara, whom I had baptized in another place, and for whom I beg my wife's pardon; I also beg my wife not to abandon her, and when she is old enough, to do her best to marry her to a good person." [95] Fearful of how untutored ex-slaves might dispose of property willed to them, another planter bestowed upon "Perpetua, who was my slave and is now free and in my company" and upon his children by her only the usufruct of land and buildings in their lifetime and prohibited the sale of such property.[96] In practice the best wishes of considerate planter fathers ran into the resistance of legal wives and their

[93] Inventory, 1855, deceased: Felix Antonio Barboza, executrix: Quiteria María de Jesus, Fazenda Unknown. APV, 1855.

[94] Inventory, 1874, deceased: Pedro Correa e Castro, executor: Antonio Agricola de Pontes, Fazenda do Tinguá. CPOV. In another instance, the daughter of a former slave woman was appointed the heir of her planter father. APV, 1872.

[95] José Correa e Castro. APV, 1876. Similarly, Inventory, 1870, deceased: Domingos Justino Pereira da Fonseca, executrix: Purcina María da Luz Paixão, Fazenda Unknown, CPOV.

[96] Inventory, 1879, deceased: Antonio Francisco Apolinari, executor: Antonio Botelho Peralta, Situação Unknown, CPOV.

children. Through protracted law cases, the ignorance of planters' amazias and their children, and the tendency of plantation society to keep Negroes in their place, the testamentary provisions for the latter were often circumvented.[97]

This is the portrait of Vassouras plantation society in the nineteenth century. It was divided sharply into the free and the slave, into marked levels of class and hierarchy. The political, social, and economic elite provided leadership for other classes to follow. It was, above all, a society where the possession of wealth was as essential as social origin, and where the elite usually possessed both.

As long as the coffee plantation functioned adequately, little social mobility developed. Three factors, however, slowly undermined social rigidity—economic decadence, emancipation, and miscegenation—and began to transform society more rapidly at the close of the nineteenth century. Without wealth, the planter and his descendants saw status slip away, while the ex-slave commenced his slow integration into freedom as wage laborer. And because the Negro freedman's change of status was imperceptible, social friction and racial prejudice were minimized. Within respective social spheres, slowly changing Brazil offered opportunity to all free men, whether white, mulatto or black. Although many planters refused to recognize illegitimate offspring, even to the extent of seeing them, hoe in hand, toiling on the coffee slopes in the slave labor gangs, or selling them, a minority assumed some responsibility for the children they brought into the world: legitimizing and educating them, granting them inheritances which their children by their legal wives hotly contested. Actually, one of the greatest factors in bridging the gap between the planter and the slave was miscegenation, and its result, the children born of such inter-racial relations. In the long run they were to provide the factual basis for the Brazilian melting pot.

[97] An example of the failure to carry out requests made in behalf of a planter's children by slave women is in Inventory, 1863, deceased: Claudio Gomes Ribeiro de Avellar, executor: João Gomes Ribeiro de Avellar, Fazenda Guaribú and others, CPOV; also, Inventory, 1873, deceased: Estevão Pimenta de Moraes, executor: José Voyano, Fazenda Manga Larga, CPOV.

CHAPTER VII

Patterns of Living

SLAVE life on the average Vassouras plantation of approximately eighty to one hundred slaves was regulated by the needs of coffee agriculture, the maintenance of sede and senzallas, and the processing of coffee and subsistence foodstuffs. Since the supply of slaves was never adequate for the needs of the plantation either in its period of growth, prosperity, or decline, the slaves' work day was a long one begun before dawn and often ending many hours after the abrupt sunset of the Parahyba plateau.[1]

Cooks arose before sunup to light fires beneath iron cauldrons; soon the smell of coffee, molasses, and boiled corn meal floated from the outdoor shed. The sun had not yet appeared when the overseer or one of his Negro drivers[2] strode to a corner of the terreiro and reached for the tongue of a wide-mouthed bell. The tolling of the cast-iron bell, or sometimes a blast from a cowhorn or the beat of a drum, reverberated across the terreiro and entered the tiny cubicles of slave couples and the separated, crowded tarimbas, or dormitories, of unmarried slaves. Awakening from their five- to eight-hour slumber, they dragged themselves from beds of planks softened with woven fiber mats; field hands reached for hoes and billhooks lying under the eaves. At the large faucet near the senzallas, they splashed water over their heads and faces,

---

[1] When the available pool of slave labor tended to diminish through death and disease, planters became more solicitous of their labor. Caetano da Fonseca's advice to planters that "work . . . be regulated according to daylight hours" reflects a viewpoint different from that of earlier period when slaves were more numerous and cheap. *Manual*, p. 104.

[2] Drivers (Capatazes) were slaves who supervised field gangs. Feitores (overseers) were free men, generally mulattoes or Portuguese, working for wages.

moistening and rubbing arms, legs, and ankles. Tardy slaves might appear at the door of senzallas muttering the slave-composed jongo which mocked the overseer ringing the bell:

> That devil of a *bembo* taunted me
> No time to button my shirt, that devil of a bembo.

Now, as the terreiro slowly filled with slaves, some standing in line and others squatting,[3] awaiting the morning *reza* or prayer, the senhor appeared on the veranda of the main house. "One slave recited the reza which the others repeated," recalled an ex-slave. Hats were removed and there was heard a "Praised-be-Our-Master-Jesus-Christ" to which some slaves repeated a blurred "Our-Master-Jesus-Christ," others an abbreviated "Kist." [4] From the master on the veranda came the reply: "May-He-always-be-praised." The overseer called the roll; if a slave did not respond after two calls, the overseer hustled into the senzallas to get him or her. When orders for the day had been given, directing the various gangs to work on certain coffee-covered hills, slaves and drivers shuffled to the nearby slave kitchen for coffee and corn bread.

The first signs of dawn brightened the sky as slaves separated to their work. A few went into the main house; most merely placed the long hoe handles on their shoulders and, old and young, men and women, moved off to the almost year-round job of weeding with drivers following to check stragglers. Mothers bore nursing youngsters in small woven baskets (*jacás*) on their backs or carried them astraddle one hip. Those from four to seven trudged with their mothers, those from nine to fifteen close by. If coffee hills to be worked were far from the main buildings, food for the two meals furnished in the field went along—either in a two-team ox-cart which slaves called a *maxambomba*, or in iron kettles swinging on long sticks, or in wicker baskets or two-eared wooden pans (*gamellas*) on long boards carried on male slaves' shoulders. A few slaves carried their own supplementary articles of food in small cloth bags.

Scattered throughout the field were shelters of four posts

---

[3] Ribeyrolles, *Brasil Pitoresco*, II, 33.
[4] Pradez, *Nouvelles Études*, pp. 80, 85.

and a grass roof. Here, at the foot of the hills where coffee trees marched up steep slopes, the field slaves split into smaller gangs. Old men and women formed a gang working close to the rancho; women formed another; the men or young bucks (*rapaziada nova*), a third. Leaving the moleques and little girls to play near the cook and assistants in the rancho, they began the day's work. As the sun grew stronger, men removed their shirts; hoes rose and fell slowly as slaves inched up the steep slopes. Under the gang labor system of *corte e beirada* used in weeding, the best hands were spread out on the flanks, *cortador* and *contra-cortador* on one, *beirador* and *contra-beirador* on the other. These four lead-row men were faster working pace-setters, serving as examples for slower workers sandwiched between them. When a coffee row (*carreira*) ended abruptly due to a fold in the slope, the slave now without a row shouted to his overseer "Throw another row for the middle" or "We need another row"; a feitor passed on the information to the flanking lead-row man who moved into the next row giving the slave who had first shouted a new row to hoe. Thus lead-row men always boxed-in the weeding gang.

Slave gangs often worked within singing distance of each other and to give rhythm to their hoe strokes and pass comment on the circumscribed world in which they lived and worked— their own foibles, and those of their master, overseers, and slave drivers—the master-singer (*mestre cantor*) of one gang would break into the first "verse" of a song in riddle form, a *jongo*. His gang would chorus the second line of the verse, then weed rhythmically while the master-singer of the nearby gang tried to decipher (*desafiar*) the riddle presented. An ex-slave, still known for his skill at making jongos, informed that "Mestre tapped the ground with his hoe, others listened while he sang. Then they replied." He added that if the singing was not good the day's work went badly. Jongos sung in African tongues were called *quimzumba*; those in Portuguese, more common as older Africans diminished in the labor force, *visaria*. Stopping here and there to "give a lick" (*lambada*) of the lash to slow slaves, two slave drivers usually supervised the gangs by criss-crossing the vertical coffee rows on the slope and shouting

"Come on, come on"; but if surveillance slackened, gang laborers seized the chance to slow down while men and women slaves lighted pipes or leaned on their hoes momentarily to wipe sweat away. To rationalize their desire to resist the slave drivers' whips and shouts, a story developed that an older, slower slave should never be passed in his coffee row. For the aged slave could throw his belt ahead into the younger man's row and the youngster would be bitten by a snake when he reached the belt. The overseer or the master himself, in white clothes and riding boots, might ride through the groves for a quick look. Alert slaves, feigning to peer at the hot sun, "spiced their words" to comment in a loud voice "Look at that red-hot sun" or intermixed African words common to slave vocabulary with Portuguese as in "*Ngoma* is on the way" to warn their fellow slaves (*parceiros*), who quickly set to work industriously. When the driver noted the approaching planter, he commanded the gang "Give praise," to which slaves stood erect, eager for the brief respite, removed their hats or touched hands to forehead, and responded "Vas Christo." Closing the ritual greeting, the senhor too removed his hat, spoke his "May He always be praised" and rode on. Immediately the industrious pace slackened.[5]

To shouts of "lunch, lunch" or more horn blasts coming from the rancho around 10 A.M., slave parceiros and drivers descended. At the shaded rancho they filed past the cook and his assistants, extending bowls or *cuías* of gourds split in two. On more prosperous fazendas, slaves might have tin plates. Into these food was piled; drivers and a respected or favored slave would eat to one side while the rest sat or sprawled on the ground. Mothers used the rest to nurse their babies. A half hour later the turma was ordered back to the sun-baked hillsides. At one P.M. came a short break for coffee to which slaves often added the second half of the corn meal cake served at lunch. On cold or wet days, small cups of cachaça distilled from the plantation's sugar cane replaced coffee. Some ex-slaves

---

[5] Couty observed the slaves' automatic greeting and the use of shouts to keep in step ("cris poussés . . . pour les tenir en haleine"), although he misunderstood the patterns of the jongo mestre cantor and the chorus. *L'Esclavage*, p. 47.

reported that fazendeiros often ordered drivers to deliver the cachaça to the slaves in a cup while they worked, to eliminate a break. *Janta* or supper came at four P.M. and work was resumed until nightfall when to drivers' shouts of "Let's quit" *(vamos largar o serviço)* the slave gangs tramped back to the sede. Zaluar, the romantic Portuguese who visited Vassouras, wrote of the return from the fields: "The solemn evening hour. From afar, the fazenda's bell tolls Ave-Maria. (From hilltops fall the gray shadows of night while a few stars begin to flicker in the sky). . . From the hill descend the taciturn driver and in front, the slaves, as they return home." Once more the slaves lined up for rollcall on the terreiro where the field hands encountered their slave companions who worked at the plantation center (sede).[6]

Despite the fact that the economy of the fazenda varied directly with the success of its coffee production, a high percentage of plantation slave labor, which some estimated at fully two-thirds,[7] others at one-half of the labor force,[8] was not engaged directly in field work. "On the plantation," Couty judged, "everything or almost everything is the product of the Black man: it is he who has built the houses; he has made the bricks, sawed the boards, channeled the water, etc.; the roads and most of the machines in the engenho are, along with the lands cultivated, the products of his industry. He also has raised cattle, pigs and other animals needed on the fazenda." [9] Many were employed in relatively unproductive tasks around

---

[6] A. E. Zaluar, "Scenas da Roça," *O Vassourense*, May 14, 1882. Most of this reconstruction of a day in the field is based upon interviews with ex-slaves of Vassouras. Of the nineteenth-century observers' accounts of a slave's daily existence the following are especially useful: Ribeyrolles, *Brasil Pitoresco*, II, 33–34; Caetano da Fonseca, *Manual*, pp. 96–97; F. P. de Lacerda Werneck, *Memória*, pp. 27–28.

Lacerda Werneck reports that some planters adopted the practice of feeding their slaves only twice daily, at 10 or 11 A.M. and at 5 P.M. Indignantly he commented: "Such planters do not have their own interests at heart . . . How can a man or woman (who is even more frail) wait from five in the afternoon until 10 or 11 the following morning without food, laboring from sunrise whatever the weather, with a hoe, billhook, or ax?" *Ibid.*, p. 27.

[7] *Congresso Agrícola*, p. 163.

[8] Couty, *Biologie Industrielle*, p. 96.

[9] Couty, *Biologie Industrielle*, p. 83.

the sede as waiters and waitresses, stableboys and cooks, and body servants for the free men, women, and children.[10]

Throughout the day in front of the house could be seen the activity of the terreiro. From his shaded veranda or from a window the fazendeiro watched his slaves clean the terreiro of sprouting weeds, or at harvest time revolve the drying coffee beans with wooden hoes. Until the hot sun of midday drove them to the shade, bare-bottomed black and mulatto youngsters played under the eye of an elderly "aunt" and often with them a small white child in the care of his male body servant (*pagem*) or female "dry nurse." [11] In a corner slaves might butcher a pig for the day's consumption while some moleques threw stones at the black turkey buzzards which hovered nearby. Outside the senzella a decrepit slave usually performed some minor task or merely warmed himself in the sun. From the engenho came the thumping sound of the pilões and the splash of water cascading from the large water-wheel. In the shade of the engenho an old slave wove strips of bamboo into mats and screens.[12] Washerwomen, beating and spreading clothes to bleach in the sun, worked rhythmically "to the tune of mournful songs." [13]

Behind the main house, the páteo enclosed on all sides offered a shelter from outsiders' eyes, a place to be at ease. Here and in the rooms around it the lives of the free and slave women blended together. Washerwomen chatted as they dipped their arms into the granite tank in the center of the páteo or stretched wet clothes to bleach on the ground, and through the door of the kitchen slaves occupied with the unending process

[10] Ribeyrolles, *Brasil Pitoresco*, II, 36.

[11] For the care of the planter's children, there were: (1) the *ama de leite*, a slave woman who nursed the master's child, generally chosen from among those slave women who gave birth at the same time; (2) the *ama seca*, a slave soman who cared for the master's child after weaning; and (3) the *pagem* or male slave companion who played with the growing children, taking them on trips, to and from school, and on hunting excursions.

[12] In his novel of plantation life Américo Werneck depicts many of these activities in considerable detail, viewing the plantation through a highly colored and romantic prism. *Graciema*, I, 61.

[13] A. E. Zaluar, "História de Um Fazendeiro," *O Vassourense*, November 19, 1882.

of food preparation could be seen at long wooden work tables. From a small porch opening on the páteo, or from the dining-room window, the mistress of the house, *sinhá* (or more informally, *nhanhá*), in a dressing gown, leaned on the railing and watched, maintaining a flow of gossip with her slaves or reprimanding some. Yet, despite the close contact between free and slave, locks on the doors of pantries and cupboards and the barred windows of both gave mute testimony to the faith of the mistress in her slaves. Life for the female house slave often seemed easier in comparison with that of a field hand; indeed, many of the *mucamas* or household female slaves were chosen from the field gangs. Yet they felt they had less liberty than the field hands since they were constantly supervised. A former pagem put the case succinctly: "Of course life in the household was always better. But many a sinhá beat her mucamas with a quince switch." [14]

The dining room, with its close relation to kitchen, páteo, and sleeping rooms, was probably the general place of family congregation on those fazendas which did not have special sewing and sitting rooms. Bedrooms were small and sparsely furnished and, in the case of the windowless alcovas, entirely dark. In the house the younger women and maiden aunts sewed and embroidered, gossiped, and made delicacies for feast days, while the mistress of the household took a direct hand in the management of affairs. Usually an active sinhá carried the keys to pantries, which were opened twice daily to dole out food for the household's main meals, and to linen, china, and silver closets. Under her direction, slaves made beds, arranged disorder, swept, and moved dust from one point to another with feather dusters, while nursemaids took charge of the younger children and wet nurses satisfied squalling infants.

At meal times, which occupied a large part of the day, diners sat on both sides of the long extension table, the fazendeiro at its head. When guests were present talk was largely between

[14] Former sinhás or free workers in plantation household service generally felt that life for the household slave or mucama was far preferable to that of the gang. This was not the way ex-slaves felt; they harped on the lack of freedom of action, the watchful eye of the mistress, her frequent beatings, and the fact they had no choice in the matter for, if they complained, they were beaten.

them and their host, while the children and dependent relatives ate in silence, speaking only when addressed. The senhor tapped his plate with a spoon to remind the waiter to change plates. A demitasse of coffee closed the meal which was followed by the inevitable toothpick taken from a silver holder. After the noon meal, while the free retired to their nap, the household slaves ate their meal, gossiped, and yawned through the washing of dishes and silverware, and, when finished, resumed the bate-papo unless the mistress or master kept them busy with small biddings.[15]

At evening roll call (*formatura*) slaves were checked and sent to evening tasks to begin what one Vassouras planter termed the "brutal system of night tasks" (*serão*), sometimes lasting to ten or eleven P.M.[16] During winter months the principal evening task—the sorting of dried coffee beans on the floor of the engenho or on special tables—was continued in the light of castor-oil lamps or woven taquara torches. Preparation of food for humans and animals was the next most important job: manioc was skinned by hand, scraped on a huge grating wheel, dried, and then toasted for manioc flour. Corn cobs were thrown to pigs, while slaves beat other ears on tables (*debrulhadores*) with rods to remove kernels to be ground into corn meal. Women pounded rice in mortar and pestle to hull it. Coffee for the following day's consumption was toasted in wide pans, then ground.[17] Slaves were sent out to gather firewood, and moleques walked to nearby abandoned groves to drive in the few foraging cows, oxen, mules, and goats. A light supper ended the serão.

In the dwelling house slaves cleared the supper table and lit castor-oil lamps or candles. The planter's family retired soon to their rooms, followed by the mucama "whose job was to carry

[15] Ribeyrolles, *Brasil Pitoresco*, II, 36.

[16] A parliamentary committee appointed to inquire into prospects for colonization of European immigrants in the Parahyba Valley reported that "the slave works without let-up ("trabalho seguido") 14 or 16, even up to 18 hours daily." *Jornal do Commercio*, February 22, 1884, cited in Delden Laerne, *Brazil and Java*, p. 98, note 2.

[17] Most fazendeiros whom Couty interviewed estimated that one-fifth of total slave manpower went into cultivation and preparation of slave food. *Biologie Industrielle*, p. 101.

water to wash the feet of the person retiring." She departed immediately to return after a short wait, received a "God-bless-you" and blew out the light.[18]

And now field hands straggled from the engenho to slave senzallas where they were locked for the night. Household help too was locked in tiny rooms located in rear of the house near the kitchen. For the slaves it was the end of a long day—unless a sudden storm blew up during the night while coffee was drying on the terreiros; then they were routed out once more by the jangling bell to pile and cover hurriedly the brown beans. Except for the patrollers, (rondantes) moving in groups on the roads and through the coffee groves to pick up slaves out without passes (guías or escriptos)[19] to visit nearby plantations or taverns, activity ceased.

(2)

With the arrival of Saturday evening and Sunday—awaited with much the spirit of the American South's "Come day, go day, God send Sunday"—came the only interruption of the work routine of plantation life. On Saturday the evening stint was usually omitted to give the labor force an opportunity to live without close supervision. Near a fire on the drying terrace, to the beating of two or three drums, slaves—men, women, and children—led by one of their master-singers, danced and sang until the early morning hours.

Even Sunday too was partially devoted to work. In morning chores, lasting until nine or ten, field hands attended to the auxiliary tasks of the plantation: hauling firewood from clearings, preparing pasture by burning the grass cover, clearing brush from boundary ditches, repairing dams and roads, and killing ever-present saúva ants with fire and bellows. Sunday was the day for distribution of tobacco cut from a huge

[18] Macedonio, O Município, March 3, 1878.

[19] A municipal regulation ordered that "Any slave found at night or at any daylight hours outside the limits of his master's plantation, or if the master lives in a hamlet, outside the boundaries of that hamlet, without written permission (escripto) of his master or members of his family, will be punished with 25 to 50 lashes." Posturas da Câmara Municipal da Vila de Vassouras, 1838, Parte III, Titulo 3, Artigo 5.

roll of twisted leaf smeared with honey, and of clean clothing for the following week's use. Chores completed, the master "gave permission"—permitted slaves to dispose of the remainder of the day until the line-up at nightfall. It was also common for planters to "give permission" on days other than Sunday to stagger the weekly day off and prevent slaves from meeting with friends from nearby plantations.

Many now scattered to small roças near the plantation center, where they raised coffee, corn, and beans. Planters gave them these plots for various reasons: they gave the slave cultivators a sense of property which, known or unknown to Brazilian masters, continued an African tradition and softened the harsh life of slavery; they provided subsistence foodstuffs which planters failed to raise in their emphasis on one-crop agriculture; and, by offering cash for the produce, planters put into slaves' hands small change for supplementary articles not provided by the plantation.[20] Often planters insisted that slaves sell only to them the coffee they raised.[21] Slaves obtained cash too when the custom became widespread among planters to pay for Sunday or saints'-day labor.[22]

Where male and female slaves cohabited, men often were accompanied to the roças by their children, while women washed, mended, and cooked, bringing the noon meal to their

[20] F. P. de Lacerda Werneck, *Memória*, pp. 24–25. When Captain José Luis da Costa Unhão died he left word in his testament that he had "moneys entrusted by slaves who earned these quantities as the result of coffee they planted and harvested with my permission." APV, 1843.

[21] Writing to his Rio factor, Lacerda Werneck advised that his slave messenger was to tie beneath his belt cash derived from the sale of "coffee of the slaves of the [fazenda] Piedade. . ." Dated December 9, 1853, at the Fazenda Monte Alegre. In Arquivo Nacional. In 1861, the Baroneza do Paty earned Rs. 4:593$209 (about $2,000 in American currency of the period) on coffee purchased from her slaves and resold in Rio. "Relatório do Estado da Nossa Caza, 1861," page 49 in Inventory, deceased: Barão do Paty, executor: Francisco de Assis e Almeida, CPOV.

[22] An entry in a plantation account book recorded, for example, "For the services of slaves on Sundays . . . 206$000." Inventory, 1886, deceased: Maria Francisca das Chagas Werneck; Couty, *Biologie Industrielle*, p. 108. The same practice was urged upon the Imperial Government, when in 1853 Conrado Jacobo de Niemeyer requested the Fazenda Nacional at Itagoahy to permit its slaves to work for a salary on their days of rest to build a canal in the vicinity. *Relatório do Presidente da Provincia do Rio, August 1, 1853*, p. 27.

mates in the field. The single men brought firewood for the cook to prepare their meal, returning at eating hours. Other slaves used the free time to weave sleeping mats or cut and sew clothing for sale. With cash or corn or beans, slaves went on Sundays to trade at nearby saloons (*tabernas*) or small country stores. On a visit to a fazenda of the province of Rio, the Swiss Pradez entered a fazenda-owned venda run by an aging slave "aunt" of the fazendeiro's confidence where he found the typical stock: tobacco and cachaça (particularly attractive to slaves),[23] notions including mirrors, straw hats, and clothing cut from cotton cloth (*Petrope*) of a quality slightly better than the coarse cloth furnished by the plantation. Outside the confines of the fazenda, he found a white taberna proprietor who served Negroes with cachaça at a *vintem* per glass. In friendly fashion the white man, to Pradez's surprise, discussed with a slave the weather, the crops, and his master, as though the slave were a "client to be maintained." [24]

More disturbing to coffee planters, and a very lucrative business to "their greatest enemies" [25]—taberna owners—was the "large-scale clandestine commerce in stolen coffee" carried on "almost exclusively at night in places heavily populated with slaves." [26] An ex-slave recounted how he used to obtain coffee for sale to a nearby taberna. After senzalla doors were locked, he climbed to the eave where tools were stored, and removed several roof tiles. Through the hole he crawled, then managed to get into the basement of the coffee storehouse. Here he drilled a hole in the floor and drained into a bag all the coffee he could carry. Then over the fazenda's outer wall and, avoiding the main road usually patrolled by rondantes,

[23] "Drunkenness must be prohibited to slaves by whipping and by other punishment once they have been exhorted not to indulge." F. P. de Lacerda Werneck, *Memória*, p. 25; Macedonio, *O Município*, November 18, 1877.

[24] Pradez, *Nouvelles Études*, pp. 82–83. "Petrope" was the "riscado petropolis" mentioned in fazenda bills. It was a coarse cotton cloth produced at the nearby mill of the Companhia Petropolitana. Inventory, deceased: Maria Francisca das Chagas Werneck, executor: Luis dos Santos Werneck, Fazenda de São Francisco, CPOV.

[25] Fazendeiros of Matto Dentro to CMV, August 13, 1843. APV, 1844.

[26] Leopoldo Nóbrega, inspector de quarteirão, Freguezía do Paty do Alferes to Delegado de Polícia do Termo de Vassouras, Vassouras, June 28, 1861. APV, 1861.

he arrived at the taberna. If the suspicious planter or his zealous overseer appeared at the door of the country bar, the taberneiro replied innocently that "No one is here." In return for the bag of coffee, the slave received a fraction of its worth in cachaça or tobacco. Not always, however, were planters put off with an innocuous "No one is here," as the following case reveals: "On the night of May 1st, Manoel, a slave belonging to the complainant, stole from the terreiro a bag of coffee and carried it away clandestinely to Ferreiros where he entered the doors of the store of Joaquim Teixeira Alves after ten o'clock."[27] This was noted by the rondantes circulating in Ferreiros, and they sealed off Alves' store. On May 2nd after dawn, in the presence of witnesses, the store was searched. The slave was found without the coffee but with 1$400 reis and a piece of tobacco given to him as payment for the stolen coffee. "Alves and his brother, who acts as his clerk, confessed on the spot and begged and pleaded not to go to jail." [28]

Fazendeiros tried to hinder the obvious collusion between their slaves and taberna-keepers, whose illegal intentions were blatant when they established tabernas on lonely roads, by demanding that the Câmara Municipal grant no licenses. They were not always successful,[29] unless they moved against the exasperating tavern-keepers without waiting for municipal authorities. "In view of the repeated thefts of coffee on the complainant's plantation perpetrated by his slaves in collusion with several nearby taberneiros for the past three years, particularly so in the past month, the complainant, Joaquim José Furtado, reports that he sought carefully for the author of these thefts with absolutely no success. But he finally learned that Renovato Borges de Siqueira, who has an unlicensed taberna near the complainant's lands, is one of those who have been buying the coffee stolen by the complainant's slaves. For this

[27] According to municipal regulations (*posturas*) all stores, except pharmacies, were forbidden "to keep their doors open for business after 10 p.m. . . . ." Título I, Artigo 9, *Posturas da Câmara Municipal de Vassouras, 1857.*

[28] Supplicante: Augusto Soares da Costa, supplicado: Joaquim Teixeira Alves. APV, 1869.

[29] Fazendeiros of Matto-Dentro to CMV, August 13, 1843. On the reverse of this petition the recording secretary of the Câmara wrote "rejected."

purpose there exists a path from that taberna to the coffee lands of the complainant cleared by the offender and the slaves to carry on the illicit traffic in coffee as proven by the coffee berries scattered on the path as well as those which have already sprouted." Furtado learned from a female slave that "one Sunday she saw Hercules, a slave of the complainant who walks hobbled with ankle chains, sell the offender a bag of coffee . . . and not the first one." [30] Some slaves were more indiscriminate in their choice of negotiable stolen goods as evinced by Manoel de Azevedo Barboza's report that a certain Luís bought from his slaves his treasured silver spoons and forks, pigs, turkeys, and chickens.[31] More than the loss of coffee,[32] however, was the continual drunkenness of slaves who stole; and in the repression of stealing and drunkenness there was fostered an "eternal, unequal, and inhuman struggle where the interests of the Senhor conflict with those of his slave, who suffers so many rigorous punishments and who flees to the forest to die by suicide, misery, eaten by worms." [33]

(3)

Diet of both free and slave population on Vassouras plantations represented the adaptation of colonial and Portuguese eating habits to local produce, and to the necessities of a large slave working force. With few exceptions basic ingredients came from each plantation or the immediate environs, could be

[30] Supplicante: Joaquim José Furtado, supplicado: Renovato Borges de Siqueira. APV, 1844. Siqueira was finally convicted of having an unlicensed taberna. Autos de Infracção de Posturas, in APV, 1844. Other similar cases were: Supplicante: José Barbosa dos Santos, supplicado: João Gonçalves. APV, 1852, and the protest of José Joaquim de Carvalho Bastos, venda-owner of Madruga, to the Câmara Municipal against charges of buying stolen goods from slaves. APV, 1883.

[31] APV, 1841. The trafficker in stolen goods was pilloried in the following comment: "One slave brought him a spoon, a knife and a fork—all of silver; to be useful to the slave he bought the loot at a very reasonable price, in view of the risks of the purchase." Macedonio, "Negocio é Negocio," O Município, October 4, 1877.

[32] Couty claimed that coffee thefts amounted to an "enormous annual loss" which fazendeiros found themselves powerless to halt. L'Esclavage, p. 22.

[33] Leopoldo Nóbrega, Vassouras, June 28, 1861. APV, 1861.

easily stored over a period of months despite summer heat and absence of any refrigeration, and were quickly prepared in large amounts for distribution to the fazenda's slaves. Couty exaggerated when he called coffee plantation diet "very perfect," but he had more than ample grounds for stating it was "the product of progressive adaptation to a series of factors difficult to modify." [34]

Five basic nutrients—corn meal, beans, manioc, bacon, and sugar—formed the core of the four daily meals served to master and slaves alike. For breakfast slaves received portions of corn meal prepared by boiling for twenty to twenty-five minutes in huge cauldrons[35] suspended over an open fire. Armed with long wooden spoons cooks stirred the steaming porridge as it gradually thickened; so strenuous was this job that the cooks were rotated weekly. With the corn meal, each slave received a mug holding some thirty centiliters of hot coffee sweetened with molasses.[36] Coffee given slaves was reported to lack aroma and flavor, since planters used beans of poor quality, which often produced a "bitter tasting" brew.[37]

Two heavy meals—lunch and dinner—considered by planters "more substantial" because of the quantity of the food served, followed in the course of work on the coffee slopes or around the main buildings. Corn meal, the "basis of slave nutrition," [38] was supplemented by boiled brown or black beans seasoned with bits of bacon and bacon grease; when served,

[34] Louis Couty, "L'Alimentation au Brésil et dans les Pays Voisins," *Revue d'Hygiène et de Police Sanitaire*, III (March 1881), 486. Couty wished to study the ". . . alimentation of peoples of whom Europeans know little and whom they too often consider in every way inferior to the civilized nations of their continent." *Ibid.*, p. 183.

[35] "A large cauldron to cook for the blacks, and kitchen utensils." Inventory, 1862, deceased: Barão do Paty, executor: Francisco de Assis e Almeida, Fazenda da Conceição. CPOV.

[36] African arrivals on Vassouras plantation probably did not find these basic articles of diet strange. Negroes from Portuguese Africa cultivated corn, beans as well as sugar cane; in fact, aguardente was widely used in Angolla. Marquez de Sá da Bandeira, *O Trabalho Rural Africano e a Administração Colonial* (Lisboa, 1873), 193; Antonio María de Castilho Barreto, "Impressões sobre Africa Occidental," *Revista Luso-Brasileira* (July 1860), I, 58; T. Peckolt, *História das Plantas Alimentares e do Gozo do Brazil* (Rio de Janeiro, 1874), p. 94.

[37] Couty, "L'Alimentation au Brésil," pp. 281, 472.

[38] Couty, "L'Alimentation au Brésil," p. 472.

the bean stew was liberally sprinkled with manioc flour, the "hunger-killer." [39] Boiled vegetables rounded out the meal as one or two of the following were heaped atop the corn meal and beans: sweet potato, squash, cabbage, turnip, or various greens.[40] To bring out the flavor of the food, cooks added only salt, pepper, or parsley. As a rule the menu for lunch was repeated at dinner. Where slaves worked late at evening tasks they sometimes received a supper of strips of jerked beef[41] (*carne secca*) which one ex-slave wistfully recalled as "three to four fingers thick" grilled then sprinkled with cornmeal or manioc flour. Occasionally, at time of hard field labor during harvest or on festive occasions slaves also received cups of aguardente known by the African term *maráfo* or by the Brazilian cachaça, caninha or paraty.[42] Slaves needed only fingers, small split gourds or *cuías*, or more rarely, spoons to aid in eating as they stood, squatted, or sat at mealtimes. With only a brief intermission to eat a heavy meal in the field and employing primitive utensils to bring to their mouths soft, boiled food, slaves earned for themselves the saying "Negroes don't eat food, they bolt it." [43]

This year-round, staple diet[44] was occasionally varied with

[39] Siqueira, *Memória Histórica*, p. 3.

[40] Botanical designations for some of the foods consumed include: *aypim* (Manihot Aypim); *batata doce* (Convolvulus Edulis); *abóbora* (Cucumis Pepo); *couve* (Brassica Oleracea); *repolho* (Brassica Sp. V.); *herva doce* (Pimpinella Anisum); *nabo* (Brassica Napus). From José de Saldanha da Gama, *Classement Botanique des Plantes Alimentaires du Brésil* (Paris, 1867), p. 11.

[41] Pound for pound, jerked beef was more expensive than fresh meat. Planters favored it for various reasons. A pound of jerked beef prepared in *saladeiros* (beef processing plants) of the Province of Rio Grande do Sul by salting, pressing, and sun-drying equaled two and one-half pounds of fresh meat. It was readily shipped and could be kept anywhere from eight to ten months without deterioration. Couty, "L'Alimentation au Brésil," pp. 183, 188–192, 195.

[42] Couty, "L'Alimentation au Brésil," pp. 289–290.

[43] "Negro não come, engole."

[44] A provincial president announced in 1859 that European colonists near the sugar center of Campos were eating the local cuisine of "beans, corn bread, manioc flour, dried codfish, jerked beef, and coffee as well as indigenous fruits." *Relatório do Presidente da Província do Rio, April 25, 1859*, p. 27. Another writer outlined his recommended foods in the daily slave diet: coffee, *rapadura* (raw sugar), beans, cabbage, bacon, corn meal, jerked beef, manioc flour, rice, greens, squash, potatoes. Caetano da Fonseca, *Manual*, pp. 96–97.

dishes slaves especially relished. Served only during Holy Week, *passóca* consisted of roasted peanuts, pounded in mortar and pestle, with manioc flour and sugar added. Reduced to a fine powder, passóca sweetened coffee or was eaten by the spoonful. *Canjica* was made with dry corn pounded slowly while a few drops of water moistened the kernels until the outer shell came off. It was then boiled in milk and flavored with peanuts, sugar, cinnamon, and clove. Sometimes masters regaled their slaves at harvest time by offering a suckling pig to those who exceeded their quota of picked beans; saints' days, too, were the occasion for distribution of barbecued pig. A variety of fruits, found wild or cultivated on coffee fazendas, supplemented the diet. There were several varieties of banana, the "poor man's bread," and of oranges, not to mention other fruits in season—mango, guava, *sapoty*, and *jaboticába*.

In keeping with other primitive plantation arrangements, cooking utensils were extremely simple. Most fazendas had two kitchens, an outdoor one for the slaves and an indoor one where food for the master's family was prepared. The outdoor cookshed contained an open fire over which could be suspended iron pots on a long rod. Nearby stood the wooden work tables, the large waist-high mortar hollowed from a tree-trunk, and its rough-hewn pestle glistening from the sliding grip of countless hands. Taquara sieves aided in separating chaff from rice or corn pounded in the mortar; for washing food there were large gamellas and small hand-size gourds. Stoppered gourds and large sections of bamboo (*taquarussú*) were used to store some foods, especially grease. The indoor kitchen differed only slightly from the outdoor one. Here a stove of brick and stone with an iron top supported on both sides provided the source of heat. Where no chimney was employed smoke blackened the tile roof and roof supports above. Over both kitchens flies hovered, on piled food, over steaming pots, and on refuse littering the ground. Infants sat or played on the floor or on tables near food. Poor sanitary conditions of both kitchens provoked a foreign resident to remark that "on leaving the kitchen it is rare not to encounter thick mud where dirty water has been poured, exhaling smells unbearable to the nose and bad for the health. . . Children early get used to the filth and grow up believing it is impossible to improve." [45]

Before the prosperous mid-century years, isolated planters ate the same unvarying fare as did their slaves. As masters, however, they could indulge themselves—a fact not lost upon their slaves who judged that "masters seemed to leave the table just in time to sit down to another meal." The master probably enjoyed not just a seasoning of bacon in his beans but rather a good cut of fresh killed pork daily. The sinhá, with the keys to both pantries—one for "dry" foods, another for wines and aguardente—saw to it that her mate was well fed. And while not above a thick slice of carne secca covered with corn meal or manioc flour, most masters were accustomed to supplement pork with dried codfish imported from Portugal, or more occasionally with beef. On the occasion of a rare visit by a wealthy planter's relative, a Rio factor or his representative, or the local priest, a fazendeiro might order a suckling pig or several chickens slaughtered. Beef was not popular since cattle were used primarily as work animals, and were slaughtered when old and almost inedible.[46]

For what he called the main Brazilian dish, *feijoada*, Couty reserved great praise. Typical of traditional Brazilian rural cuisine, feijoada was prepared by boiling beans to which were added spices and sometimes several vegetables. When almost cooked, the stew received "thick slices of carne secca from which the salt had not been thoroughly soaked." The result, he wrote, "merits the reputation that the mania for imitating Europe, or various prejudices are now tearing down." Since most large coffee plantations grew and processed sugar cane, per capita consumption of sugar among both planters and slaves was high. While sinhás would not aid in the preparation of foods, they reserved the right to make highly sweetened dishes (*doces, quitutes*) both for the immediate family and for sale or distribution at church festivals. And slaves, of course, added raw sugar to their food whenever possible. The strikingly high sugar consumption impressed Couty. "It surpasses by far

[45] C. A. Taunay, *Manual*, p. 21.
[46] Dr. Antonio Lazzarini, *O Município*, September 7, 1873.

7

European per capita consumption," he marveled, "because everyone has a sweet tooth, even the slaves, and consumption of wealthy folk is certainly considerable. The price of the best sugar is low . . . even the poor consumer can afford it." [47]

Arrival of the railroad linking rural areas with Rio, and improved communications with Europe made the capital a focal point for the dissemination of the "most up to date" or "civilized" notions of cuisine among hitherto isolated planters. Yet the total effect of foreign cuisine was a dressing-up of the basic Brazilian diet. Despite a wider use of simple sauces based on imported bunches of garlic and onions, vinegar and olive oil, planters' food was "absorbed almost plain." [48] Consumption among planters of corn meal probably dropped somewhat in favor of more wheaten products as factors forwarded wheat flour, and macaroni and biscuits appeared. Although bread was rarely baked on fazendas, bakery shops appeared in the latter half of the century in the town center and hamlets, and the sight of a baker's apprentice or slave bearing loaves of bread in a wicker basket on his head to neighboring plantations became a commonplace. Along with bread came imported butter in wooden boxes and higher consumption of Minas and Portuguese cheeses. Lack of refrigeration meant butter was soft and rancid when served. Planters' morning coffee was lightened with milk ("milk was only for main house gentry," commented an ex-slave) drawn from one or two cows on only the largest fazendas. To the most prosperous planters, foreign imports brought changes in drinking habits. Cachaça, the choice of slaves and the "poor folk," was replaced by imported French and Portuguese wines, accompanied by Havana cigars. Signs of the changing tastes of the few wealthy fazendeiros were visible in the billhead of João Antonio da Costa Carvalho in the 1880's: "Large warehouse of wines and foodstuffs. Large cellar of fine Bordeaux and Burgundy wines, Th. Roederer and Veuve Clicquot champagne, etc. Game, Meats and Fish in conserves put up by the famous packers Rodel Phillipe &

---

[47] Couty, "L'Alimentation au Brésil," pp. 474, 479.
[48] Couty, "L'Alimentation au Brésil," p. 484.

Canaud, Crosse & Blackwell. Cheeses, biscuits, vegetables, cakes, and spices." [49]

Such minor dietary modifications did not escape the notice of Vassouras' traditional minded folk. "For some time innovations of French cuisine propagated with such praiseworthy solicitude by the capital's hotels have escaped the capital's limits and become acclimated in the kingdom of the succulent and greasy recipes of our forefathers. Classic suckling pig alone has fended off the scandalous infiltration of other baked foods." [50] Couty exhorted fazendeiros to maintain the basic Brazilian diet by changing only minor details of preparation. "I deplore," he wrote in 1881, "this mania for everything European spreading to rural centers and obligating people to range far and wide for new foods and condiments which do not harmonize with their necessities and are perhaps bad for public health." [51]

(4)

As with food, so was the case with the dress of masters and slaves during the first half of the nineteenth century. For both, clothing was simple. On special occasions, as early nineteenth century portraits show, the more well-to-do families were dressed in European style.[52] It was unusual for planters to pay attention to what slaves wore, particularly in the thirties and forties when there was an adequate and relatively inexpensive inflow of African slave labor. One writer reminded planters that "The Brazilian climate, colder and more humid than that of Africa, does not agree with Africans who would not long survive were they to live in their accustomed way without clothing or shelter." [52a] Almost forty years later, a local columnist pilloried a miserly fazendeiro of Vassouras for his negligent attitude toward his slaves. To his Portuguese overseer who

---

[49] Inventory, 1889, Quintiliano Gomes Ribeiro de Avellar, executor: João Gomes Ribeiro de Avellar, Fazenda Boa Sorte, CPOV.

[50] "Um Casamento na Roça," O Município, August 20, 1882.

[51] Couty, "L'Alimentation au Brésil," p. 486.

[52] It is reported that some of the early itinerant French and Italian artists who traveled from fazenda to fazenda carried readymade canvases of elegant ladies, gentlemen, and children, requiring only the sitter's face.

[52a] C. A. Taunay, Manual, p. 10.

complained that his slave charges were a shabby lot without trousers or shirts the fazendeiro tut-tutted: "Oh, the poor things! They work hard and it is only just they have full bellies and well-covered bodies. Tomorrow you will direct them to plant cotton which we will have spun and woven to dress the poor things." Hypocritically the planter recommended: "A full belly and covered body—my overseers must always have these things in mind. Those poor creatures!" [53]

A rough cotton cloth termed by slaves "very thick," "a thick weave," or just "sacking" was ordered by planters in large bolts. Before the establishment of Brazilian cotton textile mills this cloth was handwoven in the province of Minas;[54] later manufactured cotton cloth was known as "American cotton," "Petrope," and "Santo Aleixo cotton"—the latter two textiles produced in either Petropolis or near Magé in the Province of Rio.[55] Supplementing cotton cloth were cotton flannel (*baeta*) and wool from which were fashioned warm outer garments for the cool nights of the dry season. Twice yearly, at Christmas and during the June festivals, slaves received "changes" of clothing. On one fazenda, an ex-slave recalled, male and female slaves were allowed to choose the materials they wished for their few garments from plain white or striped (*riscado*) cloth.[56]

---

[53] *O Município*, October 20, 1878.

[54] In earlier days where threads of Minas cotton were found on low branches it was proof that slaves had been in the vicinity, for before the appearance of machine-made cloth Minas cotton was considered "cheap and proper for slaves." APV, 1835; C. A. Taunay, *Manual*, p. 10. "3,093 varas of Minas cotton." Inventory, 1858, deceased: Bernardino da Silveira Dutra, Fazenda do Rio Bonito, CPOV.

Small cotton-weaving mills are reported to have developed in Minas Gerais as early as 1762; by 1785 their expanding production attracted the notice of the Portuguese government which ordered the existing shops to close, permitting only the manufacture of "coarse goods, for sacking and slaves' clothing." Affonso Costa, *Questões Econômicas* (Rio de Janeiro, 1918), p. 156, note 13.

[55] An American company constructed the Santo Aleixo mill in the município of Magé, and by 1848 had invested about Rs. 200:000$000. *Relatório do Presidente da Província do Rio, April 1, 1848*, p. 45. Among the articles of production for 1855 were "thick cotton cloths of different widths for workers' clothing and for sacking. . ." *Relatório do Presidente da Província do Rio, 1855*, p. 47.

[56] The contents of an inventory show the type of materials which went into slave garments. "Riscado suisso," "riscado petropolis," "algodão Sto. Aleixo," "algodão americano." Inventory, 1886, deceased: Maria Francisca das Chagas Werneck, executor: Luis dos Santos Werneck, Fazenda São Francisco, CPOV.

The planter's wife took charge of the cutting lest the slave seamstresses be too generous with the shears, although a planter's daughter offered another explanation: "The seamstresses did not know how to cut cloth." All work was done by hand until the sewing machine facilitated the task in the closing years of slavery.[57] Male slaves who had mates often let them make their garments; or if they were not capable, they might ask another slave to do so in his spare time in return for payment. Sometimes manumitted slaves, many of whom remained in the vicinity of their former masters, earned small amounts of cash by tailoring. Slaves undoubtedly had good reasons for giving the materials to tailors or seamstresses of their own choosing; for many masters must have had "a slave tailor, just learning his trade, who cuts and sews well or badly." [58]

Male slaves received enough material for trousers, a white shirt and a short jacket;[59] women, cloth for a long skirt which they often starched, a blouse, and head kerchiefs which "they never removed." Perhaps once every two years both women and men were presented a heavy, light blue, woolen outer cloak or *japona* for cold and rainy weather. One ex-slave recalled: "A woman's japona was shorter than a man's. Mine was made of red flannel with two pockets on the outside, lined inside with 'mericano." [60] Small children wore only shirts that fell as far as the thigh. Men completed their meager wardrobe with woven corn-shuck or straw hats. Shoes were not part of slave apparel. Once each year there were distributed woolen bed blankets. Clothes were washed each week when several women slaves were taken from field gangs and, joining washerwomen of the plantation center, soaked, whacked on stones and then spread in the sun to bleach, the soiled garments of

[57] "Singer sewing machine." Inventory, 1875, deceased: João Barbosa dos Santos Werneck, executrix: Zeferina Adelaide das Chagas Werneck, Fazenda São Luis de Cima, CPOV.

[58] Macedonio, *O Município*, March 3, 1878.

[59] Caetano da Fonseca recommended that each slave receive annually two shirts, two pairs of trousers of heavy Minas cotton and two jackets of heavy wool. *Manual*, p. 103.

[60] Chaves & Cia, 11 Rua dos Pescadores in Rio de Janeiro, sold to small country drygoods stores among other articles, "large lined or half-lined japonas." APV, 1871.

the slave labor force. Generally all mending was attended to on Saturday afternoons, and clean clothes distributed Sunday morning. Slaves added to their wardrobes by purchases and by their masters' cast-off garments.

On their fazendas, surrounded by "their own people," planters dressed in white duck trousers and cotton or linen shirts. More care went into the tailoring of their garments. On visits to inspect the slave gangs and overseers in the field, they were shod with boots and their heads were protected from the hot sun by wide-brimmed straw hats; as they sat on a shaded veranda overlooking the slaves and drivers laboring on the terreiro, they changed from boots to comfortable cloth slippers. Essentially the planter's wardrobe differed from that of his slaves in the quality of material used and the number of shirts, trousers, and short coats. In 1840, an opulent fazendeiro left on his death twelve shirts, thirteen pairs of trousers, eight assorted jackets, and a frock coat, the sign of wealth and position. When a notable visitor arrived in Vassouras, "he was immediately called upon by all who possessed a frock coat," as the local newspaper reported.[61] Increasing contact with Rio forced the planter to put aside more frequently his comfortable clothes for what European sartorial fashion dictated. During the nineties, one opulent planter was reported wearing white linen at home; when he visited neighbors, English woolens, starched high collar, French cuffs and dickie, and a black derby, a costume also worn on visits to the stifling capital in summer.

Planters' wives and daughters were equally informal in their fazenda residences. Most of the activity of the main house occurred in the back rooms around the páteo, and unexpected guests had to wait in the front rooms before presentation to the master or his family, now properly attired. A foreign lady who accompanied her husband to Vassouras, where he installed telephones on plantations, was shocked by the untidiness of fazenda matrons. "Ah, my esteemed ladies," Carmela Seoane bewailed in *O Vassourense*, "women in general and wives in

---

[61] Inventory, 1840, Luis Barbosa dos Santos, executrix: Anna Isabel de Assumpção, Fazenda unknown, CPOV; *O Município*, August 11, 1878.

particular do not realize the danger of this fatal moving about in the privacy of the home in any garment chosen at random." [62] On special occasions, such as baptisms, marriages, and church festivals, matrons and their daughters cut and stitched weeks in advance; slave seamstresses and unmarried female relatives of the planter worked too, and where needed they called upon the large number of free and slave seamstresses throughout the município.[63] Vassouras' sudden opulence in the fifties brought French modistes and their seamstresses to the town; toward the end of the century, the influence of Rio de Janeiro's French fashion shops became paramount among well-to-do plantation ladies and many preferred to visit the capital for styles and materials and, where they could afford the prices, to order the garments made there.

(5)

Hygiene and the diagnosis and treatment of disease in the município of Vassouras were of a piece with diet and dress. Exceedingly simple in a period when medicine as an inductive science was gaining recognition, general hygienic practice consisted in continuing what appeared to work and in taking tardy action only in dire necessity. A religious resignation still colored planter reaction to disease, its causes, and consequences.

Slaves were worked hard and they were not expected to last indefinitely. Proof of this was visible on all sides. At the height of Vassouras prosperity a planter sized up the situation when he wrote that "it is widely demonstrated that the average working life of a slave used in coffee cultivation is fifteen years." [64] And in view of the conditions under which slaves lived, such a statement is understandable. With respect to slave quarters, planters were said to be "unbelievably lax . . . most of their housing presents an extraordinary amount of filth

[62] August 20, 1882.

[63] The contents of the busy sewing room of a wealthy plantation in 1886 included: "one sofa, 2 rocking chairs, 8 chairs, one straw-covered stool, one wooden bench, one commode, kerosene lamps, candlestick holders, an 'American' clock." Inventory, 1886, deceased: Maria Francisca das Chagas Werneck, executor: Luis dos Santos Werneck, Fazenda São Francisco, CPOV.

[64] Siqueira, *Memória Histórica*, p. 7.

. . ." [65] Working conditions were poor and the Negro, "born to toil and forced to keep at it because of his status in society, is brought into contact with deadly conditions caused by climate." [66] He had to keep working without changing his wet clothes, and "almost always poorly dressed, he cannot fail to feel . . . the influence of frequent and rapid atmospheric variations" as humid cold weather followed heat. [67] "The Negro's food is often insufficient for the needs of his stomach. His food is rough and overworks that organ. . ." [68] In the province of Rio, "ruthless" planters fed their slaves deteriorated foodstuffs—"jerked beef . . . salt and dried fish, the basis of alimentation for slaves and poor folk, frequently eaten in putrefying condition." [69] To the minds of planters the presence of large numbers of slaves on each plantation brought more than the fear of insurrection. "Recommended and Approved," ran a Câmara resolution of 1855, "that fazendeiros carry out certain hygienic measures indispensable to the present condition of our fazendas, where as a rule slave food is bad, and the senzallas, where many people accumulate in one place, are filthy. We must try every means of spreading among them not only hygienic practices, but also the best ways to treat their physical ills. If, unfortunately, we shall have to fight an epidemic, obviously planters will be the most endangered." [70] In the absence of latrines "slaves or laborers strew human excrement everywhere," [71] coffee hulls and other substances littered brooks and streams where slaves and others drank. [72]

[65] C. A. Taunay, *Manual*, p. 21.

[66] Imbert, *Manual*, p. xx.

[67] Imbert, *Manual*, p. xx; and "Mappa Synóptico do Estado Sanitário da Província do Rio," *Relatório, May 3, 1852.*

[68] Imbert, *Manual*, p. xx.

[69] "Mappa Synóptico." Inadequate nutrition, improper clothing, and variable atmospheric conditions were reported as principal causes of disease in two municípios neighboring to Vassouras, Parahyba do Sul and Pirahy, in 1851–52. In one case the phrase "almost nudity of some slaves" was employed. Wrote a Vassouras planter in 1855: "Better clothing, better housing, better food, care during illness . . . would be enough to save many lives that are today sacrificed through laxness and carelessness." L. P. de Lacerda Werneck, *Ideas sobre Colonização*, p. 29.

[70] APV, 1855.

[71] E. Guignet, *O Município*, August 12, 1877.

[72] Presidente da Província do Rio to CMV, February 23, 1870. APV, 1870. Also, "Mappa Synoptico." Inevitably an epidemic of frightening proportion

Under such hygienic conditions, under-fed and ill-clothed slaves subject to "almost unbroken toil" fared worse than their masters. To judge by a sampling of statistics computed from plantation inventories, many plantations resembled aggregations of the sick and lame rather than agricultural establishments producing a lucrative cash crop. On the Fazenda da Conceição in 1835, for example, 26 of a slave population of 134, 19 per cent, were defective or sick, and in a sixteen-month period (1835–1837) 16 per cent died. No different were conditions on the Fazenda Pau Grande in 1848, where 31, 12 per cent of the total working force of 261 slaves, were described as "sick," "very sick," or suffering from "hernia," "chronic wounds," or "twisted legs." The proprietors of the Fazenda São Fernando could not count on fully 20 per cent of their 100 slaves in 1855; the following year on the Fazenda do Triompho, of the 64 slaves resident, 25 per cent reported "hernia," "sick in the chest," "blind," "sick intestines," "sick eyes." [73]

Sick slaves often received medical treatment from masters

spread throughout the município. A doctor, ordered by the provincial government to ascertain the causes of what appeared to be yellow fever, arrived at the town center in 1882 and found the streams traversing the town "used to be and still are the dumping place for all debris, fecal material, and filth of the area. There the material remains for a long time in view of the fact that the small volume of water cannot carry away the large quantity of material discarded there." Certain houses, he noted, held "aggregations of persons with complete lack of the simplest precepts of hygiene." As for the town's only cemetery run by the Brotherhood of the Conception and "filled with a chapel, funerary monuments, large catacombs, and perpetual tombs," he observed that in an area of forty-two by ninety-two meters, over 6,000 bodies had been interred during the previous thirty years. Residents told him that when graves were dug, gravediggers found "partly decayed bodies still exhaling a nauseating odor." Dr. J. M. Teixeira, *O Vassourense*, March 19, 1882.

[73] Inventory, 1835, deceased: Manoel Ferreira da Silva, executrix: Escolástica Cándida Ferreira da Silva, Fazenda da Conceição, CPOV; Inventory, 1848, deceased: Anna Angélica d'Avellar, executor: Barão de Capivary, Fazenda Pau Grande, CPOV; Inventory, 1855, deceased: Jesuina Polucena d'Oliveira Serra, executor: João Arsenio Moreira Serra, Fazenda São Fernando, CPOV; Inventory, 1856, deceased: Joaquim Francisco Moreira, executrix: Maria Magdalena de Castro Moreira, Fazenda do Triompho, CPOV; Inventory, 1875, deceased: João Barbosa dos Santos Werneck, executrix: Zeferina Adelaide das Chagas Werneck, Fazenda São Luis de Ubá, CPOV; Inventory, 1880, deceased: Luisa Francisca Xavier de Azevedo, executor; José Soares de Azevedo, Fazenda da Covanca, CPOV.

who did not properly understand the treatment.[74] Some masters failed to heed early symptoms of disease. "Many slaves have died victims of the cruel abandonment of planters who dismissed their ailments as feigned," penned Caetano da Fonseca in 1863. "Fazendeiros cannot be persuaded a slave is ill until the pulse is hard and the head feverish. These are the only symptoms many fazendeiros will accept as proof that a slave is ill, for they distrust all other symptoms of serious illness which ignorance hinders them from recognizing." [75] If a slave's disease was recognized as incurable, he was frequently turned loose. In 1837, a Vassouras municipal inspector demanded that "for the good of the public health Ignacio and the Black, Francisco, slaves of João Leal, who are wandering about freely, infected with leprosy" be sent to the local pesthouse.[76]

Infants probably suffered most. In 1883, an observer claimed that infant mortality was high among ingénuos—free-born slaves raised on the coffee fazendas. The number of infants one month to two years old he considered large, with far fewer six- to ten-year-olds surviving.[77] Other facts bear out the high slave infant mortality. Between 1871–1888 there were registered in Vassouras 9,310 slave births; 3,074 of these died in the same period.[78]

Most common of the diseases found on fazendas was the pulex penetrans (*bicho do pé*). Once introduced into the fleshy and calloused portion of the foot it would eat toes and sole producing ulcers and incapacitating slaves from further work —exactly what many Negroes allowed to happen.[79] Colic,

[74] Imbert, *Manual*, p. xxi.

[75] Caetano da Fonseca, *Manual*, pp. 111–112.

[76] APV, 1837.

[77] Couty, *Biologie Industrielle*, p. 111. He estimated that, of 1,000 slave births, only 120 survived the early years. An English observer commented somewhat earlier: "Among the slave class it is stated to be an admitted fact that 50 per cent of the newborn children die before attaining the age of 8." *Report by Mr. Phipps on the Trade and Commercial Relations of Brazil and on Finance.* June 24, 1872. Gt. Britain. C 636. LIX (1872), 254.

[78] Mappa Estatística dos Filhos Livres de Mulher Escrava Matriculados na Collectoría de Vassouras. February 29, 1888. APV, 1888.

[79] C. A. Taunay, "Pequeno Tratado Alphabético das Principaes Doenças que Accommetem os Pretos," Appendix, *Manual*, p. 257. This common cause of

constipation, convulsions, and whooping cough were prevalent too, but nothing was as terrifying as "Erysipelas, an endemic disease very frequent in Brazil where it is generally poorly treated resulting in elephantiasis or leonine leprosy, a horrible disease attacking many people especially the colored." [80] It was reported for 1839 that in the município of Vassouras the most common disease was "leprosy mainly in two forms. The first form is elephantiasis called popularly erysipelas. . ." [81] Classifying illness seasonally, a provincial medical tabulation for 1851–52 listed in diagnostic terms of that period the respiratory infections of winter, pneumonia, bronchitis, whooping cough, as well as rheumatism, pleurisy, angina, apoplexy, and "spontaneous" tetanus; in summer it reported there were inflammation of the lower abdomen, "light" gastroenteritis, infrequent encephalitis, chronic inflammation of the liver, scorbutic and gangrenous ulcers, measles, chicken pox, and "intermittent" fevers. Also specified for the dry months: "diarrheas, dysenteries . . . syphilis." [82]

Antonio Lazzarini, Vassouras physician-planter, offered an explanation for ever-recurring reports of intestinal disorders. "How many times on our fazendas where the culinary arts are unknown or are a rule-of-the-thumb empiricism," he diagnosed, drawing on personal experience, "how many times must there have been serious epidemics of trychinosis passing among residents as plague, the name given to all zoothic diseases hereabout? How many cases of typhoid epidemics were due to trychinosis. . .?" [83] Tracing the origins of Brazilian digestive derangements common during his tour, Guignet stormed at the "inferiority of gardens" which he compared to the "general state of Brazilian cuisine" and at the "poor Portuguese cooking traditions." In the capital as in the interior he discovered "the most absurd notions shared by well educated people." "Cooked

decreased productivity appeared in slave evaluations as "a defective foot" or "chronic sore."

[80] C. A. Taunay, *Manual*, p. 261.

[81] José André Leopoldo to CMV, December 12, 1839. APV, 1839.

[82] "Mappa Synóptico." Couty claimed most common fazenda illnesses were: pneumonia, rheumatism, malaria, diarrhea, pernicious anemia. *Biologie Industrielle*, p. 106.

[83] A. Lazzarini, *O Município*, September 28, 1873.

greens, salads, squash are believed to produce stomach ailments for which pimentos are surely the remedies. People are confident that cabbage leaves lightly cooked in hot grease, are digestible. . . ." He concluded his analysis: ". . . it is easy to show that the majority of the common claims of dyspepsia must be attributed to abuse of pimentos, vinegar and poorly prepared dishes. . ." [84]

Finally, tuberculosis took a toll of human lives from both masters and slaves. It was accepted as one of the concomitants of civilization. From planter family to planter family gossip would report that "so-and-so died phthisiky." "Cases of pulmonary tuberculosis, a disease that spreads in direct proportion with civilization, have developed on a rising scale," commented a report of 1862 on local health conditions.[85] Slaves appeared to be ready targets of respiratory infections where dehulling and winnowing of coffee by hand on sunbeaten terreiros with strainers and mortar-and-pestle raised a fine dust "prejudicial to the slaves' health" in general and, in particular, to lungs, skin, and eyes.[86]

When illness struck on isolated fazendas, free and slave in the first half of the century fell back upon local resources. The planters made the decision to treat bad cases with home remedies or to seek advice from those persons, free or slave, who had earned a recognized reputation for working cures.[87] Imbert stated the situation well: "Without outside help . . . the fazendeiros have to help themselves and must practice

[84] *O Município*, August 19, 1877.

[85] Relatório to CMV, January 29, 1862. APV, 1863.

[86] "Relatório do Estado da Nossa Caza desde 6 de Dezembro de 1862 a 6 de Dezembro de 1863," in Inventory, 1862, deceased: Barão do Paty, executor: Francisco de Assis e Almeida, CPOV. Also, "Mappa Synóptico." A recent Brazilian article by Rogerio de Camargo on the *ingazeiro* tree states that "winnowing dust . . . brings so many ills to the health of the rural laborer," including pulmonary, skin, and eye troubles. *Sombreamento dos Cafezais pelo Ingazeiro*. São Paulo, 1948.

[87] In the possession of an elderly daughter of a former coffee planter remains the bill of sale which consummated the purchase of Torquato. This slave (who was addressed as "master") served as the fazenda doctor-nurse, advising his masters "You don't have to call a doctor" while offering his own remedies. He was a slave with the specialization of "barber." The bill of sale runs: "I, signed below, have sold to Snr. Joaquim José Borges de Carvalho, a slave named Torquato, Brazilian-born, a Barber, with all his vices and ills both old and new . . . for the price of Rs. 950$000. . ." Dated Rio de Janeiro, March 2, 1850.

medicine not only for the benefit of themselves and their families but also because they cannot fail to treat their Negroes, far more susceptible to contract the diseases that afflict the human species." [88] Where fazendeiros knew little home medicine, their wives and their slaves exchanged views or finally called in the *curandeiro*, a figure of long standing in African cultures.[89] Known among Vassouras slaves as *curandeiros*, *quimbandeiros*, and *cangiristas*,[90] and to Portuguese as *feiticeiros*, curandeiros employed a variety of remedies including herbs and other substances prescribed in accordance with set rituals. For tuberculosis, *herva de Santa María*, *herva de passarinho* (bird-pest), and *herva grossa* were pounded in mortar and pestle and drunk in infusion and poured into a bath; this prescription had to be drunk in the morning on an empty stomach. For dysentery, a tea made of *sete-sangría* and white *tapoeiraba* was poured into a bath of tepid water in which the patient remained until the water cooled. The tea could also be drunk. For bronchitis and whooping cough, a syrup of boiled, sweetened, and strained *cipó-chumbo* (lantana) was taken. Scurvy, skin and liver troubles were treated with water cress.

Many curandeiros specialized in the treatment of dog and snake bites, and the wide clientele of such practitioners brought the ire of Vassouras doctors in the last quarter of the century when one wrote that "many people dare to say that only curandeiros and household invocations can cure these afflictions." [91] In the parish of Sacra Família do Tinguá, the legend was told of a man who "while he lived, worked more miracles

[88] Imbert, *Manual*, pp. xiii–xiv.

[89] At the close of the eighteenth century, a Portuguese colonial administrador on a visit to Benguella, an area of Portuguese Angola whence came many of Vassouras' African slave laborers in the nineteenth century, singled out the "wise *Zambuladores* or diviners" consulted in times of stress. Joaquim José da Silva, "Extracto da Viagem, Que Fez ao Sertão de Benguella no Anno de 1775 por Ordem do Governador e Capitão-General do Reino de Angola, o Bacharel . . . Enviado a Aquelle Reino como Naturalista e Depois Secretario do Governo," *O Patriota* (February 1813), pp. 94–95.

[90] These terms are used today in Vassouras to describe a hiercarchy of counselors for physical as well as spiritual troubles, the most powerful being the quimbandeiro followed in descending order by the cangirista (said to be a worker of evil), the curandeiro, and the *benzedor* whose province appears to be wholly physical ills.

[91] Lucindo dos Passos Filho, *O Município*, July 22, 1877.

than the water of Lourdes has done since its discovery." As the
story ran, "His house was sought by those bitten by snakes or
rabid dogs." More than such ills, however, "This good man
cured successfully . . . incurable alcoholism and the most
ineradicable passion." In his house he attended to everyone
and dispensed "the remedies required to work these miracles."
Lest his readers misunderstand, the teller of the tale acknowledged in his closing lines that "This doctor, without a diploma,
escaped the law. He was a feiticeiro." [92]

Home cures evoked frequent attacks in mid-century medical
reports, which blamed mortality of slaves and free folk on
"Abuse, ignorance and audacity of charlatans and curandeiros
and the misunderstood tolerance of authorities who afford
them aid and recommendation." [93] Even the provincial
government warned against those who "sell or distribute secret
remedies"—an allusion, no doubt, to the curandeiros' prescrip-
tions.[94] This empirical approach to medicine produced a
"mania for prescribing." "Everyone thinks he has the right to
recommend this or that remedy, ignoring that the same
symptom may be due to different causes." [95] Techniques of
homeopathic medicine employed by both licensed practitioners
and "fazendeiros and thousands of others who are strangers to
the art of healing" proved popular and many planters kept
homeopathic kits and texts for the use of their families and
slaves.[96] Despite violent attacks by licensed doctors a majority
of Vassouras' population continued to consult the unlicensed
healers. In the countryside doctors were few and inaccessible,
even when a planter was willing to call one for his slave; and
often the treatment prescribed failed to prove more efficacious

[92] *A Província do Rio*, 1883, cited in Pinto, *Fastos Vassourenses*, pp. 236–237.

[93] "Mappa Synóptico."

[94] Aureliano de Souza e Oliveira Coutinho to CMV, September 12, 1840.
APV, 1840.

[95] *O Município*, July 22, 1877.

[96] "Mappa Synóptico." In 1849, Professor of Homeopathy João Fernandes
Gomes failed to obtain a license to practice in Vassouras. Homeopathic techniques
prevailed, however, and in 1883 one fazenda, for example, contained "one
homeopathic medicine chest and two volumes of homeopathic practice." APV,
1849; and Inventory, 1883, deceased: Deolina de Jesus da Conceição Ferreira,
executor: Antonio Francisco Ferreira, Fazenda do Sertão, CPOV.

than that of the local respected healer. Medical practice still retained vestiges of medieval therapy: Vassouras barbers in the fifties still supplemented haircutting with bloodletting and toothpulling. Francisco José Martins applied in one family 287 leeches on twenty-five separate occasions, performed two bloodlettings, gave four haircuts, and pulled teeth once—in a period from December 13, 1852 to September 15, 1854. A stickler for facts, he included a separate charge for thirty-two leeches only "rented." [97]

While the curandeiro continued to exercise authority throughout the century, the growing wealth of planters and increasing slave prices caused by the end of the slave trade in 1850 stimulated more opulent fazendeiros to better care of slaves and greater attention to their ailments. Urging upon planter friends greater solicitude for their slaves during pregnancy, "more zeal and care for the newborn and children," one local planter, educated in Paris and Rome, suggested in 1855 that thereby fazendeiros could "reconcile future interests of agriculture with Christian charity." [98] Often planters set up infirmaries containing from six to fifteen beds in charge of male nurses and more rarely, of a doctor. Male nurses found their way to up-country fazendas under a variety of conditions. For example, the provincial government circulated a notice for the apprehension of Third Class Surgeon Trigant de Geneste, wanted by the French Chargé d'Affaires in Rio for jumping his ship, the Frigate *Minerva*, on April 26, 1837. When last seen he was on a road leading through the município of Vassouras in the "company of another Frenchman, Jean Bart, a mechanic employed on the fazenda of Snr. Faro. . ." [99] Or there was the French *enfermeiro* (nurse) who committed suicide in 1850 on the plantation of his employer, Francisco Luis dos Santos Vernek, leaving his last will and testament and several manuscripts.[100] A fellow Frenchman described these assistants as

[97] Bill of Francisco José Martins to Estate of José María Frederico de Souza Pinto, March 27, 1856. APV, 1855.

[98] L. P. de Lacerda Werneck, *Ideas sobre Colonização*, p. 29.

[99] Provincial Government to CMV, May 8, 1837. APV, 1837.

[100] APV, 1850; Inventory, 1856, deceased: Ambrozio de Souza Coutinho, executor: Ambrozio de Souza Coutinho, Fazenda da Estiva, CPOV.

usually former students of pharmacy who had at their disposal medicine chests containing quinine, ipecacuanha, opium, and sodium sulfate sold by local pharmacies.[101]

To aid both nurses and planters there were publications on the "art of curing and of hygiene" of the genre of *Langgard's Works* recommended in Lacerda Werneck's popular planter manual. Langgard's *Dictionary of Domestic and Popular Medicine* ("2,198 pages, elegantly printed") contained "a complete therapy, or exact description of all internal diseases and their treatment; surgery or treatment for external diseases, and detailed instruction for different operations which may suddenly be required; practical advice for pregnant women . . . care of the newborn, principal troubles of infancy." No less comprehensive was his *New Medical and Pharmaceutical Formulary or Medical Vade-Mecum* (1,222 pages) offering "a description of medicines, their preparation and effects, the illness for which they may be prescribed, method and dosage" as well as the "choice of over 2,000 selected formulas of famous authors and practitioners, ancient and modern, and indigenous medicinal plants known to date." [102] Typical of patent medicines becoming the vogue by virtue of their potent qualities, the "Leroy Remedy"—a French concoction—passed as a "violent vomitive-purgative, composed of drastic substances whose action must necessarily produce an irritation more or less noticeable." In rural areas it was handled as a panacea especially efficacious in dropsy and lung inflammations, dysentery or diarrhea. "If an unfortunate Negro suffers from a dysentery or diarrhea which makes him discharge the bowels twenty or thirty times daily, the sooner Leroy is used the better." [103]

Brazilians, however, were not to be outdone by foreign imports and soon they were credited with utilization of indigenous flora. Dr. Francisco Portella devoted articles to the analysis of *urucum* whose seeds were widely used as a spice and substitute for tomato. As an expectorant it helped "bronchitis,

[101] Couty, *Biologie Industrielle*, p. 106; *O Município*, December 14, 1873.

[102] F. P. de Lacerda Werneck, *Memória*, pp. 29–30.

[103] Imbert, *Manual*, p. xvi.

asthma, and whooping cough"; its most important application at the time was in "internal treatment of smallpox." The practical doctor also admitted that it made a potent dyestuff for cotton goods.[104] Lucrative purveying of miracle-working medicines to isolated rural folk became a side line of traveling fortunetellers. According to an advertisement in the local newspaper, Mlle Rosina Ferière (whose "fame is world-wide") carried a vast repertoire with her. From nine in the morning to ten at night she told fortunes, spoke seven languages, and sold Chinese perfumes. "Essence of Malachite (Essence of the Mandarins)" gave teeth the gleam of polished marble, destroyed tartar, protected gums, and helped mastication. After one application, "nausea disappeared, stomachaches and toothaches departed forever." Indeed a few drops in a small amount of water and "loose teeth reset themselves." So potent was the medication, according to Mlle Ferière, "a few drops in the bath cleared the skin of . . . eruptions . . . cured eruptive skin diseases such as . . . erysipelas, pustules and spots. . ." Five days of the wonder-working drops were guaranteed to cure "syphilis, dropsy, dyspepsia . . . all the sufferings, in a word, that come from impurities of the blood . . . changes of season and climate, and whatsoever imprudences of daily habits." [105]

Those more opulent planters who were aware of the changes in the European world availed themselves of the services of foreign-born and trained doctors who turned up in Brazil after the mid-century mark. Asked for his Brazilian diploma to practice on a Vassouras fazenda, Portuguese Dr. Joaquim Teixeira de Castro claimed he had graduated from the medical-surgical school of Porto and on arrival in Brazil did not take the examination of the Rio de Janeiro Medical School because "immediately after debarking I became the private and exclusive doctor of the fazendas of the Barão do Paty do Alferes where I did not treat outside cases." [106] Later it became customary for doctors to maintain offices in the town of

[104] *O Município*, December 9, 1877.
[105] *O Município*, January 20, 1878.
[106] Joaquim Teixeira de Castro to CMV, March 11, 1853. APV, 1853.

Vassouras. Dr. Lucindo Filho, a doctor in the town, advertised that he was a "specialist in births, women's diseases, heart and nervous disorders. Answers all calls in writing at any hour of the day or night in the town or outside." [107] Other doctors located themselves on plantations in key agricultural areas of the município and treated patients on neighboring plantations. Dr. João Barbosa dos Santos advertised: "General practitioner and surgeon. Residence on the Fazenda do Socego in Massambará." [108] When planter families felt that they had exhausted the services of local practitioners, they attempted to obtain advice of doctors in the capital at Rio de Janeiro by forwarding their commissários a description of their ills and requesting them to present them to doctors there. Ortigão & Cia, coffee factors, told the widow of Felix do Nascimento Costa that a Rio doctor refused to diagnose without a personal examination and would the widow kindly take the train to the capital?[109] After the coming of the railroad a very opulent planter in extreme necessity might call a doctor from Rio.

Opened in 1854 to free and slave alike, the Charity Hospital of Vassouras (*Santa Casa de Misericordia*) offered the sick a final recourse if fazenda remedies, nurses, the curandeiro, and patent medicines had brought no alleviation. Actually, the Santa Casa treated only the poor and the slaves, "those forsaken by fortune." Despite the attendance at the Santa Casa of local physicians whose number grew after 1850, fear of the institution often prevented the arrival of the sick until they were too ill for improvement. However, certain facts seemed to bear out the fear; over a twenty-eight-year period, roughly one out of seven patients to enter its doors died.[110] Lamented an attendant physician: "Dread of going to the hospital is unbelievably strong among those who need it most. There are those who still maintain in this day and age that the hospital shatters family ties, that it teaches children not to help and

[107] *O Vassourense*, February 26, 1882.
[108] *O Vassourense*, May 14, 1882.
[109] APV, 1882.
[110] *O Vassourense*, July 9, 1882.

maintain their sick and aged parents." [111] To the Santa Casa
went planters' slaves. "For 18 days of treatment in this Hospital
given the Blackwoman Eva and her minor son, Manoel,
belonging to the estate of Bernardino Días Coelho," ran a bill
sent for collection. Or the estate of another fazendeiro paid for
"41 days of board given the Black Antonio Mossambique." [112]
Dread of entering the Charity Hospital was part of the general
incomprehension of medical science's inroads upon traditional
practices. Thirty years after Vassouras received a vaccinator
paid by the provincial government, a provincial report on the
difficulties of disseminating the system of vaccination stated
that "People will not remember what happened during
previous epidemics, either the lugubrious picture of irreparable
personal losses, or the eloquence of statistics which show that
vaccinated persons escaped. Nothing has dissipated popular
prejudices." [113] Behind the persistence of rooted attitudes
toward the incomprehensible lay faith in supernatural intervention and resignation toward the ills of this world.

[111] *O Municipio*, July 5, 1877.
[112] Santa Casa de Misericordia to Consular Agent of Portugal, October 26,
1875. APV, 1875; Inventory, 1867, deceased: Francisco Correa e Castro, executrix: Laurinda Vieira Correa e Castro, Fazenda São Paschoal. CPOV.
[113] *Relatório do Vice Presidente da Província do Rio, October 4, 1866*, p. 20.

CHAPTER VIII

Religion and Festivities on the Plantation

Two strong currents of religious feeling affected the population of Vassouras plantations. Accepted as the official, state church, Roman Catholicism was the religion of the masters, of the freemen and—nominally—of Negro slaves. Yet African religious traditions formed a substratum of belief and practice among most slaves and many free folk. There were points where both conceptions of the universe reinforced each other. Where the conflict was sharp, however, African beliefs and practices tended to exist underground, or "in the woods." Both were powerful forces in the daily lives of free and slave; both colored the thoughts and actions of plantation society in Vassouras.

Influence of the Roman Catholic Church, paramount in the lives of the first residents, continued throughout the nineteenth century. When population had increased to sizable proportions at various points on the early roads of eighteenth-century Vassouras, parishes were created by the colonial government. For administrative purposes the município of Vassouras until the last years of the nineteenth century remained divided into three parishes. At the main parish churches (*matrizes*), registry of births, deaths, baptisms, and marriages were recorded. On special occasions, such as occurred when the emperor visited the town center in 1848, the Matriz of Our Lady of the Conception (Vassouras' parish church) was the showplace of the young town center. The local charity hospital was created under the aegis of the faith. Not only was baptism in the font of the Matriz a highly valued event, burial in the beaten earth floor of the Matriz was equally esteemed as late as 1846.[1] Every large plantation had an oratory usually just off the main

---

[1] Relatório of Fiscal Joaquim José da Silva to CMA, May 24, 1846. His report remarked that the floor was "dotted with recently occupied graves." APV, 1846.

entrance or salon, or occasionally a chapel was housed separately; small proprietors had portable altars containing the patron saint of the master generally kept in the master's bedroom. Tiny chapels were built along the main roads; here could often be found beautifully hand-carved wooden images of the saints surrounded by vases of flowers and new or half-burnt candles.

The presence of the religious world was always close; the first words of surprise or fear that rose to the lips of fazendeiros' wives and daughters were "Our Lady" or "Our Most Saintly Mother." Children, slave or free, encountering the aged or even their older relatives on the road or in the house, immediately asked for a blessing to which there came invariably a "God bless you." And in the few local schools, private or public, it was prescribed by law that children be taught "the Christian principles and Moral, and the Doctrine of the Roman Apostolic Religion according to their ability to understand" [2]—usually in the form of the cathechism. Recognition of man's humble position in the eyes of an all-powerful deity was perhaps nowhere more succinctly expressed than in the opening lines of a typical will: "In good health and standing upright and in my right mind and judgment, I, Pedro Correa e Castro, fearing death which unfortunately will be sure, make my testament in the following manner. First I commend my soul to God, All-Powerful Father, who created it. I beg and beseech Him by the merits of the Holy Death and Passion of His Son, Jesus Christ, and Our Lord, to accept it in the eternal Heaven when He will decide to remove it from this world. I am a Roman Catholic and was baptised in the parish of. . . As soon as I die . . . my executor will order from the day of my death to the seventh day thereafter ten high requiem masses at the customary price and two masses for the souls of my parents, another mass for the souls of my Sisters and Brothers and ten masses for the souls of my captives. . ." [3]

Into this religious ambient came thousands of African slaves,

[2] Decree creating primary schools, October 29, 1827. APV, 1827.

[3] Inventory, 1874, deceased: Barão do Tingúa, executor: Antonio Agrícola de Pontes, Fazenda do Tingúa, CPOV.

most of them between 1830 and 1850. Unlike the case of the Negro slaves shipped to northeastern Brazil, they came from diverse African localities as far apart as Angola on the west coast and Moçambique on the east. On arrival at Rio or along the provincial coast they were broken into mixed lots of men, women, and children and shipped to the rural interior where they ended up on isolated plantations and went to work. In fact, planters were urged to avoid purchasing large numbers of slaves at one time, rather to add to a good slave core slowly.[4] Under such circumstances African patterns of family life and religious practices were strained badly. Some may have been summarily baptized soon after arrival; most merely received names chosen by their new masters. Prevented by language and status from rapid integration into the whole cultural pattern of their Portuguese-speaking masters, these African "immigrants" moreover had little contact with the Roman Catholic catechism. A very few fazendeiros had resident chaplains; priests came infrequently and their contact with slaves was limited. When a priest came to officiate, wrote an observer, he arrived on Saturday night. With members of the master's family in the chapel, women grouped separately behind a half-partition or *tribuna*, and slaves further back in the big house, the priest "prayed while the Negroes sang. On the following day came the great ceremony, the mystery of the host. On their knees slaves sang as on the day before. The masters were present with their families at the symbolic sacrifice; sometimes a religious sermon closed the divine service."[5] Information gathered from ex-slaves fits into the pattern of infrequent religious services. Said one slave: "Priests came only when they were called." Or, as another remarked: "Padre came once in awhile." Wives of former planters corroborated this, one adding that on her fazenda there were two occasions when the local vicar was sure to come: on the day of the fazenda's patron saint, and for baptizing the fazenda's slaves. On the latter occasion, the planter informed the neighboring planters who promptly sent over their slave infants

[4] *Instrucções para a Commissão Permanente*, p. 10.
[5] Ribeyrolles, *Brasil Pitoresco*, II, 34.

for baptism, too. A nineteenth-century observer noted that "No one has seriously taken up the job of Catholicizing the Blacks." Further on he added that "sometimes . . . they are baptized. But most of the time they are born, live and die without having had any contact with the representatives of the Divinity." [6]

Transplanted to Brazil and functioning in the role of the occasional priest, there loomed the figure of the African "diviner" known to slaves and free folk who consulted him as quimbandeiro, cangirista, curandeiro, or benzedor.[7] As a source of counsel to slaves, a potential focal point of resistance to the slave system imposed by the master, and a mortal through whom contact was made with supernatural beings to influence human activities, the quimbandeiro had to exist *sub rosa*.[8] To Negroes he seems to have been readily identifiable, however. Among other practices, the quimbandeiro at each mealtime before touching any food set aside a spoonful for

[6] Couty, *L'Esclavage*, p. 76. This lack of contact between the slave and his senhor's faith did not differ from the situation in Africa during 1873, where it was commented that "In Portuguese East Africa where Jesuits and Dominicans have owned excellent properties and installed missions, where many friars sent from India have worked, with some slight difference the population has remained in the same pagan state in which Vasco da Gama found it." Similarly, in Angola and the Congo on the West African coast. Marquez de Sá da Bandeira, *O Trabalho Rural Africano e a Administração Colonial*, p. 129. Alleged lack of success or apparent inertia of these orders in catechising Africans may have reflected the tenacity of African religious beliefs where in 1785 the Angola *zambulador* was "one of the most important personages in society and nothing is done without his counsel. . ." Joaquim José da Silva, "Extracto da Viagem," pp. 94–95.

[7] Reconstruction of the spiritual world of the African or Brazilian-born Negro slave (*crioulo*) of the nineteenth century is difficult because African religious survivals in the Vassouras area, weakened by the heterogeneous origin of Africans introduced there, have interacted with Catholicism and other religious elements for more than a century. Spiritualist terms and interpretations—particularly those of Allan Kardec—have been widely spread. Nevertheless, frequent references to quimbandeiros and their obvious focal role in the life of the slaves of the area make imperative discussion of this figure who continues in only slightly modified form as counselor and medical consultant in the município of Vassouras.

[8] Once recognized by the master of a plantation, slave "diviners" were removed. "I decided to remove from among our slaves the mulatto slave Ciro, in view of his bad character and the consummate skill that he has always shown in the science of divination, in which he was held and proclaimed as a renowned pontifex." Baroneza do Paty "Relatório do Estado da Nossa Casa desde 6 de Dezembro de 1862 a 6 de Dezembro de 1863," in Inventory, 1862, CPOV.

spiritual helpers. If any food dropped from his mouth or spoon in eating it was never touched by the quimbandeiro for it was a sign that the "spiritual guides" were hungry too. The quimbandeiro enjoyed great powers of invisibility. As a slave he had to appear at daily "forma" or line-up; yet he was described as capable of appearing with fellow slaves when in fact, informants were certain, he was miles away giving advice. Meetings could be arranged for a group to meet in the woods with the quimbandeiro on saints' days or rest days. Nocturnal meetings were also held in slave senzallas where "not even the nearby Portuguese feitor could hear" because of the "powers of the quimbandeiro." People clapped hands and sang as the quimbandeiro "worked" with certain "saints" to solve problems, physical or mental. Chief among slaves' problems were how to "break the master's sternness" or how to "prevent a beating ordered by the master"—aspects of the system of supervision and polícia dominating their existence. In return for counsel, visitors brought food or cash; even planters were said to be not above consulting a quimbandeiro directly or indirectly when affairs of the heart were involved. But when fearful of the possibility of organized insurrection, planters joined by local police quickly swooped down upon any noticeably large slave gatherings. "Slaves from several fazendas massed in nocturnal meetings known as *Cangerês*," explained a provincial report on activities in Valença across the Parahyba River from Vassouras. "There they celebrated mysterious ceremonies which everywhere the sons of Africa believe, in their crude superstition, can cure certain diseases, prevent corporal punishment and bring money." When calmer planters sized up the situation they realized the "true purpose of the meetings," and more "discipline" and "vigilance" were recommended.[9] Even after abolition came to Vassouras, however, municipal regulations tried to prevent meetings of "sectaries of fetichism in private homes."[10]

Forms of African religious expression only superficially

---

[9] Incident reported in the Parish of Santo Antonio do Rio Bonito, November, 1861, *Relatório do Presidente da Província do Rio, May 4, 1862*, p. 7.
[10] *Codigo de Posturas da PMV, 1890*. APV, 1890.

changed by contact with the Catholic faith were countenanced where no insurrection was scented. The daughter of Brazil's pioneer nineteenth-century entrepreneur, Barão de Mauá, married a New Englander named Hayes; on their plantation, located in the Province of Rio, the slaves "organized a church of their own, and have chosen a priest from their own number." The priest was an aged Negro and "his change from a secular to a clerical costume was made by simply wearing his shirt outside his trousers." Services opened with a "general shout, and then a long, silent prostration of all hands upon the floor." At a signal from the "priest," a hundred Negroes arose and "commenced a chattering song, which must have been first sung in their native wilds." African elements of possession appeared in profusion as the Negro slaves "squatting upon their haunches, which favorite position they have assumed as an innovation upon kneeling, clapped their hands, wagged their heads and rolled their eyeballs to this savage melody." Apparently the words were "African" and the Catholic element was the chorus of "Santa Maria, ora pro nobis." The "priest" had no trouble in directing the meeting at whose conclusion he "crossed himself in every direction, then threw himself down and rose again." Songs accompanied the ceremony and in the absence of the powerful influence of the African drum, the "congregation, standing, beat time both with hands and feet, like David 'praising God in the dance.' " The young Negro women were described as "turbaned" with elaborate African arrangements of hair "à la Mozambique" or in "waterfalls." [11]

African and Brazilian Catholic beliefs found a common meeting ground in the intimate, personal attitude toward saints. Both Africans and Brazilians trusted in an Omnipotent Being ruling the universe; but it was through earthly yet holy representatives of this Being that humans communicated hopes and aspirations. Fazendas were named after the patron saint of the founder, and large or small, every fazenda respected its religious sanctuary, its capella, kept scrupulously clean with walls frequently painted an egg-shell blue and with white lace and colorful flowers adorning the altar. And atop the altar, a

[11] John Codman, *Ten Months in Brazil* (Boston, 1867), pp. 90–92.

hand-carved saint's figure flanked below by smaller carved figures and French or Italian religious engravings. In hours of need and comfort here was the material representative of the Omnipotent Being, a figure whose appurtenances and shelter were kept spotless and bright. The material and personal approach appeared in the promises made to saints in return for favors to be granted; such promises were scrupulously observed. For, as one aged planter's wife phrased her religious sentiment: "No one can afford to joke with a saint." Saints were woven into the fabric of conscious living and, when they did not accompany residents, they were acutely missed. A planter moved wife and family from one fazenda to another more distant one, and he packed only the figure of Our Lord Crucified on the Cross, leaving in the abandoned chapel figures of Our Lady of Pain, Our Lady of the Passos ("She is said to suffer a lot, they say"), Saint Sebastian, and the Child Jesus. To the end of her life, the planter's wife worried about the statue of the Child Jesus, constantly declaring, "I don't want to die without my saint."

Syncretism of African and Catholic religious belief through the concept of a here-and-now deity was documented by those who arrived in Brazil from Europe. Taunay emphasized that certain Catholic elements could be used in catechizing the Africans. "Belief in one God and in his Saints, among the latter several of their own color," he wrote in 1839, "saints which do not disdain the lowly slave, maintain happiness and hope in the hearts of Blackmen." A traveler well-acquainted with the culture area from which Africans were torn and transported to Brazil, Richard Burton was struck in the Province of Rio and elsewhere in Brazil by the use of "Our Lady of the Rosary, an invocation much affected . . . by slaves and Negroes." Remembering his African experience, he noted that the rosary beads "seem to awaken the Negro's sense of home," and explained that Popó beads "comprise his finest finery and his riches." [12] Slaves kept, in their senzallas, figures of Saint George, Saint Benedict with black face and hands, Saint Sebastian, Saint Cosme, and Saint Damian ("these are Africans from the

[12] *Explorations*, I, 83, and note.

African coast, White children of Black parents"). "Most preferred" was Saint Anthony, described as "always on the table of the quimbandeiros." Saint Anthony frequently held in his left arm a small Black child who sat upon a peg or nail from which he could be easily removed. The child played an important role for if a slave wished to obtain a request, he removed the child while promising to return it only after the request was performed. No one could see the act of seizing and hiding the child, lest the wish not be granted.

On the knee of an aged slave, "Father" João or "Aunt" María,[13] children, free and slave, were introduced to another element of the supernatural world, *Sacy*, highly reminiscent of the west African *Legba* or trickster who has often been mistaken for the African counterpart of the Devil. Sacy or Sacy Pererê, as he was frequently called, loved to play pranks, mischievous in intent, sometimes unpleasant in outcome. No one accurately described his appearance although his general outlines everyone knew. He was said to be a short Negro, one-legged, always smoking a pipe as did most Negro slave men and women; one usually found him sitting on the swinging door of a gate in the field. Sacy intrigued the Portuguese schoolmaster who resided in Vassouras and reported that "Those very respected authorities in all such ponderations, our Old Women, blame Sacy's influence for most of the annoyances that hinder our lives and which the usual causes cannot explain." A fazenda dog was found inexplicably dead out on the terreiro—a sure sign of Sacy. Or the lamp went out unexpectedly—the work of Sacy. Suppose a young girl awoke with a headache and "regretted" she could not go to school; one could be sure Sacy had been around. If the cook's special dish, placed on the sideboard to cool, disappeared, or the family spendthrift asked for a loan when money was short—blame it all and more upon Sacy's deviltry. Those who crossed Sacy's path (or was it the other way?) said they often saw him in the guise of a "little Negro wearing a red hat, making faces at travelers or sitting astraddle an old gate, or atop the fazenda water-wheel when it stopped

[13] In Brazilian folklore these wise Negroes, found on "all" fazendas, were addressed as Pai (father) João and Tía (aunt) María.

turning." If a muledriver made camp in the midst of an open field fine for grazing his animals, and the following morning discovered his pack mules worn with hunger and fatigue, he would say without a moment's hesitation, "Sacy spent the night riding my animals to exhaustion." [14] Or a composer of jongos, exceedingly proud of his ability, might encounter Sacy in the early evening; engaging in a song-bout (*desafio*) with Sacy, the jongueiro would walk on forgetting where he was or what he was about. With the facility and simplicity so much a part of the storyteller in a society of oral tradition, the African "aunt" or "father" spun tales of Sacy the Trickster.

(2)

Lay in theme, yet built around African religious elements of drum, soloist, responding chorus, and dancers, the *caxambú* occupied an intermediate position between religious ceremony and secular diversion. Saturday nights and invariably saints' days—slaves called them "festival days" (*dias de pagode*)—were the occasion for requesting fazendeiros' consent for caxambú. At an early date, planters feared caxambú probably as a convenient meeting place for many slaves under the direction of older, hence more astute and respected, slaves. In municipal regulations, first of 1831 and later in 1838,[15] planters attempted to restrict such occasions, which they grouped under the heading of "dances and candomby," to slaves belonging to one fazenda lest the meeting afford opportunity to "organize occult societies, apparently religious, but always dangerous, by the ease with which some clever Negro may use them for sinister ends." Yet planters also realized that slaves needed diversion, that "it is barbarous and unreasonable to deprive the man who toils from morning to night. . ." from amusing himself, and that "Africans in general deeply enjoy certain amusements." [16] Out of this complex of African religious drive, slave diversion,

---

[14] "Sacy," *O Vassourense*, December 7, 1882.

[15] Projecto de Posturas da CMV, 1831, Parte III, Título 3, Artigo 5. APV, 1831; Posturas da CMV, 1838, Parte III, Título 3, Artigo 8. APV, 1838.

[16] *Instrucções para a Commissão Permanente*, pp. 11–12.

and planter enlightened self-interest evolved the slave caxambú.[17]

Days before a caxambú was to be held with the permission of the master, word circulated among the fazenda slaves. The news spread among slaves of nearby plantations, through conversation in a roadside taberna or venda, when a slave visited another plantation on his master's business, or traveled subtly disguised in cryptic jongo verses sung by field gangs of neighboring plantations as they worked on coffee slopes. On such an occasion slaves did not wait for formal invitation. After the chores were completed, wood from a derrubada, piled on the drying terrace, was lit. A drum "couple" (*casal*), sometimes joined by a third drum or "caller" occupied one side of the fire; on the other side sat the old Negroes, generally Africans, whom one ex-slave called the *macota* ("people from Africa, wise persons"). To the large, deep-booming drum of the "couple" slaves gave the name *caxambú*; the companion drum, smaller and higher pitched (although one drummer said it "speaks louder than the larger drum") was called *candongueiro*.[18]

A warm-up period generally preceded the caxambú. Drummers tapped out rhythms or beats with the flat and heel of the palm, experimenting with companion drummers while jongueiros (versifiers) hummed to themselves and the drummers

[17] As late as 1890, caxambú (often termed *batuque*) was prohibited in town streets and in any house located within town limits. Elsewhere in the município, as is the case to this day, police permission had to be previously obtained. *Código de Posturas da PMV, 1890*, Título 5, Artigo 122. APV, 1890.

Tradition of the caxambú has survived in Vassouras although it is fast disappearing as former slaves become fewer. Jongos composed during the caxambú are still sung throughout the Parahyba Valley. For jongos still current in the municípios of Cunha and Taubaté, State of São Paulo, see Alceu Maynard Araujo, "Jongo," *Communicação a Commissão Nacional de Folclore do Instituto Brasileiro de Educação, Ciencia e Cultura*, May 24, 1948 (Document 22); Alceu Maynard Araujo and Manuel Antonio Franceschini, "Documentario Folklorico Paulista. I. Danças e Ritos Populares de Taubaté," *Publicações do Instituto de Administração*, XXXIII (July 1948), 26–29.

[18] Great care went into the manufacture of the two or three drums used. First a red-leafed *mulungú* tree was cut down and a section cut out. With an adze, the drum-maker hollowed out one end deep enough to hold castor oil which he then ignited. When fire had burned deep into the mulungú, it was extinguished and the inside scraped clean. Across the open end a piece of freshly dried and scraped cowhide was pulled taut and secured.

the verses they would try out. To assure an even, high reson-
ance, drummers hauled their instruments close to the fire
briefly where heat tautened the leather top. Supervising the
whole session, was the "king (rei) of caxambú" sometimes
joined by his "queen." On wrists and ankles king and queen
alone wore nguízu which produced an accompaniment to the
drumbeats when they danced. Participants walked first to greet
the king and kissed his hand. Then the king began the caxambú.
Dressed in what one ex-slave called a red flannel outfit and hat
bearing a cross, the king entered the dancing circle (roda) and,
approaching the drums reverently, knelt with bowed head and
greeted them. Arising, he sang the two lines of his jongo riddle,
the drummers swung into the batida, while assembled slaves
repeated the refrain, clapped hands, and entered the dancing
circle. Male slaves, dressed in white pants and possibly a striped
shirt, women in loosely-hanging blouses and full skirts, kerchiefs
on their heads, danced around each other without physical
contact. Dancers moved in a counter-clockwise circle. As they
tired, they danced toward members of their sex and invited
them to take their places by touching the palm. Even children
entered the circle to imitate the motions of their elders. With
the first riddle sung, and drumming and dancing under way,
the king withdrew into the background leaving the circle to
another jongueiro who would try to decipher the riddle with
two more lines and to introduce his rhymed riddle ("one line
weighed upon the other"). Yet if trouble sprang up between
contesting versifiers, the king returned immediately and silenced
the drums by placing his palms atop them. "He did not wish
to have any disturbance in the dancing circle," the son of a rei
de caxambú explained.[19]

[19] Details for the picture of the caxambú were gathered by oral interrogation
and observation of the infrequently held caxambús in the município of Vassouras.
   Two travelers have left tantalizingly brief records of Negro caxambú. Writing
in 1859, Ribeyrolles said that "On Saturday night after the last chore of the week
is completed, and on holy days which bring rest and relaxation, the slaves receive
one or two hours for dancing. They gather on the terreiro, call to each other, fall
into groups, arouse themselves and the fun begins." To the sound of the "Congo
drum," he saw the batuque and the lundú. Brasil Pitoresco, II, 37. Couty in 1883
referred to "those curious dances where the jongo, the caninha verde or other
special dances are jigged all night long by mulatto women very often attractively

The caxambú was a sanctioned opportunity to indulge in sly, deft, often cynical comment on the society of which slaves were so important a segment. The system of polícia and constant supervision tended to break spirit and will of the African immigrant and his children; the caxambú with its powerful rhythms, its almost complete lack of planter supervision, the use of African words to cover too obvious allusions, and occasional swigs of warm cachaça, gave slaves a chance to express their feelings towards their masters and overseers and to comment upon the foibles of their fellows. In this context, jongos were songs of protest, subdued but enduring. Jongo form —that of the riddle—lent itself well in phrasing the slaves' reactions, for, as with all riddles, the purpose was to conceal meaning with words, expressions, or situations of more than one possible interpretation. Words were often African, undoubtedly more so in the nineteenth century when Vassouras fazendas contained many Africans who spoke their own tongue to themselves and a "mixed up" (*atrapalhado*) Portuguese to their masters and overseers. Persons were replaced by trees, birds, and animals of the forest. There was a premium on terseness; the fewer the words, the more obscure the meaning, the better the jongo, one not readily deciphered by contesting jongueiros, or one which could be repeated to depict a multitude of situations. The few jongos presumed to date from slave days cannot be held up as a mirror of slave society, however. In the first place, they are too few; secondly, the incidents or situations that inspired them have ceased to exist. Those that have survived have done so by virtue of their intended vagueness. For their meanings, for the objects of their derision, there is only the explanation offered by the few surviving slaves who still sing them.

Each new jongueiro stepped close to the drums placing a hand on the large drum or caxambú to silence it temporarily,

dressed, at any rate always clean." *Biologie Industrielle*, p. 108. Describing festivities near the coffee-growing area around Cataguazes, Minas Geraes, in the early nineties, Julio Suckow wrote: ". . . on the terreiros, almost always near the former senzallas, the Blacks danced the jongo, beating the caxambús violently with their palms, composing desafíos, and tippling cachaça." "Uma Impressão Desoladora," *Gazeta de Notícias*, September 3, 1908.

and then began his verses. The drummer on the flatter sounding small drum, or candongueiro, experimented to catch the correct beat for the rhymed verses, and when he satisfied the jongueiro, the large booming caxambú was "called" to join. Blending words and drum accompaniment was explained as "The candongueiro sings first, to set the beat for the caxambú." Boastfully, the new jongueiro might open with

So large a terreiro	(Terreiro tamanho
Like a big city,	Cidade sem fim,
So many famous jongueiros	Tanto jongueiro de fama
Flee from me.	Corre de mim.)

He might allude to a planter family squabble over land near the Belém railroad station, between Joaquim de Souza Breves and his uncle.

Breve' fights Moraes every day	(Breve' com Moraes toda dia 'ta demandando
Every day he fights over land in Belém.	Todo dia 'tá demandando por causa de terra de Belém.
He says, The land is mine, I'll put a marker in the middle.	Terra sendo meu, boto divisa no meio.)

Before the dispute could be settled the land gave out along with its coffee trees. To which another jongueiro, aware of the situation, could answer

Monkey came and the coffee bushes died,	(Macaco veio, Macaco veio, cafesaes ja morreu,
What do we eat now?	Comê quê?)

The following jongo on the *embaúba* tree and the planter colonel typifies the double meaning aspect of jongos:

With so many trees in the forest	(Com tanto pau no mato
The embaúba is a colonel.	Embaúba é coronel.)

According to one ex-slave informant, the embaúba was a common tree, useless because it was punky inside. Many planters were known as colonels because they held this rank in the National Guard. By combining the two elements, embaúba and colonel, the slaves turned out the superficially innocuous but bitingly cynical comment.

Many a jongueiro substituted the monkey (*macaco*) for the Negro slave when describing repressive measures against slaves, as in

Monkey doesn't die by lead,	(Macaco não morre com o chumbo,
He dies in a loop when beaten.	Morre no laço de bater.)

According to the explanation of an aged ex-slave, the following jongos singled out a slave for informing to his master on his fellow slaves.

His tongue is loose,	(Tem lingua leco-leco, tem
His tongue is loose,	lingua leco-leco,
That little bird has a tongue.	Passarinho tem lingua.
Look at that Angola bird with a loose tongue.	Vaya passarinho d'Angola qu'êle tem lingua leco-leco.)

Relations between the sexes received attention from slave jongueiros. An ex-slave vouchsafed that Ramalhete and Jardim in the following refer to a man who leaves in the morning to work with his field gang whereupon another man enters his quarters and finds his wife there.

I don't understand why mama	(Eu não sei que tem mamae
Keeps playing tricks on papa.	Anda brincando com papae.
Ramalhete is in harness	Ramalhete 'tá na canga
Jardim is in the corral.	Jardim 'ta no curral.)

Here is a case, according to an aged jongueiro, of a slave woman who had sexual relations with her master. The sinhá D. María was the master's legal wife.

I'm in bad with sinhá D. Maria,	(Eu 'tou má com sinhá D. Maria,
But I get along with sinhó Breves.	Mais 'tou bem com o senhó Breves.)

The lines of the rebuttal were coldly practical in the analysis of the situation.

You may be in bad with D. Maria,	(Voce 'tá ma com a D. Maria,
But D. María has credit in the town store. Get along.	Mais D. María tem crédito na cidade. Arruma là.)

8

PART FOUR

DECLINE

CHAPTER IX

The Crumbling Economy

THE prosperous edifice erected by coffee planters in the years immediately preceding and following 1850 held within it elements of destruction. Forebodings of ruin appeared fitfully even during the prosperous years, as unsuccessful plantations were transferred to creditors and as loans taken to obtain slaves to produce more coffee could not be amortized. Later, coffee prices fluctuated, slaves were scarce and expensive, and virgin slopes slowly gave way to denuded hills covered with aging, overgrown coffee groves. Plantations in more fortunate circumstances maintained production by purchasing machinery to compensate for an aging and inefficient labor force. Yet those planters who remained debtors for slave purchases made during the prosperous years, and those who joined them in debt to purchase machinery, faced a worsening capital market in the late seventies and throughout the eighties. They could neither pay off accumulated debts nor obtain new loans from hardheaded, practical bankers. Despite extensive acreage most of the loans to plantations were based on the value of slave property; and the imminence of abolition—sudden or gradual, but in any case, inexorable—left planters with no worthwhile collateral.

(2)

Within two decades of the prosperous fifties, the seeds of decline sown by early coffee planters of Vassouras began to mature. Expanding coffee groves and good prices smoothed the temporary slumps of the sixties. In the seventies, however, the political, social, and economic structure that the older generation of fazendeiros had erected with their slaves began to crack; self-confidence faded and doubts of the future blossomed into enduring fears.

As the edifice trembled, the new generation of planters, sons of the pioneer fazendeiros, sought facile explanations for their predicament. Some blamed diminishing slave labor; others, failure to utilize fully modern coffee processing equipment; and still others, lack of cheap agricultural credit. Amid the welter of jeremiads, ranging from self-criticism to despair, only a few voices focused the attention of planters of Vassouras as well as of neighboring municípios, on the decaying state of land and coffee trees. "It is an immensely grave error to suppose that our inadequate production stems solely from lack of slave labor and credit," warned a planter from nearby Parahyba do Sul in 1878. "Only those who neither think nor study, only those who neither follow nor examine attentively and closely our system of mining the land without art or science, the course of our agriculture, meteorological revolutions and climatic changes which Brazil has suffered in the last quarter-century— only they can baldly espouse such a proposition." [1] Brushing aside the "thousand and one absurd comments" [2] proffered to explain worn-out soil, aging coffee trees, and declining or stationary coffee production, while coffee trees consumed more dwindling virgin forest reserves, Manoel Ribeiro do Val ended his address to fellow planters at the Agricultural Congress: "Only those who study, plant, yet fail to harvest during these past twenty-five years can imagine the negative effects of our system of planting."

Heedless of earlier warnings voiced against routinism (rotina) in agricultural methods, two generations of fazendeiros in Vassouras—fathers and sons—continued to direct slaves to cut down and burn virgin forest, plant carelessly young coffee bushes or improperly chosen seed, then hoe and harvest year after year as though they would always have "virgin soil,

[1] Congresso Agrícola, p. 163. Ten prominent planters represented Vassouras at this Congress assembled at the request of the Imperial Minister of Agriculture to "examine and discuss the diverse and most urgent problems that they believe concern agricultural improvements. . ." The Congress was limited to planters drawn from the grande lavoura (large plantations producing coffee or sugar for export) of four provinces: Rio de Janeiro, São Paulo, Minas Geraes, and Espirito Santo, the economic core of the Brazilian Empire in the latter half of the nineteenth century. Ibid., pp. 1, 26, 167.

[2] Luiz Correa de Azevedo, "Da Cultura do Café," p. 252.

producing in any spot abundant harvests of anything planted, and therefore not requiring any fertilizer." In 1855, Capanema foresaw: "In the uplands where the production of coffee is excellent in a few years the tired soil will have to be abandoned for more distant fertile zones." [3] Another indication of agricultural conditions appeared in 1863 when an observer reported that "harvests were becoming smaller through loss of soil fertility, planters redoubled the number of weedings and bought more slaves only to harvest little. . ." [4] Limited reserves of virgin forest demanded new techniques conflicting with those which had worked successfully thirty years previously. Elsewhere in the Parahyba Valley of 1863 there were municípios which had completely exhausted all virgin forest in the space of twenty-five years to plant ever-widening coffee groves.[5] Ten years later the theme of the age-old techniques based on the axe, fire, and the hoe wielded by forced labor was still attacked. One writer declaimed that "For 372 years a routine and wasteful system of agriculture which raises to the level of a system production based on the axe and billhook, clearing virgin forest and burning it, tears from fertile Brazilian soil the elements of greatness and prosperity of future generations." [6] Or as a local newspaper summarized, when fazendeiros instilled in their sons "interest and love for the agricultural life," they merely succeeded in passing on routine techniques inadequate in an area of diminishing forest reserves.[7]

Twenty-five years after the Baroneza do Paty wrote caustically of Vassouras planters' unprogressive methods, a planter of the município of Cantagallo, situated lower in the Parahyba Valley, dissected the current psychology with which sons were imbued. The coffee bush "is only something to make money, but not a crop affording occupation and happiness to those

[3] G. S. de Capanema, *Agricultura*, pp. 2, 4.
[4] Luiz Torquato Marques d'Oliveira, *Novo Méthodo da Plantação, Fecundidade, Durabilidade, Estrumação e Conservação do Café* (Rio de Janeiro, 1863), p. 6.
[5] Caetano da Fonseca, *Manual*, p. 13.
[6] Nicolau Joaquim Moreira, *Notícia sobre a Agricultura do Brasil* (Rio do Janeiro, 1873), p. 6.
[7] *O Município*, December 13, 1874.

who come after us." With little thought of the future or how to avoid disaster, they lived from "year to year at the will of nature." Concentrating solely on filling "vast storage bins" on their fazendas, planters as a rule turned a deaf ear to study or investigation of meteorological changes in the area; to those who interposed that modern discoveries of other lands might apply to coffee agriculture they answered with a shrug, "I have done things this way, let the next generation do as it pleases." [8] Conditions worsened in the eighties, abolition obliged former slaveholders to pay freedmen salaries, yet fazendeiros continued their long-castigated agricultural techniques based on the man with the hoe, believing that the "theory of extensive cultivation consists in tearing from the soil a unit of production at the very lowest possible cost." [9] Fifty years after the president of the Province of Rio had criticized routinism and its consequences, the governor of the State of Rio stated flatly that routinism in techniques was the product of an ignorance which could find no excuse in a "love of tradition and century-old empiricism." [10]

To the devastation wrought upon virgin slopes by axe, fire, and hoe, the saúva ant added its destructive work. Neither ditches, laboriously dug by a "half-dozen blacks to extinguish only one ant heap," nor water, nor the combination of heat and smoke blown by large and expensive bellows into sealed ant canals sufficed. [11] By mid-century Vassouras' Câmara had to report that "ants have progressed frightfully in this município . . . causing great harm to agriculture." [12] Inspired by a reward offered to anyone discovering a method to eliminate the saúva ant, several insecticides appeared on the market. The most widely used was compounded and sold under the brand name "Capanema." [13] Instead of allowing the mixture to saturate thoroughly the food-ball (*bolo*) at the center of the ant colony, most planters mixed Capanema with water, poured

[8] Correa de Azevedo, "Da Cultura do Café," pp. 242, 249, 251–252.

[9] *O Paiz*, March 23, 1893.

[10] Quintino Bocayuva, *Mensagem do Governador*, p. 76.

[11] C. A. Taunay, *Manual*, p. 105.

[12] APV, 1849.

[13] The provincial decree offering the reward was No. 980 of October 13, 1857. *Relatório do Presidente da Província do Rio, June 1, 1860*, p. 22.

it into the ant canals, then backed off and applied fire, thrilling at the series of apparently effective explosions that followed. How effective these measures proved can be judged by the descriptions of whole coffee groves covered with ant canals contained in inventories from 1870 onward. Damage caused by the saúva, added to the effect of unexpected plagues of grass-hoppers, bird-pest, butterfly-blight (White Coffee Leaf Miner), and unseasonably heavy torrential rains, prodded one suffering planter of 1876 to commiserate with his neighbors: "No one can imagine the enormously incalculable losses . . . that these add to our already overburdened coffee agriculture which must struggle against so many difficulties." [14]

With the ravages to the forest-covered slopes of Vassouras came erosion and climatic changes. Up and down the Parahyba Valley the tale was the same, as nature supplemented the destructive work of man. So bad was the situation at Entre-Rios on the Parahyba River near Vassouras, that Burton in 1867 claimed the surrounding area to be "cleaned out for coffee. . . The sluice-like rains following the annual fires have swept away the carboniferous humus from the cleared round hilltops into the narrow swampy bottoms. . . Every stream is a sewer of liquid manure, coursing to the Altantic, and the superficial soil is that of a brick-field." The blame for all this he laid to the large proprietor, to the techniques inherited from the Indian and "Inner Africa, and perpetuated by the slovenly methods of culture everywhere necessary where slave labour is em-ployed." [15] Confirming this opinion, twenty years later another observer bemoaned the loss of rich topsoil washed into narrow rock-lined streams; where terraces existed along river bottoms invariably the land was an unproductive clay. "All the humus is carried away by the currents and only clay, the heaviest element, is deposited forming a compact and worthless sediment." [16]

---

[14] *O Municipio*, November 26, 1876.

[15] Burton, *Explorations*, I, 42.

[16] F. Belisário, cited in A. d'E. Taunay, *História*, VII, 297. Delden Laerne observed that "On the whole . . . the amount of alluvial soil washed away is alarming, throughout the Rio Zone." *Brazil and Java*, p. 282.

The effects of mass destruction of forests soon became apparent, and as early as 1859 a provincial report commented on the "irregularity of the seasons" as a factor in the "decadence and weakening" of coffee trees compared with the development and production of earlier trees.[17] Fifteen years later a resident of Vassouras claimed that the "mass felling of trees on all the elevated points of the Province" explained the end of regular, periodic rainfall that hitherto had been observed.[18] At the Agricultural Congress it was reported that "in the good old days" abundant rains fell from the beginning of August to the end of May with only a fortnight of hot dry weather (*veranico*) during the whole period. The situation had changed completely. "Today we must endure an eight- to nine-month dry spell and only three to four months of rain." Meanwhile the veranico had become a "terror" to the fazendeiros who judged that the drought had "almost purposely come to parch the plant watered by the black sweat of slavery."[19] In 1887, fazendeiros of the region complained to Göldi that it rained less and far more irregularly than before. Doubting the actual diminution of rainfall, and lacking time and instruments to make his own observations since planters of the Valley had never kept continuous records, Göldi obtained reports on the meteorology of the city of Rio de Janeiro. His earlier doubts were justified: "With regard to quantity it does not rain less than heretofore. The total number of days of rainfall has shrunk; the relative quantity of rainfall during one day has increased; rainfall no longer follows the chronological rules that formerly obtained." He did not fail to discern the effect of increased rainfall on denuded coffee slopes where "torrential rains satisfied the vegetation only briefly" and instead of wetting the soil, water ran off quickly, stripping the thin layer of fertile earth from the hillsides.[20] "Each time it rains," wrote an observer in 1878, "a waterfall descends to the base of each row of coffee trees," aided in its descent by the parallel lines of trash

[17] *Relatório do Presidente da Província do Rio, August 1, 1859*, p. 23.

[18] *O Município*, January 18, 1874.

[19] *Congresso Agrícola*, pp. 163–164.

[20] Emilio A. Göldi, *Memória sobre Una Enfermedad del Cafeto en la Província de Rio de Janeiro, Brasil* (Mexico, 1894), pp. 92–93.

left by the slaves weeding between the coffee rows. "Just imagine what it must be like if the hill is steep and high and the soil sandy!" [21]

Although planters had always been aware of the relatively rapid aging of their coffee groves, the presence of unused virgin soil veiled the inevitable consequences of indiscriminate consumption of the forest and poor agricultural maintenance. First the upper slopes planted in coffee were denuded of fertility, as decayed vegetation "borne downward by torrential rains, fertilized the lower slopes." Then came a more serious development when lower slopes which formerly provided "abundant harvests" turned sterile.[22] Of Cantagallo in 1877— a município whose conditions were similar to those of Vassouras —a resident wrote that "age and decrepitude" of coffee groves menaced planters' fortunes. Most of the groves had so aged that the bushes produced "nothing or little." Although worried by the dispiriting appearance of "dried limbs extending over the hillsides," some planters were unwilling to blame anything but "the destiny of coffee plants, others pointed to the bad weather and others to coffee pests and drought." [23] Of Vassouras it was remarked in 1882 that "today the coffee bushes are extraordinarily deteriorated . . . formerly it was not surprising to find 1,000 coffee bushes producing 100, 200 and up to 300 arrobas of milled coffee . . . while today this proportion is reduced to 50 per 1,000." [24] Of the coffee zones of the Province of Rio almost ten years later a report spoke of the "slow falling off in productive capacity of our agricultural areas." [25]

In the last three decades of the nineteenth century, many planters cut back their gnarled and rachitic-looking coffee bushes to within a few inches of the ground to revive them.[26]

[21] Miguel Alamir Baglioni, *O Eresipho do Cafeeiro. Breve Estudo d'Esta Infecção Epiphytica* (Campos, 1878), p. 41.

[22] Caetano da Fonseca, *Manual*, p. vii.

[23] Correa de Azevedo, "Da Cultura do Café," pp. 227–229.

[24] *O Vassourense*, June 25, 1882.

[25] *Relatório do Presidente da Província do Rio, August 1886*, p. 10.

[26] The technic as practiced in the Rio area was described by Delden Laerne, *Brazil and Java*, p. 296. A large proportion of Vassouras planters thus pollarded their trees as revealed in inventories which enumerated groves of *café decotado*.

Most remained immobile, neglected "soldiers" rising and descending the slopes in columns as far as the eye could see, a testimony to the phrase "There are no lands that will satisfy the coffee planter." [27] Amid evaluators' comments such as "in bad condition," "in bad condition and old," or "without fruit," [28] inventories of the number of coffee trees on each fazenda showed graphically what was happening to the countryside. Few fazendas in the seventies and eighties were as badly off as one small fazenda whose coffee groves "no longer have any value in view of their condition." [29] More typical of the wasting away of large fazendas' coffee trees was the case of the "Guaribú" which had in 1863 about 402,000 bushes (315,000 over 16 years old), valued at Rs. 70:660$000. Slightly over a quarter-century later there remained 193,000 bushes (96,000 over 27 years old), valued at but 21 per cent of the former price.[30] In 1878 when it was judged that a "coffee grove of 10 to 15 years is, as a rule, completely lost and its soil forever ruined," [31] and when gaps appeared in the aging, closely planted groves as less robust trees succumbed in a "fight for life, . . . for air and sunlight," [32] a plantation such as the São Fernando faced a dismal future with 125,000 trees over 12 years of age and of these, 75,000 over 30.[33] When Ezequiel de Araujo Padilha died in 1880, he left his wife and heirs 197,000 bushes—132,000 over 14 years, and of these, 104,000 over 25.[34] The crisis in Vassouras coffee agriculture became more severe until by 1891 three fazendas for example

[27] Baglioni, *O Eresipho do Cafeeiro*, p. 48.

[28] Inventory, 1873, deceased: Estevão Pimenta de Moraes, executor: José Voyano, Fazenda Manga Larga, CPOV.

[29] Inventory, 1873, deceased: Antonia Thereza de Jesus, executor: Antonio Thereza de Jesus Cortes, Fazenda Unknown, CPOV.

[30] Inventory, deceased: Barão do Guaribú, executor: Barão da Parahyba, Fazendas Guaribú, Antas, Boa União, Encantos, CPOV.

[31] Baglioni, *O Eresipho do Cafeeiro*, p. 48. In view of the consensus among Baglioni, Burlamaque, and Delden Laerne, who wrote in the last half of the century, 15 years has been accepted as the year of marked drop in productivity per bush.

[32] Couty, *Biologie Industrielle*, p. 22.

[33] Inventory, 1879, deceased: José Ferreira Neves, executor: Candida Marcondes Neves, Fazenda São Fernando, CPOV.

[34] Inventory, 1880, deceased: Ezequiel de Araujo Padilha, executrix: Alexandrina de Araujo Padilha, Fazenda Sta. Eufrazia, CPOV.

could muster 446,000 bushes all over 20 years and no younger groves to report (Table 15).

TABLE 15. Number and age of coffee bushes on selected Vassouras plantations, 1856–1891.

Year	Plantations	Number of trees[a]	Remarks
1856	Triompho	120,000	100,000 14–22 years
1862	Manga Larga	479,000	400,000 "old, pruned"
1862	Palmeiras	142,000	100,000 "little fruit"
1865	Piedade	160,000	120,000 "old"
1874	Parahyba	345,000	120,000 "gaps"
1875	São Luis de Ubá	321,000	273,000 over 10 years
1879	Ponte Funda	14,300	8,300 over 16 years
1879	São Fernando	188,500	125,000 over 12 years
1880	Covanca	53,000	46,000 over 30 years
1880	Sta. Eufrázia	197,000	132,000 over 14 years
1882	Sta. Eufrázia	75,000	55,000 over 15 years
1883	Várzea	141,000	87,000 over 20 years
1885	Victória	337,000	275,000 over 13 years
1887	Bella Vista	141,000	69,000 over 20 years
1890	Sta. Eufrázia	272,000	165,000 over 14 years
1891	Piedade	46,000	all over 25 years
1891	Manga Larga	120,000	all over 23 years
1891	Monte Alegre	280,000	all over 20 years

[a] The number of a plantation's coffee bushes was likely to be overestimated to increase the value of aging plantations in the event of sale. Individual trees were not counted: an alqueire of coffee groves was judged to contain a fixed number of trees with some allowance for gaps. Where accurate records of coffee plantings did not exist, it is probable that groves were older than the age agreed upon for inventory purposes.

Source: Inventories, APV and CPOV.

Under the beating rains of summer and the annual rough harvests and weedings, defertilized and aged coffee bushes no longer produced fruit and were abandoned. Some were used for firewood, others were cut down, and the rest withered away. The situation was not lost upon the members of the Vassouras Câmara, one of whom wrote the Sociedade Auxiliadora da

Indústria Nacional in 1862 that "Coffee bushes replaced age-old trees of the forest and today there is not left the slightest vestige of either forest or coffee" on some "entirely bare hillsides." Yet he stated that thirty years before virgin forest covered most of the area.[35] To the Câmara in 1868, the Sociedade Auxiliadora sent a request for information: "Has the sterility . . . of some localities been due to the barbarous destruction of virgin forests?" As if to answer this almost rhetorical question, a Rio newspaper reported in 1870 that the old coffee-producing municípios of the Parahyba Valley—and it named among seven others, Vassouras—"have their fazendas worn out and their slaves aged, or are already partly so affected." [36] At the Agricultural Congress of 1878, Vassouras, again cited as once the richest coffee-producing município, was said to be declining only because of soil exhaustion.[37] By 1883, it and neighboring districts were described as "half exhausted." On his dreary trip by train through these municípios, Delden Laerne alleged that "For hours long one may steam past naked morros, studded with gigantic grey besoms, mournful relics of coffee-plantations once so splendid that they might almost have been said to bear gold." [38] For the bare slopes, a Vassouras planter counseled in vain rapid reforestation by large-scale planting of eucalyptus trees.[39]

The farsightedness of local observers of the sixties undoubtedly led them to exaggerate conditions—the lack of reserves of forest lands, aging coffee bushes, bare hills, and the invasion of weeds (*capim membeca, capim gordura, capim d'Angola, samambáia,* and *massambará*)—in order to instill in planters an awareness of their fate. Virgin forest, however, did not disappear completely, although the last decades of the century witnessed a marked and rapidly growing decline in the proportion of virgin forest to other lands—coffee lands, coffee lands abandoned to pasture (*pasto*) and to various succeeding stages of

---

[35] Secção da Agricultura da Sociedade Auxiliadora da Indústria Nacional to Ministério de Agricultura, Commercio e Obras Públicas, 1862. APV, 1862.

[36] *Jornal do Commercio*, July 6, 1870.

[37] *Congresso Agrícola*, p. 162.

[38] Delden Laerne, *Brazil and Java*, p. 283.

[39] *O Município*, June 14, and October 4, 1874.

secondary growth (*capoeira fina* or *capoeirinha, capoeira, capoeirão, capeirão grossa*). With the growing scarcity of virgin soil, went a corresponding increase in its price per alqueire, maintained

Figure 4. Land prices per alqueire[a] in Vassouras, 1840–1895

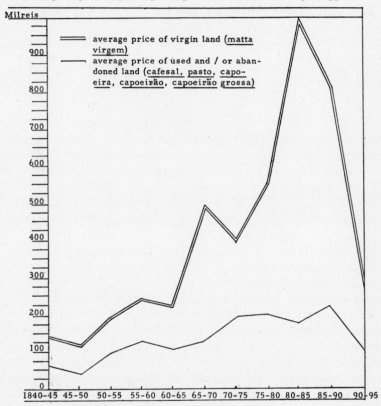

Sources: Inventories and testaments, CPOV and APV.

[a] Roughly equivalent to 12 acres.

until the mid-eighties.[40] In 1869, the 53 alqueires of the fazenda "Cachoeira" occupied in coffee and pasture were priced at Rs. 5:300$000; 50 alqueires of virgin forest land brought a price

[40] One alqueire is the equivalent of approximately 12 acres.

almost four times that, or Rs. 20:250$000.[41] The closing decades saw a steadily decreasing amount of land on Vassouras coffee fazendas available for new plantings (Table 16). As a sub-delegate of police in the município wailed after apprehending

TABLE 16. Virgin forest on selected Vassouras plantations, 1879–1895.

Year	Plantation	Area in virgin forest (alqueires)	Per cent of total area	Total land area (alqueires)
1879	São Fernando	13	9	137
1880	Sta. Eufrázia	50	27	185
1887	Bella Vista	10	9	114
1888	Boa Vista	0	0	112
1890	Sta. Eufrázia	23	12	190
1891	Piedade	0	0	500
1891	Manga Larga	2	4	57
1891	Freguezía	60	17	360
1891	Secretário	70	13	534
1895	Matto Dentro	0	0	100

Source: Inventories, CPOV.

several men for burning a neighbor's secondary growth: "The município's cultivated land is reduced and no one can try new plantings because the soil is sterile and only produces weeds." [42]

One solution for the problem of soil exhaustion was the consolidation of property to take advantage of remaining virgin soil and productive groves. In some cases, management of the holdings of an extended family was entrusted to one resident member while the others departed for government service, the professions or business in the capital. An incomplete Vassouras cadaster suggests how far concentration of landholdings had progressed by the end of the eighties. Fully 20 per cent of the

[41] Inventory, 1869, deceased: Baroneza do Ribeirão, executor: Barão do Ribeirão, Fazenda Cachoeira, CPOV.

[42] J. Caravana, September 1887. APV, 1887.

proprietors in two parishes owned 70 per cent of their parishes' area, or all the fazenda-sized property. In other words, forty-one proprietors—banks or individuals—controlled 4,715 alqueires of a total registered area of 6,631 alqueires (Table 17).

TABLE 17. Land distribution in Vassouras, 1890.

Proprietors		Size of holdings (alqueires)	Total holdings	
Number	Per cent		Alqueires	Per cent
26	13	over 100	3,765	57
15	7	51–100	950	13
28	14	26– 50	945	14
22	11	16– 25	390	6
17	8	11– 15	179	3
41	20	6– 10	264	4
56	27	1– 5	138	2

Source: Compiled from data forwarded from the parishes (freguezías) of Nossa Senhora da Conceição and Sacra Familia. Since two of the areas of greatest property concentration—Paty do Alferes and Ferreiros—sent fragmentary returns, the actual concentration of ownership was higher. The data were reported in "Relação de Todos os Proprietários de Terras . . . Intendencia Municipal de Vassouras . . . em Março de 1890." APV.

(3)

The aging and abandoned coffee groves, the diminishing or vanishing reserves of virgin soil, and the spreading expanses of weed- and saúva-covered hills did not undermine the economic and social edifice of Vassouras as did the changing nature of the "living instruments of labor" [43] at the core of each fazenda's existence—the slaves. In post-1850 Brazilian society, the age, health, number, and price of African and Brazilian-born slaves functioned as the most sensitive barometer of economic prosperity or uncertainty.[44] As the most important single element of fazenda wealth, the value of slave property accounted for more than 50 per cent of total fazenda capital over a thirty-year

[43] *Relatório do Presidente da Província do Rio, September 8, 1875,* p. 24.
[44] This was not true of the preceding period of ample land reserves, fazenda self-sufficiency, large slave importations, and cheap slave prices.

period commencing with the prosperous fifties and terminating in the wavering eighties. Indeed, slave property rose to an all-time high of 73 per cent of plantation wealth in 1857–58, far outvaluing the combined value of land, coffee groves, dwelling quarters, and other construction as well as machinery.[45] Planter confidence in continued ownership of slave laborers

Figure 5. Ratio of slave, land, and coffee grove evaluations to total plantation evaluations, 1850–1886

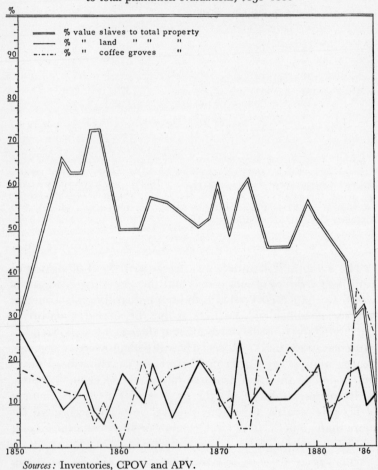

Sources: Inventories, CPOV and APV.
[45] See Figure 5.

was only slightly shaken in the early seventies by the Rio Branco law which calmed them with the words of Title 1: "The law regulating slavery remains. . ."

Confidence did not mean lack of sensitivity to variations in the supply of slaves available for coffee plantations, even in years before the mid-century mark. Taunay wrote in 1839 that "America devours the blacks: if continued importation were not supplying them, the race would shortly disappear from our midst." [46] Four years after cessation of the African trade a provincial report marked the "growing deficiency of slave labor as well as high slave prices," citing the other side of the coin, daily slave mortality on fazendas. [47] About the same time, a Vassouras planter predicted "infallible decadence" for coffee planters unless something were done to "fill the awful vacuum willed to us by the end of African colonization." He recognized, too, that slave prices would rise disastrously. [48] Those eager to liquidate large outstanding obligations profited, however, from the sale of slaves, as a planter's widow advised the Vassouras court when she expressed the desire to dispose of the "most salable property . . . my slaves. . ." [49] Those who held on to their slaves were fully aware of the potential losses they might sustain. "By the natural course of things," wrote another widow, aware of dangers latent in her labor force, "the mass of our property always tends to diminish through slave deaths and infirmities. . ." [50] Planters lost colossal fortunes and sank into "infallible ruin" through the "immense death rate to which slaves are subject," warned another in 1860. [51] Slave property in 1863 was classified as destined to "ruin and to complete disappearance," unlike cash which made a more suitable legacy for orphaned children. [52] A new development of the late

[46] C. A. Taunay, *Manual*, p. 16.

[47] *Relatório do Presidente da Província do Rio, May 2, 1854*, pp. 4, 17.

[48] L. P. de Lacerda Werneck, *Ideas sobre Colonisação*, pp. 8, 47.

[49] Inventory, 1856, deceased: Joaquim Francisco Moreira, executrix: Maria Magdalena de Castro Moreira, Fazendas Floresta and Victoria, CPOV.

[50] Inventory, 1862, deceased: Anna Joaquina de São José Werneck, executor: Ignacio José de Sousa Werneck, Fazendas Recreio, Pindobas, Palhas, CPOV.

[51] F. P. de Lacerda Werneck, *Memória*, p. 23.

[52] Inventory, 1856, deceased: Joaquim Francisco Moreira, executrix: Maria Magdalena de Castro Moreira, Fazendas da Floresta and Victoria, CPOV.

sixties influenced planters' thoughts concerning their slaves: to the understanding that "a good part of the slaves are old or infants, liable to disappear," was added the realization that the "abolitionist spirit is spreading and tends to reduce the price of slaves." Worst of all, "soon there will not be enough slaves to attend to plantation needs," it was noted in one inventory.[53] Shortly thereafter insurance companies played upon the fears of planters with statements spread through local newspapers as: "We propose to indemnify slave-owners . . . for damages caused by the death or forced liberty of slaves." [54]

Instability of the slave labor force of Vassouras plantations was underscored by two facts which presaged more effectively than words events to follow. On local plantations of the 1860's only 40 per cent of the total slave labor force consisted of prime field hands of an age capable of working the over-extended coffee groves; the remaining slaves were below fifteen or over forty. During the forties, however, the eighteen-to-forty-year-olds had comprised 62 per cent of the slave population.[55] Sensitive to the internal composition of the slave force and to the external threat posed by abolition (which Beaurepaire Rohan in 1878 predicted would come within ten years),[56] slave prices, the second factor, began a meteoric, unbroken descent—from a peak average price of approximately Rs. 1:925$000 in 1877 to Rs. 850$000 in 1887. The only comparable rate of change had taken place twenty-five years earlier, when the end of the African trade had sent slave price quotations soaring from Rs. 630$000 on the average to a high of Rs. 1:350$000 in three years (Figure 6).

[53] Inventory, 1870, deceased: José Ignacio de Lacerda Werneck, executor: Manoel Peixoto de Lacerda Werneck, Fazenda da Conceição, CPOV.

[54] *União. Seguros da Vida de Escravos. As Indemnizações são Pagas logo Depois da Morte dos Escravos Segurados* (Rio de Janeiro, 1876), p. 5. Another company was the Auxiliador do Trabalho Nacional e dos Ingénuos. Both companies advertised in *O Município*, November 23, 1876 and August 9, 1877.

[55] See Figure 3.

[56] Beaurepaire Rohan, "O Futuro da Grande Lavoura," p. 246; Correa de Azevedo, "Da Cultura do Café," p. 263. Couty advised coffee planters to take the example of Ceará's emancipation of slaves and prophesied "The legal demise of slavery in 1889" (March 27, 1884); he reported that São Paulo planters thought "inescapable" the disappearance of slave labor "before ten or twelve years" (May 22, 1884). *Le Brésil en 1884* (Rio de Janeiro, 1884), pp. 290, 405.

Little evidence supports the belief that declining slave prices in the late seventies and eighties affected planters' willingness to supplement their aging and dying slave labor force, despite

Figure 6. Average price of male and female slaves aged twenty to twenty-five years, 1822–1888

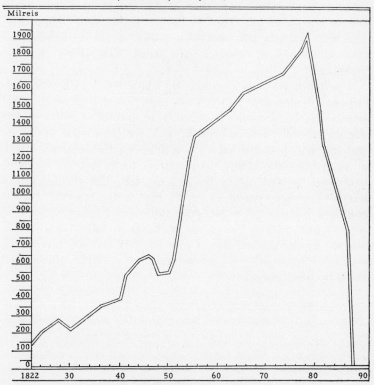

Sources: Inventories and testaments, CPOV and APV.

the absence of comments in Vassouras inventories on the subject. By tradition and practice coffee planters could not separate their fazendas from the slave force working them; this attitude flavored their thoughts about any possible emancipation. Slavery, they agreed in the late seventies, was one of those "evils" from which "Divine Providence alone can save us." [57]

[57] Visconde de Cayrú, quoted by Christiano B. Ottoni, *O Advento da República no Brasil* (Rio de Janeiro, 1890), p. 9.

In the early eighties Couty accused planters of Rio and São
Paulo of having done nothing to change their labor from slave
to free field hands or to colonists, blaming their "social characteristics . . . their mental and intellectual habits." He reported
one ingrained slaveholder as saying: "My children who will
inherit from me will do as they see fit; but as for me, I cannot
get used to other laborers." [58] To them, the whole complex of
owning a fazenda and producing coffee meant ownership and
direction of slaves, otherwise the word "fazendeiro" had no
meaning.[59]

The temptation to augment the slave force with new purchases was dangled before Vassouras planters as local newspapers in the seventies continued to publish reports of the
departure of slave ships from Brazil's northern ports to Rio de
Janeiro, which coincided with articles on the increasing lack
of available slave labor.[60] Any failure to buy slaves seems to
have been caused purely by lack of cash. The complaint, "I
haven't enough slaves to work my coffee groves," [61] was
common because planters could not muster good security to
cover loans. "There are plenty of slaves for sale," admitted a
planter at the Agricultural Congress. "What our agriculture
needs is long-term credit at low interest"—sentiments echoed
there by other speakers.[62]

[58] Couty, *Pequena Propriedade,* pp. 35–36.

[59] In the *Jornal do Commercio* of Rio, Beaurepaire Rohan wrote: "Our fazendeiros,
accustomed from childhood to handling slaves, cannot understand the idea of
laborers other than mere successors of slaves. They do not understand that large-
scale agriculture can exist on other than large fazendas of huge holdings, with
hundred of laborers who cultivate the soil for one owner. And, since they realize
the impossibility of finding free labor willing to tolerate the passive fate of slaves,
they believe there is no other way to obtain salvation." Reprinted in *O Vassourense,* July 2, 1882.

[60] Departure notice announced in *Diário de Notícias* of Bahia, June 7, 1877, and
reprinted in *O Município,* February 25, 1877.

[61] Inventory, 1877, deceased: Commendador Gabriel José Pereira Lima,
executrix: Maria José Pereira Lima, Fazenda Maravilha. APV, 1877. Correa de
Azevedo of Cantagallo observed in 1877 of Rio de Janeiro and São Paulo planters
that "slave labor seduces them, and behold how they fill themselves with burden-
some debts to obtain them. . ." "Da Cultura do Café," p. 265.

[62] *Congresso Agrícola,* p. 182. Similarly, Beaurepaire Rohan, "O Futuro da
Grande Lavoura," pp. 247–248.

Consequently, the slaves already in planters' hands tended to remain there, and the children of slave mothers, eventually to be freed by the Rio Branco law of 1871, were no exception. Between September 1873 and July 1882—on which date Vassouras' slave population totaled 18,630—fazendeiros emancipated with or without conditional clauses 425 slaves while 55 were liberated by outright purchase. For the period December 1871 to February 1888, in which 9,310 ingénuos were registered in Vassouras, 64 ingénuos were liberated "by accompanying their freed mothers." [63] Judged as a response to "imagination rather than to reality," the Rio Branco law in the eyes of many contemporaries failed to provide any education for ingénuos if freed at the age of eight in return for compensation. "Nursed on slave milk, living in the midst of slaves," no child was born a slave after 1871 but as one author outspokenly declared, "all the children of slave mothers continued to be raised as slaves and exactly in the same conditions in which they would be if the law of 1871 did not exist." [64] Planters accommodated themselves to the legal modifications in their slave property caused by the law, and with the phrase "only their services" or "probable services" appended, proceeded to list and price ingénuos with all other slaves. [65]

Attempts to break out of the tightening circle of coffee monoculture and the purchase of slaves who, once bought, "file down the road to the cemetery," [66] took the form of suggested cultivation of different crops and increased productivity through improved machine processing of coffee. News of high cotton demand in European markets as civil war in the United States reduced southern states' exports coincided with

[63] *Relatório do Presidente da Província do Rio, 1883*, and Mappa Estatística dos Filhos Livres de Mulher Escrava, Matriculados na Collectoria de Vassouras, February 29, 1888. APV, 1888.

[64] Francisco Belisário, cited in Taunay, *História*, VI, 110; *Congresso Agrícola*, p. 72.

[65] Inventory, 1873, deceased: Estevão Pimenta de Moraes, executor: José Voyano, Fazenda Manga Larga, CPOV. Inventories continued to evaluate ingénuos as late as 1883, with the last ingénuos' evaluation noted in 1885. Fifteen priced ingénuos were enumerated in Inventory, 1883, deceased: José Ribeiro Leite Zamith, executor: João Ribeiro dos Santos Zamith, Fazenda da Varzea, CPOV.

[66] Beaurepaire Rohan, "O Futuro da Grande Lavoura," p. 247.

planter stoicism or disheartenment in the face of widespread losses to the coffee crop in 1861 and 1862 induced by the butterfly-blight.[67] With the faint hope that civil war would divert to Brazil the "torrent of immigration that annually flows to the United States," provincial authorities in 1861 circulated the report of a Brazilian consul urging the wider cultivation of cotton.[68] That same year Vassouras' Câmara agreed that dependence upon coffee as the sole money crop was fraught with peril since virgin forest was disappearing and "under the present system of cultivation (it will not change in the coming twenty years) coffee . . . only prospers in virgin soil." Unlike coffee or sugar, which the Câmara designated as "colonial products," cotton's short harvest period of forty to fifty days discouraged planter interest; coffee was gathered up to six months after the first berries were ready. And then there remained the insoluble problem: would cotton grow in "lands called worn-out?" [69] For the next three years the provincial government periodically forwarded to the município circulars promoting the cultivation of cotton, including the distribution of Pernambuco cotton seeds and imported American varieties.[70] One result was the purchase and setting up of a cotton gin on the fazenda Santa Rita in 1864; and after initial enthusiasm, the cotton boom faded.[71]

Attended by more fanfare, and more attractive to Vassouras planters since the production and primitive processing of cane had always been continued on the larger fazendas to supply plantation personnel with sugar and aguardente, the sugar *central* boom burst upon the município in the seventies. The news appeared in a letter advising the Câmara that the

[67] Secção de Agricultura da Sociedade Auxiliadora da Indústria Nacional, 1862. APV, 1862.

[68] José Ricardo de Sá Rego to CMV, Nictheroy, August 23, 1861. APV, 1861.

[69] Joaquim José Teixeira Leite to Presidente da Província do Rio, November 24, 1861. APV, 1861.

[70] Presidente da Província do Rio to CMV, February 8, and April 21, 1865. APV, 1865.

[71] Raposo, *História*, p. 163. For a detailed analysis of the cotton boom in another area of Brazil, São Paulo, during the European cotton famine of the sixties, see Alice P. Canabrava, *O Desenvolvimento do Algodão na Província de São Paulo, 1861–1875* (São Paulo, 1951).

it emerged as a direct source of funds to the "agricultural industry . . . which . . . has lacked regular credit facilities." [103] During the remaining decades of the century local mortgages continued to be made but their importance proportional to funds obtained directly from banks in Rio declined.[104]

Circumstances attending the growing dependence of planters of Vassouras and other municípios of the "valley of slavery and coffee" upon Rio's private and public banking facilities were not favorable to those seeking financial aid. As dependency and need mounted, lending institutions became increasingly cautious. Two major considerations apparently motivated this reluctance: over-solicitous legislation protecting the borrower-planter from the consequences of default; and realization of the economic decline developing in the older coffee-growing areas.

Writing in 1857, a Vassouras planter belabored his friends for their indifference toward fulfilling signed obligations requiring prompt repayment of capital and interest. He did not mince words as he elucidated the reasons why. "The law fortified and armed landed property with so many exemptions and prerogatives that legal seizure became almost impossible. The *senhor* of land . . . is invulnerable and inaccessible to his creditors." [105] The mortgage law of 1863 and supplementary Imperial decrees of 1865 creating rural credit companies furthered this protection by allowing the "unscrupulous debtor to turn himself into the creditor of his creditor." According to these laws, no loan could exceed an amount equal to half the security offered by the mortgager. Where the mortgager failed to fulfill his obligation, and the mortgagee obtained judicial approval for foreclosure, the former handed over his

[103] *Instituição de Crédito Territorial* (Rio de Janeiro, 1857), p. lv.

[104] As early as 1860 the transition from local to extra-local financing of planters was obvious in the settlement of the estate of the president of the Banco Commercial e Agrícola. While important local planters owed him approximately Rs. 250:000$000 the greater part of his estate or Rs. 913:000$000 had already been invested in stocks of the Banco Commercial e Agrícola, the Pedro Segundo Railway, and other non-agricultural esterprises. Inventory, 1860, deceased: João Evangelista Teixeira Leite, CPOV.

[105] L. P. de Lacerda Werneck, *Estudos sobre o Crédito Real e Hypothecário seguidos de Leis, Estatutos e Outros Documentos* (Rio de Janeiro, 1857), pp. 9–10.

9

property, demanding the restitution in cash of half the property's value. "This is not just a simple hypothesis," added a writer of 1884. "Such abuses have already occurred." [106] Even a customarily restrained foreign visitor of the same year commented that "nowhere in all the world—at least not in Netherland India—are agriculturists granted so many legal securities to enable them to cultivate their lands in peace, as in Brazil." [107] A third observer was more outspoken in denouncing the Brazilian mortgage laws as "defective" and "made in favor of the fazendeiro who wished to keep all the rights." [108]

In the brief which planters entered against the prevailing conditions surrounding their attempts to obtain loans, no mention was made of legal favoritism, excepting the verbose and vague statements of provincial reports in 1859 and 1860 that agricultural advancement was hampered by "hindrances to the development of credit fostered by legislation inadequate for the protection of agriculture." [109] Complaints centered on the seemingly onerous terms banks exacted: high interest rates and complete amortization within a short period. As the largest source of mortgage funds, the Bank of Brazil became the most vulnerable target. Planters figured they had to repay more than 17 per cent of the original loan each year: amortization of 8 per cent annually, 9 per cent per annum interest, and full amortization at the end of six years. [110] At the Agricultural Congress of 1878 planters—with one notable exception— hammered away at the theme of the prevailing short amortizing periods and high interest rates. [111] There were also suspicions of the urban moneylenders, "the men of capital who wish to profit from their funds and the better to achieve their ends, ensnare the careless." The planter was pictured as asking for

[106] Miguel Antonio da Silva, "Agricultura National: Estudos Agrícolas," *Revista Agrícola do Imperial Instituto Fluminense de Agricultura*, VIII (December, 1877), p. 141, and "Retrospecto Commercial de 1884," *Jornal do Commercio*, p. 4.

[107] Delden Laerne, *Brazil and Java*, p. 227.

[108] Couty, *Le Brésil en 1884*, p. 372.

[109] *Relatórios do Presidente da Provincia do Rio, August 1, 1859*, p. 23; *June 1, 1860*, p. 21.

[110] Silva, "Agricultura Nacional," pp. 141–142.

[111] *Congresso Agrícola*, pp. 78–79, 182, 235.

funds, hat in hand, only to find the capitalists "impose their onerous conditions when they are certain of the agriculturists' urgent need."[112]

Manoel Ribeiro do Val, planter of Parahyba do Sul, provided the exception. A planter, sharing the planters' growing misgivings of the future, he espoused the cause of the practical leaders of banking institutions. Opening with references to visibly declining municípios, he demolished one by one the illusions nurturing the hopes of his friends, and he closed with warnings of ruin. His comments on planter concern over rural credit difficulties provided the core of his analysis: "There has been talk of the creation of a mortgage bank to provide rural credit secured by landed property. . . Well, let's see if the majority of those who really need capital to liquidate their debts . . . offer in return sufficient guarantees for amortization over extended periods with their coffee groves and slaves." Nor did he leave his audience uncertain about his conclusions. "It is clear that at the end of twenty years the greater part of coffee groves turned old and exhausted . . . will carry both the projected bank and the nation's credit to ruin." [113]

Evidence in Vassouras notarial archives and published reports backed up the contentions of Ribeiro do Val, and impressed any banker's representative with the growing precariousness of local agricultural conditions. Phrases such as "burdened with an enormous debt," "the estate could not pay its obligations," and "my debt is such that forced collection would consume the whole inheritance" cropped up in the fifties, sixties, and seventies.[114] In these decades, planters failed to meet obligations, though some staved off foreclosure by refunding scattered debts into one large obligation. One report of the eighties claimed that "very few" planters were debt-free.

---

[112] Correa de Azevedo, "Da Cultura do Café," p. 264.

[113] *Congresso Agrícola*, p. 164.

[114] Joaquim Pinheiro de Souza, APV, 1857; Inventory, 1862, deceased: Anna Joaquina de São José Werneck, executor: Ignacio José de Souza Werneck, Fazendas Recreio, Pindobas, Palhas, CPOV; Inventory, 185, deceased: Luiza Maria de Noronha, executor: José de Souza Werneck, Fazenda Unknown, CPOV; Inventory, 1879, deceased: José Ferreira Neves, executrix: Candida Marcondes Neves, Fazenda São Fernando, CPOV.

A planter possessing anywhere from 80 to 100 slaves, the number employed on an average large Vassouras plantation, and owing approximately 200 contos, "cannot possibly retrieve himself, not even if prices are exorbitantly high." [115] Couty divided fazendeiros of the coffee zone into three categories: a small number of planters completely debt-free and holding government bonds; a slightly larger group barely solvent; and a third group comprising the majority of large planters who were without resources to meet their debts contracted with commissários, the banks, and the wealthier planters. Their situation was hopeless; already overburdened with debt, "they realize they cannot replace the slaves that die, or improve their machinery, or expend the money to install free imported laborers. . . All progress as far as they are concerned is impossible." Nor could their lands, houses, and slaves find buyers if offered for sale. Under such circumstances, foreign banks quickly withdrew funds from the mortgage loan market after exploratory investments around 1872 had been made.[116]

To survive, the unsalable coffee fazendas of the Parahyba Valley, which still provided dwindling returns to their owners, had to satisfy their creditors somehow. Vast credits came from the government's Bank of Brazil which more than doubled its loans to planters of the province of Rio in the brief period of 1877 to 1883. From the Bank's coffers the first and second largest sums awarded in the province of Rio went to the neighboring municípios of Valença and Vassouras, two of the oldest coffee-producing areas (Table 18).

The pump-priming occurred despite temporarily declining overseas coffee markets, the competition of cheaper coffee grown in São Paulo's expanding groves outside the Parahyba Valley, and lower production in the worn-out debtor areas of the province. A summary of market conditions of 1878 pointed to the diminishing consumption of coffee abroad as industrial

---

[115] Delden Laerne, *Brazil and Java*, pp. 217, 225.

[116] Couty, *Le Brésil en 1884*, 95–96, 196–198. Writing during the same months, Delden Laerne divided coffee planters into "coffee growers free from debt (20 per cent)," those barely capable of settling their debts (30 per cent), and those "hopelessly involved, and beyond all possibility of retrieving themselves (50 per cent)." *Brazil and Java*, p. 224.

production slowed and the fears of large-scale warfare in Europe spread, and to the consequent depressing effect on coffee quotations.[117] Coffee production in other areas of the world cut Brazilian percentage of world production from 49.4 per cent in 1855, to 45.9 per cent as of 1878.[118] Four years later the belief circulated that low quotations could be traced only

TABLE 18. Mortgages of the Banco do Brazil in the Province of Rio and in Vassouras, 1877 and 1883.

| | Province of Rio | | Vassouras |
	1877	1883	1883
Number plantations mortgaged	294	351	44
Value of plantations	—	45,313:690$	6,916:208$
Total of bank loans	14,316:693$	32,712:165$	4,735:501$
Percentage of total value in loans	—	72	68

Sources: O Município, October 14, 1877; Delden Laerne, Brazil and Java, pp. 218–219.

to production exceeding the "present demands of consumption." [119] In 1883, São Paulo production matched Rio's for the first time; three years later, after ten years' unbroken upswing, it surpassed Rio's.[120] One small Vassouras planter advised the court settling his wife's estate in 1883 that debts totaled more than 12 contos and "it is not possible to liquidate them since there is no coffee to be found in the groves this year nor in the lands of neighbors; in fact, there is a total lack of coffee." [121]

While the plantation's real assets (casco da fazenda) of houses, machinery, land, and coffee changed slowly in value, rapid slave depreciation cast a pall over fazendas years before

[117] "Retrospecto Commercial de 1878," Jornal do Commercio, p. 11.
[118] "Retrospecto Commercial de 1880," Jornal do Commercio, p. 4.
[119] "Retrospecto Commercial de 1882," Jornal do Commercio, p. 3.
[120] Roberto C. Simonsen, Aspectos da História Económica do Café (São Paulo, 1940), Graphico 1.
[121] Inventory, 1883, deceased: Deolina de Jesus da Conceição, executor: Antonio Francisco Ferreira, Fazenda do Sertão, CPOV.

abolition by reducing the security upon which planters depended for loans. It evoked from one Vassouras fazendeiro the comment that there had been "an extraordinary decrease in agricultural values"; from another the confession that his son could not settle his debts since his security "comprised merely a second-rate agricultural establishment considerably depreciated in view of present circumstances." [122] Further, in the minds of Vassouras planters, who felt that the institution of slavery was inseparable from the operation of their aging, high-cost-of-production plantations, the drop in slave values confirmed the fear that they were approaching their economic demise. Others, years earlier, had perceived that "all plantation property has nothing readily salable except the Negroes, they are the clearest, the most liquid of their capital. . . The real assets have little value." [123] In 1882 it was discerned that a planter could not sell the accumulated capital represented by cultivated land "since only the slave has value, only the human cattle which till it." [124] Reflecting the importance of slaves in securing mortgage loans, the amount granted by hesitant bankers tended to hover at the evaluation of the slaves and not at that of the remainder of a fazendeiro's property.[125] One year before the advent of abolition, as slave prices sank to the level attained before 1850, a Vassouras planter heard his mortgagee declare in court that "in view of the present situation in which slaves are depreciated and perhaps will be valueless shortly, the fazenda will lose its value too if shorn of its slaves." [126]

The inventories of two of the oldest coffee-growing fazendas in Vassouras provide good examples of the effects of a half-century of coffee agriculture (Tables 19, 20). In 1863, "Guaribú" was priced at Rs. 635:377$000, representing real assets and slaves; during the next quarter-century the slaves

[122] Inventory, 1885, deceased: Ignácio de Avellar e Almeida, executor: Barão da Cananea, Fazenda Unknown, CPOV.

[123] Pradez, *Nouvelles Études*, pp. 238–239.

[124] Couty, *L'Esclavage*, pp. 61–62.

[125] See tables in Delden Laerne, *Brazil and Java*, pp. 218–223; Couty, *Le Brésil en 1884*, p. 88.

[126] Execução que Fazem Miranda, Monteiro e Cia contra Antonio Baptista Correa e Castro e Mulher, 1887, CPOV.

alone fell in value from Rs. 441:530$000 to Rs. 45:600$000; in 1890, the fazenda was worth Rs. 66:691$000. In 1880, the heirs and the Imperial Treasury waged a bitter struggle

TABLE 19. Depreciation of Fazenda Guaribú, 1863–1890.

Property	1863	1874	1880	1887	1890
Slaves	441:530$	282:170$	282:170$	45:600$	
Coffee	70:650$	70:650$			
Land	41:150$	43:000$			
Houses	16:168$	14:026$	134:876$	42:798$	42:798$
Other[a]	65:879$	24:875$	24:963$	23:893$	23:893$
Total	635:377$	434:721$	442:009$	112:291$	66:691$

[a] Includes furniture, harvested coffee, animals, gold, and silver, although all these items were not always listed.

Source: Inventory, 1863, deceased: Barão do Guaribú, executor: Barão da Parahyba, Fazenda do Guaribú, CPOV.

TABLE 20. Depreciation of Fazenda Taboões, 1880–1888.

Property	1880	1888
Slaves	130:005$	
Coffee	23:200$	5:880$
Land	15:000$	7:000$
Houses	15:480$	10:370$
Other	9:207$	3:875$
Total	192:892$	27:125$

Source: Inventory, 1880, deceased: Felisberta Avellar Vieira, executor: Joaquim Xavier de Castro, Fazenda dos Taboões, CPOV.

over the amount of inheritance taxes, and some of the evaluations may have been excessively high that year. The drop in the eighties, however, was typical of other fazendas, such as "Taboões." In this case the estate lost 130 contos of slave property when emancipation was decreed.

Private banking institutions which had distributed little or no capital in mortgage loans to coffee planters now restricted "idle or restless" investment capital to public bonds.[127] Vassouras planters in the pre-emancipation months of 1888 petitioned the Imperial Government to "intervene in our behalf at credit establishments to help our agriculture" and suggested a debt moratorium of five years.[128] Sensitive to the demands of the politically powerful coffee planters, shorn of their slave property by uncompensated abolition one year earlier, the Rio provincial government in 1889 tried to stimulate private banks to furnish planters their needed funds by guaranteeing 6 per cent interest to agricultural companies they might create to spur the settlement of foreign immigrants.[129] One month after the founding of the Republic the national government promised similar favors to banks creating a separate mortgage portfolio for loans on landed security.[130] Temporary measures at best, these attempts to supply planters with funds were not successful. Banks had no wish to tie up funds in "hypothecary letters . . . subject to great depreciation." Noting the instability of formerly dependable government bonds as the Republic succeeded the Empire, private banks utilized the proffered funds for non-agricultural projects with a higher, quicker return.[131]

[127] "Retrospecto Commercial de 1885," *Jornal do Commercio*, pp. 3–4.

[128] Reunião dos Lavradores de Vassouras, March 20, 1888. APV, 1888.

[129] *Relatório do Presidente da Província do Rio, October 1889*, p. 9. The economic steps of the provincial government reflected essentially political moves by the Imperial Government. "Visconde Ouro Preto on coming into office proceeded to give an immense extension to the system of 'Credits to Agriculture and Kindred Industries,' in the hope that such a policy would bring back to their allegiance the disaffected planters whom the Emancipation Act had caused to join the opposition to the Imperial Government; and between June and November 1889, it entered into agreements with seventeen banks for further advances to agriculture, for a total sum of 172,000,000 milreis, of which the Government was to furnish one-half. . . Under these contracts the banks are not obliged to contribute their own share of the advances until they have placed the whole amount furnished to them by the Treasury." Hugh Wyndham, *Report on the Finances of Brazil for the Year 1889 to March 1890*. Rio de Janeiro, March 29, 1890. Gt. Bratiin. C 5895. LXXIV (1890) 21–22.

[130] *Mensagem do Governador do Estado do Rio, September, 1896*, pp. 35–36.

[131] *Mensagem do Governador do Estado do Rio, September, 1897*, p. 81; A. d'E. Taunay, *História*, VI, 195, 200. The republic's first Minister of Finance, Ruy

In accepting funds from sources outside the boundaries of the município—funds which came in sizable amounts principally from the sole banking institution willing to furnish rural credit, the Bank of Brazil—Vassouras planters divorced themselves from the era of personal finance. Henceforth, few moratoria were forthcoming, as they formerly had—from understanding friendly planter-bankers, if the defaulter begged off on his interest and amortization payments alleging poor harvest, sudden illness in the family, or unexpectedly high fazenda overhead. The Bank felt neither family ties nor the obligation to keep a friend's plantation operating. On the other hand, it did prove lenient in the seventies and early eighties— by some extensions of time for repayment and by appointing defaulting planters as administrators of their property in behalf of the bank. But as agricultural decline in the município intensified in the years immediately preceding abolition, the Bank foreclosed on planter defaulters. Its direct responsibility was, after all, to the government rather than to private individuals.

An era was drawing to a close for the majority of Vassouras fazendeiros as May 13, 1888 approached. Those who somehow had managed to ward off banks, factors, or other creditors, could probably describe their insecure way of life during the preceding years as did one planter settling his wife's estate three days after the abolition of slavery was decreed. "I thought it convenient not to settle the estate as long as the slave problem was not completely solved. . . The income of the plantation has been small these past years and I have spent it on maintaining the plantation, feeding and clothing the slaves and my family. By extinguishing slavery in Brazil the law of May 13th of this year erased from the fazenda's assets the value of my slaves. There is practically nothing left for distribution among the heirs." [132]

Barbosa, had decided opinions on the value of the steps taken by Ouro Preto. Commented Hugh Wyndham: "Senhor Ruy Barbosa . . . denies that this expenditure has afforded the least benefit to the real interests of agriculture, and declares that he would gladly have put a stop to it at once, but for the fear that such a proceeding might have created a powerful opposition to the infant Republic." *Report*, p. 22.

[132] Inventory, 1888, deceased: Felisberta Avellar Vieira, executor: Joaquim Vieira Xavier de Castro, Fazenda dos Taboões, CPOV.

CHAPTER X

Abolition and Aftermath

WORRIED and confused groups of planters gathered in the halls
and on the steps of the columned municipal courthouse (*Paço*)
of Vassouras on March 20, 1888. Some stood in clusters on the
granite steps fronting on the municipal garden and its majestic
baroque fountain erected in the prosperous 1840's. Beyond the
houses enclosing the opposite side of the rectangle of garden
they could see the red earth which marked the Estrada da
Polícia winding its way above the denuded hills of the Serra de
Matacães to Sacra Família and, leagues further, to the capital
where momentous events affecting Vassouras proprietors were
being discussed. To the right of the Paço and atop the steep
rise which dominated the town stood the Church of Our Lady
of the Conception with its two gracefully bulbous towers
crowned with weathercocks. Warm, wet summer was yielding
to dry winter weather of cloudless bright skies; those coffee
trees of the município still bearing fruit promised the first
bountiful harvest in years. Around the fountain, filling buckets
of water from serpentine spouts, slaves, men and women,
conversed. Undoubtedly they knew that the troubled planters
gathering in the Paço had come to discuss the imminent
emancipation of their slaves. Slowly the planters moved indoors
to the stuccoed main salon; but from the open balcony doors
heated words and uncontrolled voices told of their fears for
their slave property and for the picking not only of this but of
other coffee harvests.

Since the early months of the year the "great question" of
emancipation developing over two troubled decades occupied
the thoughts of slaveholding planters and their adversaries, the
abolitionist "anarchists" of Brazil's urban centers, to the
exclusion of all else. Violence between planters and abolitionists

in the sugar-center of Campos in the Province of Rio, organized abandonment of São Paulo coffee fazendas by slaves who traveled by road and railway to the fugitive encampments of Cubatão in the coastal range between Santos and São Paulo,[1] precipitated the March meeting. The local newspaper refrained from commenting on the threat that uncompensated emancipation posed to planters' fortunes already reduced to the security of slave property. Rio newspapers, however, particularly one conservative organ reflecting the views of anti-abolitionist planters of the Province of Rio, supplied Vassouras planters daily with news of emancipation developments. *Novidades* at the end of January undoubtedly expressed the sentiments of Vassouras planters who accepted the "righteousness" of abolition but did not wish it to come "in a jet" and without compensation: "It is true that there exists no essential divergence between ourselves and those who wish . . . ardently that slavery disappear from the Empire as soon as possible. The divergence is only in the *modus faciendi*: we believe that to open all the dikes right now and free the 500 or 600,000 slaves who still exist is not only an economic and social error, but also amounts to preparing the ruin of the nation by bankruptcy and disorder." [2]

This delaying position, undoubtedly a radical departure eighteen years earlier when it had been officially phrased by a conciliatory parliamentary commission, was untenable in 1888. Slave violence to masters and overseers was mounting, passive resistance to orders was widespread, and jails had been assaulted to take vengeance upon slaves suspected of attacking planters.[3] Firmiano José Antonio da Silva, a carpenter and the free son of a slave, was accused in Vassouras of "instigating illicit slave meetings" and there inciting slaves to indiscipline, theft, and disorganization of plantations of the vicinity.[4]

---

[1] *Os Deputados Republicanos na Assemblea Provincial de São Paulo. Sessão de 1888.* (São Paulo, 1888), pp. 74, 82, 137.

[2] January 31, 1888.

[3] Couty, *Pequena Propriedade*, p. 40; *Relatório do Presidente da Província do Rio, August, 1885*, pp. 8–9; A. d'E. Taunay, *História*, V, 166. Taunay described the assaults on local jails as "lynchings in the public squares."

[4] APV, 1888.

Tension between the free and the slave was communicated to local police authorities who were charged with imprisoning fugitive slaves without legal orders and whipping them.[5]

Unsettled by spreading social ferment, the planters received no guidance from *Novidades*. On February 9, 1888, this newspaper acknowledged that São Paulo using immigrant labor would make progress while coffee planters of Rio remained beset by "climate, the lack of pecuniary elements, precarious conditions of worn out lands, diminishing yields, etc." Yet forgetting this incisive analysis of differing conditions in both provinces, three weeks later, it attributed Rio's ingrained resistance to abolition and its slowness in adopting immigration as a substitute for slave labor to the "natural prudence of the genuine Rio planter . . . where the São Paulo planter blindly adopts the newest fad. . . The Province of Rio chooses slow, moderate and profitable evolution, judging what is to be gained and substituting what must infallibly be lost." [6] *Novidades* admitted that such conservative Rio political leaders as Paulino de Souza could not retard abolition and opined that "slavery can no longer be counted upon." [7] Aside from publishing unconfirmed notices of armed slave insurrections in the municípios of Barra Mansa and Rezende near Vassouras, coupled with laments about the promising harvests threatened in early March by slave disorganization in Rio where "the slave works only as long as he is a slave," *Novidades* held out no program except "go slow" on emancipation.[8] It was in the midst of such a defeatist atmosphere that early in March printed announcements were circulated in the town and on plantations, inviting planters to meet in the Paço on March 20 and discuss a "matter of great concern to the agriculturists of the município." [9]

[5] A local attorney charged that "In recent months we have noted many abuses committed by some police authorities. The population of this town, for example, on a certain day of last February at two o'clock in the afternoon overheard the anguished groans of Negroes detained as fugitives and whipped in the prison." APV, 1888.

[6] February 28, 1888.

[7] February 16, 1888.

[8] February 21 and March 12, 1888.

[9] There exists in the APV a document dated March 20, 1888 supplying many

More than 200 planters sat or stood in the main salon as the Barão de Massambará proposed that the Barão de Santa Maria act as president. The latter deferred to Manoel Peixoto de Lacerda Werneck, deputy to the Imperial Assembly as well as a prominent planter of the município of Vassouras. After summarizing the rise of abolitionism and dwelling at length on the Rio Branco law of 1870 and the Sexagenarian law of 1885, Lacerda Werneck pointed to the "necessity of adopting measures which might attract both the national and foreign laborer to the município of Vassouras." [10] There was probably nothing startling in these proposals; the bombshell that for a while threatened to turn the calm meeting into a mob scene developed when another planter took the floor. José de Vasconcellos tried to evaluate the significance of the encampments of runaway slaves at Cubatão in São Paulo and the popularity of the abolitionist, Silva Jardim, who was moving up and down the Parahyba Valley, addressing audiences in the town centers. Concluding his impromptu speech, Vasconcellos warned that the only path to avoid the abrupt disorganization of plantation slave labor, if emancipation came overnight, was voluntary liberation of all slaves within the município before any official emancipation. As a hum of protest spread through the planter audience, one of the largest slave and property owners of the município, Christóvão Correa e Castro, arose. Perhaps to calm those planters irked by Vasconcellos' address, Correa e Castro discussed the various ways to keep the freedman or the immigrant on Vassouras plantations, as paid day laborer or share-cropper, as a person hired for a certain job (*empreiteiro*), or as renter of land. He was "open to suggestion," and would accept Vasconcellos' proposal if he did not feel that "he had to maintain the precepts of class solidarity which he had long considered holy." [11]

particulars of what was described as a "Meeting of Fazendeiros." Some of the details cited by Raposo were not found in the APV document and it is possible that what was located there is only a part of the full account. Both Raposo and the document discovered have been used in this account of the proceedings. Raposo, *História*, pp. 237–238.

[10] Reunião dos Fazendeiros, March 20, 1888. APV, 1888.

[11] Reunião dos Fazendeiros; Raposo, *História*, p. 237.

No sooner had Correa e Castro resumed his seat, than another planter expressed the widespread trust that they had in Paulino de Souza who had promised early in January that planters could count on five more years of slavery. And turning toward Vasconcellos he told him he would soon pay him back for his "levity . . . and mad ideas." Several planters ran over to strike Vasconcellos and only the intervention of Correa e Castro prevented him from being "smashed up." [12] The final speakers counseled planters not to be "panicked" by developments in São Paulo and elsewhere and reaffirmed their confidence in the promises of Paulino de Souza, and in the "Public Authorities who would safeguard the interests of the Province."

In the closing minutes of the meeting, the planters agreed to summarize their attitude toward oncoming abolition. As a last testament on the eve of officially decreed emancipation, it bore witness to the fear and disheartenment, the sense of personal grievance, and the groundless hope that somehow a great social revolution might come without financial loss to those who had profited most and now were about to lose irrevocably, which Vassouras planters and their counterparts shared. "Although the recent events have produced a certain disheartenment and provoked apprehensions justified naturally by the injustices by which the planter class has been victimized, still the fazendeiros of Vassouras trust in the solicitude and patriotism of public authorities, confident that the substitution of slave labor which is sincerely desired by all will come with due caution and accompanied by those measures which the most ordinary prudence and the example of other nations whose labor, as is ours, consists of slaves, recommend. . . For the benefit of those persons who failed to appear at this meeting let it be inscribed that . . . the ardent desires of the planters of Vassouras are not against the liberation of the slave race but that such liberation come without perturbation and conflict, without shaking the wealth of the public, without danger to our fellow-citizens, by pacific and orderly means as all Brazilians desire."

The drama of abolition drew quickly to a climax for planter and slave alike. There were instances of fazendeiros who freed

[12] Raposo, *História*, p. 238.

their slaves en masse in the remaining months of slavery, some in return for baronies bestowed by the Imperial Government, others in the hope that grateful slaves would remain on the plantation. Said *Novidades* bitterly of those who boasted of planter magnanimity toward their slaves: "No one freed his slaves out of the conviction that ownership was illegal; rather out of desire for recompense or out of the speculative, ingenuous hope of gratitude." [13] Perhaps the ingrained resistance of many planters was mirrored in the reply of a planter who snapped back at members of a commission which toured the province of Rio urging the voluntary liberation of slaves. "I prefer to see my mother rot than sign a letter of liberty for my slaves. I shall wait for the government to reimburse me for them." [14]

On May 4, the Princess Regent in the annual royal address urged immediate emancipation. Five days later she proposed the law abolishing slavery. "At this moment," editorialized *Novidades* in repetitive and disoriented fashion, "it is almost impossible to point out all the consequences of this dictatorial act of the excellent heiress to the Brazilian throne. . . The hour of reason has not yet arrived. We have nothing to say, therefore. . . Deeply and painfully we feel that the proscription of calm, the exile of reason has been decreed. . . Promises, words, ideas have been forgotten. . . We have fulfilled our duty and we confess that we remain impenitent." [15] Four days later, on May 13, slavery was abolished.

Intransigent to the last remained the nine deputies of the Province of Rio, joined by six senators who voted against the proposal of the Princess Regent.[16] To the leader of the fifteen, the Barão de Santa Maria, as president of the Vassouras Câmara, sent thanks for their last-ditch stand. For in the eyes of conservative, slaveholding planters, the Conservative party had served in the last years of anti-abolitionist resistance as the

---

[13] June 20, 1888. On May 11 a Vassouras plantation's slaves were withdrawn from auction because "it seems ridiculous under present circumstances to continue to offer slaves for sale." CPOV.

[14] *Monitor Campista*, June 26, 1888, cited in *Novidades*, June 30, 1888.

[15] May 9, 1888.

[16] *Novidades*, May 11, 1888; Alberto Brandão, *O Brasil* (Rio de Janeiro, 1896), p. 22.

protector of "extremely valuable interests" and the bulwark of "resistance to precipitation in the solution of this grave problem." Yet even the Conservative party failed to maintain its "obligation" to the planters in the parliamentary defense of planter interests. In the closing paragraph of the message to Conservative party leader Cotegipe, the Barão returned to the argument of March 20, the counsel of moderation and delay. "If our protest had been listened to, emancipation would have come to an end at the opportune moment, without the brilliance of so important a social evolution darkened by the shadow of discontent (more than justified) of all classes directly or indirectly prejudiced, especially the class of planters, the most numerous, which has been surprised and condemned to incalculable losses by the sudden disorganization of labor on its agricultural establishments." [17] Only one municipal councilor abstained from the message of thanks.[18]

On May 13 and 14 *Novidades* failed to appear for sale at newspaper kiosks in the city of Rio. In the interior towns and countryside the reception of the emancipation decree (the "Golden Law") was entirely different. For the slaves, "captivity ended." Word of "liberty" traveled by slave grapevine from fazenda to fazenda; a planter's son was reported to have hurried from fazenda to fazenda shouting, "From now on we are equal, we are one." Some planters sent word to their overseers to order the labor gangs to return immediately to the main house; one planter announced to his slaves gathered before him: "Today we are equal, we are one. You will henceforth be paid for your work." Many planters are said to have wept as they asked their slaves to remain for the coffee harvest.

As captivity ended, a new-found sense of liberty, of freedom to escape from the plantation with its overtones of forced labor, discipline, and unending surveillance, surged in its place. A mass exodus from the plantations occurred as slaves—men, women, and children—moved along the backroads, stopping to ask for friends and relatives, resting near the roadside

[17] CMV to Cotegipe, 1888. APV, 1888.
[18] Raposo, *História*, p. 240.

taverns for dancing, jongo-singing, and talk. "Each one sought his own destiny like cattle in pasture." Said one Negro when his ex-master asked him to stay: "Thank God, you can stay here, senhor, you can stay here with your 'leg broken,' for I'm going away." An ex-slave woman explained why she would not stay on the plantation where she had been born and raised: "I'm a slave and if I stay here, I'll remain a slave." In Parahyba do Sul, word spread that, according to a new governmental decree, ex-slaves were to serve out seven more years of slavery. The next day approximately sixteen plantations were left bare of freedmen.[19] To fazendeiros who urged slaves to stay on as sharecroppers, freedmen replied that they had worked enough and they they needed to "rest now and if they fall ill the Princess Regent will take care of them." [20]

Three nights and three days the drums could be heard reverberating as freedmen rejoiced at the caxambú. These were held near the tabernas and vendas, where articles of clothing representing the freedmen's changed status could be bought: hats, suits, shoes, and umbrellas were eagerly sought. Jongueiros turned to the events of the Thirteenth of May for inspiration, referring to the wavering attitude of the emperor ("stone") toward abolition, praising the action of his daughter ("queen"):

> I stepped on the stone, the stone tottered
> The world was twisted, the Queen straightened it.
>
> (Eu pisei na pedra, pedra balanceou
> Mundo 'tava torto, rainha endireitou.)

Or a jongo recounted the surprise which slaves experienced when the happy news was announced:

> I was sleeping, *Ngoma* called me
> Arise people, captivity is over.
>
> (Eu 'tava dormindo, *Ngoma* me chamou
> Levanta povo, cativeiro ja acabou.)

Bitterness, resignation, and retribution appear in another verse

---

[19] *Novidades*, July 12, 1888.
[20] *Novidades*, November 12, 1888.

and reflect how deeply slaves had resented the subservience imposed by the master's authority:

> In the days of captivity, I endured many an insult
> I got up early in the morning, the leather whip beat
> me for no reason.

> But now I want to see the fellow who shouts to me from
> the hilltop
> "Say, God bless you, master"—no sir, your Negro is a
> freedman today.

> (No tempo do cativeiro, aturava muito desaforo
> Eu levantava de manhã cedo, com cara limpa levo o couro.

> Agora quero ver o cidadão que grita no alto do morro
> "Vas Christo," seu moço, está forro seu Negro agora.)

Sobering reality gradually replaced the joyous Thirteenth and the caxambú-filled days that followed. A state of affairs where "ex-slaves wandered in groups along the roads, with no destination, sleeping in the ranchos or under the open sky" could not long endure. Happy, hungry, and in the tattered clothing belonging to them on the day of liberation, the freedmen began to look for work. Some tried to work for Negroes who had been liberated by their masters in the years preceding 1888 and who had managed to obtain small lots of property (sitios) where they carried on subsistence agriculture.[21] Others merely changed plantations, "always moving onward" as one freedman described it, or "one day here, one day there, always changing," or "we exchanged plantations." But woe to the planter who told freedmen how bad he felt about their plight; word soon reached the abolitionist press which seized upon such commiseration as "an attempt to re-enslave the freedmen."[22] Still other freedmen moved into the town center searching for work of a non-agricultural nature which might confirm their legal separation from their masters and the plantations. Old and decrepit slaves, for whom many ex-masters in many cases felt no responsibility, fared worse. Begging from house to house and from plantation to plantation, a few managed to live out the few remaining years. Despite the

[21] *Novidades*, May 30, 1888.
[22] *Novidades*, June 2, 1888.

optimistic speeches of the handful of Vassouras politicians who had favored abolition,[23] the Thirteenth of May "brought hunger and death to the aged freedmen." [24] A novelist wrote of a blind slave in a book based upon Vassouras experience: "The Great Law found him blind, what good did it do him? . . . Now he's dying in the dark, today he eats, tomorrow he starves, just as God wills. Liberty . . . of course! People dying right and left—the turkey buzzards enjoy that." [25] Unattached freedmen ("young bucks") drifted off to areas in São Paulo and eastern Rio where planters could afford higher wages than those offered by local planters. Most Vassouras slaves, with their mates and children, slowly flowed back to the plantations where they came to terms with planters eager to save their coffee harvest.

(2)

Certain factors operated upon planters eager to secure harvest labor and upon restless freedmen, shaping the immediate and eventual forms of land utilization and labor relationships. Dominant among these was the unbroken supremacy of large holdings—plantations of more than fifty alqueires—in the município of Vassouras.[26] In the first days after emancipation rumor was current of a distribution of small plots of land to the ex-slaves, but nothing ever materialized and the freedmen "kept mum," according to one of them. Yet this unfulfilled hope found its way into the jongos of the caxambú disguised in the embittered metaphor developed by African tradition and Brazilian Negro servitude:

> Ay, she did not give us a chair to sit on
> The Queen gave me a bed but no chair to sit on.
>
> (Ahi, não deu banco p'ra nos sentar
> Dona Rainha me deu cama, não deu banco p'ra me sentar.)

---

[23] "Today our labor will undergo a transformation . . . soon in this fertile land we will see the outstanding results of labor whose only driving force is self-stimulation." From a speech by Sebastião de Lacerda on May 14, 1888, published in *O Vassourense*, May 20, 1888.

[24] *Novidades*, June 19, 1888.

[25] Coelho Netto, *Banzo* (2nd ed., Porto, 1927), pp. 17–18.

[26] Relação de todos os proprietarios de terras da . . . Intendencia Municipal de Vassouras . . . em Março de 1890. APV, 1890.

Other factors also helped determine the fluid labor arrangements between ex-slaves and former masters during the next
two or three years. Fazendeiros had never kept large local cash
reserves to meet payments, for the Rio commissários had
always paid up-country planters' bills. Cash payment to slaves
for extra work on Sundays or saints' days had been easily
handled. But to pay a large labor force weekly or even monthly
wages on short notice proved difficult.[27] Drafts on Rio factors
had always been based on future harvests; now, not only was
the harvest of 1888 doubtful, those of the future seemed
imperiled as organized labor seemed headed for disintegration.
Rio factors feared the worst and the banks where they dis-
counted planter bills were even more dubious.[28] Most planters
had no other source of ready cash and the few "whose circumstances are favorable may be able to pay wages during this
harvest, but not afterward." [29] The crucial problem posed by
the nature of coffee agriculture and plantation economy was
how to keep labor on a year-round basis to weed the groves,
plant new trees where possible, and raise foodstuffs. Observ-
ing no way of maintaining a labor force such as previously
existed, planters considered the possibility of abandoning their
fazendas. "Panic," *Novidades* philosophized, "is as catching as
laughter."[30]

In making arrangements with ex-slaves, planters were
favored by the fact that freedmen desperately needed money to
feed, house, and clothe themselves and their families, if they
had any. Coelho Netto, the novelist who lived in Vassouras
during the post-abolition years, put into words the helplessness
which seized many Negro freedmen in the years after 1888:
"The Negroes were dying of hunger along the roads, they had
no shelter to turn to, no one wanted them, they were perse-

[27] One economic journal estimated that the creation overnight of rural labor on
a salaried basis necessitated fifty million milreis above normal circulation or 25 per
cent increase in the circulating medium. Unfortunately no facts were offered to
substantiate the statement. *Conjuntura Econômica*, II, (August 1948), 24–25. This
estimate is found too in Caio Prado Junior, *História Econômica do Brasil* (2nd ed.,
São Paulo, 1949), p. 228.

[28] *Novidades*, June 8, 1888.

[29] *Novidades*, June 2, and June 8, 1888.

[30] June 5, 1888.

cuted." [31] In the pages of *Novidades*, only too ready to generalize on the evil consequences of "precipitous" emancipation, planters aired their dissatisfaction in dealing with foot-loose freedmen sorely needed to gather the harvest. "From the majority of planters," reported *Novidades* darkly, "we get word of the indiscipline and bad comportment [of freedmen] which planters tolerate because they need to harvest coffee." [32] Apparently "bad comportment" meant that the liberated Negro would not work as hard as he had formerly; he turned up for work after lunch (10 A.M.), and once he picked enough for his needs, he departed. [33] In his new sense of liberty the freedman equated fixed and long hours of work with slavery and therefore not "compatible" with freedom. [34] An article by a Vassouras planter who began administration of a fazenda on the day after emancipation provides an index to planters' outmoded conceptions of their own and their freedmen's role in the "new era." Baldly he put the proposition that the freedmen required more and not less supervision than the former slave; for his part, the ex-slave should not think that emancipation meant "the suppression of all the obligations he formerly fulfilled toward his master. He must not think that liberty means no obligatory hours of work." [35]

What constituted "obligatory hours of work" was at the heart of the changing labor situation which Vassouras planters at first refused to accept in much the same fashion that they resisted emancipation until governmental decree stripped them of their slaves. Five years earlier an observer had tried to explain why planters considered the ex-slave field hand "lazy." Since field slaves worked anywhere from fourteen to eighteen hours daily in the coffee groves, the fact that ex-slaves worked six to seven hours daily discouraged planters of 1884 with the

[31] Coelho Netto, *Banzo*, p. 26.
[32] May 30, 1888.
[33] *Novidades*, June 8, 1888.
[34] *Novidades*, August 11, 1888. Writing in 1883 Couty observed similarly that freedmen avoided gang labor in coffee groves. For them the concept of "regular and daily" labor implied a "dishonorable idea." *Biologie Industrielle*, p. 118.
[35] André Werneck in an article published in 1888. Documentos Referentes a Familia Werneck. Arquivo Nacional.

idea of depending upon the labor of freedmen. He reminded planters that European colonists would not work more than four or five hours per day exclusively on coffee, attending to only one-third of the coffee bushes maintained by slaves.[36]

Further aggravating the problem was the shortage of labor. Aside from those ex-slaves, usually the younger ones who could not adjust to the new conditions into which emancipation thrust them—whom an embittered and disillusioned abolitionist later termed "young men wandering on the roads or lounging at the vendas and liquor shops, gossiping, gambling or becoming intoxicated" [37]—the largest reduction in available labor stemmed from the reluctance of many newly emancipated women to return to the field gangs. "They just didn't want to grab the hoe handle again." Observed a planter, "Immediately after the emancipation act 50 per cent of the laborers, the part represented by women, stopped working." [38] Cooks, washerwomen, dishwashers, housecleaners, and caretakers of children —most of the female personnel who had performed the auxiliary services vital to the maintenance of an integrated and effective slave labor force—abandoned their plantations. The increase of manpower in these subsistence activities now performed in family units directly affected the labor supply for the main crop, coffee; at harvest time, however, when planters paid a flat piecework rate for picked coffee, the women often returned to work. Finally, many freedmen who left for work in the coffee areas outside the município must have taken along their mates, as occurred in the nearby Parahyba Valley município of Rezende.[39]

To former slaveholders of Vassouras who conveniently forgot the worsening economic conditions of their plantations in the seventies and eighties, blaming the troubles of 1888, 1889, and 1890 solely upon the decree emancipating slaves, the sight of

[36] Delden Laerne, *Brazil and Java*, pp. 348, 215, 374.

[37] Quintino Bocayuva, *Mensagem do Governador, September, 1902*, p. 130.

[38] Pedro Días Gordilho Paes Leme, "A Grande Propriedade e o Chim," *Revista Agrícola do Instituto Fluminense de Agricultura*, XXII (December 1891), 49.

[39] João de Azevedo Carneiro Maia, *Notícias Históricas e Estatísticas do Município de Rezende* (Rio de Janeiro), pp. 253–254. This author claimed an "extraordinary number of marriages" among freed folk after May 13, 1888.

former slaves apparently lounging unconcernedly in front of liquor shops or the small hovels which a few built among the cultivated groves provided a constant goad.[40] Planters reared in the tradition that all Negroes were supposed to work during daylight hours could not fail to view in loitering freedmen "vagabonds" and "depredators," or, as Quintino Bocayuva later phrased it, "an element of perturbation and an example of laziness and insubordination which merely serve to corrupt those workers who fulfill their obligations."[41] Reflecting the current mentality of planters, the director of the state treasury, Alberto Brandão, former schoolmaster of one of Vassouras' private secondary schools, prepared a report for the governor of the State of Rio urging that "an article of the Criminal Code be applied to force the freedmen . . . to return to the plantations they had abandoned."[42] Brandão's proposal might have gone unnoticed but for the fact that the *Sociedade Central de Immigração* of Rio inserted a letter of protest in a Rio newspaper, since Brandão's recommendations for alleviating the shortage of agricultural labor bypassed immigration as an alternative. "We are not in agreement with you, in relation to the first measure you propose, a measure which seeks in the severity of the laws and in coercion a way of providing labor for abandoned plantations; a measure which takes advantage, through the application of force and threats, of that idle segment of the

[40] Ex-slaves' reaction to freedom, and the bitterness of planters toward "loafing" freed folk who refused to work in the field gangs of coffee fazendas were current long before the days following the Thirteenth of May. At the Agricultural Congress of 1878 one planter urged that the Imperial Government "correct and force to work" freedmen loitering in groups of four, five or six at the doors of every liquor shop as well as freedwomen who, it was believed, "move to the slums to loaf or indulge in vice." Joaquim Leite Brandão in *Congresso Agrícola*, p. 182.

[41] *Mensagem do Governador do Estado do Rio, September, 1902*, p. 133.

[42] *Gazeta de Notícias*, January 13, 1890. In Brandão's defense it must be stated that his recommendations to the governor were entirely consistent with his previously stated views on slavery. When the Imperial Senate rejected the proposal of Conselheiro J. J. Teixeira Junior prohibiting slave trading among provinces of the Empire (1877), Brandão applauded. Later Martinho Prado Junior of São Paulo's provincial assembly urged a prohibitive tax be levied on slaves imported into that province. Rejected by the provincial president, it was re-introduced in 1879. When the powerful Club da Lavoura of Campinas (São Paulo) threw its weight against the measure (1879) Brandão again registered approval. *O Município*, June 7, 1877, March 2, and March 9, 1879.

population which you term . . . the shiftless and by whom you mean the freedmen of the Thirteenth of May." [43]

Having stirred up a hornet's nest, Brandão forwarded a restatement of his ideas. Aside from a condescending reference to "unrestricted liberty of work," he minced no words. "If we repress loafing, much manpower now useless will have to return to the abandoned plantations and since the majority of men living in the interior are field hands, they will resume their former profession." [44]

Comment in equally direct terms came from a Vassouras planter on January 17. A. P. de Lacerda Werneck accused Brandão pointedly of advocating "enslaving the freedmen of the Thirteenth of May and compelling them to work on the very fazendas they had quit because of bad administration there." Nor did he mince words: "See here, a man . . . who thinks this technique, which he calls 'open and generous,' is going to help agriculture is truly amazing!" [45] Despite the adverse reception given Brandão's report, a Vassouras councilman proposed the adoption of municipal regulations to enforce labor contracts two years to the day after the meeting of March 20, 1888.[46] During the following year, another Vassouras planter suggested that those individuals convicted of "minor transgressions"—meaning the "vagabonds and depredators"—be put to work on agricultural establishments. Protest against Brandão's ideas probably inspired this planter to add that it would not be advisable to let such measures be interpreted as a plan "to prolong by more or less subtle means the accursed state of slavery." [47]

Despite the social and economic turmoil generated by the Thirteenth of May, planters and ex-slaves worked out a *modus vivendi* within a few months. To be sure, for the next two or three years the forms of labor on coffee plantations remained fluid, reflecting the carry-over of traditional methods of working

[43] *Sociedade Central de Immigração* to Alberto Brandão, dated January 10, 1890, in *Gazeta de Notícias*, January 11, 1890.

[44] *Jornal do Commercio*, January 15, 1890.

[45] *Jornal do Commercio*, January 17, 1890.

[46] Sergio Werneck to CMV, March 20, 1890. APV, 1890.

[47] Paes Leme, "Organização Agrícola," pp. 5, 7.

the coffee groves by gangs of men and women, the restlessness of liberated Negroes and their reaction to gang labor, and the shortage among planters of cash for paying wages. Yet the essential fact soon emerged—alarmist articles of the planters' press to the contrary—that the "new era," preceded by years of bitter controversy, did not cause total disorganization of the labor force. The coffee harvest of 1888 was not lost and, according to one source, coffee exports for 1888 rose 48 per cent over those for the previous year.[48] As a Rio provincial report presented in August of 1888 phrased it officially, emancipation came "pacifically . . . without beclouding the order and tranquillity which must reign in a well-constituted society." [49] Eighteen months later in concluding a series of articles on abolition's aftermath, a Rio newspaper gave an equally serene appraisal. "The slaves were liberated, and no pains were taken to care either for the freedmen or for those who depended on their labor. Left to their own devices, both groups settled matters as well as they could and—wonderful resurgence of our land!—the freedmen did not turn into vagabonds and malfactors as some prophesied." [50]

In the first post-abolition harvest and through the spring of 1888 all the forces of pre-abolition decades in Vassouras brought planter and freedmen to terms on the basis of gang labor. Of the agricultural laborers in the Rio area—French, German, Italian, Spanish, and Portuguese immigrants, migrating Mineiros from the contiguous area to the north of the State of Rio, and Negro freedmen—the "preponderant element" was the Negro liberto with the tradition of the labor gang and, in many cases, of the small plot of subsistence crops. To that large group of planters raised in the traditions of blind routinism, the Negro liberto offered the "great service of continuity

[48] Total exports in bags of 60 kilos were as follows: 2,241,755 (1887) and 3,330,185 (1888). However, no mention was made of the inclusion of stocks of coffee from the harvest of 1887 in exports for the following year. "Retrospecto Commercial de 1888," *Jornal do Commercio*, pp. 3, 45; Antonio Gomes Carmo, *Reforma da Agricultura Brazileira* (Rio de Janeiro, 1897), p. 27. For the rapid reorganization of plantation labor in São Paulo following emancipation, see Luz, "A Administração Provincial de São Paulo," p. 98.

[49] *Relatório do Presidente da Província do Rio, August, 1888*, p. 17.

[50] *Gazeta de Notícias*, January 14, 1890.

of labor." He was, in the words of a Vassouras planter, "without any reservation the best rural worker we possess because of his perfect adaptation to coffee culture, his greater degree of resistence to climatic conditions, his eminently malleable qualities, besides his habits of sobriety in food and dress and other advantages which give him unquestionable value as an instrument of labor." [51] Not that other forms of labor were overlooked by planters; in addition to the salaried gang or turma worker (camarada), planters experimented with share-cropping (*colono parceiro*), jobbing (*colono empreiteiro*), and renting (*arrendatário*) of land.[52] The drastic alternative to large property and gang labor, division of plantations and sale of lots to small freedmen proprietors, was avoided. Whether by traditional modes of thought or by personal experience, Vassouras planters reasoned that the "indigenous workers"—Brazilian-born freedmen—would not be suitable as small proprietors because of the "very indolence of the climate, or even more, by the ignorance deriving from the condition under which they lived until only a little while ago." These factors, it was believed, left the ex-slaves without "ambition or stimulus" and consequently the large fazenda could use them only for wage labor.[53] Wrote one Vassouras planter some months after passage of the "Golden Law": "Since the Law of the Thirteenth of May of last year, which so profoundly changed agricultural conditions, I have fought and still fight to have organized labor, using every legal means to keep in order men habituated to constant tutelage and who have been abruptly handed over to their own control." [54]

Wherever possible, planters sought to house their freed field hands near the plantation main buildings or sede. In this way reorganization of pre-abolition plantation routine encountered the least possible amount of innovation; supervision of the

[51] Paes Leme, "Organisação Agrícola," p. 4.
[52] Reunião dos Fazendeiros, March 20, 1888. APV, 1888. Two years later the same alternatives were proposed as "a jornal, de empreitada ou parcería, em terra arrendada ou comprada." Angelo de Amaral, *Tres Cartas* (Rio de Janeiro, 1890), p. 51.
[53] *O Vassourense*, January 18, 1891.
[54] Christóvão Correa e Castro to CMV. APV, 1889.

gangs, performance of the auxiliary services of food preparation, clothes washing, and the care of children seemed to be re-channeled into former molds. Most ex-slaves working on fazendas had no place to move to immediately; they remained in the former slave quarters or senzallas which were now called "employees' or camaradas' dormitories." On one plantation, the old separated tarimbas or sleeping quarters of male and female slaves were termed "rooms for male employees" and "dormitories for unmarried freedwomen." Yet in an inventory of plantation property drawn up twelve years after the Thirteenth of May, freedmen's quarters near the sede still appeared as "One house . . . . which used to be a senzalla." [55]

Although the purchase and preparation of food for breakfast and supper now depended upon free field hands, the planter was still prepared to supply gang laborers with meals when work was in progress on the coffee slopes. An ex-slave who took the job of cook on the plantation where he had been raised as an ingénuo reported that he cooked "for the field gangs, for the children of mothers who worked in the fields, for the masons and carpenters, and for the 'folk who lived upstairs' (the planter and his family)." Naturally the daily wage of those supplied with meals was lower than that of those who managed to arrange their own. Those furnished with food were paid *a molhado* and the others *a secco*, the latter receiving on the average 50 per cent more in wages or Rs. 1$800 compared to Rs. 1$200 daily.

In their efforts to maintain the pre-abolition pattern of centralized plantation services with the least possible contact with potentially disorderly outside elements, many planters opened their own stores to sell food, clothing, and assorted

[55] "30 sections of slave quarters in front of the terreiro, which serve as a dormitory." Inventory, 1889, deceased: Quintiliano Gomes Ribeiro de Avellar, executor: João Gomes Ribeiro de Avellar, Fazenda da Boa Sorte, CPOV. "A house divided into dormitories for employees, a house covered with tile (the old senzallas), a house covered with tile, floored, serving as infirmary and dormitory for unmarried freedwomen." Inventory, 1890, deceased: Alexandrina de Araujo Padilha, executor: João Antonio Dias, Fazenda Santa Eufrázia, CPOV. "One house covered with tile, with five sections which used to be a senzalla." Inventory, 1900, deceased: Manoel Peixoto de Lacerda Werneck, executrix: Evalina Teixeira de M. Werneck, Fazenda Monte Sinai, CPOV.

drygoods. According to *Novidades*, two months after abolition,[56] planters did not entertain hope of profiting as merchants, rather to provide newly liberated plantation personnel from their own vendas as formerly they had used the fazenda dispensary for their slaves. For a day's labor, planters exchanged supplies, a technique that reduced the volume of cash needed to pay wages to freedmen who otherwise would immediately set off for already established vendas. Vassouras planters judged mutually satisfactory an arrangement that supplied "goods at reasonable prices, which profits the worker and the planter—for the former achieves a maximum quantity of needed goods with his earnings, while the latter does not have his organized labor interrupted by the frequent departures of his men to the tavern." [57] Fazendeiros may also have tried to protect freedmen from becoming the prey of sharp dealing venda proprietors of the vicinity. Nevertheless, planters frequently sold useless but bright and attractive articles at exorbitant prices to ex-slaves unacquainted with the perils of a cash economy. One ex-planter was reported to have rationalized his sales technique thus: "The government robbed me of my slaves. Now the Negroes are going to pay me back."

Pre-abolition patterns of life and labor could not be totally reimposed. The Thirteenth of May gave the ex-slave freedom of movement, freedom to choose his own boss (*patrão*) and his place of residence, if it failed to give him any small property. Many ex-slaves with mates and children often preferred to move away from the sede, from the vigilance and patriarchalism of the senhor—from the outward forms of slavery. In planter descriptions of the clients who traded at their vendas, the labor force was composed of "workers and colonos"—the

[56] July 12, 1888.
[57] Christovão Correa e Castro to CMV. APV, 1889. ". . . keeping the workers away from the taverns. . ." Joaquim Gomes Ribeiro de Avellar to CMV, February 21, 1890. APV. ". . . a small stock which almost exclusively supplies my workers and colonos. . ." Francisco José do Amaral to CMV, 1890. ". . . a small commercial establishment whose purpose is to offer foodstuffs almost exclusively to my colonos and workers. . ." Widow and Heirs of Augusto Baptista de Mello to CMV, June 1, 1890. ". . . a store or small shop with the sole aim of furnishing my workers and colonos. . ." Visconde de Cananea to CMV, February 21, 1890. CMV, 1890.

workers residing in dormitories, the colonos with their families scattered in groups (*colônias*) of small huts throughout the surviving coffee groves.[58] As resident day laborers (*colonos camaradas*) these freedmen worked six days per week in the labor gangs on a salary basis. Between the rows of coffee surrounding their houses, they raised beans and corn which they sold to the fazendeiro or exchanged at an outside venda. Their mates prepared food, washed clothing, and kept house; their children tended the corn and bean patches and a few chickens and pigs.

Not all coffee planters in the months after emancipation were able to retain enough freedmen as camaradas or colonos camaradas to care for their groves, harvest the crop, and prepare the groves for the next season's harvest. In leaving certain planters, ex-slaves were motivated sometimes by restlessness, more often by the fact that these planters were associated in their minds with "bad captivity," or by the attraction of higher wages dangled before their eyes by enterprising labor contractors or *empreiteiros*. Empreiteiros, many of whom were Portuguese, contracted with planters whose slaves had deserted to furnish the necessary gang labor for any agricultural tasks at a flat rate. Picked up from the pool of unemployed freedmen wandering in the towns, the itinerant gangs averaged fifty men. No unmarried women were included. The empreiteiro provided the gangs with food, and lodged them in ranchos located in the midst of the coffee groves; when the job or jobs were finished, the labor contractor and his gang moved on to another plantation. Although these organized gangs seemed a more promising alternative to the "maggots of freedmen who gather a few baskets of coffee and exchange them for alcohol and jerked beef at the nearest store," there was one drawback. Empreiteiros made their profit by deceiving their gang laborers, by paying them less than promised. In turn, the freedmen often stole what coffee had been harvested and handed over to the

[58] In Minas Gerais, Negro freedmen reacted similarly. Pierre Denis noted that "Since abolition the black agricultural population has acquired new habits; its dwellings are now scattered. The negro habitations . . . are scattered all over the area of the fazendas, distributed at hazard, in the neighborhood of the springs or along the roads." *Brazil*, p. 317.

planter by the labor contractor, then fled.[59] In the middle of
the harvest of 1888, *Novidades* even accused abolitionists of
having "incited the slaves with thoughts of liberty" in order to
siphon off part of their wages as freedmen by "hiring them out
on their account to the agriculturists." [60]

Supervision of labor gangs, now composed of freedmen,
suffered modifications as some outward forms reminiscent of
slavery were dropped. Feitores—the hated overseers—became
foremen (*apuntadores*)[61] because four times daily they made a
notation (*ponto*) in small books to check on the gang members'
attendance. The bacalhao or whip was eliminated; instead, the
foremen moved about armed with a long stick and a muzzle-
loading shotgun. "There was no discipline," as one ex-foreman
expressed it, "and the foreman had to impose respect and
authority because the Negro field hand no longer tolerated the
impositions of vigilance. The field hand often reacted violently." Another foreman said he moved about armed because
he was "afraid of a fight." A third, who carried a revolver,
feared he might be assaulted if he found himself in an argument
with freedmen in a spot isolated from the remainder of the gang.

As in the days of slavery, the work day began before sunrise
and ended at sunset. Planters paid weekly or monthly wages.
But whereas under slavery the field hand who hoed his row of
coffee to the top of the slope was ordered by the overseer to
help his neighbor or to begin a new row, under freedom, the
hand who worked better than the others might finish his row,
then wait at the top smoking a cigarette. Group feeling, however, animated the newly freed slaves and strengthened the
slave pattern of the slowdown. One foreman said he once
approached a man who worked hard and well and proposed to

[59] *Novidades*, June 8, 1888.

[60] August 9, 1888.

[61] ". . . apuntadores (the name designated for those in charge of the labor
gangs, the feitores of the slave sysyem). . ." Sylvio Ferreira Rangel, "O Café,"
O Brasil. Suas Riquezas Naturaes. Suas Industrias (Rio de Janeiro, 1908), II, 44. Of
the coffee plantations in southern Minas Geraes Pierre Denis wrote: ". . . it is
impossible in Minas to obtain a constant effort from the negroes unless the supervision is incessant. They are therefore organized in gangs, with a foreman or
overseer to each gang. Except that they carry no whip, these overseers are what the
guards were in times of slavery." *Brazil*, p. 318.

increase his wages if he kept up the good work. Nearby, several field hands overheard the conversation and shouted "let's get together." Once his fellow field hands talked to him, the field hand in question slowed down.

After the turmoil of the months following emancipation and the improvisation of labor gangs from camaradas, colonos-camaradas, or empreiteiro-led gangs, organization of remaining fazenda coffee production crystallized in the form of share-cropping or parcería, supplemented by jobbing. By the middle of 1890 sharecropping had become widespread in the município of Vassouras and one Vassouras planter was even moved to denounce the unsupervised freedman sharecropper (colono parceiro or meieiro) as "given over solely to the ignorance in which he was raised, full of the vices he acquired in the slave regime, habituated to the hoe and the billhook. . . Hence the need of the proprietor's intelligent direction." In almost the same breath the writer admitted that the "direction" of slave days consisted of individuals—fazendeiros or overseers—who "in the majority could not explain how they did things. They did them mechanically, and consequently could not teach others." [62] Such individual protests failed to deter the diffusion of the cropping system whose advantages appealed to both fazendeiros and freedmen. Of the two predominant forms of coffee production in the State of Rio in 1897, sharecropping was evaluated as more "frequent" than jobbing (*empreitada*); both persisted during the years of remaining coffee production in the município of Vassouras, as in municípios of the Parahyba Valley.[63]

The share system apparently satisfied the freedmen's desire to avoid constant supervision and to enjoy the semblance of small property. In the process whereby "coffee turned into halves" a camarada or colono-camarada would approach his patrão or foreman and inform him he wanted to work a piece of land in a certain corner of the coffee groves. Planters

[62] A. P. de Lacerda Werneck, *A Lavoura e o Governo. II Apelo aos Fazendeiros* (Rio de Janeiro, 1890), pp. 7–8.

[63] Empreitada was often called *empreitada paulista* since it was applied widely in the São Paulo coffee growing areas, whence it spread to sections of the State of Rio. Arrigo de Zettiry, *O Estado do Rio* (Rio de Janeiro, 1897), pp. 83–86.

generally approved because the new system kept cash transactions, whether weekly or monthly wages, to a minimum, and
presented the planter with the added labor force of the colonos'
wives or "companions" (*companheiras*) who willingly supplemented the work of their mates. Sharing also helped fix the
freedmen to one place; and while the less profitable groves
could be worked on shares, the younger remaining groves could
absorb the sharecropping colono as day laborer, when necessary
several times weekly.[64] Where the sharecropper was able to
cultivate corn or sugar cane beyond his subsistence needs,
planters stipulated that in addition to "halves" on coffee, there
be "thirds" of large subsidiary crops. Colono sharecroppers
could produce for their needs but generally sold their subsistence
crops—the coffee always was handed over to the plantation
proprietor—to a nearby venda for cash. When they needed the
foodstuffs, they returned to the venda and repurchased them
at higher prices. Some, of course, saved their produce where
storage facilities were available, but these were few. At the end
of the year, when the main cash crop, coffee, was delivered to
the fazendeiro, little surplus was left after the storekeeper's bills
were met.

There was no fixed method of sharing. In some cases, the
patrão and the sharecropper (colono-meieiro) walked over the
land and divided the groves or other crops into two to avoid
any differences at the time of division. Or, at the harvest when
the mature berries were piled in small dumps on the drying
terrace, the proprietor chose his share. A third method was to
divide the bagged coffee in the engenho after processing was
complete. Whatever the form of sharing, it was the planter who
sold all the coffee to his Rio factor and who distributed the cash
payments due to each of his sharecroppers.

Forms of gang labor subsisted among sharecroppers when
more labor was required than that mustered by the sharecropper and his family. If a colono-parceiro had a crop which
he could not handle on time, the patrão might pay extra wage
laborers recruited from among the other residents. This supple-

[64] It was the colono's double role as sharecropper and day-laborer that confused
the forms of labor in the post-abolition years.

mentary labor was called a "help" and its cost was deducted by the planter. The *mutirão*, on the other hand, was organized without the intervention of the patrão although with his consent. A sharecropper asked his planter if he would dispense the labor of men slated to work for the plantation on a certain day. The sharecropper then called his neighbors, killed a pig and several chickens, and worked and fed them for the day. Women and children came along, too. In the evening at the end of the day's labor there would be dancing, jongos, and drumming at a caxambú.

Under the other predominant form of working the fazendas after abolition, the empreitada, planters delimited an area containing several thousand coffee bushes. A contract was made between fazendeiro and colono-empreiteiro: in return for the weedings and general care of from 3,000–5,000 bushes, the fazendeiro promised to pay a fixed quantity per bush. At the time of harvest, each arroba of coffee gathered by the contratista or his family was paid at a fixed rate. "With this pact," one observer wrote, "the colono has absolutely no right of possession over the coffee he harvests." [65]

From the welter of labor forms which emerged from pre-abolition roots and which began to crystallize by the early nineties, the coffee planters of Vassouras undoubtedly profited as long as coffee prices remained high enough to work remaining groves profitably. Salient among their advantages was the fact that planters avoided any division of their large holdings. Full legal control of land and crops was unmodified. A more decisive advantage stemmed from the fact that planters were dealing with freedmen unused to a money economy. Only yesterday freed from the forced labor of servitude, Negro freedmen tended to accept cash in any amount as adequate return for their services. This attitude was strengthened by the development of resident labor which as colono-camarada or colono-meieiro could have a separate home removed from the

---

[65] Zettiry, *O Estado do Rio*, p. 86. Fazendeiros also employed the colono-empreiteiro, sometimes called *colono-contratista*, to perform specific jobs at a fixed rate, such as clearing land for the planting of coffee, or draining terraces lying on the edges of small streams.

former master's eye, and where foodstuffs for daily consumption were raised. Cash, therefore, in large amounts was useful but not an absolute necessity, in their essentially subsistence economy.

Planters used short-weighting techniques at harvest times to widen the margin between cost and profit. Each freedman carried his basket of coffee to the end of his coffee rows and poured out the berries. Later the planter sent out his ox-cart to collect the harvested berries. Presumably the basket used to measure each freedman's pile held 48 liters; but there were instances where fazendeiros insisted on using large baskets, some holding from 60 to 70 liters. Yet from fazenda to fazenda the price per basket poured into the fazendeiros' collecting cart was fixed. Few freedmen could count exactly the number of baskets as they were put into the cart. Moreover as the measuring basket was filled, then placed in the cart to be poured, the man measuring leveled the top of the basket to obtain an even measure. The excess remained in the cart and only the basketful was counted. Repeated when measuring corn by volume and not by weight, the process was known as "weeping." It was, of course, true that a basket of coffee often held more than mature berries. Stones, dirt, and twigs found their way into the cart as in the days of slavery. And a certain amount of coffee stealing by freedmen from the coffee terraces was common. Finally, where coffee was divided into shares and proprietor and sharecropper looked over the piles, the planter chose first. When freedmen reacted to short-weighting, or planters felt the presence of certain freedmen to be undesirable, planters with little ceremony sent around an ox-cart, loaded the colono's belongings and dumped them at the limits of the fazenda. Nor did neighboring planters welcome troublemakers.

(3)

Immersed in the problem of saving their homes and lands through satisfactory reorganization of available labor, in the year following abolition planters looked with apathy, if not bitterness, upon the disintegration of the monarchy in which they had once seen the "guarantee of their slave property." Although the Imperial Government tried to insure the allegiance of disaffected planters in the last years of the Empire by wide-spread distribution of titles (Table 21), the planters' reaction intensified as hope for indemnification of lost slaves withered. "The pact between the monarchical regime and the classes which formerly defended and upheld it was destroyed." [66] Two months after emancipation, one newspaper of the State of

TABLE 21. Distribution of baronies and other titles in Brazil, 1880–1889.

Year	Barons	Total titles granted
1880	13	15
1881	31	31
1882	33	34
1883	29	29
1884	16	16
1885	13	13
1886	17	18
1887	34	36
1888	69	84
1889	92	92

Source: A. d'E. Taunay, *História*, VIII, 228–240. Of the 92 baronies granted in 1889, it should be noted, 75 per cent were conferred in the five months, June 7 to November 15, 1889.

Rio printed its conviction that "only the republic can maintain order in Brazil, only the republic can allow the expansion of powerful national forces." [67]

Overnight Vassouras' tiny group of tolerated republicans swelled to include the majority of embittered planters. A published announcement invited the "republican citizens" of Vassouras to a meeting on July 1 to "explain the fundamental ideas of the program and measures for the organization of the party." [68] Signed by almost fifty of the most important land-holders of the município, the republican manifesto of July 1

[66] *Monitor Fidelense*, July 4, 1888.
[67] *Monitor Fidelense*, July 7, 1888.
[68] *O Vassourense*, June 17, 1888.

attacked the monarchy as an element that had usurped the powers of the legislature and had "exonerated itself from obedience to the inspirations of public thought." The monarchical regime, the manifesto averred, had turned into a "reign of fictions, lies, hypocrisy." The "centralizing power" of the monarchy had subordinated the other governmental powers and bred "moral and political anarchy." As for the future, only the republic held out the hope of creating institutions in harmony with the nation's "necessities." [69] Republican meetings multiplied in Vassouras and in the other disgruntled municípios of the Parahyba Valley where Silva Jardim and other abolitionist-republicans spread the new gospel.[70] Membership of large numbers of formerly monarchical-minded planters, and the "class of commissários, whose interests are identified with those of the planters," led one observer to call the political converts "plutocratic neo-republicans with a penchant for great social inequalities." [71] When the republic was called into existence on November 15, 1889, the event caused little disturbance in the area aside from the usual festivities and optimistic proclamations.[72] Unflurried by the news, fazendeiros and freedmen tried to work out some means for mutual survival.

[69] *O Vassourense*, August 5, 1888.

[70] *Monitor Fidelense*, July 28, 1888; *O Isothérmico* (Vassouras), August 25, 1888.

[71] Ottoni, *O Advento da República*, pp. 78–79.

[72] *O Vassourense*, November 24, 1889.

CHAPTER XI

Epilogue

IF abolition and the advent of the Republic quickened the tempo of development in the expanding coffee-growing areas of São Paulo by creating opportunities for European immigrant laborers, it only emphasized in the minds of Parahyba Valley planters the instability of their economy and the inevitability of its decline. Assertion of the forces of decline, evidenced in the three decades preceding the Thirteenth of May, continued to undermine the whole structure of Vassouras plantation society. The rising coffee prices of the early 1890's supported many planters of Vassouras as they attempted to achieve some stability through reorganization of their labor force. But the drop in coffee prices in the latter half of the decade ushered in rapidly the transition to Vassouras' new economy—cattle-raising—and gave the area full membership in the community of the "dead towns" [1] of the eroded and devastated Parahyba Valley.

In the nineties the coffee groves of Vassouras were only a shadow of what decades before had been the pride and the fortune of local planters. "We know that the main crop, the origin of our agricultural wealth, has decreased very, very much," wrote two Vassouras planters to the municipal Câmara at the end of 1890. "We know that large areas of our lands are becoming useless or are so mishandled that they give insignificant returns. We know all about this just as we are aware of

---

[1] In a short essay published in 1906 and entitled "The Dead Towns," Monteiro Lobato highlighted the decadence of the once opulent coffee towns of the Parahyba Valley. As he wrote in one brief paragraph: "There, everything was, nothing is. Even the verbs are not conjugated in the present. Everything is past tense." José Bento de Monteiro Lobato, *Urupês. Outros Contos e Coisas* (Artur Neves, ed., São Paulo, 1943), p. 137.

the impoverishment of our município and its visible decadence." [2] Formerly masked by the use of slave labor working
long hours daily on both productive and over-aged groves, the
progressive contraction of the number of producing coffee trees
was accelerated by slave emancipation and the switch to wage
labor. A Portuguese immigrant who arrived in Vassouras in
the mid-nineties found most of the land in secondary growth

TABLE 22. Estimated coffee production in the State of Rio,
1891–1896.

Year	Production (kilograms)	Index
1891–92	97,521,461	100
1892–93	80,874,199	83
1893–94	67,661,197	69
1894–95	60,855,314	52
1895–96	59,934,167	51

Source: Mensagem do Governador do Estado do Rio, September 1902, pp. 137–138.
These statistics are only indicative of the crisis, since many of the figures given
during the nineties for coffee production in the State of Rio are contradictory.

or low weeds; the older coffee groves were being abandoned in
order to concentrate labor on those groves that could still pay
the cost of wages and transport and leave a margin of profit.
Production of coffee, stated the Rio governor's report in 1896,
was "reduced by the exhaustion of soil appropriate to this type
of crop." [3] a note repeated in the following year's report with
more somber overtones. "The State of Rio which for many
years has been based upon coffee monoculture is almost
exhausted and needs an agricultural and industrial transformation. . . Rio's coffee production has declined notoriously since
1888." (Table 22.)[4]

Desperately seeking an exit from the "dark blind alley which
we have long been preparing," [5] some planters attempted to

[2] Christóvão Correa e Castro and Pedro d'Alcántara Leite Ribeiro to Intendencia Municipal de Vassouras, December 24, 1890. APV, 1890.

[3] *Mensagem do Governor do Estado do Rio, September, 1896,* p. 41.

[4] *Mensagem do Governador do Estado do Rio, September 1897,* pp. 85–86.

[5] Luíz Pereira Barretto, *O Século XX sob o Ponto de Vista Brasileiro* (São Paulo,
1901), p. 30.

restore their land's fertility through the use of the plow and fertilizer in the form of manure or the hulls of processed coffee beans. What might have produced some advantages twenty years earlier, however, was worthless in exhausted soil. Transporting fertilizer in ox-carts along coffee paths cut in the sides of steep slopes proved "extremely expensive" and neither oxen nor plow could profitably till the bare, tired hills. "But when by the application of supreme energy these processes were carried out, only one torrential downpour was needed to wash away the freshly plowed sandy soil and to leave it more sterile than before." [6] Local attempts were no less pitiable as Vassouras planters with no experience in growing coffee in once-cultivated soil tried the impossible. One planter is reported to have placed young coffee bushes in the gaps of his aging groves. "They grew, but not very high." He turned to a stretch of secondary growth spreading through groves abandoned fifteen to twenty years before. He ordered the young trees and low brush cut carefully, the branches trimmed to insure proper and even drying. Then the cleared section was permitted to decay for one month; no firewood could be removed. The section was fired and planting begun. With each seedling went a small amount of fertilizer in the form of coffee hulls. "Nothing happened. The new coffee grove died before it bore any fruit, only growing to about 18″ in height." Said the disheartened planter to his friends: "I'm worn out too. Coffee will never grow here again, the land is like a banana tree because it yields only one bunch of bananas."

Planters were caught between the blades of a scissors and the pressure mounted in the course of the last decade of the nineteenth century. Falling coffee production of the Rio area was one blade; the other, inability to pay satisfactory wages to hold freedmen or immigrant labor tempted by better wages elsewhere. On the one hand planters, molded in the tradition that the slave laborer be worked to the maxmium for the lowest possible cost, continued to "pay insufficient wages to their laborers . . . and to reimburse the labor of the colono . . . at a price barely superior to the cost of maintaining the slave laborer." Hence, "the constant struggle on the part of the

[6] Gomes Carmo, *Reforma*, p. 3.

planter to restrict the colono's gains to a minimum in every indirect way possible."[7] There was another element in Vassouras planters' reasoning. "It is known that in gang labor each worker handles today 4,000 coffee bushes which produce on the average 80 arrobas which, calculated at the price of Rs. 5$000, total Rs. 400$000. Now, if the annual wage of a worker is Rs. 300$000, we should have only a surplus of Rs. 100$000 subject to unforeseen expenses, interest, etc., etc."[8] Planters thereby concluded that it was throwing good money after bad to maintain those fazendas where the productive trees were few.

The times were changing, and the Negro's new freedom to choose his occupation and to accept the best wages restricted the planter's freedom in making terms with his laborers. The nearby, expanding capital of the Republic offered many opportunities for domestic servants at higher wages than those proffered by ex-masters. Industrial expansion, both in industries already existing or of recent creation, provided an equally powerful magnet for footloose agricultural labor.[9]

A new development closed even more forcibly the scissors' blades: higher wages paid by agricultural companies formed within the município of Vassouras through the amalgamation of foreclosed or insolvent plantations. Operating through the private banks, the Republican government stimulated the formation of the agricultural companies by granting the banks non-interest-bearing loans to match the sums which the banks loaned to planters at fixed, low interest rates. In turn, the state governments attempted to channel the banks' funds to those planters "disposed to amalgamate several fazendas into one enterprise."[10]

Although doubts were raised in 1890 about the eventual destination of the Republican government's total disbursement

[7] *O Paíz*, March 23, 1893. Compare the statement made four years later: "Once abolition came, [planters] had to deal with freedmen and to find some method of retaining them for their crops. Certainly, that method was not to try all the time to pay as little as possible, always lowering wages. . ." Gomes Carmo, *Reforma*, pp. xi–xiii.

[8] *O Vassourense*, January 18, 1891.

[9] Paes Leme, "Organização Agrícola," p. 8.

[10] "Retrospecto Commercial de 1890," *Jornal do Commercio*, p. 4.

of more than 43,000 contos for such companies,[11] pressure to match wages scales of the heavily capitalized agricultural companies brought immediate denunciations from Vassouras planters. A deep, rankling bitterness, focused on the state governor, fairly boiled from the indignant article which one planter inserted in a newspaper of the capital. "And so today I am going to part with my fazenda, because I have to sell it! And the bread of my children, my tranquillity and everything that made up my life, (because at my age I cannot begin a different career)—all these I must sell to the companies which Snr. Portella [the governor] invented to protect the planters, to use his own words." With limited resources, the planter continued, he could not compete with the "powerful capital" behind such companies. Moreover, since the Portella regime guaranteed 6 per cent of the capital, the companies could augment their operating capital by eliminating a dividend at any time and throwing upon the state government the onus of making good the default. The capital, in the form of a better wage scale, siphoned away freedmen from more modest plantations. "Didn't Snr. Portella see that I will be shorn of my laborers?" asked the writer. And he immediately explained: "Obliged to pay at least thirty times the interest rate demanded of large companies for borrowed capital, I cannot afford the wages offered by those companies." As far as this planter was concerned, the companies only cloaked the schemes of those "clever planters who petitioned and scrambled for concessions so that other planters would have to sell their properties for a bagatelle (just the way they want to buy up mine), or keep them without a labor force." [12] Not all Vassouras planters felt so. One who wished to sell out wrote that "important companies or enterprises supplied with large capital, aim to acquire fazendas or rural establishments in order to maintain and work them conveniently, something which the actual proprietors,

[11] "Retrospecto Commercial de 1890," *Jornal do Commercio*, pp. 5–6. The charge was soon made that the number of private banks mushroomed merely to receive the "gratuitous advances of the Treasury." "Retrospecto Commercial de 1889," *Jornal do Commercio*, p. 6.

[12] Clipping of André Werneck, dated August 18, 1890 in Documentos Referentes a Familia Werneck, Arquivo Nacional.

who as a group entirely lack the necessary funds, will not be able to achieve." [13] Another played upon those very concessions and favors to try to pry from the state government a law forcing unemployed freedmen to labor on the plantations of the favored agricultural companies.[14]

Beset by the problem of obtaining cash to pay wages to plantation laborers, planters fell back upon their factors for help.[15] Here, too, were signs of the changing times. Planters who had received financial aid from their factors in earlier crises now discovered that the commissário, too, was menaced by the aftermath of emancipation. The planters' merchant friends at Rio, once lavish with their hospitality, treated them "with a certain lack of confidence" while some tried to disguise their scorn.[16] As intermediaries, on the one hand, between planters and exporters, and, on the other, between planters and bankers, factors perceived that their dual role was superfluous. Their resources available for advances to up-country planters had shrunk; few banks were willing to extend long-term or short-term credit to factors whose only collateral consisted of bills signed by planters mired in insolvency. Typical of the straightened circumstances of once opulent figures was the financial situation of a Vassouras resident who prior to his death had been both factor and later, planter. Immediately after his death his wife asked the probate judge for permission to contract a loan of 130 contos for six months at 10 per cent interest with the Bank of Brazil to cover the debts which her deceased husband had incurred as a partner in two commission houses. In November 1892, the total debts of the estate amounted to 214 contos. She returned to the Bank of Brazil in the following month to plead to have 100 contos of debt scaled down; but the Bank proved obdurate, gave her a two-months' moratorium and insisted that 155 contos be paid at the end of the mora-

[13] Letter, August 22, 1890 in Inventory, 1889, deceased: José Caetano de Almeida, executor: Teofilo Teixeira de Almeida, Fazenda da Victoria, CPOV.

[14] Paes Leme, "Organização Agrícola," p. 7.

[15] Inventory, 1889, deceased: José Caetano de Almeida, executor: Teofilo Teixeira de Almeida, Fazenda da Victoria, CPOV.

[16] Moritz Lemberg, *Brasilien Land und Leute* (Leipzig, 1899), cited in *Mensagem do Governador do Estado do Rio, September 1902*, p. 79.

torium. "No arrangements whatsoever may be made with other banking establishments, and even were this possible, it would have to be on very onerous conditions." She finally located one "capitalist" who offered to advance her 150 contos for three to four months at 10 per cent interest plus a second mortgage on urban real estate in her possession in Rio de Janeiro.[17]

Unable to obtain from factors the cash advances so badly required as their labor force shifted from slavery to freedom and wages, planters were reported to have felt "suddenly bereft of their natural guardians." [18] The precarious economic situation of the planters and their factors played into the hands of the coffee syndicates and exporters who, hitherto "tributaries of the coffee factor intermediaries," proceeded to circumvent the now helpless factors to purchase directly from planters harried for funds to cover the costs of production and to clear or amortize their obligations. "The large exporters, both rich and foreign in their majority and manipulating their own funds as well as those placed at their disposal by overseas syndicates whose intermediaries they are, send into the interior of the coffee producing states numerous agents charged with purchasing from the planters part or all of his harvest for cash, while they refuse to pay the same price for coffee consigned to the commissários of Rio de Janeiro." Between traditional factors and the coffee exporters the battle for consignment of up-country planters' coffee shipments was joined in 1895;[19] seven years later the struggle culminated in the "rout of the factors" who not only saw their shipments of coffee from the interior dwindle, but also could not reduce the debts accumulated in advances made to up-country planters since the latter suspended further coffee consignments. Concluded the governor's report for 1902: "In general lines this is the present situation of our agriculture, handed over with arms and legs bound to the triumphant speculation of capitalism." [20]

---

[17] Inventory, 1891, deceased: Visconde de Arcozello, executrix: Viscondessa de Arcozello, CPOV.

[18] *Mensagem do Governador do Estado do Rio, September, 1902*, p. 50.

[19] *Mensagem do Governador do Estado do Rio, September, 1897*, pp. 78–79.

[20] *Mensagem do Governador do Estado do Rio, September, 1902*, p. 51. W. G. Wagstaff of the British diplomatic service at Rio de Janeiro watched closely the elimination

Foreclosures of insolvent plantations furnished the final scene of the drama of social and economic disintegration at the close of Vassouras' cycle of coffee agriculture. History's hindsight lights up the seemingly inexorable forces which made of once productive plantations abandoned hulks grounded at the base of treeless hills. To the human participants in the drama, however, possible eviction from the property of their fathers and grandfathers made it imperative to scrape together the last bit of cash to meet interest and amortization payments and learn how to carry on when foreclosure notices came from the Vassouras courthouse.

The pattern of the decade of mortgage foreclosures in Vassouras—the decade of the nineties—was repeated in countless cases. Only the minor details varied. For example on December 6, 1889, José Caetano Alves and María Francisca de Souza Alves, his wife, signed a mortgage contract with the Banco de Crédito Real do Brazil. The Bank evaluated the property (234,000 coffee bushes) at Rs. 70:000$000, judged the annual revenue to be Rs. 17:500$000 and then offered the pair Rs. 35:000$000 in cash to be repaid in fifteen years, 6 per cent interest and amortization of Rs. 1:787$170, payable every six months. Interest rate of all overdue installments was to rise to

of the coffee intermediaries. In 1897, he reported that in 1895, "mention was made of the fact that exporters had initiated the system of buying direct from the planters without the customary intervention of commission agents, baggers and brokers. Business in this form has greatly increased; commission houses are no longer able to afford planters the assistance and facilities which they require, and they have therefore lost their control of the crops. It is argued that as this innovation prevents the compilation of market statistics as to sales, deliveries, available supply, stock, current prices, etc., the planter practically negotiates in ignorance of the real value of his coffee, and that this circumstance, together with his want of resources, places him quite at the mercy of the exporter. No doubt the planter would much prefer the reestablishment of the old order of business." Wagstaff then turned to criticism of "speculation." "Some profess to discern in this new movement of the exporter not merely an ordinary commercial proceeding adopted to promote his interests in a perfectly legitimate manner, but rather an act of coercive speculation, to which, and not to excessive production, they desire to ascribe the great fall in prices." A commission, after examination of planters' charges, determined that the planter was "responsible for the situation, inasmuch as he has devoted himself exclusively to the disproportionate extension of coffee cultivation neglecting all other kinds of produce, with the result that he is dependent upon foreign supplies for his food and other necessaries." *Report on the Trade and Commercial Activities of Brazil for the Year 1897.* Gt. Britain. C 8648. XCIV (1898), 7.

9 per cent. Keenly cognizant of the rural proprietor's labor problem, the Bank made detailed stipulations in the mortgage contract that "the mortgagers promise to administer the mortgaged property well, making all due repairs for its preservation and improvement and maintaining the property in a state of proper functioning with the proper number of laborers so that the present annual income of Rs. 17:500$000 will never

TABLE 23. Loans and arrears of selected Vassouras plantations, 1878–1895.

Date of original loan	Amount	Date of foreclosure	Amount outstanding	Percentage of amount outstanding on loan
1878	35:000$000	1891	72:451$000	207
1881	15:000$000	1891	20:331$900	136
1884	20:000$000	1893	63:509$700	318
1889	20:000$000	1894	24:266$900	121
1894	70:000$000	1895	78:797$330	113

Sources: Credor: Banco do Brazil, devedor: Manoel Machado Guimarães e mulher; Credor: Banco do Brazil, devedor: Luiz Antonio de Aguiar e sua mulher; Credor: Banco de Crédito Real, devedor: Virgilio José de Avila e mulher; Credor: Banco de Crédito Real, devedor: Antonio Furquim Werneck de Almeida e sua mulher; Credor: Banco do Brazil, devedor: Lindorf Moreira de Vasconcellos. All in CPOV.

diminish and . . . to give the Bank the right to examine, supervise and even intervene in the administration of the mortgaged property." All biannual payments were promptly paid until 1896, when coffee prices on the world market dropped. There then remained an unpaid balance of Rs. 21:326$893. Within one year, after having skipped two payments, incurred a fine for default of payment and suffered 9 per cent interest on the capital of the arrears, the mortgagers had a debit of Rs. 28:880$640. When a representative of the Bank with his distrainor arrived at the plantation on December 11, 1897 he was greeted by the widow of José Caetano Alves, her daughter, and son-in-law. The plantation was reported "in bad condition." Of the 234,000 coffee trees of 1889, only

60,000 remained. On December 18, 1899 the property was offered for sale at its 1889 evaluation; by February 1900, no prospective buyer had appeared. As successor to the Banco de Crédito Real do Brazil, the Banco Hypothecário do Brazil posted a new selling price at a 10 per cent reduction, or Rs. 63:000$000. On March 6, 1900 the property was offered for a 20 per cent reduction, or Rs. 56:000$000. When no buyer appeared at the third public sale, the property was offered to the highest bidder, the Banco Hypothecário, which paid Rs. 18:000$000.[21] Other cases of planters falling into arrears are even more extreme (Table 23). By the end of the decade most of the coffee plantations of the State of Rio were mortgaged or controlled by the mortgage sections of hypothecary banks and "those that are not totally abandoned, as can be observed on a large scale in our state, endure a miserable existence." [22]

(2)

Abandoned to grass, and stretching up and down the rounded hills, the rachitic files of aged and unproductive coffee trees had no peaceful interment. Such vast expanses of rolling hillsides could not be left in unprofitable abandonment. On the path of those who almost a century before had moved backward toward the coast from the frontier areas of the Minas gold fields came a second invasion of settlers from Minas. This time they did not come to learn to handle a new crop. This time they brought with them cattle, whose meat and milk could provision the expanding population of the capital of the Republic. In Vassouras as in other municípios of the Parahyba Valley, the new settlers found pasturage cheaper than in the southern portions of Minas. Easily they could turn loose their cattle to feed on the grasses—*capim angola, capim membeca, capim gordura*—spreading quickly through the untended coffee groves. As a resident expressed the change: "Pasture invaded the coffee groves." One planter was shipping milk out of the município

---

[21] Credor: Banco de Crédito Real do Brazil; devedor: José Caetano Alves e sua mulher, María Francisca de Souza Alves, CPOV.

[22] *Mensagem do Governador do Estado do Rio, September 1902*, p. 79.

as early as 1889;[23] in keeping with the changing times the first rolls of barbed wire were purchased by Vassouras' municipal authorities in October 1893.[24] A report for 1899 talked seriously of the need for polyculture and cattle-raising,[25] and in 1902 another prophetic report called cattle-raising the "future guarantee of our prosperity and greatness" and noted that "intelligent planters have recently tried to enlarge the area set aside for the raising of cattle." [26]

The cattle moved in and the people of Vassouras—planters and their families, freedmen and their families—moved out. For the ex-master and his family there were two paths: to the new coffee growing regions of São Paulo and eastern Rio de Janeiro; or to the payroll of the municipal, state, and federal governments as civil servants. As agricultural crises multiplied in the second half of the nineteenth century in rural Brazil, the flow of planters' sons into government service had swelled in volume and brought comment at the Agricultural Congress of 1878. According to the analysis of one minister of agriculture, planters no longer directed their sons into the uncertain future of agricultural pursuits, they prepared them for the professions. "Since our society cannot absorb all the trained professional people, there remains for them only recourse to civil service positions." [27] A quarter century later, as the exodus from the municípios of the Parahyba Valley increased, the "attraction of the civil service offering a fixed remuneration" was judged a "phenomenon inherent in all impoverished societies, in all countries disturbed by deep, serious crises. Where agriculture is on its deathbed; where commerce feels paralyzed; where industry does not prosper; where labor grows scarce, social parasitism develops." [28]

The freedmen and their families were made superfluous by ever-dwindling coffee groves which in turn required less labor,

[23] Inventory, 1889, deceased: Estevão Rodrigues Barbosa; executor: Augusto C. de Freitas, Fazenda Santa Eugenia, CPOV.

[24] APV, 1893.

[25] *Mensagem do Governador do Estado do Rio, September 1899*, p. xlvi.

[26] *Mensagem do Governador do Estado do Rio, September 1902*, pp. 96–97.

[27] *Congresso Agrícola*, p. 127.

[28] *Mensagem do Governador do Estado do Rio, September 1902*, p. 20.

and by the transformation of the abandoned groves into pasture for cattle-raising, which also could employ only a minimum of the available labor supply. As the last planter descendant of several generations of Vassouras fazendeiros had to write in his municipal report of 1913: ". . . the excess population must seek employment in other regions, and jobs are readily found because of the nearness of our município to the Federal Capital and to the State of São Paulo which is still developing a prosperous coffee agriculture." [29]

On foot along the dusty roads, in carts, on mules or horses, and by train, the exodus took place. For some the past became a fond remembrance where roseate memories were stored to regale the first generation of the twentieth century. For others the past stood for discipline, overwork, servitude. There was no middle ground in the two conceptions. But the future promised one group the chance to recoup fortune and status, the other the opportunity to remove gradually the scars of servitude's stocks and lash. Over both hovered the heritage of the past: "We are paying for the errors which we accumulated for over a century." [30]

And so they left the rolling hills of Vassouras, those hills where could be seen the cordilleras to the north, to the west, to the east, and to the south. The heritage willed to them could be found in the "bald expanse of the horizons of the Parahyba or . . . the rugged profile of the hills. There the onlooker remains transfixed before the abominable devastation that in the short period of a half-century destroyed forever a marvelous and majestic forest treasure without leaving behind in its place wealth, comfort, activity, flourishing industry, the fertile labor of small property, commercial expansion—all the signs of the perpetual strength of a flowering civilization." [31]

[29] Joaquim Ribeiro de Avellar, *Relatório Apresentado a CMV* (Barra do Pirahy, 1913), p. 21.
[30] Luiz Pereira Barretto, *O Seculo XX*, 30.
[31] Gomes Carmo, *Reforma*, p. 3.

The Legacy

In one century, the município of Vassouras and the major portion of the extensive Parahyba Valley were the scene of a complete economic cycle which started with tropical forest and terminated with denuded, eroded slopes. Once exploited, the lands of an internal frontier were abandoned to grass, weeds, and cattle. Paralleling the ruthless use of natural resources was an equally ruthless exploitation of man, both a part of the heritage willed to twentieth-century Brazil. Despite the toll of human and natural resources, however, the Brazilian coffee plantation nurtured the change that swept over Brazil during the nineteenth century. To be sure, Brazil in 1900 was still a land where localities barely removed from the few coastal towns resembled areas of the seventeenth- or eighteenth-century Portuguese colony.

Nevertheless Brazil had changed, and the coffee cycle of the Parahyba Valley was one of the most effective elements in the change. The cultivation, processing, and export of coffee to overseas markets carried Brazil into the currents of international trade that Western Europe and the United States widened and deepened in the nineteenth century. In the last decades of the eighteenth century and throughout the next century, agricultural and industrial innovations in Western Europe and in the United States facilitated the growth of population, thereby creating new and larger markets for the products of field and factory. To the water and steam driven factories in the distant English midlands and on the European continent, Brazil shipped its raw cotton; and for the tables of the multiplying population in lands on both shores of the North Atlantic, Brazil furnished the desserts—sugar, tobacco, and coffee. Brazilian sugar and tobacco suffered from the competition of other producing areas of the world during the nineteenth century; on the other hand, Parahyba Valley coffee maintained a dominant position in world markets until the end of the century when its exhausted lands could not match the output of the fresh soil of nearby São Paulo. And there the coffee cycle began anew, to repeat the onslaught on virgin forest and to cut a similar swath in search of new lands.

The sailing and steam driven ships which carried the coffee of Vassouras and of the Parahyba Valley to overseas markets returned laden with the elements of change: immigrants, food-stuffs, hardware, books, and luxuries. Coffee financed the telegraph and railroad lines that stretched from the ports into the interior; it financed the forced entry of African slaves from Angolla and Moçambique and drew the Portuguese, Italians, Spaniards, Frenchmen, and Germans of Europe; it brought merchants, doctors, carriagemakers and blacksmiths, opera stars and dressmakers, agricultural journals, medical manuals and *L'Illustration*, pine flooring from Riga and rooftiles from Marseilles, butter, bacon, and cod, English textiles and Swedish iron, patent medicines, French perfumes and wines. Coffee financed the sojourn abroad of planters' sons in Lisbon, Paris, and London and returned them, *doutores*, to cities thinly veneered with European culture and to the countryside of pack-mules, ox-carts, slave quarters, and black and mulatto children scampering about amid the flies of kitchens of the big houses. It returned them to the coffee fazenda.

Above all, the rapid adaptation of coffee cultivation in the Parahyba Valley committed Brazil, newly emerged from colonial dependence upon the Portuguese metropolis, to a continuation of colonial patterns of large property, Negro slavery, patriarchicalism, and accentuated class divisions. While the coffee fazenda drew Africans and Europeans to Brazil, it failed signally to provide equal opportunity. The Negro field hand and house-slave were not integrated into Brazilian society and, unprepared for freedom, slave men and women were left to fend for themselves after emancipation.

The coffee plantation of the nineteenth century was more than a unit of production and a way of life. For better and worse it left an indelible imprint upon the minds of all who left the Valley to work out their destiny elsewhere in Brazil.

APPENDIX

GLOSSARY

BIBLIOGRAPHY

INDEX

APPENDIX

Exchange value of Brazilian currency in United States dollars, 1825–1900.

Year	Value of milreis (U.S. dollars)	Value of conto (U.S. dollars)
1825	1.05	1,050.00
1850	0.58	580.00
1875	0.55	550.00
1900	0.19	190.00

Source: Adapted from Julian S. Duncan, *Public and Private Operation of Railways in Brazil* (New York, 1932), p. 183.

One conto equals 1,000 milreis. The sign $, used as follows: 153:247$320, means 153 contos, 247 milreis, and 320 reis.

Brazilian equivalents of measures*

Distance:

    Palma = 0.22 meter (8.66 inches)
    Vara   = 1.09 meters (3.57 feet)
    Braça = 2.19 meters (7.18 feet)
    Legua = 6.56 kilometers (4.08 miles)

Area:

    Alqueire (Rio) = 4.84 hectares (11.96 acres)

Weights:

    Libra   = 0.45 kilogram (0.992 pound)
    Arroba = 14.40 kilograms (31.7 pounds)

Volume:

    Alqueire = 13.5 liters (14.3 quarts)

* Adapted from Charles van Lede, *De la Colonisation au Brésil*, p. 221.

Estimated population of Brazil, 1798–1900

Year	Slave	Free	Total
1798	1,500,000		
1800	1,000,000	2,000,000	3,000,000
1808			2,419,406
1817	1,930,000		
1819	1,107,389	2,488,743	4,396,132[a]
1823	1,147,515	2,813,351	3,960,866
1830			5,340,000
1850	2,500,000	5,520,000	8,020,000
1854			7,677,800
1864	1,715,000		
1872	1,510,806	8,419,672	9,930,478[b]
1873	1,542,230		
1874	1,409,453		
1875	1,410,668		
1880	1,368,097		
1882	1,272,355		
1883	1,211,946		
1884	1,240,806		
1885	1,000,000		
1887	637,602		
1888	500,000		
1890			14,333,915
1900			17,318,556

[a] Includes 800,000 Indians.
[b] Census of 1872.

Sources: Adapted from Ciro T. de Padua, "Um Capítulo da História Económica do Brasil," *Revista do Arquivo Municipal de São Paulo,* XI (1945), 175; Caio Prado Junior, *História Económica,* p. 330; T. Lynn Smith, Brazil, *People and Institutions* (2nd ed. Baton Rouge, 1954), p. 128; F. J. Oliveira Vianna, "Resumo Histórico dos Inquéritos Censitários realizados no Brazil," *Recenseamento do Brasil,* **1920** (Rio de Janeiro, 1922), I, 404–405, 414.

Slave population of Brazil by province, 1819–1887

Province	1819	1823	1872	1873	1882	1885	1887
Corte			48,939	47,084	35,568	28,000	
Minas Geraes	168,543	215,000	370,459	311,304	279,010	226,000	191,252
Rio de Janeiro	146,060[a]	150,549[a]	292,637	301,352	268,881	218,000	162,421
São Paulo	77,667	21,000	156,612	174,622	139,500	128,000	107,829
Espírito Santo	20,272	60,000	22,659	22,207	29,717	15,000	13,381
Bahia	147,263	237,458	167,824	165,403	132,200	158,000	76,838
Pernambuco	97,633	150,000	89,028	106,236	84,700	66,000	41,122
Sergipe	26,213	32,000	22,623	33,064	26,173	20,000	16,875
Alagoas	69,094	40,000	35,741	36,124	29,439	22,000	15,269
Parahyba	16,723	20,000	21,526	25,817	20,800	16,000	9,448
Rio Grande do N.	9,109	14,376	13,020	13,634	10,051	7,000	3,167
Amazonas	6,040		979	1,545	1,716		
Pará	33,000	40,000	27,458	31,537	25,393	18,000	
Maranhão	133,332	97,132	74,939	74,598	60,050	48,000	
Piauhy	12,405	10,000	23,795	23,434	18,091	14,000	
Ceará	55,439	20,000	31,913	33,409	19,588		
Paraná	10,191		10,560	11,240	7,668	5,000	
Santa Catarina	9,172	2,500	14,984	15,250	11,049	8,000	
Rio Grande do S.	28,253	7,500	67,791	98,450	68,708	49,000	
Goiás	26,800	24,000	10,652	8,800	6,899	5,000	
Matto Grosso	14,180	6,000	6,667	7,051	5,600	4,000	
Total	1,107,389	1,147,515	1,510,806	1,542,230	1,272,355	1,000,000	637,602

[a] Rio de Janeiro and Corte (now, Distrito Federal).

Sources: Oliveira Vianna, "Resumo Histórico dos Inquéritos Censitários realizados no Brasil," pp. 404–405, 414; Padua, "Um Capítulo da História Económica do Brasil," pp. 156–157, 163, 165.

Free and slave population of Brazil by province, 1823 and 1872

Province	1823			1872		
	Free	Slave	Total	Free	Slave	Total
Corte	425,000	215,000	640,000	226,033	48,939	274,972
Minas Geraes	301,999[a]	150,549[a]	451,648[a]	1,669,276	370,459	2,039,735
Rio de Janeiro	259,000	21,000	280,000	490,087	292,637	782,724
São Paulo	60,000	60,000	120,000	680,742	156,612	837,354
Espírito Santo				59,478	22,659	82,137
Bahia	434,464	237,458	671,922	1,211,792	167,824	1,379,616
Pernambuco	330,000	150,000	480,000	752,511	89,028	841,539
Sergipe	88,000	32,000	120,000	153,620	22,623	176,243
Alagoas	90,000	40,000	130,000	312,268	35,741	348,009
Parahyba	102,407	20,000	122,407	354,700	21,526	376,226
Rio Grande do N.	56,677	14,376	71,053	220,959	13,020	233,979
Amazonas				56,631	979	57,610
Pará	88,000	40,000	128,000	247,779	27,458	275,237
Maranhão	67,704	97,132	164,836	284,101	74,939	359,040
Piauhy	80,000	10,000	90,000	178,427	23,795	202,222
Ceará	180,000	20,000	200,000	689,773	31,913	721,686
Paraná				116,162	10,560	126,722
Santa Catarina	47,500	2,500	50,000	144,818	14,984	159,802
Rio Grande do S.	142,500	7,500	150,000	367,022	67,791	434,813
Goiás	37,000	24,000	61,000	149,743	10,652	160,395
Matto Grosso	24,000	6,000	30,000	53,750	6,667	60,417
Total	2,813,351	1,147,515	3,960,866	8,419,672	1,510,806	9,930,478

[a] Rio de Janeiro and Corte.

Source: Oliveira Vianna, "Resumo Histórico dos Inquéritos Censitários realizados no Brasil," pp. 404–405, 414.

GLOSSARY

The following terms are defined according to local usage although some have additional meanings in Brazilian Portuguese.

aggregado Freeman, non-rent-paying tenant, dwelling on a plantation at the planter's sufferance.

aguardente Sugar brandy or *cachaça*.

alqueire See Brazilian equivalents of measures, page 293.

amazia Cohabitation without religious or legal sanction.

apuntador Gang foreman (post-abolition).

armazem Large storehouse, warehouse.

arreiador Leader of a pack-train.

arroba See Brazilian equivalents of measures, page 293.

bacalhao Codfish, also whip (slang).

bate-papo Small talk.

braça See Brazilian equivalents of measures, page 293.

cachaça Sugar brandy.

cafesal Coffee grove.

camarada Freeman, day laborer, usually employed in gang labor. See *colono-camarada*.

Câmara Municipal Town council.

Caminho Novo One of two roads traversing Vassouras in the eighteenth century.

capataz Slave drivers.

capoeira Secondary growth, amsller than *capoeirão*.

capoeirão Secondary growth of about twenty to thirty years.

casa de tropa Animal shed.

casa de vivenda Planter's main residence.

casco da fazenda Real assets of a plantation, excluding slaves.

caxambú Negro slave festival based upon drumming, versifying, and dancing.

certão Unexplored forest.

chiqueiro Pigpen.

colono-arrendatario Renter (post-abolition).

colono-camarada Resident day laborer.

colono-empreiteiro Resident laborer hired for specific jobs (post-abolition).

colono-meieiro Sharecropper on halves.

colono-parceiro Sharecropper.

commissário Factor handling planters' coffee exports. Also importer on planters' accounts.

compadrío Godparenthood.

conto See Table of Brazilian currency, page 293.

curandeiro Negro healer or diviner.

cuia Bowl used by slaves, made from a gourd.

despolpador Coffee depulping machine.

eito Cultivated areas of a plantation.

empreitada Jobbing, a system of paying resident labor for specific tasks.

empreiteiro Labor contractor. See also *colono-empreiteiro*.

engenho de pilões Coffee processing equipment for dehulling.

fazenda A plantation.

fazendeiro Planter, proprietor of a fazenda and, before 1888, slaveholder.

feiticeiro Negro healer or diviner. See *curandeiro*, *quimbandeiro*.

feitor Plantation overseer.

formatura Rollcall or lineup of slaves at dawn and nightfall.

grande lavoura Large-scale or plantation agriculture. See also *pequena lavoura*.

herva-de-passarinho Bird-pest, a coffee blight.

Iguassú Port on Guanabara Bay where coffee was transshipped from muleback to small coastal vessels for the port of Rio.

ingénuo Free child of slave mother, born after 1871.

jongo Impromptu rhymed verses sung at caxambú. Also, slave work songs.

legua See Brazilian equivalents of measures, page 293.

liberto Emancipated Negro or Mulatto.

mascate   Pack-peddler.
mata virgem   Virgin forest.
matriz   Principal parish church.
moinho de fubá   Corn mill.
moleque   Negro or Mulatto male child.
monjollo   Pounding mill.
mucama   Female household slave.
muda   Coffee seedling.

noruega   Hillside receiving minimum sunlight.

pagem   Male slave used as body servant.
paiol   Corn crib.
parceiro   Fellow worker, companion; also sharecropper.
parcería   Share-tenancy.
pasto   Pasture.
Paty do Alferes   First parish founded in Vassouras (1726).
pequena lavoura   Small scale or subsistence agriculture.
pilões   Pestles, parts of coffee processing equipment. See *engenho de pilões*.
pobreza   The class of free poor.
pombeiro   See *mascate*.
posse   Possession, occupancy; hence, squatter's rights.
posseiro   Squatter.

quimbandeiro   Negro slave healer or diviner.

rancho   Shelter for muleteers and pack animals; country store, shelter, and pasturage. Also small farm or *situação*.
rapadura   Raw sugar.
roça   Small cultivated plot.
rondante   Patroller.
rotina   Routinism.

Sacra Família   Second parish founded in Vassouras (1750).
saúva   Species of ant.
sede   Nucleus of plantation buildings containing planter's residence, slave quarters, storehouses, coffee processing equipment, and drying terraces.
senhor   Planter.
senzallas   Slave quarters.
serão   Evening chores on plantations.

Serra Acima   Uplands north of Rio de Janeiro's coastal lowlands.

Serra da Mantiqueira   Mountain range north of the Parahyba River.

sesmaría   Royal land grant.

sinhá   Form of *senhora* employed by slaves to address adult female members of their owner's family.

sitiante   Small property owner, proprietor of a *sitio* or *situação*.

situação   Property up to thirty alqueires in size.

soalheiro   Hillsides receiving maximum sunlight.

taberna   Country tavern.

tarimba   Slave bed; also synonym for *senzalla*.

terreiro   Coffee drying terrace of mud, stone, or macadam. Also cleared area around rural houses.

travessías   Short trunk roads.

tronco   Stock for punishing slaves.

tropeiro   Muleteer.

tulha   Storehouse.

venda   Country store.

ventilador   Winnowing machine.

BIBLIOGRAPHY

Manuscript Sources

Sesmarías
1. National Archives, Rio de Janeiro.
2. Documents in Medição Judicial da Fazenda das Palmas and das Cruzes, CPOV.

Inventories and Testaments
1. Cartório do Primeiro Offício, Vassouras.
2. Archive, Prefecture of Vassouras.

Civil and Criminal Cases
1. Cartório do Primeiro Offício, Vassouras.
2. Archive, Prefecture of Vassouras.

Official Publications

Relatório do Presidente da Província do Rio, 1841–1889.
Mensagem do Governador do Estado do Rio, 1889–1906.

Newspapers

Vassouras
1. *O Município,* 1873–1879.
2. *O Vassourense,* 1882–1891.
3. *O Isothérmico,* 1886–1888.

Rio de Janeiro (capital)
1. *Aurora Fluminense,* 1828–1831.
2. *Gazeta de Notícias,* 1888–1908.
3. *Jornal do Commercio,* 1870–1890.
4. "Retrospecto Commercial," 1870–1900, *Jornal do Commercio.*
5. *Novidades,* 1887–1889.

Other Works

Adamson, T., *Report on the Commercial Relations of the United States and Foreign Countries for the Year 1878. Brazil.* Washington, 1879.
Agassiz, Louis, *A Journey in Brazil.* Boston, 1868.
Amaral, Angelo de, *Tres Cartas.* Rio de Janeiro, 1890.

Antonil, André João (João Antonio Andreoni, *S. J.*), *Cultura e Opulencia do Brasil por suas Drogas e Minas*. A. d'E. Taunay, ed. São Paulo, 1923.

Artigo de Officio. *Caminho de Ferro Entre o Municipio da Corte e a Província de São Paulo*. Rio de Janeiro, 1840.

Artigo Separado da Convenção Assignada em Londres aos 28 de Julho de 1817, addicional ao Tratado de 22 de Janeiro de 1815. Rio de Janeiro, 1818.

Baglioni, Miguel Alamir, *O Eresipho do Cafeeiro. Breve Estudo d'Esta Infecção Epiphytica*. Campos, 1878.

Baillie, [Consul], *Report on . . . Brazil*. Gt. Britain. Accounts and Papers. C 3222. LXX (1863).

Barauna, João L., *Estado Actual de Propriedade no Brasil*. Rio de Janeiro, 1889.

Barros, Domingos Borges de, "Memória sobre o Café," *O Patriota*, V (May 1813), 3–15; VI (June 1813), 31–43.

Beaurepaire Rohan, Henrique, "O Futuro da Grande Lavoura e da Grande Propriedade no Brazil," Appéndice, *Congresso Agrícola*. Rio de Janeiro, 1878.

Bellegarde, Pedro d'Alcántara and Conrado Jacobo de Niemeyer, *Relatório da Carta Chorográphica da Província do Rio de Janeiro, 1858–1861*. Rio de Janeiro, 1863.

Bernardes, Nilo, *Notas Preliminares sobre os Aspectos Morfológicos do Municipio de Paraiba do Sul*. Resumo de Comunicação Apresentada a IV Assembleia da Associação dos Geográfos Brasileiros em Goiânia. December 1948.

Brandão, Alberto, *O Brasil*. Rio de Janeiro, 1896.

Breve Notícia Sobre a Primeira Exposição de Café do Brasil. Rio de Janeiro, 1882.

Burlamaque, F. L. C., *Catechismo de Agricultura*. Rio de Janeiro, 1870.

———, *Manual de Máquinas, Instrumentos e Motores Agrícolas*. Rio de Janeiro, 1859.

———, *Monographia do Cafeseiro e do Café*. Rio de Janeiro, 1860.

Burton, Richard F., *Explorations of the Highlands of the Brazil*. 2 vols. London, 1869.

Caetano da Fonseca, Antonio, *Manual do Agricultor dos Géneros Alimentícios*. Rio de Janeiro, 1863.

Camargo, Rogério de, *Sombreamento dos Cafezais pelo Ingazeiro*. São Paulo, 1948.

Canabrava, Alice P., *O Desenvolvimento do Algodão na Provincia de São Paulo (1861–1875)*. São Paulo, 1951.

Capanema, G. S., *Agricultura. Fragmentos do Relatório dos Commissários Brazileiros a Exposição Universal de Paris em 1855.* Rio de Janeiro, 1858.

Carneiro de Campos, Frederico, *Apontamentos Estatísticos sobre a Provincia do Rio de Janeiro.* Rio de Janeiro, 1862.

Carneiro Maia, João de Azevedo, *Notícias Históricas e Estatísticas do Município de Rezende.* Rio de Janeiro, 1891.

Carvalho de Moraes, José Pedro, *Relatório apresentado ao Ministério da Agricultura, Commercio e Obras Públicas.* Rio de Janeiro, 1870.

Castilho Barreto, Antonio María, "Impressões sobre Africa Occidental," *Revista Luso-Brazileira,* I (July 1860), 57–62.

Código Criminal do Império do Brazil. Rio de Janeiro, 1830.

Codman, John, *Ten Months in Brazil.* Boston, 1867.

Coelho Netto, Paulo, *Banzo.* 2nd ed. Porto, 1927.

Congresso Agrícola. Collecção de Documentos. Rio de Janeiro, 1878.

Conselheiro do Povo ou Collecção de Fórmulas. 2 v. 2nd ed. Rio de Janeiro, 1853.

Correa de Azevedo, Luiz, "Da Cultura do Café," in F. P. de Lacerda Werneck, *Memória.*

Correa de Mattos, Bernardino, *Machina Brasileira de . . . para Descascar e Preparar Café.* Rio de Janeiro, 1876.

Costa, Affonso, *Questões Económicas.* Rio de Janeiro, 1918.

Costa Pereira, José Veríssimo da, "Os Traços Essenciais da Paisagem do Vale Médio do Paraíba," *Boletim Geográfico,* I (November 1943), 131–137.

Couty, Louis, *Étude de Biologie Industrielle sur le Café. Rapport Adressé à M. le Directeur de l'École Polytechnique.* Rio de Janeiro, 1883.

———, "L'Alimentation au Brésil et dans les Pays Voisins," *Revue d'Hygiène et de Police Sanitaire,* III (1881), 183–195; 279–294; 470–486.

———, *Le Brésil en 1884.* Rio de Janeiro, 1884.

———, *L'Esclavage au Brésil.* Paris, 1881.

———, *Pequena Propriedade e Immigração Européa.* Rio de Janeiro, 1887.

Delden Laerne, C. F. van, *Brazil and Java. Report on Coffee Culture in America, Asia and Africa.* London, 1885.

Denis, Pierre, *Brazil.* Bernard Miall, tr. New York, 1911.

Escritório Técnico Paulo de Assis Ribeiro, *Settlement Possibilities in the State of Paraná.* São Paulo, 1949.

"Evolução da Conjuntura no Brasil-Republica até o Início da Primeira Guerra Mundial," *Conjuntura Economica*, II (August 1948), 23–29.

Favilla Nunes, J. P., *Recenseamento do Estado do Rio de Janeiro feito em 30 de Agosto de 1892*. Rio de Janeiro, 1893.

Ferreira, Felix, *Província do Rio de Janeiro. Noticias para o Immigrante*. Rio de Janeiro, 1888.

Ferreira de Aguiar, João Joaquim, *Pequena Memória sobre a Plantação, Cultura e Colheita do Café na qual se expõe os Processos seguidos pelos Fazendeiros d'esta Província desde que se planta até ser exportado para o Commercio*. Rio de Janeiro, 1836.

Ferreira Rangel, Sylvio, "O Café," *O Brasil. Suas Riquezas Naturaes. Suas Indústrias*. 3 v. Rio de Janeiro, 1909.

Ferreira Soares, Sebastião, *Elementos de Estatística comprehendendo a Theoria da Sciencia e a Sua Applicação a Estatística Commercial do Brasil*. 2 v. Rio de Janeiro, 1865.

——, *Esboço ou Primeiros Traços na Crise Commercial da Cidade do Rio de Janeiro em 10 de Setembro de 1864*. Rio de Janeiro, 1865.

——, *Notas Estatísticas sobre a Producção Agricola e Carestia dos Géneros Alimentícios no Império do Brazil*. Rio de Janeiro, 1860.

Ferreira Vianna, Antonio, *A Crise Commercial do Rio de Janeiro em 1864*. Rio de Janeiro, 1864.

Freire Allemão, Francisco, "Quaes são as Principaes Plantas que Hoje se Acham Acclimatadas no Brazil?" *Revista do Instituto Histórico e Geográphico Brasileiro*, XIX (1856), 539–578.

Furquim de Almeida, Caetano, "Carestia de Géneros Alimentícios," Annexo K, *Relatório do Presidente da Província do Rio de Janeiro, August 1, 1858*.

Göldi, Emilio A., *Memória sobre una Enfermedad del Cafeto en la Província de Rio de Janeiro*. Mexico, 1894.

Gomes Carmo, Antonio, *Reforma da Agricultura Brasileira*. Rio de Janeiro, 1897.

Goulart, Maurício, *Escravidão Africana no Brasil (Das origens a extinção do tráfico)*. São Paulo, 1949.

Graham, Maria, *Journal of a Voyage to Brazil and Residence There during Part of the Years 1821, 1822, 1823*. London, 1824.

Instituição de Crédito Territorial e Agrícola da Província do Rio de Janeiro. Rio de Janeiro, 1858.

Instrucções para a Commissão Permanente nomeada pelos Fazendeiros do Município de Vassouras. Rio de Janeiro, 1854.

Imbert, Jean Baptiste Auguste, *Manual do Fazendeiro ou Tratado Doméstico sobre as Enfermidades dos Negros, Generalisando as Necessidades Médicas de Todas as Classes.* 2nd ed. Rio de Janeiro, 1839.

Itier, Jules, *Journal d'Un Voyage en Chine en 1843, 1844, 1845, 1846.* Paris, 1848–53.

James, Preston E., "The Surface Configuration of Southeastern Brazil," *Annals of the Association of American Geographers,* XXXIII (September 1933), 165–193.

Lacerda Werneck, A. P. de, *A Lavoura e o Governo. II Apelo aos Fazendeiros.* Rio de Janeiro, 1890.

Lacerda Werneck, Francisco Peixoto de (Barão do Paty do Alferes), *Memória sobre a Fundação e Costeio de Uma Fazenda na Provincia do Rio de Janeiro.* 4th ed. Rio de Janeiro, 1878.

Lacerda Werneck, Luiz Peixoto de, *Estudos sobre o Crédito Real e Hypothecário seguidos de Leis, Estatútos e Outros Documentos.* Rio de Janeiro, 1857.

————, *Idéas sobre Colonisação precedidas de uma Succincta Exposição dos Principios Geraes que Regem a População.* Rio de Janeiro, 1855.

Lavollée, Charles Hubert, *Voyage en Chine.* Paris, 1853.

Leal, Victor Nunes, *Coronelismo, Enxada e Voto.* Rio de Janeiro, 1949.

Leclerc, Max, *Lettres du Brésil.* Paris, 1890.

Lede, Charles van, *De la Colonisation au Bresil. Mémoire Historique, Descriptif, Statistique et Commercial sur la Province de Sainte-Catherine.* . . . Bruxelles, 1843.

Leite Brandão, Joaquim Eduardo, *Dissertação sobre o Cafeseiro.* Rio de Janeiro, 1842.

Leite Ribeiro, Domiciano, *Reminiscencias e Fantazías.* 2 v. Vassouras, 1885.

————, *Trovas de um Quidam.* Rio de Janeiro, 1862.

Lèze, M. R., "Indústria Agrícola. Cultura e Indústria do Café no Brazil," *Revista do Instituto Fluminense de Agricultura,* XXII (September 1891).

Lima, Ruy Cirne, *Terras Devolutas,* Porto Alegre, 1935.

Luz, Nicia Vilela, "A Administração Provincial de São Paulo em Face do Movimento Abolicionista," *Revista de Administração,* VIII (December 1948), 80–100.

A Machina de Seccar Café Taunay-Telles. Pareceres da Imprensa, Agricultores, Proffissionaes, Etc. Rio de Janeiro, 1881.

Magalhães, Basílio de, "García Rodrigues Paes," *Revista do Instituto Histórico e Geográphico Brazileiro,* LXXXIV (1918), 9–40.

Maia Forte, José Matoso, "O Centenário de Quatro Municípios Fluminenses," *Revista da Sociedade de Geografía do Rio de Janeiro*, XXXVI (1932), 160–165.

———, "A Fazenda do 'Secretário' em Vassouras." MS in Archives of the Serviço do Património Histórico e Artístico Nacional, Rio de Janeiro.

———, "Introdução a Corografía de Vassouras," *Revista da Sociedade de Geografía do Rio de Janeiro*, XLVIII (1941), 24–33.

———, *Memória da Fundação de Vassouras (Do início do povoamento a creação da villa)*. Rio de Janeiro, 1935.

Manchester, A. K., *British Preeminence in Brazil. Its Rise and Decline*. Chapel Hill, 1933.

"Mappa Synóptico do Estado Sanitário da Província do Rio," *Relatório do Presidente da Província do Rio, May 3, 1852*.

Marques d'Oliveira, Luiz Torquato, *Novo Méthodo da Plantação, Fecundidade, Durabilidade, Estrumação e Conservação do Café*. Rio de Janeiro, 1863.

Martonne, Emmanuel de, "Problemas Morfológicos do Brasil Tropical Atlántico," *Revista Brasileira de Geografía*, V (October–December 1943), 523–546.

Maynard Araujo, Alceu, "Jongo," *Communicação a Commissão Nacional de Folclore do Instituto Brasileiro de Educação, Ciencia e Cultura. May 24, 1948* (Documento 22).

Maynard Araujo, Alceu, and Franceschini, Manuel Antonio, "Documentario Foklorico Paulista. I. Danças e Ritos Populares de Taubaté," *Publicações do Instituto de Administração*, XXXIII (July 1948), 26–29.

Milliet, Sérgio, *Roteiro do Café e Outros Ensaios*. 3rd ed. São Paulo, 1941.

Milliet de Saint-Adolphe, J. C. R., *Diccionário Geográphico, Histórico e Descriptivo do Império do Brazil*. 2 v. Paris, 1845.

Ministério da Fazenda, *Auxílios a Lavoura. 1889*. Rio de Janeiro, 1889.

Ministério dos Negocios da Agricultura, Commercio e Obras Públicas, *População Escrava e Libertos Arrolados. Estatistica Organizada a Vista dos Dados da Mátricula e do Arrolamento Encerrados a 30 de Março de 1887*. Rio de Janeiro, 1888.

Monteiro Lobato, José Bento de, *Urupês. Outros Contos e Coisas*. Artur Neves, ed. São Paulo, 1943.

Moreira, Nicolau Joaquim, *Breves Considerações Sobre a História e Cultura do Cafeeiro e Consumo de Seu Producto*. Rio de Janeiro, 1873.

Moreira, Nicolau Joaquim, *Notícia sobre a Agricultura do Brasil*. Rio de Janeiro, 1873.

Murtinho, Joaquim Duarte, *Introdução ao Relatório do Ministério da Indústria, Viação e Obras Públicas*. Rio de Janeiro, 1897.

Nabuco, Joaquim, *Um Estadista do Império*. 2 v. 2nd ed. Rio de Janeiro, 1936.

Noronha Santos, Francisco Agenor de, *Meios de Transporte no Rio de Janeiro*. 2 v. Rio de Janeiro, 1934.

Oliveira Vianna, F. J., "Resumo Histórico dos Inquéritos Censitários realizados no Brasil," *Recenseamento do Brasil*. . . 1920 (5 v. Rio de Janeiro, 1922–1930), I, 404–405, 414.

Os Deputados Republicanos na Assemblea Provincial de São Paulo. Sessão de 1888. São Paulo, 1888.

Ottoni, Christiano B., *Esboço Histórico das Estradas de Ferro do Brazil*. Rio de Janeiro, 1866.

——, *O Advento da República no Brasil*. Rio de Janeiro, 1890.

Padua, Ciro T. de, "Um Capítulo da História Económica do Brasil," *Revista do Arquivo Municipal de São Paulo*, XI (1945), 135–190.

Paes Leme, Pedro Gordilho Días, "A Grande Propriedade e o Chim," *Revista Agrícola do Instituto Fluminense de Agricultura*, XXII (December 1891), 49–55.

Paes Leme, Pedro Días Gordilho, Joaquim Mariano Alvares de Castro, Arthur Getulio das Neves, "Organização agrícola; Parecer sobre a Organização Agrícola do Estado do Rio de Janeiro," *Revista Agrícola do Instituto Fluminense da Agricultura*, XXII (June 1891), 3–29.

Paula Cándido, Francisco de, *Clamores da Agricultura no Brazil*. Rio de Janeiro, 1859.

Peckolt, T., *História das Plantas Alimentares e do Gozo do Brazil*. Rio de Janeiro, 1874.

Pereira Barretto, Luis, *O Século XX sob o Ponto de Vista Brazileiro*. São Paulo, 1901.

Phipps, E. C. W., *Report on the Trade and Commercial Relations of Brazil and on Finance*. Gt. Britain. Accounts and Papers. C636. LIX (1872).

Pinto, Jorge, *Fastos Vassourenses*. Vassouras, 1935.

Pizarro e Araujo, José de Souza Azevedo, *Memórias Históricas do Rio de Janeiro e das Províncias Annexas*. 9 v. Rio de Janeiro, 1820–22.

Plano de Huma Estrada de Ferro desde o Município da Corte até a Villa de Rezende. Rio de Janeiro, 1839.

Posturas da Câmara Municipal da Vila de Vassouras. Rio de Janeiro, 1857.

Pradez, Carlos, *Nouvelles Études sur le Brésil*. Paris, 1872.

Prado Junior, Caio, *História Económica do Brasil.* 2nd ed. São Paulo, 1949.

Ramos da Silva, Pedro, "Carestía de Géneros Alimentícios," Annexo K, *Relatório do Presidente da Província do Rio, August 1, 1858.*

Raposo, Ignácio, *História de Vassouras.* Vassouras, 1935.

Rau, Virginia, *Sesmarías Medievais Portuguesas.* Lisboa, 1946.

Rebouças, André, *A Lavoura Nacional.* Rio de Janeiro, 1884.

Recenseamento da População do Império do Brazil a que se Procedeu no Dia 1o. de Agosto de 1872. Quadros Estatísticos. 23 v. Rio de Janeiro, 1873–1876.

Recopilação do Custo, Despezas e Rendimento de Hum Estabelecimento da Cultura do Caffeiro. Rio de Janeiro, 1835.

Relatório da Commissão Encarregada da Revisão da Tarifa em Vigor que Acompanhou o Projeto da Tarifa. . . Rio de Janeiro, 1853.

Relatórios das Operações de Auxílios a Lavoura, Julho a Dezembro de 1889, pelo Fiscal do Governo Junto ao Banco de Crédito Real do Brasil. Rio de Janeiro, 1890.

Relatório apresentado pela Directoria aos Accionistas da Estrada de Ferro de D. Pedro II em 31 de Janeiro de 1857. Rio de Janeiro, 1857.

Resumo Chorográphico da Província do Rio de Janeiro e do Município da Corte. Rio de Janeiro, 1841.

Reybaud, Charles, *Le Brésil.* Paris, 1856.

Ribeiro de Avellar, Antonio Gomes, "A Prole da Família Avellar a Contar de Antonio de Avellar e sua Mulher D. Antonia da Conceição." MS in possession of D. Marianna de Albuquerque. Avellar, Estado do Rio, Brasil.

Ribeiro de Avellar, Joaquim, *Relatório Apresentado a Câmara Municipal de Vassouras.* Barra do Pirahy, 1913.

Ribeiro Filho, Raimundo, "Caracteres Físicos da Bacía do Paraíba," Ministério da Agricultura (DNPM), *Anuário Fluviometrico* (No. 4, 1943), 21–80.

Ribeyrolles, Charles, *Brasil Pitoresco.* Gastão Penalva, tr. 2 v. São Paulo, 1941.

Rodrigues Cunha, Agostinho, *Arte da Cultura e Preparação do Café.* Rio de Janeiro, 1844.

Rodrigues d'Oliveira, Luiz, "Banques et Institutions de Crédit," in F. J. de Santa-Ana Néry, ed., *Le Brésil en 1889.* Paris, 1889.

Roure, Agenor, "A Escravidão (De 1818 a 1888)," *Jornal do Commercio,* September 28, 1906.

Sá da Bandeira, Marquez de, *O Trabalho Rural Africano e a Administração Colonial.* Lisboa, 1873.

Saint-Hilaire, Auguste de, *Voyage dans les Provinces de Rio de Janeiro et de Minas Geraes.* 2 v. Paris, 1830.

Saldanha da Gama, José de, *Classement Botanique das Plantes Alimentaires du Brésil.* Paris, 1867.

Scully, William, *Brazil; its Provinces and Chief Cities; the Manners and Customs of the People.* London, 1866.

Silva, Joaquim José da, "Extracto da Viagem, Que Fez ao Sertão de Benguella no Anno de 1775 por Ordem do Governador e Capitão-General do Reino de Angola, o Bacharel . . . Enviado a Aquelle Reino como Naturalista e Depois Secretário do Governo," *O Patriota* (January 1813), 97–100; (February 1813), 86–98; (March 1813), 49–60.

Silva, Manoel Joaquim da, "Carestía de Géneros Alimentícios," Annexo K, *Relatório do Presidente da Província do Rio de Janeiro, August 1, 1858.*

Silva, Miguel Antonio da, "Agricultura Nacional," *Revista Agrícola do Imperial Instituto Fluminense de Agricultura,* VIII (December 1877), 133–142.

——, "Agricultura Nacional," *Revista Agrícola do Imperial Instituto Fluminense de Agricultura,* X (March 1879).

Silva, Moacir, *Kilómetro Zero. Caminhos Antigos e Estradas Modernas.* Rio de Janeiro, 1934.

Simonsen, Roberto C., *Aspectos da História Económica do Café.* São Paulo, 1940.

Siqueira, Alexandre Joaquim de, *Memória Histórica do Município de Vassouras.* Rio de Janeiro, 1852.

Soares, Caetano Alberto, *Memória para Melhorar a Sorte dos Nossos Escravos lida na Sessão Geral do Instituto dos Advogados Brazileiros no dia 7 de Septembro de 1845.* Rio de Janeiro, 1847.

Sociedade Central de Immigração, *Divisão em Lotes das Fazendas Hypothecadas.* Rio de Janeiro, 1885.

Souza Silva, Joaquim Norberto de, "Memória Histórica e Documentada das Aldeas de Indios da Província do Rio de Janeiro," *Revista do Instituto Histórico e Geográphico Brazileiro,* XVII (1854), 301–552.

Spielman, Henry W., "The Coffee Future of Brazil." Rio de Janeiro, 1946. American Embassy. Report No. 249 (unpublished).

Taunay, Affonso d'Escragnolle, *História do Café no Brasil.* 15 v. Rio de Janeiro, 1939–43.

Taunay, C. A., *Manual do Agricultor Brazileiro, Obra Indispensavel a Todo o Senhor de Engenho, Fazendeiro e Lavrador.* 2nd ed. Rio de Janeiro, 1839.

Tavares Bastos, Aureliano Candido, *A Província; Estudo sobre a Decentralização no Brasil.* Rio de Janeiro, 1870.

Teixeira Junior, Jeronymo José, *Elemento Servil.* Parecer e Projecto de Lei. Rio de Janeiro, 1870.

Teixeira Leite, Carlos, and Guilherme de Almeida Magalhães, *Proposta Feita aó Governo Imperial Relativamente a Estrada de Ferro D. Pedro II.* Rio de Janeiro, 1868.

Tratado da Abolição do Tráfico de Escravos em Todos os Lugares da Costa da Africa. . . Rio de Janeiro, 1818.

Tschudi, J. J. von, *Viagem às Provincias do Rio de Janeiro e São Paulo.* Eduardo de Lima Castro, tr. Biblioteca Histórica Paulista. V. São Paulo, 1953.

União Seguros de Vida de Escravos. As Indemnizações são Pagas logo depois da Morte dos Escravos Segurados. Rio de Janeiro, 1876.

Vasconcellos, J. M. P. de, *Arte Nova de Requerer em Juizo Contendo Uma Grande e Preciosa Copia de Formas de Petições.* Rio de Janeiro, 1855.

——, *Livro das Terras.Collecção da Lei.* 4th ed. Rio de Janeiro, 1885.

Vasconcellos, Max, *Vias Brasileiras de Communicação.* Rio de Janeiro, 1928.

Vellozo de Oliveira, Henrique, *A Substituição do Trabalho dos Escravos pelo Trabalho Livre.* Rio de Janeiro, 1845.

Wagley, Charles, *Amazon Town. A Study of Man in the Tropics.* New York, 1953.

Wagstaff, W. G., *Report on the Trade and Commercial Activities of Brazil for the Year 1897.* Gt. Britain. Accounts and Papers. C 8648. XCIV (1898).

Walsh, Reverend R., *Notices of Brasil in 1828 and 1829.* 2 v. London, 1830.

Werneck, Americo, *Erros e Vicios da Organização Republicana.* Petropolis, 1893.

——, *Graciema.* 2 v. 2nd ed. Rio de Janeiro, 1920.

——, *Problemas Fluminenses.* Petropolis, 1893.

Werneck, Francisco Klörs, *História e Genealogia Fluminense.* Rio de Janeiro, 1947.

Wilberforce, E., *Brazil Viewed Through a Naval Glass: With Notes on Slavery and the Slave Trade.* London, 1856.

Wyndham, Hugh, *Report on the Finances of Brazil for the Year 1889 to March, 1890.* Gt. Britain. Accounts and Papers. C 5895. LXXIV (1890).

Zaluar, Augusto Emilio, *Peregrinação pela Provincia de São Paulo, 1860–1861.* Rio de Janeiro, 1862.

Zettiry, Arrigo de, *O Estado do Rio.* Rio de Janeiro, 1897.

INDEX

Abolition, 250–258

African slave trade: end of, 20, 29–30, 52 n. 59, 62–65; contraband, 64–65, 69–70. *See also* Slave trade

Aggregados: as laborers in clearing forest, 32; and subsistence crops, 48, 57; in elections, 57 n. 11; described, 57–58, 119; attack large planters, 58–59; as storekeepers, 86

Agricultural companies, 280–282

Agricultural Congress of 1878, 123, 230, 242–243

Agricultural techniques, 48, 50, 51, 215–217 *passim. See also* Coffee cultivation

Amazia: among slaves, 155–156; among free poor, 156; between planter and slave, 157–160; offspring of, 159–160, 160 n. 97

Araujo Padilha family, 16, 121

Architecture: of plantation, 22–23, 39–45

Avellar e Almeida family, 16, 121

Banco Commercial e Agrícola, 20, 238, 239

Banco de Crédito Real do Brazil, 284–286; succeeded by Banco Rural e Hypothecário do Brazil, 286

Bank of Brazil: established, 19 n. 43; and Souto crisis, 238–240; and mortgage loans, 240–241, 242, 244, 249; mentioned, 282. *See also* Credit

Banks, 19, 20, 52, 238–239. *See also* individual banks; Credit

Barão do Paty. *See* Lacerda Werneck, Francisco Peixoto de

Brandão, Alberto: on status of women, 152; on forced labor, 263–264

Caetano Alves family, 16, 285–286

Caminho Novo, 7–8, 11 n. 20

Cattle, 277, 286–287

Caxambú, 205–209

Charity: and Brotherhood (*Irmandade*), 123; and mendicancy, 129; and school for poor girls, 130–131. *See also* Charity Hospital

Charity Hospital of Vassouras, 123, 194–195

Climate, 4–5, 216–218 *passim*

Clothing, 143–144 *passim*, 179–183

Coffee cultivation: and large plantation, 16–17; early methods of, 23–25; techniques in the fifties, 31–36, 162–165; and scarcity of virgin forest, 45; reduces subsistence crops, 46; life of bush, 46; pests attack, 51–52, 216–217, 232; declining productivity in, 219–221; attempts to diversify, 231–233; attempts to revive in nineties, 278–279. *See also* Soil; Virgin forest

Coffee prices, 53, 82, 239, 244–245, 277

Coffee processing: drying, 35–36, 38 n. 20; milling and sorting, 36–37; improvements in, 233–236, 237–238

Coffee production: of Rio area (1792–1860), 53; in São Paulo, 245; in nineties, 278

Colonization, 59, 61

Commerce, 85, 95, 111–114. *See also* Country stores; Roads; Peddlers; Vassouras

Commissários. See Factors

Conservative party: and abolition, 255–256

Coroado Indians, 9, 57, 120

Correa e Castro family, 16, 120

Correa e Castro, Christóvão, 253

Correa e Castro, Pedro, 159, 197

Cotton, 231–232

Country stores, 9, 81, 85–86; illicit activities of, 86–87, 171–173; railroad effects, 111–112

Credit: in early settlement, 17–19; end of slave trade expands, 19–20; factor as source of, 47, 52; growing scarcity of, 52–53, 213, 236; at Agricultural

HARVARD HISTORICAL STUDIES

(Early titles now out of print are omitted)

47. *William Farr Church*. Constitutional Thought in Sixteenth-Century France. 1941.

48. *Jack H. Hexter*. The Reign of King Pym. 1941.

49. *George Hoover Rupp*. A Wavering Friendship: Russia and Austria, 1876–1878. 1941.

51. *Frank Edgar Bailey*. British Policy and the Turkish Reform Movement. 1942.

52. *John Black Sirich*. The Revolutionary Committees in the Departments of France. 1943.

53. *Henry Frederick Schwarz*. The Imperial Privy Council in the Seventeenth Century. 1943.

54. *Aaron Ignatius Abell*. Urban Impact on American Protestantism. 1943.

55. *Holden Furber*. John Company at Work. 1948.

56. *Walter Howe*. The Mining Guild of New Spain and Its Tribunal General, 1770–1821. 1949.

57. *John Howes Gleason*. The Genesis of Russophobia in Great Britain. 1950.

58. *Charles Coulston Gillispie*. Genesis and Geology: A Study in the Relations of Scientific Thought, Natural Theology, and Social Opinion in Great Britain, 1790–1850. 1951.

59. *Richard Humphrey*. Georges Sorel, Prophet without Honor: A Study in Anti-intellectualism. 1951.

60. *Robert G. L. Waite*. Vanguard of Nazism: The Free Corps Movement in Postwar Germany, 1918–1923. 1952.

61. *Nicholas V. Riasanovsky*. Russia and the West in the Teaching of the Slavophiles. 1952.

62. *John King Fairbank*. Trade and Diplomacy on the China Coast: The Opening of the Treaty Ports, 1842–1854. Vol. I, text.

63. *John King Fairbank*. Trade and Diplomacy on the China Coast. Vol. II, reference material. 1953.

64. *Franklin L. Ford*. Robe and Sword: The Regrouping of the French Aristocracy after Louis XIV. 1953.

65. *Carl E. Schorske*. German Social Democracy, 1905–1917. The Development of the Great Schism. 1955.

66. *Wallace Evan Davies*. Patriotism on Parade: The Story of Veterans' and Hereditary Organizations in America, 1783–1900. 1955.

67. *Harold Schwartz*. Samuel Gridley Howe: Social Reformer, 1801–1876. 1956.

68. *Bryce D. Lyon*. From Fief to Indenture: The Transition from Feudal to Non-Feudal Contract in Western Europe. 1957.

69. *Stanley J. Stein*. Vassouras: A Brazilian Coffee County, 1850–1900. 1957.